Closing the Slaughterhouse

The Inside Story of Death Penalty Abolition in Virginia

Dale M. Brumfield

ABOLITION PRESS

RICHMOND, VA.

Abolition Press
P.O. Box 12222
Richmond, Va. 23241

Publisher's Note: Notice: the information in this book is true and complete to the best of our knowledge. It is offered without guarantee on the part of the author or the publisher, Abolition Press. The author and Abolition Press disclaim any and all liability in connection with the use of this book.

Front and Back cover by Doug Dobey at Dobey Design, Richmond, Va.
Back photo courtesy of the M. Watt Espy Papers, M.E. Grenander Department of Special Collections & Archives, University at Albany, SUNY.

Closing the Slaughterhouse: The Inside Story of Death Penalty Abolition in Virginia/ Dale M. Brumfield -- 1st ed.
First published 2022.
1. Capital Punishment – Virginia   2. Prisoners – death row
Manufactured in the United States of America
ISBN 9780578286860

Also by Dale M. Brumfield

Memoir
Three Buck Naked Commodes: and 18 More Tales from a Small Town

Fiction
Remnants: A Novel about God, Insurance and Quality Floorcoverings
Trapped Under the Pack-Ice (eBook)
Bad Day at the Amusement Park (eBook)
Standers
Naked Savages
Theme Park Babylon

Non-fiction/history
Richmond Independent Press: A History of the Underground Zine Scene
Independent Press in D.C. and Virginia: An Underground History
Virginia State Penitentiary: A Notorious History
Railroaded

Anthologies
Richmond Macabre (Iron Cauldron Press, Phil Ford & Beth Brown, editors)
Richmond Macabre II (Iron Cauldron Press, Phil Ford & Beth Brown, editors)

Web
http://www.dalebrumfield.net
https://medium.com/@dalebrumfield
https://muckrack.com/dale-brumfield
https://www.instagram.com/brumfield.dale
https://www.facebook.com/dale.brumfield.1

For everyone who worked to abolish Virginia's death penalty.

CONTENTS

Introduction

By Sister Helen Prejean

> There is no place today for the death penalty in this commonwealth, in the South, or in this nation.
> —Virginia Gov. Ralph Northam, on signing the law abolishing the death penalty, March 24, 2021.

The death penalty in America is increasingly becoming a freak occurrence for a good reason. Executions are secretive spectacles of sanctioned judicial homicide, which teach the permissibility of killing people to solve our social problems woes. Since the dawn of American society, state governments have killed thousands attempting to justify their destructive anger by the supposed benefits these killings would bring to the rest of society.

After executing more of its citizens than any other state, including Texas, Virginia just became the latest state to realize the ineffectiveness and barbarity of the death penalty. On July 1, 2021, it became the first southern state to abolish it.

Capital punishment is entirely and absolutely cruel and unusual. It is a sadistic, lingering relic of the earliest days of penology, when branding in the hand, punching holes through the nose, and lopping off ears, among other equally bizarre corporal punishments, were commonplace.

Proponents of the death penalty claim it is needed to punish "the worst of the worst." Those are rarely the ones executed. It is applied randomly at best and discriminately at worst, with race, poverty, education, zip code, and the quality of counsel the deciding factors. It continually violates the constitutional guarantee of the equal application of the law because of its disproportionate imposition on minorities or those whose victims were white.

Legal executions send the unmistakable message that life ceases to be sacred when it is considered beneficial to take it. Proponents insist that the violence is legitimate and justified by pragmatic concerns that appeal only to those who wield the legal authority to kill.

Capital punishment epitomizes the tragic inefficiency of a final, reactive resort to violence after proactive solutions to complex social problems have failed or, worse, were never attempted.

I applaud the Commonwealth of Virginia for abolishing the death penalty and congratulate Virginians for Alternatives to the Death Penalty, the Virginia Interfaith Center for Public Policy, the Virginia ACLU, the Virginia Catholic Conference, bill patrons Del. Mike Mullin and Sen. Scott Surovell, the capital defense attorneys, vigil attendees, and all donors and supporters over the years who never gave up hope. This bold act will spark conscience and active hope in citizens across the land to end this futile, torturous punishment.

Sister Helen Prejean is the author of the 1994 book "Dead Man Walking: An Eyewitness Account of the Death Penalty in the United States," which ignited awareness of America's death penalty worldwide. Her second book, The Death of Innocents: An Eyewitness Account of Wrongful Executions," was published in 2004. "River of Fire: My Spiritual Journey" was released in August 2019.

PART I: DEATH

Foreword: The Thomas Wansley Story

A Textbook Case of Corruption and Racial Injustice in the 20th Century

'Get a Negro – any Negro – and kill him; burn him for raping these white women. Our women.' So you see, in '62, someone had to cry – someone had to die. And hence, (Dec. 8, 1962) I became the victim of circumstances.
-Thomas Wansley, excerpt from a letter to his attorney, reprinted in *The Southern Patriot*, Sept. 1972.

The page one headline seemed almost a benign afterthought – "Preliminary Hearing Set Thursday for Negro Charged in Rape Cases." However, the accompanying story, cynically created by the publishers of the *Lynchburg Daily Advance* in the Nov. 10, 1962 edition, contained particular buzzwords, loaded phrases, and flat-out false assertions, such as that Wansley had confessed to four attacks. It seemed intended less to report the capture of a suspected rapist but more to embarrass, intimidate, and send a message to Lynchburg's Black community.

And this was just the beginning. The Lynchburg courts, law enforcement, and the white-owned local press would go on to meticulously construct a public and personally damning narrative about this Black teenager with no prior records, criminalizing him long before his first 1963 trial and long afterward.

In the early 1960s, Lynchburg was racially divided and struggling with civil rights. In 1960, six students – four white, two Black – staged a sit-in at Patterson's Drug Store protesting the segregation of the lunch counter. They were arrested, and a hostile judge, Joseph McCarron, sentenced them to 30 days in jail, where they served 21 days total. Afterward, the students faced ostracism from their friends, families, and churches.

The Elks Club in 1962 was still producing Blackface minstrel shows as fundraisers. White School Board administrators advised Black parents to keep their kids out of E. C. Glass High School because "they would not be happy there," although two Black students – a boy and a girl – finally integrated the school the following January. The *Lynchburg News* newspaper canceled its annual spelling bee when Black children entered.

Rev. Greta Crosby, a Harvard Law School graduate and Minister of the Unitarian Universalist Church in Lynchburg, wrote in 1963 that she and a Mrs. Boulware created a summer enrichment program for Black youth that "included a number of field trips to broaden their experience and aspirations."

The first trip was to the *Lynchburg News* newspaper building. While there, the Black children were not allowed to ask any questions. Crosby wrote that her friend put a positive spin on the visit, imploring the children "to observe the different kinds of jobs, even if there were no Negroes doing them, because now the children could begin to aspire to any one of them, even to owning the newspaper."

Black ownership of the two Lynchburg papers would have been the longest of shots. Carter Glass III, the grandson of Carter Glass, published both papers, and both were steeped in racism. The senior Glass, who referred to Blacks as an "ignorant and trashy population," was the owner and editor of the *Lynchburg News* at the turn of the twentieth century. More significantly, he was the architect of Virginia's 1902 Jim Crow Constitution.

Glass announced at the 1900 Virginia Convention that "We are here to discriminate to the very extremity of permissible action under the limitations of the federal constitution, with a view to the elimination of every negro voter who can be gotten rid of, legally, without materially impairing the numerical strength of the white electorate."

In 1938, former Howard University Professor and Historian Robert E. Martin called Glass "the dominant and guiding spirit behind the movement to completely eliminate the negro by constitutional provision" from participation in Virginia politics.

Carter Glass III seemed to be following in his grandfather's footsteps, based on news stories he chose to run regarding the plight of this recently arrested, soft-spoken, bespectacled young Black man. Former civil rights leader Bruce Smith reported in a 2021 interview that "I didn't know until the fall of 1966 that civil rights leaders in Lynchburg felt that the manhunt, arrest, trial, and conviction of Thomas Wansley was, in reality, a counter-attack by the white racist power structure on Lynchburg's Black Community in response to the sit-in movement that took place the year before, while I was still in high school."

As Smith professed, there was far more to the Wansley case than just another Black juvenile ramrodded through a tangled and bewildering maze of hearings, trials, appeals, and retrials, then ordered put to death on bogus rape and robbery charges against white women. This incident did not occur in 1890 Jim Crow – this was 1961, and the case became one of the more outrageous modern-day examples of a malicious and putrid collaboration between Virginia's entrenched white aristocracy, bigoted southern law enforcement, biased courts, and the local white racist mainstream press, working hand-in-hand to subjugate Blacks and keep them in their place.

And, of course, looming over Wansley – in a chilling repeat of hundreds and hundreds of cases that came before him – was the racist use of Virginia's death penalty.

In short, the Wansley case highlighted Virginia's continuous, unrelenting quest to wield judicial homicide to silence young Black men. This pursuit reached back at the time over 350 years and would continue another 60 years afterward.

Even the Lynchburg Museum noted on their website in 2021 that "If there were a moment in Lynchburg's history that could have resulted in a lynching, the Wansley case would have been it. Thankfully, no such horror occurred."

An Affair Gone Horribly Wrong

Thomas Wansley was a 16-year-old who worked as a dishwasher at the Virginia Grill. He had missed so much school as a child due to a chronic scalp condition he was continually held back until he finally dropped out in the sixth grade, too embarrassed to continue. Wansley's father was deceased, and his mother worked as a companion and maid for an elderly white woman.

On Dec. 8, 1962, two policemen confronted Wansley at his job. After a short questioning, they charged and arrested him for the Dec. 5 rape and robbery of a white woman named Annie Carter and the mid-November rape of another Japanese-American woman, Kyoko Fleshman. They also charged him with a third attempted rape and the robbery of $1.37 in bus change.

Wansley had no prior arrests and had never been in any trouble. What led the police to him?

Wansley told his attorney, Reuben Lawson, that he had been having a consensual affair with Fleshman, who lived not far from where he worked. One night her husband unexpectedly came home and almost caught them. Wansley escaped through a window, and Fleshman told her husband she had been raped.

Fleshman tried to get Wansley to resume the affair a few days later, but he prudently declined her invitation. But when the attack on Carter occurred, Fleshman threatened to tell police that Wansley had raped her and probably the other woman if he refused to resume the affair. Still, Wansley declined, so she contacted the police and told them she knew who raped her and Annie Carter. That ID led to his subsequent arrest, trial and conviction.

Let the Railroading Begin

> Capital punishment must "be limited to those offenders who commit a narrow category of the most serious crimes" and whose extreme culpability makes them "the most deserving of execution."
> -U.S. Supreme Court, *Kennedy v. Louisiana*, (2008), quoting *Roper v. Simmons*, (2005).

During the investigative period, Wansley went under the jurisdiction of the Lynchburg Juvenile and Domestic Relations Court, where police interrogated him for about five hours with no lawyer present.

While Wansley's certification hearing was scheduled on Dec. 13, Juvenile Court Judge Earl Wingo stated publicly days earlier that he had already decided that Wansley should be tried as an adult, an allegation Wingo later tried to walk back. But accordingly, the juvenile court determined that the 16-year-old was to be tried as an adult. On Dec. 18, Dr. John G. Novak, a court-appointed psychiatrist, briefly questioned Wansley and reported that he was competent to stand trial.

After a brief hearing in January 1963, Wansley was officially certified to the Corporation Court of Lynchburg for trial as an adult. This decision was significant because in Juvenile Court, Wansley could not get a death sentence – but tried as an adult assured he would.

Wansley's lawyer, Reuben Lawson, requested a continuance when a court reporter did not show up for the Feb. 7, 1963 trial. He was bizarrely overruled, so no transcript of that trial was created. Lawson also objected when prosecutors introduced new evidence concerning Wansley's mental health, but the judge again overruled with no proceedings recorded by a reporter.

The victim, Annie Carter – who had been unable to pick Wansley out as her attacker in a lineup days earlier – took the stand and admitted she was "not too sure" that her attacker had been Wansley.

Nevertheless, the all-white jury sentenced Wansley to death for the Carter rape and twenty-years imprisonment for a robbery of $1.37 from her. Five days later, Wansley was found guilty of raping Fleshman and received a second death sentence.

"The death penalty for rape is a tool of the racists and bigots," wrote Miami-based ACLU lawyer Tobias Simon in 1965. "Its purpose is to impose punishment upon Negroes where the methods of the lynch mob and the Ku Klux Klan have failed or fallen into disrepute."

Five weeks before the trial, a vital defense witness, Sylvester Dickerson, who was to testify that he was also an acquaintance of Fleshman's and had supposed proof of Wansley's innocence, was found stabbed to death. A white man, Elmon Baldwin, was arrested and charged with Dickerson's death.

Then, on Mar. 23, 1963, Wansley's attorney Lawson dropped dead. This unexpected death created a nightmare scenario in that since no court reporter had transcribed the first trial, no defense attorney had heard the testimony. The law stated that in the event of an appeal, where there was no transcript of the original trial, the defense and the prosecutor had to agree on what was said. With Lawson deceased, this agreement was impossible.

Lawson's replacement was Norfolk attorney Leonard W. Holt, a member of the legal committee of the Southern Conference Educational Fund (SCEF).

(In response to this fiasco, in June 1964, the General Assembly passed a law prohibiting the trials of persons charged with a felony if there was not a court reporter present.)

These events, coupled with ten incidences of error, including the absence of transcripts and the court's refusal to grant continuances, led the Supreme Court of Virginia to reverse the sentences and grant a new trial for October 1966.

The retrial drove the racist Lynchburg press into a frenzy of recriminations and accusations. They continually referred to Wansley as the "twice-convicted rapist" in daily stories even after the sentence reversals. When the press learned that famed New York attorney William Kunstler would be defending Wansley on a *pro bono* basis, the papers went full-blown Joseph McCarthy on him by repeatedly accusing him of being a communist.

"Man Linked with Red Fronts Makes Talk for Negro Rapist" headlines trumpeted. "Kunstler Has Record of Commie Front Links."

"Back then," Bruce Smith explained, "If you were an activist and weren't called a communist, you weren't trying hard enough."

Wansley was experiencing firsthand a troubling history lesson that emerged in the early days of the twentieth century, that of Black men stereotyped as sexual savages preying upon Southern white women.

"That trope goes back to 'Birth of a Nation' and 'The Clansman,' Thomas Dixon's book, which was made into a play," observed Catherine Read, a Fairfax Democratic party activist and public radio host, in a 2021 interview. "When the play 'The Clansman' opened in Atlanta in 1912, it caused race riots. But that started the trope that the main threat to civilization was these aggressive Black men threatening white women, and it persists today."

The premiere of "Birth of a Nation" marked a significant shift in the stereotyping of Black men, from depicting them as shuffling, buffoonish stereotypes as Sambo and Jim Crow to brutish, marauding savages. In the film, the Ku Klux Klan could only tame this terrifying Black beast by lynching him, thus protecting their white women.

"In this country, Black men still equal danger," explained Read of the label that ensnared Tom Wansley and so many others like him into today. "Even if it's Tamir Rice playing with a toy gun in a park. The police, within 30 seconds, shot him dead. Because Black and male equal dangerous. It is a bias we still own culturally."

Southern civil rights activist and writer Anne Braden, in her 1972 essay "Free Thomas Wansley: Letter to White Southern Women," explained that Carter and Fleshman's behaviors were another troubling continuation of the Jim Crow-era practice of white women falsely accusing Black men of rape and assault due only to their "revered" status as a "white Southern woman." It was a designation that, according to her, led not just to women's subjugation but inevitably to those accused Black men's executions, life-long imprisonment, or even their lynchings.

In her blunt introduction, she wrote:

> Whether we like it or not, [Wansley] is in prison because of us. He is a victim of the myth of white Southern womanhood. We didn't personally put him in prison – just as we did not create the myth. But by remaining silent, as Black men died or went to prison because of it, we have helped to fasten its shackles on ourselves.
> For Wansley is imprisoned on a charge of rape. Rape – the cry that for the last 100 years in the South has undergirded the myths about women and made it impossible for us to fight for our own freedom. Rape – traditionally a crime in the South if the accused was Black, and the alleged victim was white, but never a crime, if the victim was Black and the attacker, was white, and scarcely noticed if both parties were white, or both Black.

Of the embedded mythology of "white Southern womanhood," Braden explained:

> I believe that no white woman reared in the South – or perhaps anywhere in this racist country – can find freedom as a woman until she deals in her own consciousness with the question of race. We grow up little girls – absorbing a hundred stereotypes about ourselves and our role in life, our secondary position, our destiny to be a helpmate to a man or men. But we also grow up white – absorbing the stereotypes of race, the picture of

ourselves as somehow privileged because of the color of our skin. The two mythologies become intertwined, and there is no way to free ourselves from one without dealing with the other.

"Not a Sick Boy"

What was particularly infuriating to Lynchburg's Black community was that only a few months before the Wansley case, a police officer, C. W. Snow, caught a white man named George Brooks raping an 11-year-old Black girl. Unlike Wansley, the system treated Brooks with dignity and respect. He was released on a $5,000 bond after his arrest, and the court generously granted him a mental examination that stretched on for weeks.

The court found Brooks guilty of rape and perjury, then Wansley's judge, Raymond Cundiff, sentenced him to five years in prison. Brooks was released after serving two years – arrested, convicted, sentenced, and released back into society before Thomas Wansley could even get a fair trial.

Rev. Virgil Wood, president of the Lynchburg chapter of the Southern Christian Leadership Conference, circulated a flyer comparing the two cases, with the headline "Lynch-burg lives up to its name!" Cundiff was so enraged by the handout he cited Rev. Wood for contempt when he showed up at Wansley's second trial.

Wansley again went to trial on the Carter robbery charge. Along with fellow attorneys Philip Hirschkop and Charles Mangum, Kunstler identified over 89 procedural errors in his original trial. These included not changing the venue based on the sensationalized stories and editorials against Wansley in the local press, the racist jury selection that produced an all-white jury, the segregation of the Lynchburg courtroom, and the absence of a court reporter during the hearings. They also noted the unconstitutionality of Virginia's race-based sentencing for rape.

Cundiff denied a request for a mental evaluation for Wansley after commonwealth's attorney Royston Jester III simply declared that Wansley "was not a sick boy."

The defense was also hamstrung by the court's absolute refusal to cooperate with them. Before the trial, Holt asked the court clerk, H. Martin, to mail Kunstler a copy of the records of the previous trials. Martin replied, "Judge Cundiff says he does not think it would be proper of us to deliver a copy of records like the one in question to a foreign lawyer."

Kunstler was from New York.

Kuntsler and Hirschkop tried to find Kyoko Fleshman, who had identified Wansley as her rapist, to put her on the stand and admit that she had fabricated the charges. As soon as she heard that Wansley's lawyers were looking for her, she left Lynchburg. They tracked her to the West Coast, then to Hawaii. When they located her there, she fled to Japan (where she was still a citizen) and could not be extradited. And there she remained, refusing to respond to pleas to tell the truth and save Wansley's life.

She only signed an affidavit that stated she would not return to Lynchburg "under any circumstances."

Just after the first two trials, *New South Student* reporter Carl Braden asked Lynchburg Chief of Police Major P. O. Brooks, who claimed to be no relation to George Brooks, the white man convicted of the rape of the underage Black girl, about the discrepancies in the treatment of a white against a Black by law enforcement in these two cases. Brooks nonsensically answered that the white man's sex with the 11-year-old had been consensual but was only charged as rape because she was a juvenile.

He then said he was more concerned with Wansley's purported victim, Carter, in that she allegedly had been a white 59-year-old virgin.

In the summer of 1965, when it appeared Wansley would get new trials, Police Chief Brooks committed suicide.

An Abolition Movement Emerges

As news of Wansley's case spread, white people started speaking out. One of them was Rev. Crosby, who was also secretary of the Lynchburg Council on Human relations. She accompanied a delegation to Richmond to confront Gov. Albertis Harrison regarding the Wansley case. She also founded a local, interracial death penalty abolition group called "Death to Death."

Rev. Crosby told the June 6, 1963 edition of *Jet* Magazine of their meeting that "We prepared to tell the governor that we were not asking for the execution of a white man or the saving of one Negro, but the abolishment of all capital punishment." She added that the death sentence was a carry-over from the primitive "eye for an eye" concept. "How can you apply that to rape?"

She wrote a letter to the editor of the *Lynchburg News,* which posited, "No white man has been executed for rape in the Commonwealth of Virginia ... would Wansley now be awaiting execution if he were white?"

Jet reported that Gov. Harrison promised to look into the Wansley case and surprisingly urged the Death to Death organization to go public to encourage the General Assembly to repeal all capital punishment laws.

William Kunstler confronted the jury during closing arguments in the 1966 robbery trial. He paced in front of the jury box and asked if they had seen the movie "Twelve Angry Men." He summarized Henry Fonda's role as the courageous, lone juror who saw reasonable doubt and dared to say so in court. Then, as he slowly passed his hand across the jury again, they sat transfixed as he asked, "Which one of you will play Henry Fonda?" Then he turned and took his seat.

A unanimous jury was required, but they returned deadlocked at 11-1. A lone white man, forever unknown, played the Henry Fonda role.

The appeals court then sent Wansley's case back to the state court for yet another retrial on the Carter rape charge. In a hearing to change the venue, Kunstler, Hirschkop, and Charles Mangum – who suspected the House Unamerican Activities Committee (HUAC) was feeding lies about Kunstler to the Lynchburg newspapers – called Editor Carter Glass III to testify.

Glass admitted on the stand that he had indeed gotten files on Kunstler from Virginia Representative and former Gov. William Tuck, a segregationist and current Vice-

Chairman of HUAC. The disclosure led the *Washington Post* to muse that not only Wansley but the press was also on trial. Still, the court denied the change of venue, and another trial began in March 1967.

All 61 prospective jurors, who had filed into the packed courtroom past a mural that depicted enslaved Black people planting tobacco, claimed they had heard of the trial and read the articles about the "rapist" Wansley and Kunstler's alleged involvement with communist activities. Wansley's frustrated attorneys again asked for the trial to be moved out of Lynchburg. Again, the court refused. They finally chose 12 jurors and one alternate.

The trial lasted five days. Victim Annie Carter again took the stand and claimed she could positively identify Wansley, even though four years earlier she could not. When asked how both statements could be factual, she replied, "Well, naturally, I've seen his pictures in the newspapers, and I've seen him in court since then."

Kunstler moved for a mistrial after a juvenile probation officer, Lee Read, described that after Wansley's initial arrest, he overheard a supposed "confession" to his mother that he slept voluntarily with Fleshman. Read then testified that commonwealth's attorney Jester encouraged him to disclose this "half-truth" specifically to mislead the jury. By the time Kunstler finished his intensive cross-examination, Read appeared emotionally devastated.

Also, as Kunstler pointed out, it was improper and completely unethical for Read, a juvenile officer, to testify against a juvenile whose rights he was supposed to be protecting.

During this trial, hundreds of people gathered outside the courtroom to chant, pray, sing protest songs, and hear speeches by local and national leaders. Two hundred high school students cut classes to attend, and when school administrators threatened them with detentions and suspension, their parents took even more children out while filing a class-action suit in U.S. District Court. They claimed in the lawsuit that their children were being deprived of their First Amendment right "to protest a gross miscarriage of justice."

Female students from Lynchburg's predominantly white Randolph-Macon College volunteered to tutor until the suit settled. Ultimately, the school district buckled, promising that detention periods would only provide the students tutoring until they caught up.

Back inside, closing arguments revealed a stark contrast between the prosecution's old Jim Crow Virginia style vs. the defense's progressive new Virginia style. Jester, a tall, southern gentleman-type with white hair and a deep, booming voice, pounded the table and lectured the jury about the attack on "this sweet little lady" whom he continually referred to as "Miss Annie." He insinuated the old southern patriarchal refrain (as described by Anne Braden) that she was the traditional symbol of white Virginia womanhood, who had been outraged by a Black man. He then demanded the death penalty to "spank" Wansley and "show other people what they can expect" from such crimes.

Kunstler took a softer, more objective approach, dispensing with any Deep South race-baiting. He asked the jurors to remember that this was the most explosive of crimes in the Jim Crow South – a Black man's rape of a white woman. He asked them to draw their verdict from the evidence or the lack of it, not by emotion.

After three hours of deliberation, the jury found Wansley again guilty of rape and sentenced him to life in prison, plus 20 years. Supporters were shocked, but at least death was now off the table.

To the Penitentiary and Beyond

Historians and psychologists offer many potential explanations for the differences in capital punishment's popularity between the South and other regions: the South's tradition of lynching, Southern evangelical religions, the region's prolonged rural/frontier experience, a history of racial subjugation, the loss of the civil war, and a siege mentality that places blame on others.

-Dov Cohen & Richard E. Nisbett, "Self-Protection and the Culture of Honor: Explaining Southern Violence." Published in *Personality & Social Psychological Bulletin,* 1994.

While confined in the State Penitentiary as his case wound through appeals, Wansley became an outspoken prison rights activist and was one of the five plaintiffs in *Landman v. Royster*, a groundbreaking prison rights case settled in 1971 that transformed the corrections department in Virginia and nationwide. In addition, he was also a plaintiff in *Mason v. Peyton*, which was settled in 1974 and desegregated the entire Virginia prison system.

Wansley's role as a plaintiff in *Mason v. Peyton* had severe repercussions from the racist white power structure inside the prison. Although he was a model prisoner before a 1968 work stoppage, the fact he was a co-plaintiff with Leroy Mason in that suit, he was padlocked in his cell. Later, when the other striking prisoners were released from confinement, and despite his early request to go back to work, he remained locked in his cell, 24 hours a day, from July 19, 1968, through Apr. 1, 1969.

Penitentiary officials gave no reasons for Wansley's harsh confinement. There was no hearing, and he had no opportunity to confront the officials who ordered his quarantine. When the court asked the penitentiary superintendent why Wansley was in padlock, he stated in his deposition, "... in my judgment, I think that is where he should be."

"Tom Wansley was a great guy. Very quiet," recalled Calvin Arey, who was also incarcerated in the penitentiary from 1965 to 1972. He, along with Wansley, was one of the original five plaintiffs in *Landman v. Royster*. "Wore glasses. Not a troublemaker sort."

Arey added, "It wasn't easy in those Jim Crow days for a young Black man to stand up for civil rights, especially in the prison system."

On Jan. 3, 1973, Federal District Court Judge Robert Merhige Jr. finally handed down a reversal that determined that Wansley did not receive any fair trials guaranteed him by the Constitution due to local press coverage, courtroom negligence, and the continuous denial of his constitutional rights. Merhige's opinion dealt heavily with what he called juvenile court official Read's "breach of the trust" in failing to protect the rights of a child, as required by state law, and testifying against his own charge at the trial. This act alone, Merhige held, would have been "fatal" to the state's case.

He ordered that Virginia either retry him or free him. They elected to retry.

A Danger to Virginia's Women

On Jan. 11, Wansley again went in front of Circuit Court Judge Cundiff. One of the more infamous courtroom scenes in Virginia history unfolded at this trial when Kunstler told Cundiff that with so much doubt now about Wansley's role as the attacker, he should be released on bail. Cundiff refused, declaring that releasing Wansley "would be to endanger every woman in the state of Virginia."

Kunstler didn't miss a beat, stating, "I think you did it deliberately and willingly when you violated your oath of office; it was to lynch Thomas Wansley and do it a little less bloodily than with a rope."

Cundiff angrily replied that he would not "exchange his conscience" for Kunstler's. Kunstler countered that the essence of the case was the truth, not conscience, and he would not trade his truth for that of the judge. The remark drew a burst of applause from the predominantly Black spectators.

An infuriated Cundiff ordered the courtroom cleared, with many, including Kunstler, dragged out forcibly. But unfortunately, bail for Wansley was denied.

After the trial, Kunstler and Hirschkop immediately returned to Judge Merhige, who on Jan. 17 granted a federal writ of habeas corpus and freed Wansley on $10,000 bail.

"A (Temporary) Miracle has been Performed."

Once freed, Wansley went to work briefly with activists Bruce Smith and Lynn Abbott at the Woody Guthrie Community Center on Floyd Avenue in Richmond. Smith recalled that "Lynn Abbott and I split our salaries at the Woody Guthrie Center and hired Tom to work with us, concentrating on helping other, newly released long-term prisoners find their way back to life as an ex-convict while advocating for prison reform with the Prisoner's Solidarity Committee (PSC). Wansley provided expert guidance to people in and coming out of custody in Virginia prisons."

However, in November, the U.S. Supreme Court refused to review the conviction, and Wansley returned to the penitentiary. The brief that the Supreme Court dismissed called Wansley's conviction "A classic case of the selective prosecution, conviction, and punishment of a young Black man in Southern states accused of sex crimes against white women."

Despite a motion accompanied by a national campaign to pardon him, including rallies on Wansley's behalf in Lynchburg, Norfolk, and Richmond, and a petition to free him that contained over 15,000 signatures, Gov. Linwood Holton in 1974 denied the motion.

"Many Black leaders were left with a bitter taste in their mouths concerning Governor Holton," the March 22, 1974, *Muhammad Speaks* magazine wrote. Worse, the NAACP had recently given Holton a "Brotherhood" award.

Wansley's mother, Willie Mae Thornton, openly wept as she read Holton's two-page letter, in which he claimed he did not consider her son's case "extraordinary."

"The petition campaign succeeded in gaining broad support from Black and white citizens, independents, and people of both major political parties, including influential Republican women in Virginia," Bruce Smith explained. "But Holton backed off. Virginia's first Republican governor since Reconstruction seemed to be intimidated by his right-wing, former Dixiecrats from Lynchburg, who had just joined the Republican party after the Democrats decided to leave Jim Crow politics behind."

Free Wansley!

> If they knew that when they laid hands on one of us they'd have to face all of us – they wouldn't mess with any of us ... You can only let Mr. Wansley go to the electric chair if you don't recognize that he is part of you, recognize he's black- and that's the reason they're picking on him. If Mr. Wansley dies, I blame you."
>
> -Civil rights activist Stokely Carmichael, quoted in *The Southern Patriot*,
> April 1967.

In direct contrast to the mainstream press that sought to malign, condemn, and convict Tom Wansley (and even William Kunstler) through the court of public opinion, the growing left-wing counterculture and Black Power movements instead raised awareness of the grotesque inequities of the case. Chicago, Boston, New York, and even San Diego held rallies in Wansley's defense. Civil rights leader Stokely Carmichael spoke on his behalf at a rally at Lynchburg, originally scheduled to be held at all-white Lynchburg College until administrators found out that Blacks would be attending.

Student artists, writers, and activists organized. They used the pages of the *Virginia Weekly*, a Charlottesville-based underground newspaper, the *Southern Patriot*, *The Great Speckled Bird* in Atlanta, *The New South Student*, *Muhammed Speaks*, and the feminist newspaper *Triple Jeopardy*, among others, to tell the incredible and unvarnished story of Wansley's sham arrest, conviction, death sentences, and spurious imprisonment.

The coverage gained traction and induced more people and organizations to rally behind Wansley. Bumper stickers declaring "Free Wansley!" appeared on vehicles, suitcases, backpacks, and guitar cases. The case was championed by the Southern Conference Education Fund (SCEF), the Student Nonviolent Coordinating Committee (SNCC), Virginia Students Civil Rights Committee (VSCRC), the Southern Student Organizing Committee (SSOC), and the NAACP, among others.

Dr. Martin Luther King Jr. visited Wansley early on in the Lynchburg jail and told him to be patient and "learn to read and write" because he would need to help the attorney that the Southern Christian Leadership Council (SCLC) would hire for him. Student-led pickets vocally confronted the Lynchburg newspapers over their "commie-baiting" tactics and the media blackout of the case directed at the city's Black community.

"... I was on the Thomas Wansley Defense Committee," Beth Marschak recollected in 2021. "Some of us, including Willie Dell (who in 1973 was the first African-American woman elected to Richmond city council), met with Gov. Holton to try and get a pardon. He was cordial and gave everyone a chance to talk. My argument was [that] even if Tom was guilty, the sentence was disproportionate, and he should be freed. After listening to everyone, Holton thanked us for coming to see him with our concerns and said he would look into it."

"I was also in the Prisoner Solidarity Committee, which did leafleting at the state prison on Spring Street and Belvidere," Marschak continued. "Even did a few press conferences about Wansley and racial segregation at the prison."

On Feb. 2, 1974, Wansley married Earlinda Walker at the James River Correctional Center, but they divorced on Sept. 27, 1977. He married twice more after that.

Thomas Wansley was eventually fully released late in 1977. Bruce Smith offered to accompany him out of the country to Angola, Africa via Montreal, but after consideration Wansley elected to stay in Virginia. He went to work as a truck driver in Harrisonburg.

Unfortunately, because of his horrific experiences under Virginia's crushing criminal justice system, Wansley became an alcoholic later in life and died in Harrisonburg on Aug. 24, 2003.

Despite the notoriety of the case, Thomas Wansley was not the last Black man in Virginia sentenced to death for the rape of a white woman. There would be three more, with the last one, Cecil Wood, sentenced to death in 1972. None of them, however, were executed.

No Monsters

> A couple of years ago, as it was becoming apparent that the [Virginia] death penalty might finally fall, I did an informal survey among Hampton Roads area activists, Black and white, young to our age, the whole gamut of political views and experience. I could not find one person who had heard of Tom Wansley.
> - Al Long, former Charlottesville-area Southern Students Organizing Committee [SSOC] member, in a 2021 email.

Thomas Wansley lost 15 years of his life through this racist judicial firestorm. Still, unlike so many other young Black men who came before and after him and experienced similar treatment, he did not lose his life in the electric chair. Others with names forgotten to history – Hampton, Smith, Green, Davenport, Gillespie, Gilbert, Fleming,

Traynham, Breckenridge, Parker, Goins, Noel, Barbour, Sitlington, and hundreds of others – never had an activist speak up for them, or receive coverage and guest columns in counterculture newspapers, or have a Kunstler or a Hirschkop represent them.

Many of these men committed horrific crimes, but almost none were the monsters they were painted. They were overwhelmingly impoverished, broken, abused, substance-abusing, or intellectually disabled young men, who could only sit in bewildering curiosity at the legal circus unfolding with breakneck speed around them, guilty or not, with no one to speak on their behalf.

Then, when everyone finished yelling and pointing at them, the angry white people paraded from a small room after a brief wait of sometimes only minutes. They pronounced the defendant unworthy of life in polite white Virginia society.

Yes, many of those in this book deserved harsh punishment. But 400 years of Virginia's racist, mob-driven, reactive capital punishment system entangled so many innocent and undeserving victims – such as Thomas Wansley, among countless others – under the toxic guises of protecting their white women or of being "tough on crime." With so many of them, their guilt or innocence was irrelevant.

According to the Death Penalty Information Center, Virginia leads the nation with 1,390 executions between 1608 and 2017. In the modern era, starting in 1976, Virginia institutionalized and streamlined the parade to the death chamber more efficiently than any other state. The U.S., on average, executed about 16 percent of inmates who received a death sentence. A breathtaking 73 percent of all who received death sentences between 1977 and 2017 in Virginia were executed, leading the nation by far (Texas is second at 50 percent). Between October 1995 and January 1996, Virginia had an execution scheduled roughly every ten days.

By 1999, in a twisted and dangerous quest to accelerate the killing even more, Virginia whittled the capital appeals process down to less than five years, when the national average was almost ten years. The Supreme Court of Virginia and the Federal Fourth U.S. Circuit Court of Appeals most always upheld capital sentences passed in the lower courts.

Virginia executed more women (94) and more enslaved people than any other state (about 736, or 87 percent of all enslaved people executed nationally). Virginia also appears to be one of the leaders in killing juveniles whose ages have been verified between 11 and 17, with 16 executions. However, hundreds of those executed between 1608 and 1900 had no age recorded.

Death was the Virginia Way. And now, thanks to the work of dozens of people over almost five decades, it's over.

And it's one hell of a story.

Welcome to the Slaughterhouse

A New World, a New Set of Rules

The first person executed in the new English-speaking world was Capt. George Kendall, a member of the Jamestown Council. He was executed by firing squad for either conspiracy, treason, or both in 1608, only one year after the founding of Jamestown. The council curiously buried him with full military honors.

The distinction of "first execution" almost went to Kendall's accuser, James Read, a blacksmith convicted of mutiny, then cursing and threatening (or even punching) a Council leader, who punched him first. "For this, he was condemned to be hanged," wrote Edward M. Wingfield, the colony's first president.

In short, Read went "prison snitch" and saved himself just seconds before his hanging by declaring Kendall the ringleader of a conspiracy with the Spanish against the British.

In his 1608 letter "A True relation of such occurrences and accidents of note, as hath hapned at Virginia, since the first planting of that Collony by John Smith," which was later published without his knowledge or permission, Smith wrote:

> [Having] thus by Gods assistance gotten good store of corne, notwithstanding some bad spirits not content with Gods prouidence, still grew mutinous; in so much, that our president hauing occasion to chide the smith for his misdemenour, he not only gaue him bad language, but also offred to strike him with some of his tooles. For which rebellious act, the smith was by a [j]ury condemned to be hanged, but being vppon the ladder, continuing very obstinate as hoping vpon a rescue, when he saw no other way but death with him, he became penitent, and declared a dangerous conspiracy: for which, Captaine *Kendall*, as principal, was by a [j]ury condemned, and shot to death.

Kendall objected to the sentence. Being a man of influence, he confronted President John Ratcliffe and pronounced that since his real name was Sicklemore, he was not worthy to pronounce judgment against him. Captain John Martin instead declared him guilty and ordered his execution by firing squad.

In 1996 archaeologists working on unearthing the original Jamestown fort found the skeleton of a young white man buried behind a wall. Skeletal damage indicated the man was shot several times, then buried in a coffin, a luxury reserved only for gentlemen. Historian Nancy Egloff said of the skeleton, "A lot of evidence points to Kendall."

In 1609, after Chief Powhatan moved west to Orapakes, he tried two colonists for an unknown crime who had fled Jamestown. When Powhatan pronounced punishment after a short trial, the two hapless traitors were dragged just a few yards to a log and executed with clubs.

In 1610, Sir Thomas Gates sentenced a mutinous colonist, Henry Paine, to death while stranded on Bermuda after the shipwreck of the *Sea Venture*. Gates had previously pardoned other mutineers but decided to make an example of Paine. He also granted Paine's request to be shot rather than hung, which was punishment for commoners and considered lowbrow.

William Strachey wrote in 1625 that "Our Governour [Sir Thomas Gates], who had now the eyes of the whole Colony fixed upon him, condemned him [Paine] to be instantly hanged; and the ladder being ready, after he had made many confessions, hee earnestly desired, being a Gentleman, that hee might be shot to death, and towards the evening he had his desire, the Sunne and his life setting together."

Paine's execution was followed years later by Daniell Frank, who in 1621 was charged and convicted with George Clark for stealing a calf from former Gov. Sir George Yardley. Both were sentenced to death. On March 3, 1622, Frank became the first man hanged in the new world. His accomplice Clark, however, received a last-minute reprieve.

There is a notation in the National Death Penalty Archive that a person named Francis Lymberley was executed en route from England to Virginia in 1616. Further details are lacking.

Non-Clergyable Offenses

The first colonists arrived in Jamestown wielding a royal charter and accompanying orders under English common law, which prescribed the death penalty for various crimes. Some, such as rebellion and mutiny, were considered treasonous, and others, such as murder, rape, and adultery, were deemed non-treasonous and "non-clergyable" offenses. "Benefit of clergy" was a mechanism by which first-time offenders could obtain partial clemency for some crimes, then receive a reduced sentence. While benefit of clergy was available for misdemeanors, manslaughter was the only felony or capital crime for which the benefit of clergy was allowed. The death penalty – rendered by 12 "honest and indifferent" men – was mandatory for non-clergyable offenses with a guilty verdict.

Those early "honest and indifferent" men were sparing with the use of the death penalty, given the horrendous conditions under which the colonists lived and the accompanying high death rate by illness and starvation. Of the 105 English gentlemen, soldiers, tradesmen, and servants who arrived in Jamestown on May 13, 1607, more than one-half of them died that first summer. With little news of those hardships reaching England, clueless pilgrims kept sailing to the new world, with 525 dying in the first three years.

According to Gov. Percy, "There were never Englishmen left in a forreigne Countrey in such miserie as wee were in this new discovered Virginia."

In the spring of 1611, Sir Thomas Dale and 300 soldiers arrived in Jamestown. They were horrified at what they found – starvation, death, a breakdown of social hierarchy, and worse, a lack of order and discipline that boded poorly for the British investors. The despotic Dale quickly declared martial law, issuing draconian military regulations that supplemented existing civil orders that Gov. De La Warr had decreed in 1610. The following year these collective orders were printed in London with the title "For The Colony in Virginea Britannia. Lawes Divine, Morall and Martiall, &c."

Though enduring harsh disapproval of his methods, Dale functioned as a European-style tyrant from 1611 to 1619, imposing unforgiving punishments of forced labor and the liberal use of corporal punishment. His laws also stipulated sometimes horrific death sentences for an astonishing 54 specific offenses. One unnamed Jamestown colonist, caught stealing a few ounces of oatmeal, was allegedly tied to a tree, had a long "bodkin" (a blunt needle) forced through his tongue, then left to starve to death.

Many historians believe, however, that other than the first five years, Dale's system was intended to frighten colonists into obedience than serve as a legitimate criminal code. For example, adultery was a non-clergyable capital offense, but there is no evidence Dale imposed any death sentences for it. The same applies to other crimes such as bigamy, blasphemy, cursing, hog-stealing (first or second offense), price-gouging, pocket-picking, and misappropriation, or selling colony commodities for personal profit.

The meticulous research of death penalty historian M. Watt Espy tentatively confirmed this assumption, although record verification is difficult. He confirmed only around ten executions in Virginia from 1608 to 1700 for espionage, theft, sodomy, rape, murder, arson, and three unknown crimes.

On the other hand, illness and malnutrition claimed far more able bodies than the death penalty. By 1624, of the 7,549 who settled the colony, only 1,095 remained – an 85% death rate.

The execution of Richard Cornish in 1624 for sodomizing a young apprentice sailor displayed these harsh criminal justice statutes under which early lawbreakers endured. Cornish was convicted and executed based on the testimony of a single witness, forcing two men, Thomas Hatch and Edward Nevell, to critically speak out against what they considered a hasty and unlawful decision.

Leaders did not take their critiques kindly. Hatch, a servant of Gov. Yardley, was ordered to be "whipt" for speaking up, then "sett upon the pillory and there to loose one of his eares." His servitude to Yardley was reset to zero, leaving him to start all over.

Nevell fared even worse – he was ordered to stand in the marketplace "with a paper on his head shewing the cause of his offense." Then, both of his ears were cut off. He then received the unusual punishment of servile status for life.

By 1631 the governing body of Jamestown, which in 1624 had made the settlement a royal province, seemed to understand that harsh capital punishment laws were counterproductive to the new world's success. Edward Wingfield wrote in "A Discourse of Virginia" that "[Were] this whipping, lawing, beating, and hanging, in Virginia, knowne in England, I fear it would [drive] many well affected myndes from this [honorable] action of Virginia."

To attract more "well affected mynds," a 1631 revision enacted 61 statutes into Virginia law, with not one capital. A 1643 revision and another in 1658 combined prescribed almost 200 new statues, with only one capital. A final revision in 1662 enacted 142 new laws with only one capital.

But punishments were still harsh when enacted. Thomas Hellier, a white man but a lifelong bound servant (white slave) due to a conviction for theft in England, killed his master, Cutbeard Williamson, his wife and maid with an ax on their perhaps appropriately named Charles City plantation "Hard Labour." Hellier hanged on Aug. 5, 1678. Then, as a warning to others, his body was displayed crucifixion-style with his arms outstretched, left to the vultures and seagulls, on Windmill Point at the mouth of the Rappahannock River.

Capital punishment in those times was about revulsion and fear, with deterrence a distant third. The *Virginia Gazette* declared that capital punishment was a way of "counterbalancing temptation by terror, and alarming the vicious by the prospect of misery." An executed criminal was "an example and warning, to prevent others from those courses that lead to so fatal and ignominious a conclusion."

The capital crime of piracy became an epidemic off the Virginia coast between 1699 and 1730. Many of those convicted and executed, like Hellier, received the added degradation of being gibbeted or hung on display for months or even years. In May 1700, three pirates, John Houghtaling, Cornelius Frank, and Francois DeLaunee, were gibbeted in Elizabeth City. In 1718, fourteen members of Blackbeard's army were also gibbeted along the Capitol Landing Road in Williamsburg. In November 1720, six more were strung up in a veritable gauntlet of rotting, dangling corpses.

When authorities finally took down their bleached and picked-over bodies, they threw them into an open trench.

From 1700 to the American Revolution, piracy cases were heard by royally-appointed Admiralty judges because regular land-based courts had no jurisdiction over crimes committed on the high seas. The last verified executions in Virginia for piracy were Thomas Reed and Edward Clements, who were hanged in Richmond on April 26, 1852, on brand new gallows built by well-known Richmond architect and civil engineer W. A. Powell.

The Ordeal of Being Female in Colonial Virginia

According to the M. Watt Espy collection in the National Death Penalty Archive, since the founding of Jamestown, Virginia has executed 94 enslaved and free women, over twice as many as runner-up Massachusetts, and accounting for about one-fourth of all female executions nationwide.

Seventy-eight of these Virginia women were Black (both free and enslaved), eleven were white, and the remaining five, their races unknown. Only two white women have been executed in Virginia since 1774.

The first two women to show up in Jamestown were Mistress Forrest and her maid, Ann Burras, who arrived with Christopher Newport in September 1608. While more women began showing up sporadically in 1609, it wasn't until the 1620s that significant numbers of women were recruited, coerced, or forced to travel to the new colony across the Atlantic.

Life was especially arduous for this handful of Jamestown women during the "starving times" of 1609-10. They had no influence, no power or rights, yet were expected to manage a household and feed their families under a husband who controlled all aspects of their lives.

So subjugated were these women during this time that an unnamed starving English gentleman believed he was entitled to save his own life by killing and cannibalizing his pregnant wife. According to Capt. John Smith's diary, he proceeded to "ripp the childe out of her woambe and threw itt into the River and after chopped the Mother in pieces and salted her for his foode." When questioned about her absence, he claimed she ran away.

After parts of her mangled body were discovered, and still insisting the law permitted his heinous act per his upper-class comportment, he was "hanged by the Thumbes with weightes att his feete a quarter of an howere before he wolde Confesse the same." He was reportedly then, under a British Colonial custom reserved only for specifically heinous crimes that disturbed the social order, burned at the stake.

The Plight of Jane Champion, the First Woman Executed

As if being shipped from their homeland into impoverished, squalid conditions, then constantly reminded of how weak and inferior they were was not degrading enough for these women, the additional criminal stigma of pregnancy outside marriage compounded their suppression and societal fears. Infanticide, however, was the worst and considered a capital crime.

Unmarried pregnant women faced probable execution no matter what path they chose. The church taught that the murder of an unbaptized infant was the killing of its eternal soul, for the unbaptized had no place in heaven. A Jamestown preacher named Foxcroft reminded parishioners "[that] monstrous fact being detected, has brought to her yet greater shame, by an infamous execution, as a murderer."

"Pride has tempted many a young woman to destroy the fruit of her own body," he thundered from the pulpit, "that she may avoid the scandal of a spurious child ...."

It is not clear when Jane arrived in Jamestown or when she married her husband, a wealthy landowner named Percival Champion. But sometime around September of 1630, Jane had a brief affair with another colonist named William Gallopin. She soon discovered she was pregnant and – knowing what trouble she was in – went to great pains to conceal her illegitimate pregnancy from the colony.

Sometime in late 1631 into early 1632, Jane gave birth to a possibly stillborn baby, but it didn't matter. According to the law, she and her paramour both were guilty of infanticide, and they both faced execution.

The minutes of the Jamestown court state, "Wm. Gallopin & Jane Champion wife of Percival Champion Indicted by Gd. Jury for murder & concealing ye death of ye sd. Jane's child supposed to be got by ye sd. Wm. pleaded, found guilty by petty Jury & sentenced to be hang'd."

While the record attests that the court sentenced William to hang, no record confirms it. Jane's hanging, however, is verified by researchers Espy and Victor Streib.

Jane Champion's execution set a brutal precedent for colonial women convicted of the capital crime of infanticide. The very next year, on June 24, 1633, another white James City County woman, Margaret Hatch, was hanged for allegedly killing her illegitimate infant. Hatch initially claimed she was pregnant again to delay her execution, but a "jury of matrons" examined her and concluded she was not.

The laws at the time stipulated that if a woman gave birth with no midwife present, her execution was mandatory if the baby was dead, even if she claimed it was stillborn.

There were only a few other cases of non-slave women executed in colonial Virginia. Martha Sharp hanged for child murder in early June 1767. According to the June 11 *Virginia Gazette*, she "... denied the crime for which she suffered, and laid it upon the father of the child."

Killing Enslaved People

The sweeping criminal justice reforms of 1797 applied only to freemen and did not affect capital crimes governing enslaved people. Thus, they faced an even harsher iron fist of Virginia justice.

The ship *White Lion*, commanded by John Colyn Jope, introduced slavery to America in late August 1619 when it arrived at Point Comfort near Chesapeake. Jope brought "20 and odd Negroes," believed to be from Angola, who he sold in exchange for food and provisions. Four days later, the *Treasurer* arrived, and its captain, Daniel Elfrith, sold three of the enslaved Africans aboard.

Since slavery was not yet lawful in the new world, the Blacks worked as indentured servants with no contracts until 1661, when slavery was made legal.

In 1682, Virginia became the first state to implement a set of rigid "slave codes" to regulate these new arrivals. These codes defined enslaved people as property with no legal rights. They also mandated their servitude as lifelong, with harsh punishments prescribed for numerous violations, including the death penalty.

By 1690 two separate legal systems had emerged, one for free men and one for the enslaved. By that year, runaways could be killed if they failed to return after being ordered to by proclamation. In 1691, the first offense of hog stealing was made a capital crime for slaves only, although it was repealed in 1699. Subsequent laws include a statute enacted in 1723 which stated that if more than five enslaved people planned an insurrection, they were guilty of conspiracy, a capital crime without benefit of clergy. This law was amended in 1748 to include five conspirators or fewer. In 1765, manslaughter was a clergyable offense for slaves only if another slave was the victim. Another provision that year prescribed castration for an enslaved male for the attempted rape of a white woman.

The first recorded enslaved man executed in Virginia was Tony, who hanged in Henrico County around April 7, 1688, for an unknown felony. According to the Henrico County Order Book, ten shillings were paid "for building a gallows for ye negro executed in this county by his Excellency's command." Tony's hanging was followed in 1693 by that of Tom Cary (Swan), a slave hanged in Northampton County for robbing and setting fire to a house belonging to Thomas Richards.

Tom Cary was the first enslaved man convicted in the recently established court of Oyer and Terminer ("Listen and Determine"). Until the 1690s, slaves and free Blacks, when accused of a felony, were tried in Jamestown at what was first called the Quarter Court, then the General Court. However, as the settlement expanded, the Assembly created Oyer and Terminer "for the speedy prosecution of slaves ... without the sollemnite of jury." This "speedy prosecution" may be considered the forerunner of Virginia's later "rocket docket."

From two to six local justices presided over these courts, depending on who was available. Witnesses testified against the slave, who defended themselves with no legal counsel. Convictions had to be unanimous, and there were no appeals.

Sarah (Custis), the first enslaved woman to be executed, was tried in a court of Oyer and Terminer in Northampton in 1705. She intentionally set fire to her owner's barn and house, which, unknown to her, contained several barrels of salt and gunpowder – which undoubtedly resulted in a spectacular and high-profile conflagration.

The codes also upheld the use of deadly vengeance against slaves by their white owners – basically awarding them a license to kill. In 1705, a Virginia code stated that "if anyone with authority correcting a slave killed him in such correction, it shall not be accounted felony, and the killer would be freed as if such accident had never happened." However, as property, many enslavers considered it unwise to kill a living asset they needed to keep their farm profitable. Thus, private capital punishment inflicted by owners was mainly anecdotal.

Over time, lawmakers carved out exceptions. According to the April 21, 1775, *Virginia Gazette*, William Pitman, a white man, came home in a drunken rage and "tied his poor negro boy by the neck and heels," beat him viciously with a grapevine, then stomped him to death "for a trifling offence."

"This man has justly incurred the penalties of the law, and we hear will certainly suffer," the article pointed out. "Which ought to be a warning to others to treat their slaves with moderation and not give way to unruly passions."

Pitman's son and daughter testified against him, and he was found guilty. He hanged on Dec. 5. No more whites were executed for crimes against Blacks until 1997.

Despite Pitman's aberrant behavior, the Commonwealth of Virginia became a wholesale killer of slaves, executing far more than any other state, with about 736 killed between 1641 and 1865. In his study "Slave executions in the United States: A descriptive analysis of social and historical factors," researcher Adalberto Aguirre, Jr., found that Virginia, during the 1790 – 1865 antebellum period, executed nearly three times as many enslaved people as all other Upper South states combined. "The comparably exorbitant number of slave executions in Virginia is most likely an outcome of its history as a slave state and having a sizable proportion of slaves in its population." By 1850, Virginia's 66 death penalty-eligible crimes for its enslaved population undoubtedly played a significant role.

Another option for certain crimes committed by slaves not sentenced to death was transportation to another state, usually for a set amount of time, such as seven or 14 years. The punishment for returning before that time was execution. After the term was up, most slaves could not afford to return; therefore, the penalty amounted to banishment.

Between 1801 and 1858, Virginia transported an estimated 900 condemned slaves out of state.

Slave executions were also costly to Virginia taxpayers, who ultimately, under the 1705 law, owed reimbursements to slave owners through the treasury when a slave was executed or transported out of the state. Lawmakers amended this law in 1801 under Rule 43. Once sentenced, a Virginia court jury would assess a monetary value on the slave, depending on their age, sex, strength, and future value as a worker. Many jurisdictions reimbursed slave owners for considerably less than the total value as a costly reminder to the owner to manage and control his assets properly.

There is little to no extant recordkeeping by county sheriff's offices of slave executions. Still, executions can be confirmed by county auditor records of payments made to the owners or their estates. The Library of Virginia stores many of these records.

The 1831 House of Delegates auditor's office records that from 1819 to 1830, Virginia paid out $124,785 for the execution or transportation of 313 slaves, with an average dollar value of $398.67 each.

Slave reimbursements skyrocketed to as high as $4,000 each during the civil war but were payable in quickly depreciating Confederate money.

The Virginia criminal code of 1848 dramatically reinforced slave codes and increased the number of capital crimes for which only slaves could be executed. Chapter XII, section 1 ominously stated that any slave who committed any offense that would get a free person three years or more in the penitentiary would be punished with death.

Capital crimes for which slaves could be charged and executed expanded over time to include numerous categories of murder, rape, attempted rape, suspicion of rape, administering poison to whites (including ground glass and other foreign elements in food or drink), preparing and administering medicine to a white person, arson, livestock theft, burglary, highway robbery, and numerous categories of assaults, attempted assaults, even threats of assaults.

Since burglary and armed robbery were capital crimes only for slaves, the law was amended immediately after emancipation to also allow freemen to be executed for these crimes. The goal was to threaten formerly enslaved people with hanging if they attempted to take the property of their former masters by force.

For non-capital offenses in which a free person would be imprisoned for less than three years, the slave would be punished with "the stripes" (whippings), not exceeding 39 lashes at any one time. One unnamed slave in 1854 was convicted of aiding and abetting a murder. Rather than execution or transportation, he was whipped 39 lashes on the first day, 15 on the second, 15 on the third, 15 again on the fourth, and 39 on the fifth. Slaves could also be whipped for using "menacing language or gestures" toward a white person, going from home without a pass, carrying a gun, or attempting to preach.

Many of the crimes considered capital were exceedingly minor. A Frederick County slave named Bob, belonging to Margaret and Sarah Wilson, hanged on June 1, 1786, for breaking into a house and stealing a pair of shoe buckles and a shirt belonging to another slave. One Nottoway County slave, Phill, property of Phillip Greenhill, was hanged in 1789 for stealing a single silver spoon.

Harsher Penalties for Enslaved Women

Virginia executed the oldest enslaved woman in America. Sixty-five-year-old Nellie (Green) hanged along with her daughter Betsy and 18-year-old grandson James on Feb. 13, 1857, in Prince William County for the ax-murder of their owner, George E. Green. Two other juveniles, Elias and Ellen, were convicted but not hanged due to their "extreme youth."

Nellie was valued at $300, and Betsy and James at $800. This hanging was Virginia's first and only execution of three consecutive generations of one family.

Ax murders by women were rare, as poisoning was a far more pervasive threat to white owners of enslaved women – several cases in particular point out the dangers of poisoning, both to the owner and the slave. In 1772, an enslaved woman named Judith, who belonged to Nathanial Harrison of Prince George County, was tried for "Suspicion of feloniously administering poisonous medicine with intention to destroy the family" of Lewis Scarbrough in Brunswick County. She was found guilty and hanged on June 26. A companion male slave was also accused but acquitted.

In 1803, Princess Anne County slave siblings Charity and George were found guilty of attempting to poison the Thomas Lawson family by mixing arsenic in a pot of coffee. The family was sickened but did not die. Both hanged on Oct. 28.

A better-documented poisoning case with a grislier result was that of an enslaved woman named Eve in Orange County. Zachary Lewis, attorney for the King, informed the court of Oyer and Terminer that Eve, a "slave woman lately belonging to Peter Montague, late of Orange County, Virginia, had, on Aug. 19, 1745, poisoned Mr. Montague, and that he had languished to Dec. 27 of the same year," when he died.

Eve pleaded not guilty, but witnesses testified against her, and the court found her guilty. The court ordered the sheriff to carry out the execution the following Wednesday. The June 1896 *Virginia Historical Magazine* stated that Eve was "drawn upon a hurdle to the place of execution, and be there burnt." The court determined her to be worth $200, payable to Montague's widow.

The smoke of the burning of Eve at the stake was reportedly visible over a large extent of the Orange County countryside.

Boiling to death and burning alive were punishments in England and Virginia reserved for slave women who committed the crime of "petit treason," a lesser form of high treason which included poisoning and killing one's owner. This cruel law originated in 1531 when a cook named Richard Roose, in the Bishop of Rochester's kitchen in central London, poisoned seventeen people – two fatally – with porridge. British Parliament then passed an act declaring poisoning as treason, and Roose was convicted, then retroactively boiled to death.

While there were two, maybe three burnings, there are no records of anyone in Virginia boiled to death.

More than one slave woman made an ax their weapon of choice. The Feb. 25, 1737

Virginia Gazette reported a slave woman who belonged to a family named Prudden was found guilty of the murder of her owner's wife with a broad-ax. Like Eve, she also was burned alive after confessing to the crime. "... [the slave] lately killed her Mistress in Nansemond, upon her Tryal, confes'd the fact, receiv'd Sentence of Death, and is since burnt."

The Gov. William Cabell papers record the 1806 case of two female slaves, Crease and Sall (alias Sarah), who were the property of Daniel Morrissette in Manchester. They allegedly despised Morrissette's wife, Martha, because of her "shrewishness." One day, while plowing, Sall crushed Martha's head with an ax after a particularly harsh reprimand. She and Crease hid the body until nightfall, when they retrieved it, dragged it to the banks of the James River, and dismembered it, throwing the pieces into the river. An investigation recovered only one leg.

Crease hanged on May 30. Sall received a pregnancy respite but was ultimately hanged on July 11, 1806, on gallows built directly over the murder scene.

Outside of the slavery era, on April 22, 1881, a crowd of 100 spectators gathered outside an enclosure beside the Lunenburg County Jail for the hanging of a Black woman, Lucinda Fowlkes, who in January had murdered her husband, William, with an ax, after years of beatings and verbal abuse.

The Ghastly Consequences of Slave Revolt

Except for a few isolated but well-publicized uprisings, slave revolt in Virginia was not nearly as widespread as in other areas, particularly the Deep South, but the early punishments were shockingly brutal. The Surry County Order Book, 1691–1713, records two enslaved men named Salvadore (a Native American) and Scipio (a Black man), who were executed on May 2, 1710, for planning Virginia's first insurrection. The revolt failed when a third slave lost his nerve and turned in the other two, gaining a reprieve for himself.

Surry chronicled just how brutal their punishment was:

> [Salvadore was to be] hanged and his body disposed of, *viz*, his head to be delivered to the sheriff of James City County and by him sett up (put on display) at the city of Williamsburg. Two of his quarters likewise delivered to the sheriff of New Kent County be sett up in the most publick place of the said county, and the other two quarters to be disposed of and sett up as the justices of the County of Surry shall think fit to direct.

Scipio's body was similarly mutilated, with pieces sent to Gloucester, Lancaster, New Kent, and King & Queen counties to display as warnings.

As evidenced by the treatment of Salvadore and Scipio, the public display of a dismembered and decapitated body was, like gibbeting, designed to induce fear, disgust, and hopefully, deterrence. In 1763, an Augusta County court ordered that Tom, convicted of killing his owner, "be hanged by the neck until he be dead and ... then his head be severed from his body and af'xed on a pole on the top of the hill near the road that lead from this Court House."

(Similarly, a few miles south in Rockbridge County, a slave named York was hanged in 1786, not for insurrection but for killing a fellow slave. In a strange and gruesome coda, the judge inexplicably ordered York's head cut off and placed on a pole at a fork in the road between Lexington and "Mr. Parton's house.")

Peter, a slave belonging to John Riddle in Orange County, was tried, convicted, and immediately hanged on June 23, 1737, for murdering his owner. After hanging, his head was placed on a pole near the courthouse "to deter others from doing the like." Later, tradition states that the head was moved to the banks near a river, and for decades the area was known as Negro Head Run.

This incident, however, is disputed. The June 1894 edition of the *Virginia Magazine of History and Biography* dismisses the incident, falsely insisting that "It is safe to assert that this is wholly untrue, and that no such barbarous punishment ever took place in Virginia." The 1907 book "A History of Orange County, Virginia" by William Wallace Scott states of the rumor that "If true, the incident must have occurred before the county was formed."

The 1930 book "Criminal Law in Colonial Virginia" notes that in 1767, four Black men in Arlington County attempted unsuccessfully to "poison their overseers." After being hanged, they were decapitated, and their heads were placed on the courthouse's chimneys. This incident is also recorded in the Jan. 11, 1768, *Boston Chronicle*.

The Aug. 2, 1750 *Pennsylvania Gazette* notes that a Northumberland County "negro boy" was found guilty of aiding and abetting the murder of his owner, Col. Pressley. Oyer and Terminer sentenced him to be hanged, then drawn and quartered, but there is no direct evidence in Virginia records that he was.

Post-mortem punishments, such as quartering and beheading, seemed to be inflicted strictly at the court's whim, with no guiding legal standards. A revolt in 1730 resulted in four unnamed slaves being hanged in Princess Ann County, but the courts dispensed with any other abuses of the bodies. The Princess Ann Order Book, 1728-1737, records that Sheriff Francis Mosely was paid 1,910 pounds of tobacco for carrying out those executions.

In January 1778, three Amelia County slaves, listed as Simon, Old Bristol, and Young Bristol, were hanged for murdering their owner, John Ford, also with no additional desecration.

In October 1799, two Georgia slave traders, Joshua Butte and Harris Spears traveled to Southampton County to purchase "a parcel of negroes" to join a slave gang they were "driving" back South. Several of the 15 slaves armed with "sticks, knives, and pistols" attacked Butte and Spears a few hours later. They cut the men's throats "ear to ear" and threw their bodies into a nearby pond.

The Nov. 2, 1799 *Augusta Chronicle* reported that five culprits, Hatter Isaac, Old Sam, Young Sam, Jerry, and Isaac, were arrested, convicted, and sentenced to death by the Southampton Court. Young Sam pleaded benefit of clergy because of his age, so he received 39 lashes and was branded in the hand. Isaac died in prison while awaiting execution because of a jurisdictional dispute between Virginia and Georgia, but the remaining three all hanged on Nov. 25, 1799. The court valued them between $260 and $316 each.

Slave justice was not only brutal but swift in those days. Although it was customary to wait ten days between sentencing and execution, the January 1899 *William & Mary College Historical Magazine* recorded an entry from the "Diary of John Blair," which stated that an unnamed James City County slave burglarized a house on Sept. 29, 1752. He was captured, tried, convicted, and hanged on Oct. 1.

Death Without Dignity

> When the trap springs, he dangles at the end of the rope. There are times when the neck has not been broken, and the prisoner strangles to death. His eyes pop almost out of his head, his tongue swells and protrudes from his mouth, his neck may be broken, and the rope many times takes large portions of skin and flesh from the side of the face that the noose is on. He urinates, he defecates, and droppings fall to the floor while witnesses look on.
> -From *Campbell v. Wood*, petition for writ of certiorari, U. Supreme Court,
> May 26, 1994.

Hanging seemed almost respectful compared with states' execution methods such as Louisiana, which in 1730 executed eight slaves by "breaking on the wheel." This was a barbaric and excruciating punishment in which the executioner tied the prisoner spread-eagle to a wagon-like wheel, then crushed their arms and legs with a club, hammer, or iron bar. Frequently the executioner would inflict further torture by "weaving" the still-living, shrieking victim's shattered limbs throughout the wheel spokes before delivering a final, fatal blow to the chest, head, or abdomen.

Louisiana executed 24 slaves in assembly-line fashion on April 15, 1795, for planning an insurrection at Point Coupeé. This revolt ended the importation of slaves from the West Indies. Louisiana executed another 16 slaves in January 1811 in an unknown manner. South Carolina executed 35 slaves for insurrection in 1822, with a stomach-churning 22 hangings in one day on July 26.

Southern states were not alone in inflicting gruesome punishments for slave revolts. In 1712, New York executed 21 slaves convicted of insurrection by breaking on the wheel, burning, hanging, and hanging in chains. New York executed another 33 slaves in 1741 by hanging and burning alive.

Gabriel's Rebellion

In August 1800, a crowd of almost one thousand Virginia slaves led by Gabriel (Prosser) planned a well-coordinated uprising against enslavers, federalists, and Richmond merchants. Quakers, French, women, and children were intended to be spared.

The enslaved were well-armed. Gabriel, his brothers, and other blacksmiths worked undercover for weeks turning scythe blades into twelve dozen swords. They also created 50 spears and numerous musket balls.

Planning to march under a banner that read "Death or Liberty," Gabriel's Rebellion was scheduled for Saturday, Aug. 30. However, Gabriel canceled the revolt due to hours-long torrential rain that made meetings impossible and roads impassable.

Two slaves reportedly saw the storm as an omen and told Mosby Sheppard of the planned attack led by "Prosser's Gabriel." Gov. James Monroe mobilized the Richmond Light Infantry Blues, and they quickly began arresting culprits, including Gabriel, who fled but was caught aboard the schooner Mary in Norfolk a week later. The governor interrogated him personally, but he refused to divulge any information. He and twenty-six other co-conspirators were then incarcerated in September at the State Penitentiary and Henrico County Jail.

Ten of the conspirators hanged on Sept. 12 and 15, with Gabriel hanged on Oct. 7, and the last, Peter (Claiborne), was hanged two weeks later. One defendant committed suicide before his arraignment. Eight others were transported outside of Virginia, and a few others were pardoned or found not guilty.

In 2007, Gov. Tim Kaine informally pardoned Gabriel to recognize his convictions for liberty and revolution.

Thomas Jefferson's Aversion to the Death Penalty

After ten hangings in the Gabriel Rebellion, Gov. James Monroe asked Thomas Jefferson if, in his opinion, more executions were needed to prevent similar rebellions. Jefferson, who for over 20 years worked tirelessly to reform Virginia's archaic criminal justice laws, responded that "there is a strong sentiment that there has been hanging enough. The other states and the world at large will forever condemn us if we indulge a principle of revenge or go one step beyond absolute necessity."

Sentencing in those early courtrooms was notoriously arbitrary. A Culpeper man named John Floy in 1751 was found guilty of manslaughter and, for punishment, was burned in his hand. Two months earlier, a Spotsylvania man named William Johnson was found guilty of stealing a watch and was sentenced to death. On April 18, 1751, an "old offender" from Southampton, John Hill, was tried for his fourth crime: horse stealing – a capital offense. He had once even broken out of the Norfolk prison, robbed a store, then returned to his cell to evade suspicion. Upon sentencing on May 9, Hill petitioned for an "honors clemency," arguing that "tho' a brother should sin seventy times seven," on his repentance he "should be acquitted." The Virginia Gazette reported the court ruled that "Christianity obliged us to forgive him."

However, Christianity did not oblige that same court to forgive Lowe Jackson, as it sentenced him to death for counterfeiting.

Thomas Jefferson personally disliked capital punishment and lobbied tirelessly to restrain its use. He agreed with the Pennsylvania Quakers that the legitimate object of all punishment should be discipline, repentance, and reform rather than vengeance. As early as August 1776, he wrote, "Punishments I know are necessary, and I would provide them, strict and inflexible, but proportioned to the crime."

"Death," he added, "might be inflicted for [murder] and perhaps for treason."

While serving in the Virginia General Assembly from 1776 to 1779, Jefferson drafted a long-awaited revision of the penal laws, titled "A Bill for Proportioning Crimes and Punishments in Cases Heretofore Capital." He added that non-capital crimes could be punished by "working on high roads, rivers, and other projects in time proportionate to the offense."

The General Assembly, however, not only had reservations about Jefferson's somewhat unusual theories regarding extended incarceration, labor, and solitary confinement but were distracted by the war with Britain, and the bill died. Another bill introduced by James Madison in the 1785 General Assembly session (while Jefferson served as Ambassador to Paris) to amend Virginia's outmoded laws and incorporate "labor by public works" gained the support of the judges of the General Court. They wrote, "as men, we cannot but lament that the laws relating to capital punishments are in many cases too severe." Nonetheless, a single vote defeated the bill in the House of Delegates.

Attributing the defeat to a resurgence in horse stealing, a dejected Madison wrote to Jefferson in 1787 that "Our old bloody code is by this event fully restored."

In 1796 Jefferson finally succeeded in reforming Virginia's laws. The new code eliminated the death penalty for all crimes committed by free persons except for first-degree murder. No longer was it punishable by death to trade with Indians, steal blueberries, or kill a domestic animal without permission. The following year, construction started on the most significant building project in America south of Washington D.C. – the Virginia State Penitentiary, which opened its doors on April 1, 1800, and remained open until February 1991.

Deadly Tobacco

In colonial times, any tampering or destruction of Virginia's precious cash crop, tobacco, was declared a form of high treason, punishable by death. So severe were they about protecting the crop that in May, 1682, after bumper crops stuffed warehouses, farmers and planters asked the government to authorize a one-year cessation in planting to drive prices back up. They failed to do so, forcing prices in London to a critical low. Desperate tobacco planters, including women, in Gloucester and Middlesex County, then cut down tens of thousands of young plants. Either one or six of these "plant-cutters" were reportedly hanged to discourage the practice, but details are lacking.

It wasn't until the 1770s that the Virginia legislature stripped the treason language and enacted more exacting laws to protect their most critical source of revenue. One law passed by the General Assembly in 1778 declared three separate tobacco offenses as felonies punishable by death. These included tampering with tobacco casks, landing or unloading tobacco at some location other than a designated warehouse, and exporting tobacco under forged or counterfeited inspection certificates.

These laws expanded in 1783 by declaring capital offenses without benefit of clergy to place or remove tobacco in a cask that had already been inspected, or procure tobacco from a designated warehouse by using forged or counterfeit receipts.

Cruel and Unusual

> The death penalty cannot be useful, because of the example of barbarity it
> gives men.
>
> -Cesare Beccaria, "On Crimes and Punishments," 1764.

It is with no small sense of irony that colonial Virginia leaders led other states in declaring their opposition to "cruel and unusual punishments" only to lead the nation in executions and deliver them faster and more efficiently than any other state. George Mason in 1776 included a prohibition of cruel and unusual punishments in his draft of the commonwealth's Declaration of Rights. In 1788, during debate on the ratification of the U.S. Constitution, Mason, and his fellow antifederalists worried that the lack of common law constraints in the new Constitution would permit Congress to create "new crimes, inflict unusual and severe punishments, and extend their powers." In 1791, this Virginia prohibition became the central component of the Constitution's Eighth Amendment.

Patrick Henry emphasized that the lack of a prohibition of cruel and unusual punishments in the Constitution draft meant that Congress could use those punishments as implements of oppression: "Congress ... may introduce the practice of France, Spain, and Germany of torturing, to extort a confession of the crime," he wrote. "They ... will tell you that there is such a necessity of strengthening the arm of government, that they must ... extort confession by torture, in order to punish with still more relentless severity. We are then lost and undone."

Concessions were made, and Virginia became the first state ratification convention to propose that the U.S. Constitution be amended to include a prohibition on cruel and unusual punishments.

Fear and Loathing

Gabriel's Rebellion in 1800 had a chilling effect on Virginians, making them terrified not only of slave uprisings but of mere rumors of them. In January 1802, Gov. Monroe heard of a plot in Nottoway County, prompting the hanging of four ringleaders. Two more suspected conspiracies in 1808 and 1809 led to the hanging of an enslaved man named Jacob.

In 1805, arson and treason were added to murder as death penalty eligible crimes.

Scattered rumors of revolts continued until 1831 when a self-described mystic and avid Bible reader named Nat Turner conceived the most comprehensive uprising of all – a plan to conquer Southampton County. After recruiting several co-conspirators, Turner and his men began striking rural white homes across the county. Within 48 hours, they had accumulated a small army of 60 armed men who killed 55 people before turning their attentions to the county seat of Jerusalem for a planned coup d'état.

The Turner rebellion constituted the most significant number of white casualties in any single slave revolt in the history of the United States.

While on their march, a large posse overwhelmed Turner's army, forcing them to abandon their plans and disperse. Turner was able to escape and hid for six weeks in the swampy overgrowth of the Great Dismal Swamp before he was caught and brought to trial.

In total, 16 or 17 insurrectionists were charged with "with feloniously counselling, advising and conspiring with each other and divers[e] other slaves to rebel and make insurrection and making insurrection and taking the lives of divers[e] free white persons of the Commonwealth." They were then hanged, with a described "calm and collected" Turner dying on Nov. 11, 1831.

As an enslaved man, the court valued his life at $375.

Before the civil war, a few other notable executions include the triple hanging of Buck, Harris, and John, who were three slaves who attempted to kill their Suffolk County owner, Henry Birdsong. Harris was recommended for clemency, but the governor refused, and all three died on Sept. 9, 1853.

Exceptionally few whites were executed in the decade leading to the civil war. On Oct. 28, 1853, 30-year-old Thomas Board, a white man described as "weak-minded" and "childish on his outlook on life," was hanged for the April murder of his young nephew, Strickler Chrislip, near Philippi, Virginia (now West Virginia). After he was tried and convicted, he failed to grasp that he was about to die, only that he was about to be the center of attention. As onlookers hurriedly passed his jail cell window toward the gallows, he reportedly told them there was no need to hurry, as there "won't be any fun until I get there."

Executions of whites were, in fact, so rare in this far western side of Virginia that in 1858, a pastor named Preston Turley hanged in Charleston for murdering his wife. The press reported "the strange spectacle" of the execution of a white man in this region. "It was the first occurrence of the kind ever known to have taken place within the county." The event was so unique that the *Charleston Star* estimated 5,000 people showed up.

Capital Punishment During the Civil War

At the outbreak of the civil war, lawbreakers and laws about them channeled through three classes. For whites, the law authorized capital punishment only for treason, murder, and arson. Free Blacks could receive the death penalty for these three offenses, plus rape and attempted rape if the victim was a white woman. Finally, the state could continue executing enslaved people for dozens of other crimes outlined in the 1848 codes.

Virginia conducted 46 hangings during the war, from 1860 to 1865. Forty-three were Black men and women, all slaves. One of the three white executions was Timothy Webster, the only documented Virginia execution for war-time espionage, who died in a botched hanging before an immense crowd at Fort Lee on May 1, 1862.

The first rope came untied at Webster's hanging when the trap was sprung, and the unfortunate prisoner tumbled to the ground. The executioner quickly tied another rope, but he incorrectly placed it, and Webster's neck did not break in the fall. As he hung suspended, strangling to death, he allegedly uttered his last words, "I suffer a double death."

Isolated slave revolts continued to be a problem for their owners during the war years, although none resembled the scale of the Turner or the Gabriel rebellions of the past. Three slaves, Colin, Dick, and John, were hanged on Nov. 11, 1860, for attempting to poison their owner's family, who was regarded as one of the most prominent in Lunenburg County. The *Richmond Dispatch* reported on Nov. 15 that after the drop, Dick did not immediately die and "seemed to suffer the most excruciating agony," as he spun in a circle, "visibly agitated" while desperately trying to untie his hands.

A story published by the Nov. 28, 1974, *Amherst Progress* (and confirmed by the National Death Penalty Archive) described an uprising against a wealthy landowner named Terisha Washington Dillard, who enslaved many men and women on his James River plantation near Lynchburg. He allegedly purchased a slave from Louisiana in the 1850s, and by 1862 that transplant started sowing seeds of insurrection with the others against their owner.

In March or early April of 1863, several slaves attacked Dillard in his yard after the issuing of the Emancipation Proclamation. According to the story, a woman named Bet struck a fatal blow to his head with an ax. They then reportedly decapitated him and buried his body in the hog lot.

Once the revolt and killing were discovered, 11 slaves were tried for the murder of Dillard, with six – Armistead, Bet, George, Jane, Sarah, and Seaton – found guilty and executed in May 1863.

Even free northern Blacks could not sometimes escape Virginia's war-era slave system and capital punishment machine. One of the more insidious money-making schemes during the war was the creation of a reverse underground railroad. Captured Black Union soldiers, even free Black men, women, and children snatched off the streets, were sold "down the river" into slavery to southern plantation owners. One Free Black Ohio man, Isaac Chaney, who fought for the Union at the 1864 Battle of Saltville, was captured by Confederates and sold into slavery to a Rockbridge County man named Parsons.

After the war, Chaney and his wife – with no money or home of their own – were released from slavery but forced to become sharecroppers for John. F. Gerald, also of Rockbridge. One day Chaney and Gerald had an altercation, and Chaney reportedly killed Gerald with a club in self-defense. He was arrested and tried in a bogus trial with no defense witnesses called, then hanged twice in Libby Prison in 1866 because the rope broke on the first attempt.

In 1866, burglary, armed robbery, and rape were added as death penalty-eligible crimes. In 1868, armed robbery expanded to include "partial strangulation or suffocation, or by striking or beating, or by other violence to the person, or by the threat of presenting firearms."

Lynching and Capital Punishment During Post-War Jim Crow

After the civil war, Virginia's political and business leaders desired to abandon the constraints of the lost cause still embraced by the agrarian states of the Deep South and chart a course of industrial and manufacturing development more in common with that of the Northern states.

But old traditions died hard, and with slavery officially ended, Virginia whites sought alternative ways to maintain control of Blacks and keep them subjugated while embarking on ambitious construction projects of highways and railroads to the north and west. One solution became known as the convict leasing system, coupled with the passage of "Black Code" laws. Legislators crafted these laws specifically to entrap primarily young, Black men into frequently nonsense crimes, earning them long prison sentences, where railroad barons could lease them out to work in Western and West Virginia tunnels.

In April 1864, the U.S. Senate introduced and passed the Thirteenth Amendment by the required two-thirds majority. The amendment stated, "Neither slavery nor involuntary servitude, *except as a punishment for crime whereof the party shall have been duly convicted* (emphasis added), shall exist within the United States, or any place subject to their jurisdiction."

The "punishment for crime whereof the party shall have been duly convicted" clause remains in the amendment. Virginia and most Deep South states exploited this clause during the Jim Crow era to relegate Blacks convicted of low-level, even specious crimes to be leased out and worked – sometimes to death – on railroads, quarries, and other public works projects. The convict leasing program thus quickly became a sadistic purgatory between slavery and freedom. The white leaderships of Virginia and other southern states contended that Blacks still needed to be kept in their place and that as freemen, they worked best as they did as slaves: in groups, under the eyes of brutal overseers, in similarly degrading conditions.

With intimidation and violence utilized through forced servile labor, lynching, capital punishment, and convict leasing soon became natural extensions of maintaining white supremacy. The amendment that abolished slavery thus in a backhanded manner helped preserve it.

During the 1877 to 1930 Jim Crow era, law enforcement tactics bore many similarities to lynching. Both frequently utilized haphazard, mob violence-driven, and racially discriminatory criminal justice police methods. After a serious crime was purported to have been committed, suspects were sometimes captured not by law enforcement but by hastily thrown together posses of angry, armed white men consumed with retribution. The predominantly Black suspects – impoverished, uneducated, and helpless within the system's confines – were routinely (mis)identified by traumatized victims, likely bullied and beaten into confessing, then threatened with death, if not by mobs then by the courts.

These defendants sometimes had poor legal counsel or none at all. They cowered in holding cells while white packs lurked outside like wolves, watching for an opening. Bogus trials sometimes lasted less than one hour, and convictions frequently followed the eyewitness identification of a single witness, sometimes a child as young as ten years. Jury deliberations were mere formalities, with verdicts delivered in as little as five minutes. There were few to no appeals.

Virginia's capital punishment system during Jim Crow was thus an almost endless parade of powerless Black men railroaded into fraudulent trials and hasty convictions with guaranteed executions. And if it were not for a statute dictating a minimum of 30 days between conviction and execution to allow for appeals and examinations by the governor, those executions would have undoubtedly been carried out even faster.

Two Jim Crow Case Studies:

Hodges and Christian

An example of the harsh retribution reserved only for Black-on-white crime and the corresponding egregiously biased judicial system regarding women are the contrasting cases of Octavia Hodges, a 19-year-old white female, and Virginia Christian, a 17-year-old Black female. Both were convicted of murder while defending themselves, almost 20 years apart. The radically opposing outcomes of their cases highlight disturbing racial and gender disparities among females in Virginia's criminal justice system and the media's treatment of them.

As described in the Thomas Wansley case, white women in the American South, Virginia included, were revered as refined, pure, and virtuous creatures whose qualities had to be preserved at all costs by patriarchal white male authority. Attractive white women, in particular, were simply not considered physically or emotionally capable of committing murder and were treated as helpless and destitute victims of circumstance. And if they somehow did get a conviction, their sentences, paroles, and pardons were dictated by their degree of traditional physical beauty.

Black women, of course, got no such judicial considerations.

Octavia Hodges, a 19-year-old white Rocky Mount teenager, was the only white female in the Virginia State Penitentiary when she was admitted in the broiling summer of 1892 for murdering a sewing machine salesman named R. J. Cunningham.

Hodges claimed at her Franklin County trial that in May 1890, Cunningham entered her family's tavern heavily intoxicated and became threatening during a card game. She reportedly tried to call a police officer, but Cunningham blocked her exit. Desperate to corner the young woman, Cunningham "menacingly" raised a chair over his head. Hodges grabbed a pistol from a cupboard and shot him through the chest, severing his aorta.

Claiming self-defense, she was found guilty of second-degree murder and sentenced to six years in the penitentiary.

Clemency was discussed for Hodges almost immediately upon her admittance to prison, due almost exclusively to her striking looks and quiet, prim demeanor. Only four days after her arrival, the *Altoona Tribune* stated that "The friends of Octavia Hodges, the pretty mountain girl who has just been committed to the penitentiary for killing a sewing machine agent named Cunningham, will appeal to the governor to pardon her. The girl is only nineteen, and modest in her bearing."

Her appearance and notoriety made her a short-lived nineteenth-century celebrity. The *Richmond Dispatch* reported on Aug. 18 that "Efforts ... will be made to secure a pardon for pretty Octavia Hodges, who is serving a six-year term at the penitentiary for killing a sewing machine agent at Rocky Mount."

"A Fair Murderess" gushed a headline in the Aug. 14 *Norfolk Virginian*, "She is nineteen years old and a beauty."

"The only white female in the penitentiary is Octavia Hodges, a beautiful young woman, who was received from Franklin County," the starstruck reporter wrote. "Miss Hodges ... has black hair, large brown eyes, fair skin and refined features. Even in her prison garb she looks well."

However, the people of Rocky Mount and Franklin County knew better than fall for the gushing over Octavia. They seemed to recognize a more sinister side of the pretty young murderess. She, in their opinion, was simply batting her eyes and playing the "poor pitiful Pearl" routine to hoodwink those gullible Richmonders. On Aug. 25, the *Weekly Virginian and Carolinian* reported that "No effort will be made here now to get Octavia Hodges, the pretty young convict from Franklin County, pardoned ... It has been ascertained that she is a woman of very bad character, and the account she gave to the reporters of herself and the crime of which she has been convicted, was false from beginning to end."

Regardless of the opinions of those who knew Hodges, after serving a little over four years, Gov. O'Farrell twisted himself into a knot justifying a pardon for the comely inmate. In a report to the 1896 Report to the House of Delegates, he stated, "This woman, when convicted, was quite young and reared in most immoral influences ... The homicide was committed in her mother's house, which was a house of ill-fame, and while a game of cards was going on, and when this girl was excited by the game and her mind inflamed with liquor."

"It seems to me that clemency can properly be extended." She was released on Jan. 2, 1897.

Contrast the treatment Octavia Hodges received from the courts, the prison, and the press with that of Virginia Christian. Christian, a 17-year-old Black woman, similarly got into an altercation and murdered her white female employer, Ida Belote, in 1912. Christian had gone to Belote's house to do washing, and an argument ensued when Belote accused her of stealing a locket and a skirt. Belote threw a ceramic cuspidor at Virginia in anger, striking her on the shoulder and shattering it. The teenager rushed to protect herself by grabbing a broom handle and knocking Belote to the floor. In an attempt to stifle Belote's screams, Virginia stuffed a towel in the woman's mouth and, with the broom handle, forced it down her throat. The woman died of suffocation.

The *Newport News Daily Press* heartlessly described Virginia as "a full-blooded negress, with kinky hair done up in threads, with dark lusterless eyes and with splotches on the skin of her face. Her color was dark brown, and her figure was short, dumpy and squashy. She had some schooling, but her speech betrayed it. Her language was the same as the unlettered members of her race."

The April 11 *Newport News Times-Herald* also ran Virginia's account of the crime in verbatim racist plantation dialect to promote the image of her not being cultured enough to exist in polite white society:

I got mad an' told her if I did have it, she wasn't goin' to git it back. Den she picked up de spittoon and hit me wit it an' it broke. They wuz two sticks in de room, broom handles. She run for one, an' I for de' other. I got my stick furst an' I hit her wit it 'side de hade and she fell down. She kep' hollerin' so I took a towel and stuffed it in her mouth. I helt it there twel she quit hollerin' and jes' groaned. I didn't mean to kill her an' I didn't know I had ...

Unlike white Octavia Hodges, who was immediately suggested to be pardoned for an almost identical crime, Black Virginia Christian was subjected to a sham trial. The threat of a lynch mob loomed in case of a not guilty verdict. The jury returned a verdict of guilty of first-degree murder after only twenty-three minutes of deliberation. Trial Judge Clarence W. Robinson sentenced her to die in the electric chair.

Gov. William Mann remained unmoved by numerous attempts to commute her sentence, including an appeal from Richmond's most prominent Black woman, Maggie Walker. He wrote that "Christian's murder of her *white* (emphasis added) employer, Ida Virginia Belote, was the most dastardly in the state's history and that Christian's execution is necessary to ensure public safety.... I have therefore reluctantly reached the conclusion that there is nothing in the case which justifies executive clemency."

Christian was executed on Aug. 16, 1912.

The Gillespie Case

At sunrise on Jan. 10, 1909, Charles Gillespie allegedly attacked 19-year-old Marie Louise Stumpf, the pretty white daughter of a respected local businessman, on her way to Mass at the Catholic Cathedral on Laurel Street in Richmond. An account in the Jan. 13 *Lexington Dispatch* of this perfect storm of racial hostility stated that Stumpf "fought with the frenzy of fear for her life" in trying to escape her "savage" attacker. She was reportedly saved by a passerby who heard her screams.

Two hours after the assault, two detectives arrested and searched a man at the corner of Beech and Main Streets who partially matched the attacker's description. They reportedly found a ring and a bracelet belonging to the victim in his possession.

As word of the attack spread throughout the neighborhood later that day, a furious lynch mob gathered outside the precinct police station, demanding that Gillespie be turned over to them. But as the press explained, a Judge named Witte arrived at the station and assured the mob that Gillespie would receive a speedy trial and that he would personally summon a special grand jury to indict him as soon as Miss Stumpf was well enough to testify against him.

That assurance pacified the crowd, and it dispersed.

Knowing that mob violence in the heart of Virginia's capital city was assured if Gillespie was found not guilty, the court legally bludgeoned him, calling a procession of no less than 40 witnesses for the prosecution but not one for the defense. The judge characterized the offense as a "crime against the very womanhood of the city" and that it was of "vast importance" that justice was served. When a shell-shocked Stumpf took the stand, the judge cleared the courtroom "to spare the feelings of the young lady and her relatives." Her melancholy deposition reportedly "moved all present to tears."

After the testimony, the verdict was a foregone conclusion. The enflamed all-white jury took less than five minutes to find Gillespie guilty and sentence him to death in the electric chair. Gillespie was duly executed only 36 days after the commission of the crime.

Capital Punishment and the Links to Lynching

As evidenced by the Charles Gillespie and Virginia Christian cases, there is little disagreement that the post-civil war rise in executions was inexplicably linked to the odious influence of lynching. Virginia's "rocket docket" system, which ramrodded Blacks through rushed trials, convictions, and sentencings, played a substantial role in discerning the relationship between legal executions and extralegal lynchings during the Jim Crow era.

According to James Madison University Professor Gianluca DeFazio on that school's racial terror website, lynching was a "formidable institution to preserve white supremacy in the Jim Crow South through the systematic use of racial terror." In his 1992 paper "Race, Rape, and Radicalism: The Case of the Martinsville Seven, 1949-1951," Eric Rise wrote that "Traditionally, white southern males had invoked a paternalistic concern for white female chastity as a justification for the summary execution of suspected Black rapists. Lynching, they explained, not only punished Blacks for violating racial and sexual mores, it also spared fragile (white) women from the trauma of testifying in a public courtroom."

The 1866 legislature authorized the death penalty for any male, white or Black, convicted of rape. Since the death penalty was left to the discretion of the overwhelmingly all-white juries, death sentences became reserved only for Blacks for that crime. And in 1894, the legislature expanded the punishment to include attempted rape because of fears that failure to do so would encourage lynch mobs.

White men were indeed convicted and sentenced to death for rape in Virginia as late as 1972, but none were executed.

This "use of racial terror" applied proficiently to Virginia's frequent use of the death penalty since, as the *Newport News Daily Press* reported, long prison sentences meant nothing to Blacks. "The negro fears death," an editorial claimed, "and death alone."

Several factors make up Virginia's relatively low lynching numbers compared to other Deep South states. However, the extraordinary speed at which Virginia arrested, tried, convicted, and then executed overwhelmingly young, Black men (almost always for attacking a white person) frequently pacified angry mobs, helping keep lynching numbers low. As in the Gillespie case, these mobs were sometimes repulsed from jail steps by judges and sheriffs who pleaded with them to disperse, assuring them that the law would take its course and justice would be served. All were dog whistles for "let a legal lynching" do your work for you.

Virginia law enforcement officers, legislators, and courts were publicly critical of lynching over concerns that the commonwealth could not attract desired business connections with the Northern states. Still, lynching's lurking influence functioned behind the scenes as a fear tactic and convenient confession-extractor against the Black population. Its insidious authority contributed heavily to those assembly-line convictions and death sentences.

In addition to law enforcement and courtroom proceedings, lynching threats permeated jury deliberations and sometimes forced the mob's desired verdict. Noah Finley, for example was convicted in September 1899 for robbing and shooting at (and missing) a respected White businessman in Pulaski, Major Darst. When the jury could not reach a verdict after 15 hours of deliberation, the *Richmond Planet* reported that "a party of citizens notified them that if a verdict was not rendered by 10:00 a.m., the negro would be lynched."

And it had to be the correct verdict of guilty, which "was brought in promptly at the specified time." Finley was duly and legally executed on Sept. 15.

Also, the *Planet* reported that on the same day the Black man, Finley, was sentenced to death for robbery, a white Fredericksburg man named Edward Conway was found guilty of murdering a Black man, Clarence Scott, "in a cold-blooded assassination." Conway was not hanged for the murder but fined $10.

According to the Watt Espy File, from 1865 until 1908, when executions were centralized at the electric chair in the Virginia State Penitentiary's "A" basement, Virginia localities executed 163 people – 123 Black, 30 white, and 10 with race unknown or unstated. All but four were males.

Two of the four Black women were executed for complicity in the murder of their husbands. Barbara Miller hanged in the Henrico County Jail yard on Sept. 14, 1883. Her accomplice, Charles Lee, hanged the previous August. According to a hand-written note in the National Death Penalty Archive, her hanging was witnessed by about 100 people. The drop failed to break her neck, and she died of strangulation after 12 minutes.

Similarly, on Jan. 22, 1892, Margaret Hashley hanged in Danville for complicity in the Oct. 26, 1891 murder of her husband, George. Her accomplice, James Lyles, confessed that he alone was responsible for the murder in support of Margaret, who steadfastly maintained her innocence.

In 1904, Virginia added kidnapping as a death penalty-eligible crime.

From 1877 to 1927, Virginia executions outpaced lynchings at over a 2:1 ratio, with about 104 known extrajudicial lynchings occurring before the introduction and passage of the Virginia Anti-lynching Law of 1928. During this same period, Virginia legally executed 274, with 225 Black.

In his 1993 book "Lynching in the New South" historian Fitzhugh Brundage expressed uncertainty that speedy trials ending in legal executions effectively reduced extralegal lynchings. In Jim Crow Virginia, the two co-existed as strange bedfellows, with the identical purposes of terrorizing the Black population with a failsafe outcome of guilty and a subsequent quick death.

Terror, Mystery, and Awe: Virginia Introduces the Electric Chair

Witnesses routinely report that, when the switch is thrown, the condemned prisoner "cringes," "leaps," and "fights the straps with amazing
strength" ... the force of the electrical current is so powerful that the prisoner's eyeballs sometimes pop out and "rest on his cheek." The prisoner
often defecates, urinates, and vomits blood and drool ... Sometimes, the
prisoner catches on fire, particularly [if] he "perspires excessively." "The
temperature in the brain approaches the boiling point of water," and when
the post-electrocution autopsy is performed, "the liver is so hot that doctors have said it cannot be touched by the human hand."

-U.S. Supreme Court Justice William Brennan, dissenting in *Glass v. Louisiana*, 1985.

The General Assembly decided once and for all in 1908 that the "hurrah and holiday
air" that accompanied public hangings had to stop, as it was too tempting for Blacks to
gather, pray, chant, and celebrate the condemned prisoner's entry into the promised
land. While looking for a form of execution that was "safe, effective and dignified," they
took an acute interest in an advertisement passed among them from the Adams Electric
Company of Trenton, New Jersey, that promised a guaranteed "electrocuting plant."

"All appliances used in the construction of this Electrocuting Plant have been designed with the utmost care, and the makers guarantee absolute reliability," the ad
boasted. "The workmanship is of the best, and the entire outfit presents an elegant appearance notwithstanding the fact that it is to be used to despatch (*sic*) condemned
murderers into eternity." The flyer also claimed that the lethal electrical charge of between 1700 and 2300 volts rendered the victim unconscious in 1/240th of a second, less
than the time required for the nervous system to register pain.

The switch from the gallows to the electric chair generated debate in the General
Assembly. Southampton Del. Williams, an ex-sheriff, described hanging as a "barbaric
practice," which was always accompanied by the possibility of "hideous accidents" and
caused the condemned criminal great agony.

Henrico Del. C. Throckmorton, on the other hand, argued that although he was in
favor of moving all executions to the penitentiary, an electrical engineer told him that
the chair was as prone to uncertainty as hanging and that it caused "unspeakable agony"
to the condemned inmate.

Sen. Gravatt countered that the electric chair was more humane and "in line with
progress."

Sen. Folkes claimed that the chair was fine but that the death penalty was intended
to be a warning and should take place at the same locality as the crime.

After the bill passed on Feb. 3, 1908, the legislators voted to appropriate $1,000 to
install the necessary electrocution plant – not nearly enough, so the actual chair was
constructed of oak by inmates, using the chair at New York's Sing-Sing Prison as a model.
The Virginia Electric and Power Company assessed a service charge of five dollars for
connecting dedicated high-voltage lines which carried current to the death chamber.

While hangings generally cost local counties about $250, electrocutions would cost an estimated $50 to $150 each.

Research revealed that no inmate involved in constructing the chair was ever electrocuted in it.

On March 30, 1908, an above-the-fold story on page one of the *Richmond News Leader* underscored the electric chair's menacing influence specifically to the Black population, in that its very presence, deep in the bowels of the State Penitentiary, was indeed serving as intended as a shadowy and terrifying deterrent.

The story reported that the previous February, a "dope-soaked negro" named Robert Faulkner ran amuck in Shockoe Bottom after stealing a shotgun and a box of cartridges from Tignor's gun store at Eighteenth and Franklin Streets. Faulkner, described as "crazed with whiskey and cocaine," then shot and wounded "ten or twelve" white people before he was taken down injured by several shots from police.

While in the hospital, Faulkner became terrified that he would be electrocuted for his actions. The *News Leader*, sensing an opportunity, spared no mercy in their ghastly description of the prisoner and the fate that could await him:

> Terror of the electric chair, the grim and fearful engine of legal death ordered by the recent legislature, and haunting dread of a mysterious and colorless execution of the law somewhere within the cold stone and iron walls of the penitentiary, were too much for the African imagination, and Faulkner declared repeatedly with shudders of anticipation that he would never die that way.

Faulkner feared electrocution so much that he several times threw himself against the wall of his hospital room and clawed open his wounds in desperate efforts to take his own life. A day later, he died of an embolism.

The *Alexandria Gazette* reported that the chair was ready for use on Sept. 19, 1908.

Virginia's first electric chair victim was Henry Smith, a Black Portsmouth man. Smith, age 22, was convicted of raping a 75-year-old white woman, Catherine Powell, on Aug. 11 in Portsmouth. He also robbed her house of $15 and then "beat the old lady into a state of insensibility." He was executed on Oct. 13.

There is no record of how the electric chair functioned. Per the new law, no details could be divulged by prison authorities or by the press. Penitentiary physician Dr. Charles Carrington widely praised the new device, however, writing in the 1908 Penitentiary Annual Report that:

> [It was a] swift, sure, solemn and awe-inspiring mode of punishment, and to my mind is infinitely more humane than hanging. Absolutely nothing of the spectacular is permitted in an electrocution, and when you eliminate the psalm-singing-forgiving-your-enemies that usually, I am told, preceded a hanging, and in its stead institute a solemn, very swift mode of inflicting the death penalty, you have taken a step which will in time be powerfully

deterrent on the criminal classes.

On Dec. 10, 1908, after only two executions, the *Washington Post* reported that authorities in New Jersey intended to revive an electrocuted inmate. A consortium of doctors hypothesized that electrocution only stunned the victim and did not kill him.

"The electric chair was thought to be the perfect method of criminal execution," the article stated. "But some of the things noted in autopsies upon the bodies of electrocuted men caused physicians to doubt. A number of autopsy surgeons have been known to refuse to dissect the bodies of electrocuted men, fearing that the duty might make executioners of them."

Let the Parade Begin

While it is unknown if this experiment happened, the rumor certainly did not deter Virginia, as the introduction of the electric chair ushered in some of the busiest execution years in the commonwealth's history, with 17 electrocutions (and one hanging) in 1909 alone. Arthelius Christian, a 17-year-old Black youth, was electrocuted on March 22 for the rape and murder of a 14-year-old white girl in Botetourt County. Because of lynching threats, Christian was indicted, tried, and convicted within 24 hours of his capture near Roanoke. From opening to sentencing, his trial took a disorienting 21 minutes, forcing the press to describe it as "the swiftest execution of justice in the history of the criminal courts of Virginia."

On Nov. 15, 1909, Clifton Breckenridge abruptly confessed to Staunton Chief of Police Liscomb that he had attempted to assault the young daughter of the Staunton jailer, where he worked as a "trusty" while incarcerated for chicken theft. The system sprang into action – a special grand jury was called the next day, Nov. 16, at 11:00 a.m., and 45 minutes later returned an indictment. The trial began two hours later, at 2:00 p.m., and by 3:37 – after only 12 minutes of deliberation – the jury sentenced him to death.

Shouted threats of lynching inside the packed courtroom forced the judge to not only expedite proceedings but at one point clear the venue entirely, except for court officers and the press. The night after the verdict, fury at Breckenridge still raged, and citizens were unwilling to wait 30 days to see him die. Someone sounded the Staunton fire bell to summon a lynch mob. Several dozen men gathered and attempted to break Breckenridge out of jail, but they were driven back by the sheriff and several officers.

Breckenridge was executed on Dec. 17, 31 days after his conviction.

After the execution of Clifton Breckenridge, Virginia's system continued into overdrive. After 14 electrocutions in 1913, there were nine in 1914, 11 in 1915, and nine more in 1916. Eighteen-year-old Alfred Wright was tried, convicted, and sentenced to death so fast in an Appomattox County courtroom that his attorney insisted that such a legal travesty showed "great prejudice in the county" against his client. Judge Hundley, a former Confederate officer who had stated from the bench when court convened that he expected the trial to last "only a few minutes," ruled that the prisoner's feeling that he would not get a fair trial was insufficient, and that specific proof of unfairness was necessary before a verdict rendered under such circumstances could be set aside. The press, however, boasted of the lightning-quick trial with the headline "Virginia shows how to prevent rule of mob," showing once again the hidden, sinister influence of lynching on legal proceedings.

Wright received several respites but was executed on May 16, 1913.

Any mitigating circumstances, such as a defendant's drug or alcohol abuse or intellectual and mental disabilities, meant nothing in these courtrooms, where Black-on-white crimes were pushed through with high-speed efficiency and assured outcomes. Police arrested Benjamin Baily on May 27, 1913, for attempted assault of a six-year-old Great Falls girl. The next day, May 28, he was indicted by a special grand jury after only a few minutes of deliberation, entering a not guilty plea. The press noted that Baily "seemed to be half-witted and did not understand the few questions that were put to him."

Baily's trial was set for May 30 to placate a lynch mob. He was then tried, convicted, and sentenced to die, based solely on the testimony of the young victim, only eight days after his crime. The jury rendered a verdict in 10 minutes.

On July 25, Gov. Mann granted a respite to "investigate the mental condition of the prisoner." Baily (likely with the help of the jailer) wrote a letter to his mother, telling her that he "is well" and that he is to be "electrocuted, whatever that means." He added at the end that he wished they would "make haste and do it" because "he wants to get back home."

Baily went to the electric chair on Aug. 8. He never went back home but to the state dissecting lab.

Another Option

Before 1914, a jury in a capital murder case faced only the blunt choices of death, acquittal, or downgrading the offense. Therefore, the General Assembly amended the criminal code that year to allow life imprisonment for murder "if the death penalty was not imposed." This addition provided a much-needed legal middle ground, providing juries a pass, especially for white defendants tried for especially egregious crimes but for whom they did not deem possible to acquit nor send to their death. The change, however, was small comfort to Black men who found themselves trapped in a system seemingly explicitly tailored to put them to death as quickly as possible.

After a brief uptick, Virginia in 1919 slowed executions, with only five that year, all Black men. In 1920 Robert Williams was the lone electrocution for murder. This drop-off, coupled with the conspicuous front-page execution of Wilmer Hadley, the wealthy white society doctor, triggered a brief flurry of newspaper editorials in January 1922, denouncing capital punishment as ineffective in its current state.

"All facts tend to show clearly that the death penalty is a mere remnant, a leftover from the days when the repressive theory of criminology held sway, a vestigial organ which has ceased to function for lack of exercise," the Jan. 29 *Staunton News-Leader* lamented. "It is too rarely used to prove a very efficacious deterrent, yet its occasional use renders it a ridiculous and purposeless outrage. For as it is now applied, the death penalty is nothing but an arbitrary discrimination against an occasional victim."

This statement was especially true compared to its use against well-connected whites.

Despite the editorials, in 1922, the crime of entering a bank intending to commit larceny while armed with a deadly weapon became a death penalty-eligible crime.

By the late 1920s, any talk of abolition ceased with public anxiety over crime waves that revolved around Prohibition and the Great Depression. As a result, the number of executions nationwide rose sharply in the 1930s and the 1940s.

Lynching Outlawed

In 1928 Virginia passed the nation's first anti-lynching bill, a crucial step forward in criminal justice reform. The real power behind the bill was the fearless and sometimes brash *Richmond Planet* editor John Mitchell Jr. and *Norfolk Virginian-Pilot* editor Louis Isaac Jaffé. Jaffé was a white man whose Pulitzer Prize-winning editorials addressed rapid increases in mob violence in the twenties. Thanks to their advocacy and Gov. Byrd's endorsement, Virginia's government, and business leadership finally realized that mob violence and lynching was indeed becoming a risk to their efforts to attract industry to the commonwealth.

The law became section 4427 of the Virginia code. Its various subsections defined what constituted a mob, that lynching was murder, and that assault and battery by a mob was a felony, among other distinctions.

The first year after the passage of the anti-lynch law, Virginia continued a slow but relentless pace in executions, with four Black men executed in 1929, three in 1930, two in 1931, and two more in 1932. The only execution in 1933 was 38-year-old Frank Mann for murder.

In 1934 Possession or use of a machine gun in any crime of violence became a death penalty-eligible crime.

In 1935 Virginia executed two more high-profile notorious white men, Robert Mais and Walter Legenza, known as the "tri-state gang." After making headlines with cigarette truck hijackings, Legenza and Mais made a splash in Richmond on March 8, 1934, when they commandeered a federal reserve truck, expecting a significant score. Legenza, a textbook sadist with no regard for human life, casually murdered security guard E.M. Hubard for no reason when the truck's rear doors opened. After tossing several sacks into their car, they fled, only to find later they had murdered Hubard for bags of worthless canceled checks.

Since this was a United States mail robbery, the FBI had jurisdiction. They tracked Mais and Legenza to Baltimore, Maryland, and Mais was severely wounded in his abdomen during a brief gun battle. Legenza immediately surrendered. They were then extradited to Virginia for trial, facing capital murder charges.

Both men were promptly convicted and sentenced to death in November 1934. On Sept. 29, Mais's mother arrived at the Richmond city jail carrying a can of cooked chicken with a gun hidden inside. In a dramatic escape, officer William Toot was killed, and two other officers were wounded. Wracked with guilt over the escape and the murder of his friend and co-worker, city night sergeant Richard Duke later took his own life.

In January 1935, the FBI captured Mais and Legenza in New York City. They were again sent back to Virginia, guarded by a squad of nine handpicked officers.

Triggerman Walter Legenza had to be carried from his cell to the electric chair because both of his legs had been broken trying to escape from police. He compared himself to Robin Hood and was "bitter, cynical and jeering" until he died.

There was an unspecified malfunction with the electric chair during Mais's execution, and rumors spread it took him twenty minutes to die.

From the 1930s to World War II, federal appeals courts began reviewing state court death sentences in most states, as trial courts imposed them without any higher state or federal oversight. A handful of landmark cases, such as the 1932 Scottsboro Boys rape case (*Powell v. Alabama*), set precedents for federal appeals review based on charges that state courts had violated the federal Bill of Rights.

Capital Punishment During a World War and a Cold War

A Black Isle of Wight man named Charlie Brown, convicted of raping a 23-year-old woman, was the only execution in Virginia in 1941 as the United States entered World War II. The previous year, 63-year-old John McCann was executed for the attempted rape of a seven-year-old white Norfolk girl, one of four executions in 1940. Both killings continued the shameful precedent of the Old Dominion only executing Black men for the crime of rape or attempted rape.

As unlikely as it seems, not all men, Black or white, who received death sentences for rape between 1909 and 1940 were executed. Nine men total during that period had their death sentences commuted to lengthy prison terms, with many even receiving conditional pardons. Joseph Mickens, a Black man, was sentenced to death for rape in 1940. But in January 1942, Gov. James Price reduced his sentence to life in the penitentiary. He then received a conditional pardon in 1962, after serving twenty years.

In August 1939, Dimps Ricker, a white man, was sentenced to death in Virginia for rape. Gov. James Price, however, commuted his sentence to life in September 1939. Ricker received a conditional pardon in August 1946.

From 1940 to 1949, there were 35 executions – 28 Black, seven white.

The Sad Case of Odell Waller and the Poll Tax Jury

One of those 28 Black men executed was a Pittsylvania County sharecropper named Odell Waller, in a case that would stir Virginia deeply, raising serious questions of the relationship of economic status, race, and political power to the state's justice system

Waller, his wife Mollie, and his adoptive mother Annie on Jan. 2, 1939, moved onto farmland near Gretna managed by tenant farmer Oscar Davis to work raising wheat, tobacco, and corn. Waller's agreement stated that Davis would furnish the farm supplies and tools while Waller supplied the labor. In return, he would receive one-fourth of the cultivated crops.

A temperamental hothead, Davis was almost as destitute as Waller. He owed everyone money, including $7.50 to Waller's mother, Annie, for a month of nursing his ailing wife. Annie never got paid.

When the federal Agricultural Adjustment Administration curtailed Davis' tobacco allotment during the war, he slashed Waller's acreage and denied him his one-quarter share of the cultivated wheat.

Upon returning to Gretna from Baltimore, where he worked stringing electrical lines, Waller found his wife Mollie and his mother evicted. Enraged, he put a pistol in his pocket, confronted Davis, and demanded his 52 bags of wheat. Davis claimed he "wasn't going to get that damned wheat." What happened after that is disputed, but just as Davis put his hand in a pocket where he always carried a gun, Waller shot him four times, killing him.

With mob violence looming, Waller fled to Columbus, Ohio, where he was captured then extradited to Virginia. Despite continual threats of lynching, the presiding judge refused to grant a change of venue and set the trial to start in two days. Waller was appointed two less than competent young lawyers, Thomas Stone and Byron Hopkins. After one postponement, a jury of all-white tenant farmers found Waller guilty of murder and sentenced him to death.

A Chicago-based civil rights attorney named John Finerty, who had worked the Sacco and Vanzetti trials, took Waller's appeal and brought up a salient point: that Waller had not been tried by a jury of his peers. He argued that destitute "second-class citizens" like Waller had been barred from serving on Virginia juries because they could not afford Virginia's annual $1.50 poll tax. Juries at the time were picked almost exclusively from poll-taxpayer lists. Unfortunately, Waller's first lawyer had not submitted evidence to this point in the first trial, so due to this oversight, Finerty's appeals for a new trial were denied time and again.

The courts first denied the defense's contention that Virginia required jurors to be poll taxpayers. In addition, they held that since Waller's first two attorneys failed to show that he had not paid the tax, they nonsensically claimed that "he is in no position to complain of such discrimination, had it existed."

Many Virginians disliked an outsider like Finerty sticking his nose in the Old Dominion's criminal justice laws. Others saw the Waller case as a severe flaw in the system that needed correcting.

With the help of social activist Pauli Murray, Annie Waller became an activist and social reformer out of necessity, visiting churches and labor unions in New York and Boston for weeks in December 1940 to raise awareness of her son's dilemma and money for his legal expenses. Waller and Murray also established Waller Defense Committees supported financially by the Workers Defense League (WDL), the Brotherhood of Sleeping Car Porters, and the NAACP.

Waller's relentless activism for her son and all sharecroppers shone a spotlight on the experiences of Black families and women in the Jim Crow and "Jane Crow South" (a phrase credited to Murray). They pointed out the oppressive socio-economic conditions and inherent racial unfairness that plagued sharecroppers, their wives, and their families.

Protests favoring Waller got louder and louder, but his case continued to get turned down, despite notable Richmond attorney Edmund Preston joining Finerty. Gov. Colgate Darden Jr. granted stay after stay as the case wound through the courts. In 1941, Murray co-authored a booklet with Murray Kempton titled "All for Mr. Davis: The Story of Sharecropper Odell Waller" that further highlighted the racial and class inequities of the case. Novelist Pearl Buck, even First Lady Eleanor Roosevelt, joined her husband, President Franklin D. Roosevelt, to make a private appeal on Waller's behalf to Darden. Thurgood Marshall personally prepared an *amicus curiae* brief on behalf of the ACLU. Dozens of letters supporting Waller and decrying Virginia's discriminatory poll tax jury selection system appeared in the *Richmond Times-Dispatch* and other papers.

It was an innovative argument – perhaps too creative for rural Virginia. Their point, simply, was that equal protection of the laws demanded that a particular economic class, such as the one to which Waller belonged, not be excluded from jury service.

Compare the experiences of Odell Waller with those of white Danville farmer Robert G. Siddle. On Oct. 20, 1941, while the Waller case continued to spin its wheels, the 68-year-old Siddle fatally shot a Black sharecropper named Tom Denson over the fair distribution of a potato crop.

After a Nov. 19 trial, in the same Pittsylvania Court and under the same judge that heard the Waller case, Siddle was found not guilty in the murder of Denson.

It took the jury just eight minutes to acquit the white man for killing the Black.

While Waller languished on death row in the penitentiary, he wrote a remarkable 10-page "dying statement" to his attorney Edmund Preston. In one excerpt, he admitted to making some mistakes, but he never meant to kill Davis:

> First I will say don't work for a man two poor to pay you. He will steel and take from you. In my case I worked hard from sun up until sun down trying to make a living for my family an it ended up meaning death for me.

Despite these appeals for a stay of execution and a failed request for review by the U.S. Supreme Court, and after 630 days on death row, Odell Waller died in the electric chair on July 2, 1942. over 2,500 people attended his funeral on July 5. WDL Secretary Morris Milgram was the only white attendee.

Virginia did not abolish its poll tax until 1966. However, the Waller case did jumpstart some sweeping penal reforms during the remainder of the decade. These included the creation of a statewide Department of Corrections, abolishing the antiquated fee system of payment for sheriffs, and creating a State Parole Board. Most importantly, the 1940s saw corporal punishment finally abolished in Virginia's prisons thanks to the pioneering work of outspoken Richmond attorney Howard Carwile.

The Martinsville Tragedy

On April 23, 1951, Black students led by Barbara Johns at Robert Russa Moton High School in Farmville, Virginia, walked out to protest the dilapidated conditions of their school and inadvertently triggered a civil rights movement.

However, just weeks earlier, another seminal civil rights moment occurred when seven Black men, from just down the road in Martinsville, were executed in assembly-line fashion over two days at the Virginia State Penitentiary. They had all been sentenced to death by all-white juries for the rape of a white woman.

While the Moton walkout remains a positive, groundbreaking achievement in Virginia history that led to the desegregation of public schools, the "Martinsville seven" case was a clear and unmistakable Jim Crow-style middle finger to that pivotal movement initiated by those young students.

The Martinsville Seven case became momentous, as lawyers for the first time organized statistical evidence to prove systematic discrimination against Blacks in capital cases.

The Martinsville case began two years earlier, on the late afternoon of Jan. 8, 1949. Ruby Stroud Floyd, a white 32-year-old wife of a local grocery store manager, walked into the east section of the industrial town of Martinsville to collect six dollars for a suit and a pair of shoes she had recently sold. Floyd was a familiar figure known to some as the "Watchtower Woman" because she frequently distributed the magazine for the Jehovah's Witnesses.

Floyd was not familiar with that area, so she stopped at the home of Dan Gilmer to ask for directions to the woman's house. Gilmer urged her to return home since it was getting dark, and on Saturday night, he claimed the locals "like to celebrate and have a nice time." Floyd insisted on continuing, however, and asked eleven-year-old Charlie Martin, the son of a woman she knew, to accompany her.

At 7:30 p.m. Mary Wade, a neighborhood resident, answered a knock at her door and found Ruby Floyd, beaten and bruised, wearing only a shirt, sweater, and slip. Wade later testified, "There were scratches on her arms. Her clothes were kind of hanging off her and her hair tangled up ... Her thighs were red-rubbed like." Mary's husband Jesse testified Floyd "seemed to be scared to death."

Floyd claimed four men who paid Charlie Martin a quarter to disappear and keep his mouth shut dragged then attacked her near a secluded train track, where three others allegedly joined them.

Just after midnight, Martinsville Detective Murray Barrow arrested two young Black men, Frank Hairston, Jr., who allegedly confessed to raping Floyd, and Booker T. Millner, who admitted that he was at the scene but denied raping the woman. Based on these confessions, another Officer, A. T. Finney, arrested James L. Hairston, Howard Lee Hairston, John C. Taylor, and Francis DeSales Grayson at their homes between 3:30 and 4:00 a.m. By 7:30 a.m., the police coerced confessions from all four, although Grayson and Howard Hairston also denied raping the victim.

Early Monday morning, Jan. 10, the police arrested the final suspect, Joe Hampton. By 10:35 a.m. Sergeant Barnes claimed he had a signed confession from each suspect, in which they admitted their part in the attack and implicated the others as well.

They became the Martinsville Seven.

All these men were between eighteen and twenty years of age (except for Grayson, a World War II veteran, thirty-seven, married, and the father of five) and worked as laborers in local furniture factories. All the men were from "East Martinsville," considered the "colored" side of town, and looked on less favorably than the whiter "West Martinsville." None of the men had serious criminal backgrounds – Hampton had earlier received a suspended sentence and probation for grand larceny. Millner had been fined once for public drunkenness, and Taylor had been arrested on a minor sex charge in 1944.

Floyd immediately identified Grayson and Hampton as her rapists, but she could not positively identify the others since the attack happened at night. By April, however, all seven men faced rape charges.

Reverend Robert Anderson, the pastor of Richmond's Fifth Baptist Church and spiritual minister to John Taylor, told the *Richmond Afro-American* newspaper that at least two of the defendants informed him of improper conduct by the Martinsville police during questioning. Both men claimed they were seated in a chair and surrounded by several officers, while one allegedly held a nightstick over their heads, telling them that if they did not admit guilt, they would be beaten to death.

Police also told several of the men that their companions had already confessed and implicated them. If they did not also confess, they would be handed over to a "mob of a thousand men waiting outside to [lynch] you." These tactics recalled the ugly no-win situations law enforcement used at the turn of the twentieth century to entrap young Black men accused of "assaulting the virtues" of young white women. And again, the use of the menacing convenience of looming lynch mobs, actual or threatened, to force confessions.

Unfortunately, Rev. Anderson was unsuccessful in getting this information to Gov. John S. Battle because Battle refused to see him.

Before the trials, Martinsville Circuit Court judge Kennon C. Whittle – mindful of the circus-like 1931 Scottsboro case and not wishing to repeat it –told prosecutors and defense lawyers that all the defendants "will be tried as though both parties were members of the same race. I will not have it otherwise."

The Martinsville Seven case bore several similarities to Scottsboro, which involved nine Black teenagers falsely accused of raping two white women aboard a train near Scottsboro, Alabama, in 1931. The trials of those young men, coupled with the two Supreme Court verdicts they produced, and the international uproar over their treatment, played a prominent formative role in the rise of the civil rights movement that coincided with the Martinsville case.

Whittle also agreed to a defense request to hold individual trials except for Taylor and James Hairston, who agreed to be tried jointly. During jury selections, Whittle's admonition to "try both parties as if they were the same race" spectacularly failed when the prosecution vetoed all potential Black jurors, mainly because they opposed capital punishment.

So, in another ominous similarity to Scottsboro and numerous earlier Virginia cases, white juries were to hear all six trials.

On April 18, at the request of the court-appointed defense attorneys, the Martinsville

Circuit Court heard arguments on a motion for change of venue based on the contention that the defendants could not receive fair trials. A front-page article and op-ed in the April 19, 1949 *Martinsville Bulletin* addressed concerns that previous articles were "written for the purpose of arousing public sentiment."

"General sentiment of the citizens of the City of Martinsville [had] been so inflamed by the said newspaper accounts" that it would be impossible to "secure a jury or juries in said City free from bias or prejudice."

The court summoned 23 local citizens, Black and white, to a venue hearing, and a majority believed the defendants could get a fair trial in Martinsville. Juror H. Claybuck Lester told the court that "I have made up my mind they are guilty because they confessed." He added, "I think they could get as [sic] fair trial here as elsewhere."

Lester admitted later that his idea of a fair trial was that "they should be convicted and electrocuted."

Martinsville Bulletin editor K. L. Thompson Jr. answered defense charges that his paper had purposefully avoided inflaming the public "or exciting the community." He claimed he used the term "criminal assault" instead of "rape" and that the *Bulletin* never mentioned the victim's race or ran photos of the defendants for that very reason.

Although Judge Whittle denied the motion for a change of venue, he recognized that a critical issue in the case would be "this race question." In a pretrial meeting with counsel, Whittle expressed his regret that the case would be complicated because the defendants were Black and the victim white. Nevertheless, the trial continued as planned.

"All the focus was on civil rights and none on criminal justice," recalled Dr. Peter Wallenstein, a history professor at Virginia Tech, adding that this created a "grotesque [racial] disparity."

Ruby Floyd testified in all six one-day trials, sometimes for as long as forty minutes. She could positively identify only three of her supposed seven assailants, pointing out Joe Hampton as the first attacker and positively identifying DeSales Grayson as the last. She hesitated between James Hairston and Booker Millner as the second attacker, saying only that it was undoubtedly "one of those two." Juries also heard medical verification of Floyd's physical injuries and testimony from residents she had appealed to for help after the rape.

On the stand, each of the defendants partially or fully rejected his earlier confession. Some claimed that the police had written the confessions, and when they signed them, they did not notice that their own words had been changed. The *Afro-American*, in a Feb. 10, 1951, article headlined, "Mass Execution Ends Martinsville Case," reported that "Independent investigation by responsible citizens showed that 'confessions' had been extorted from the men after violent maltreatment by local officials."

While there was a noticeable absence of the prosecutorial race-baiting seen in similar prosecutions across the South, Virginia law (since 1848) authorized capital punishment only for Blacks not just for rape but also for attempted rape and aiding and abetting rape. Thus, all the juries took less than two hours each to convict the young men of rape, disregarding their actual roles in the Stroud attack. On May 3, 1949, those 72 white jurors also recommended the death penalty for all seven.

"There was a range of behaviors," said Wallenstein of the racist convictions. "Some clearly took part, and others hung around – no distinctions were found. White people got those distinctions. But these graduations were not made. Had they been white, none of them would have gone to the electric chair."

However, conservative southern Virginia newspaper editorials praised the fairness of the arrests and trials. "No infringement of their rights occurred," trumpeted the *Danville Register* on June 6, 1950. "The seven were tried in an atmosphere free from excitement and were represented by the ablest counsel available."

To them, the gentlemanly fairness of the "Virginia way" had prevailed – Jim Crow justice was applied respectfully and impartially.

After the convictions, Richmond-based civil rights attorneys led by Martin A. Martin and Oliver Hill represented the men in the appellate process. After Martin requested some execution statistics from the penitentiary, Superintendent W.F. Smyth Jr. admitted to him in an eye-opening letter that they had combed through 51,780 inmate records dating back to Jan. 1, 1908, and confirmed, "No white person has ever been electrocuted in Virginia for the crime of rape; or attempted rape."

It was likely the most damning statistic to fly under the radar. Since the introduction of Virginia's electric chair in 1908, all 45 men executed for rape in Virginia were Blacks convicted of attacking white women. Not one of the 808 white men convicted of rape in that same period was executed. James Briley in 1984 was the first person since 1775 to be executed for a crime against a Black (for killing Judith Barton and her son Harvey), and no white man in Virginia since Revolutionary days was executed for a crime against a Black until 1997 when Thomas Beavers was executed for the 1990 murder of Marguerite Lowery.

White rapists of white women always received prison sentences. However, the punishments for white men raping Black women during this era were absurdly lenient. The Oct. 16, 1948 *Norfolk Journal and Guide* reported that a white farmer in Amherst County, Corbett Witt, raped a pregnant nineteen-year-old Black woman. He was found guilty and fined $350.

Most shameful was the rape of a "feeble-minded colored woman" by Murrel Dudley, a white man, near Glasgow, Virginia, on Aug. 29, 1948. According to the *Journal*, Dudley was found guilty and fined a mere $20.

Martin confronted this staggering bias head-on: "The prime reason [these men] were sentenced to the electric chair was because all of them are colored, and the prosecutrix was a white woman and the juries were composed of all white men."

Gov. Battle, however, shrugged at these damning electrocution statistics in his clemency petition, writing, "No fair-minded person can read the evidence in these cases without being convinced, beyond the shadow of a doubt, of the guilt of all the defendants."

Battle purposefully ignored the point – Martin and his associates merely wanted justice applied fairly. They wanted these Black men to receive the same punishments under the law as white men convicted of the same crime.

The Supreme Court of Virginia flatly rejected their appeal, and the U.S. Supreme Court declined to hear the case. The Martinsville case became a stark reminder of the excessive punishments reserved only for Blacks who violated deep-rooted southern racial protocols. Nothing had changed.

The world responded loudly to the Martinsville case, and thousands of messages deluged Richmond to stop the executions. A two-page telegram from Russia, signed by numerous Russian writers and artists, including film director Grigori Alexandrov and composers Dimitri Shostakovich and Sergei Prokofiev, expressed "deepest indignation at this act of infamy and brutality inspired by race hatred." Many letters—especially from people in northern states—warned Gov. Battle that he was doing a grave disservice to Virginia and southern racial justice by allowing the executions to move forward. Charged terms such as "legal lynching" and "Jim Crow justice" proliferated.

Battle remained unmoved.

Even in Death, the White Man Goes to the Front of the Line

On Feb. 2, 1951, at 8:04 a.m., George Hailey, a white Halifax County man who had nothing to do with the Martinsville cases but was convicted of raping and murdering a twelve-year-old girl, was executed first in a gruesome uninterrupted sequence of five executions. A terrified Hailey fought the guards ferociously in the walk to the chamber and as they strapped him in the chair.

In stark contrast to Hailey, the first of the Martinsville defendants, Joe Hampton, was solemn and composed as he entered the death chamber. Officials declared him dead at 8:12 a.m. According to press reports, Howard Hairston followed him at 8:22 a.m. and required a second charge to kill him. Booker Milner was dead by 8:29 a.m., and finally, Frank Hairston was dead by 9:05 a.m.

The final three defendants were scheduled for execution on Feb. 5, which coincidentally was the same date in 2021 when the General Assembly finalized the vote on death penalty abolition. Gov. Battle received many more letters and telegrams, including a particularly vicious one allegedly from the National Negro Congress, a Chicago-based activist group. It stated, in part, "You white sons of bitches will suffer for crucifying these innocent boys ... Soon the glorious Negro race will revolt and rule in your place, and you will be strung up from the Courthouse flagpole and your carkass [sic] thrown to the dogs. YOU MUST DIE!!" It was signed, "Booker Carver Washington III, Grand and Imperial Regent."

On Feb. 5, at 7:35 a.m. John Taylor went to the chair. He was followed by James Hairston, who, like his brother, needed a second charge, and finally Francis Grayson. All three were dead by 8:15 a.m.

The following July 13, 1951, Ulysses Jones was executed for murder, then Floyd Joyner Jr. was executed on Dec. 12, making ten total executions in 1951 – the busiest year since 1915, with 11 executions.

A Simple Pardon

On Aug. 31, 2021 – less than two months after signing abolition of the death penalty, Gov. Ralph Northam granted a simple pardon to the Martinsville Seven. "While these pardons do not address the guilt of the seven," the Office of the Governor stated in a release, "they serve as recognition from the Commonwealth that these men were tried without adequate due process and received a racially-biased death sentence not similarly applied to white defendants."

"This is about righting wrongs," Gov. Northam said of the pardon. "We all deserve a criminal justice system that is fair, equal, and gets it right—no matter who you are or what you look like. I'm grateful to the advocates and families of the Martinsville Seven for their dedication and perseverance. While we can't change the past, I hope today's action brings them some small measure of peace."

Executions, Post-Martinsville

After the horror of the 1951 Martinsville killings, executions slowed considerably. There was only one in 1952, when Albert Jackson Jr., another Black man convicted of rape, was executed on Aug. 25.

Like the Martinsville case and so many others, the Jackson case remains a distressing commentary on the treatment of Blacks, Black women, and the mentally ill at the hands of Virginia's 1950s criminal justice system. Jackson, a 24-year-old Charlottesville native, received a less-than-honorable discharge from the U.S. Army in 1948 when he reportedly "went berserk." He returned to Charlottesville an alcoholic and could not hold a job. Later that year, he brutally raped a young Black woman, and the Charlottesville Corporation Court imposed a 10-year sentence. He went to the state penitentiary, where he received no psychiatric treatment despite a psychiatrist deeming him a "psychopathic personality" who "did not learn by experience."

In August 1950, after serving less than two years, Jackson was released by the Board of Paroles and returned to Charlottesville.

On May 5, 1951, at 11:00 p.m. Jackson attacked a white woman as she got off work on Main Street in Charlottesville. He dragged her into an alley off Second Street and raped her twice, knocking her into a ravine, where she was severely injured. He dragged her out to another alley and was in the process of raping her a third time when interrupted by a policeman making his rounds.

While the victim received treatment at Martha Jefferson Hospital, Jackson confessed to police that he raped her. He pled temporary insanity at his trial, but the jury, composed of nine white men, two white women, and one Black man, sentenced him to death.

Numerous petitions circulated both in Black and white Charlottesville neighborhoods urging Gov. Battle to commute Jackson's death sentence to life imprisonment, to no avail.

James W. Phillips, a spokesman for the parole board, defended their 1950 parole of Jackson by noting to the *Charlottesville Daily Progress* that Jackson displayed "no sign of manic or perverted tendencies" when paroled, and that "one mistake does not mean that the basic decisions are wrong."

"Besides," Phillips concluded in a printed statement that draws gasps of disbelief today, "the record indicates that the (Black) woman he was charged with raping in 1948 had a poor character."

Jackson was initially scheduled to be electrocuted on June 30, but on June 28 – in an ironic and Frankenstein-like incident – a bolt of lightning struck the State Penitentiary, shorting out a main power line. The execution date was then delayed to July 28, during which a Charlottesville judge granted a stay for the defense to appeal to Gov. Battle.

Battle predictably claimed there was "no good purpose" for further postponement, and Jackson was executed.

Throughout the 1950s, there were only two or three executions per year. There was not one execution in Virginia in 1953 or 1956.

Delaware's repeal of capital punishment in 1958 revived a national abolition movement that peaked in 1966 when for the first time, Americans who opposed the death penalty outnumbered the proponents by a slim margin of 47 percent to 42 percent. In the mid-1960s, three more states abolished the death penalty, bringing the number of states without capital punishment to 12, plus the District of Columbia.

In 1960, Virginia expanded kidnapping to include all types of abduction punished by the death penalty when the victim was a female under the age of 16 for purposes of prostitution or concubinage; or when kidnapping was conducted with the intent to extort money, for financial benefits, or to defile the victim.

In 1961, 23-year-old Lynwood Bunch became the last Black man in Virginia executed for raping a white woman. The attack occurred in Newport News almost three years earlier, in 1958. During the trial, Bunch pled temporary insanity, a claim bolstered by a Dr. Lowry, a member of the American Board of Psychiatry and Neurology, who testified that Bunch suffered "a severe type of psychiatric disorder, a schitzoid (*sic*) personality."

Bunch's father admitted on the stand he beat his son regularly as a child because he didn't get along with friends or siblings. Taking the stand, the defendant, in a low voice, freely admitted raping the woman, relating the crime in lurid details.

He received a death sentence by an all-white, 12-man jury. The Dec. 10, 1958 *Daily Press* reported that there had initially been "five potential Negro jurors." One was hard of hearing and never called. Two others stated they could never vote for the death penalty. The remaining two were dropped during peremptory challenges.

The 1965 Washington & Lee report "The Incidence of the Death Penalty for Rape in Virginia" stated that between 1908 and 1962, 1,084 Blacks were admitted to the penitentiary for rape, compared to 887 whites. However, only Blacks were executed, making it "impossible to offer any reasonable hypothesis other than racial prejudice to explain why all of those executed for rape have been Blacks."

The historical treatment of Blacks charged with rape remains the most brazen example of institutional, systemic racial bias in Virginia's criminal justice system.

Eating Our Young: Virginia's Dark History of Executing Children

> No doubt ample justice will be rendered to one whose youthful villanies have been so execrable.
> - "Diabolical Murders," *Carolina Sentinel* newspaper reporting murders committed by slave James, age 13, in Spanish Grove, Va., Feb. 2, 1822.

An enslaved girl, Rebecca, or "Beck," could well be the youngest child ever legally executed in the history of the United States. According to the Court record of Oyer and Terminer, Rebecca was "about 11 or 12" when she was hanged July 2, 1825, for the murder of four-year-old Adeline Coalter, the daughter of her owner, in what was then Monroe County, Virginia (now West Virginia).

Rebecca approached the little girl from behind and, for unknown reasons, struck her with a rock as they gathered flowers on April 13. She then hid the body in an attempt to conceal her crime.

Rebecca was tried and convicted on May 2, then hanged two months later "on the road leading to the Alexander Farm." The Court valued her at $150, payable to her owner.

Not One White

The execution of children is one of the darkest legacies of America's slavery and capital punishment systems. Nationwide, between 1642 and 1924, an estimated 102 American juveniles were convicted and executed before their eighteenth birthday. Around 20 were Virginians. All of the Virginians were Black, and all their ages have been verified as under 18 by various sources. These include court records, county auditor records, and the National Death Penalty M. Watt Espy Archive, located at the M. E. Grenander Special Collections at the State University of New York at Albany.

At least eleven of these confirmed juveniles executed by Virginia between 1787 and 1924 were enslaved.

These numbers undoubtedly vary, and there most likely have been many more. It was not common to record the ages of condemned prisoners, especially enslaved persons in Virginia, until after 1900. Even these numbers can be unreliable until the advent of social security numbers, personal ID cards, and driver's licenses.

Several states including Virginia hanged young, overwhelmingly minority children. In Arkansas, a Cherokee named James Arcene was ten years of age in 1873 when he and an adult companion named William Parchmeal murdered a Swedish storekeeper, Henry Fiegel. Arcene and Parchmeal eluded capture until 1884, when deputies arrested Arcene for selling whiskey on the reservation at Tahlequah. A deputy marshal pieced enough evidence together to charge them both for the murder. The then-21-year-old Arcene pleaded that he was only ten at the time of the crime and had no idea what he was doing. Nonetheless, he and Parchmeal were convicted and hanged on June 26, 1885.

"Both died in true Indian style," reported the July 15, 1885, *National Police Gazette* without explaining what "true Indian style" meant, "except that they were Christians and prayed before going to the gallows."

On Dec. 20, 1786, a 12-year-old "moderately retarded" Pequot Nation Native American girl, Hannah Ocuish, was executed in New London, Connecticut, for the murder of a six-year-old white girl named Eunice Bolles. Hannah was not only intellectually disabled but a product of a neglectful and abusive childhood, shuffled in and out of foster homes by her alcoholic mother. A description of her life and crime, published with a transcript of Rev. Henry Channing's day-of-execution sermon, pointed out that Hannah's mother was "an abandoned creature, much addicted to the vice of drunkenness."

Court officials eventually took Hannah from her mother and "bound her out" as a servant of a widow.

At her trial, where she pleaded not guilty, Hannah – most likely because of her youth and diminished mental capacity – appeared to onlookers and jury unconcerned about her plight. "Her conduct, as appeared in evidence in the Honorable Supreme Court, was marked with almost everything bad," Rev. Channing's appendix notes. "Theft and lying were her common vices. To these were added a maliciousness of disposition which made the children in the neighborhood much afraid of her."

Witnesses reported that Hannah "seemed greatly afraid when at the Gallows." With her last words, she "thanked the Sheriff for his kindness, and launched into the eternal World."

A 10-year-old slave boy was reportedly hanged for murder in Louisiana in 1855. A U.S. Supreme Court decision even mentioned the case, but the research of Watt Espy and the National Death Penalty Archive does not verify it.

Meanwhile, Back in Virginia ...

Bill, a 12-year-old enslaved child, was one of only three maybe four 12-year-olds to be executed in the United States. He was hanged for murder on July 30, 1791, in Woodford County, Virginia (now Kentucky). On June 25, the Court of Oyer and Terminer convened to try the juvenile accused of murdering the young daughter of a neighbor, Benjamin French. "It appearing to the Court that the said Bill is about the age of twelve years, and that he is a very sensible boy," stated a handwritten transcript. "Whereupon the Court after due consideration of the several circumstances are unanimously of the opinion that the said Bill is guilty of the felony aforesaid in manner and form as in above set forth ... Therefore, it is considered in the Court that he be hanged by the neck until dead."

Bill's owner, Ann James, was reimbursed for Bill's death. It was the last execution carried out before Kentucky obtained statehood.

Another 12-year-old enslaved child named Clem was hanged in 1787 for murdering Henry and Miles Seat, the two young sons of his owner, Hartwell Seat, in Sussex County on April 13, 1787. On that day, the boys walked to their "old master's" house, and Clem followed under the pretense of getting one of the boys to get some rice seed to plant. Clem then struck Henry with a knot wood stick, knocking him down. As Henry got up and started running, Clem clubbed Miles, then chased Henry, catching him as they crossed a fence. He then struck Henry four times with the stick, killing him.

As Clem dragged Henry to a nearby swamp, he saw Miles struggle to his feet. He reportedly dropped Henry and beat Miles to death with the same stick. He then dragged both bodies to the swamp, where he concealed them. No documents mention the motivation for the murders.

The Sussex County Court convicted Clem on April 19, finding him guilty of murder. He hanged on May 11, 1787. A Court document stated he was "valued to the court the sum of fifty pounds of current money," the amount paid to Hartwell Seat for the killing of his "property."

Rebuttable Presumption

The hangings of pre-teens Rebecca, Bill, and Clem showed Virginia's sentencing guidelines paid little consideration to the ages of those convicted of violent crimes. From the mid-1700s until the dawn of the twentieth century, the commonwealth's criminal justice system recognized that only those aged seven and under were decisively presumed to be incapable of criminal intent and could not be charged with a capital crime under any conditions. However, those aged eight to 14 were considered capable of capital crime under what was called rebuttable presumption, in which the court presumed the defendant knew right from wrong unless proven otherwise – in this case, an attenuated form of "guilty until proven innocent." New Kent County Justice George Webb wrote as early as 1736 in "The Office and Authority of a Justice of Peace" that Virginia could legitimately hang a child as young as eight for murder as long as they knew right from wrong.

In a few hanging cases, sheriffs feared children were not heavy enough for the drop to instantly break their necks. Rather than subject witnesses to the uncomfortable sight of a child slowly strangling to death, they attached weights to their feet.

One Augusta County enslaved girl named Amy, whose age is not recorded but described by historian Joseph Waddell as "quite young" was executed Dec. 11, 1812, in "Gallowstown," on the west end of Staunton.

Her hanging was steeped in a seemingly paranormal experience that remained a mystery for many years. Amy was convicted of drowning her owner, James Tate's, two-year-old daughter, Mary, in what was then called a "swill," or compost barrel. There was reportedly much public sympathy for the young girl, as many believed the baby drowned by accident. Nonetheless, she was found guilty in the County Court and sentenced to death.

According to Waddell's 1902 "Annals of Augusta County," the night after she died, an unearthly groaning awoke almost the entire town. People ran into the streets, fearing that maybe Amy had been wrongfully executed and was returning to exact revenge. Many people claimed they had seen an apparition of the girl sitting on the courthouse steps.

The event remained legend for many years before someone finally revealed the truth: a two-story building at the corner of New and Courthouse Streets (now East Johnson Street) contained a store belonging to Ben Morris. Morris had a young employee who eventually confessed to going up on the roof through a trap door the night of the execution and groaning through a large brass "speaking-trumpet," an early type of bullhorn commonly used at the time for political speeches and by firemen.

On Aug. 3, 1796, the Court of Oyer & Terminer met in Frederick County and convicted a 13-year-old enslaved child named William for setting fire to the home of his owner, Rawleigh Colston. He hanged on Sept. 16. Deputy Sheriff Griffin Taylor certified the boy's hanging and value of 70 English Pounds.

Thirteen-year-old Henry, owned by James Hunt of Mecklenburg County, was hanged on Jan. 3, 1822, for murdering Hunt's three daughters, ages 18, 12, and eight. "Seldom have the inhabitants of Virginia been presented with a more tragical scene than was witnessed in Mecklenburg," cried the news accounts of the gruesome killings by the young boy that occurred Dec. 13, 1821, near Spanish Grove.

Upon leaving for the three-day business trip in Richmond, Hunt left his two youngest girls and Henry in the care of his oldest daughter. On Thursday evening, the oldest girl chastised Henry for some unstated misconduct. That night, the girls placed their bedding by the fire and went to sleep.

At just before daybreak, Henry – "irritated by the chastisement lately received, and instigated by a diabolical desire of revenge," murdered the three sleeping girls with an ax.

After daybreak, Henry took anything considered of value, then set the house on fire as he left to cover his crime. Neighbors arrived soon afterward and managed to retrieve the girls' bodies from the flaming wreckage "before they were entirely consumed."

Henry was immediately suspected when authorities could find no trace of him nearby. They later apprehended him, weighted down by his spoils, a few miles north of Spanish Grove. He quickly confessed and reiterated his confessions when questioned by a coroner's jury the next day.

While there is no record of his trial, he hanged on Mar. 1, 1822.

Before emancipation, Virginia also executed a 17-year-old Sussex County enslaved juvenile named Allen for attempted murder on Oct. 30, 1795. Another 17-year-old Southampton County slave named Dick hanged for carnal knowledge of a four-year-old on Dec. 20, 1808. A 17-year-old Shenandoah County enslaved juvenile named Hercules hanged for burglary on Nov. 11, 1814, and a slave named Arthur also hanged at age 17 for attempted murder on June 5, 1857.

In the post-slavery era, 17-year-old Winston Green was the second person executed in Virginia's brand-new electric chair in 1908 for the crime of scaring a 12-year-old white girl. The Court interpreted his crime as "attempted criminal assault." As the girl drove a small horse and buggy down what is today Midlothian Turnpike, Green, reportedly mentally disabled, stepped into the road and stopped her horse. The girl screamed, and Green ran away.

Two gangs of men organized by the girl's father caught Green within hours. The trial took about one hour, and the all-white jury sentenced him to death in minutes. He had no legal counsel.

Sixteen-year-old Charles Beaver hanged for rape on Mar. 30, 1883. Gabriel Battaile, also age 16, hanged for rape on June 8, 1906. News accounts stated that he calmly smoked a cigarette on the gallows while the sheriff read his death warrant. On Mar. 22, 1909, 17-year-old Aurelius "Felix" Christian was electrocuted for rape and murder. John Eccles was electrocuted at age 17 for murder on Nov. 11, 1910, and 17-year-old Harry Sitlington was electrocuted for murder on Dec. 16, 1910.

Virginia Christian, the only juvenile female executed in Virginia history, was electrocuted for murdering her white employer on Aug. 16, 1912, the day after her seventeenth birthday. Percy Ellis was electrocuted at age 16 for murder on Mar. 15, 1916; Tolson Bailey was electrocuted at age 17 for robbery and murder on July 2, 1918; and 17-year-old Fritz Lewis was electrocuted for robbery and murder on Sept. 12, 1924.

A Stab at reform

While over a dozen states had reform schools in place by 1860, Illinois' Juvenile Court Act of 1899 was the first in the nation to institute a criminal justice system to deal solely with juvenile crime. The law specified that juvenile court was to treat and rehabilitate and not impose any punishment on a juvenile offender. Many other states quickly followed Illinois' example, and by 1925, all states but two had some form of juvenile justice program in place. Virginia's juvenile system was in place as part of the reforms of the 1920s.

It may seem that this seminal 1899-1925 era of evolving juvenile justice would have eliminated or at least reduced the death penalty for such young offenders. However, over 50 offenders were executed after their eighteenth birthday for crimes committed while juveniles. Many of these cases were forced not into juvenile courts, where the defendant would escape a death sentence, but due to legal complications, prosecution (mis)conduct, even public opinion (such as the threat of lynching), they were forced into criminal court, where the defendant assuredly faced a death sentence.

This scenario is how Lynchburg's Thomas Wansley got sentenced to death twice for rape in 1961 at age 16. He escaped execution and of course was later exonerated.

Fits and Starts

It wasn't until 1988 that *Thompson v. Oklahoma* maintained that execution for crimes committed at age 15 was unconstitutional. Defendant Wayne Thompson instead received a sentence of life imprisonment, an admittedly harsh punishment for a 15-year-old.

In June 1989, the U.S. Supreme Court ruled in *Stanford v. Kentucky* that states were free to impose the death penalty for convicted murderers age 16 or 17. In a 5-4 vote, the judges ruled that the death penalty for "older juvenile killers" did not violate the Constitution's ban on cruel and unusual punishment. The ruling affected about 25 of about

2,200 death row inmates across the nation, but none in Virginia

Every other nation in the world joined international agreements, such as the United Nations' 1990 Convention on the Rights of the Child, which among other rights, prohibited the execution of juveniles. The United States could not ratify the Convention because of the stubborn willingness to imprison for life and even execute children, which was a direct contravention of the Convention's Article 37.

In 2005, *Roper v. Simmons* held that execution for crimes committed at an age less than 18 was unconstitutional, forcing the U.S. to abandon juvenile executions once and for all.

This decision was too late for Virginia's Steve Roach, who was executed Jan. 19, 2000, at age 23 for the 1993 murder of Mary Hughes, a crime committed when he was 17.

Almost Executed: Richard Phillips and William Harper

On Jan. 16, 1900, army private Joseph New died from a gunshot wound during a fight at Gurley's saloon in Elizabeth City County (now part of Hampton). A well-known local boxer, Richard Phillips, was seen arguing with the victim before he was found with a rifle. He and an accomplice, Grant Watts, were arrested at the saloon.

Hours before the jury trial convened in April, with Judge Baker E. Lee presiding, Phillips' defense attorney abruptly withdrew from the case. Judge Lee then appointed Burdett Lewis as his replacement. Lewis had two hours to prepare to defend Phillips.

During Phillips' trial, Grant Watts was a witness for the prosecution and testified that he saw Phillips murder New with his rifle. Phillips conversely testified that it was Watts who shot New with a pistol.

The jurors found Watts more credible and, on Apr. 7, found Phillips guilty of murder. In mid-April, Phillips was sentenced to death. Later that month, a jury acquitted Watts during a separate trial.

In May 1901, over a year after his conviction and after several stays of execution, a special jury found Richard Phillips clinically insane. The previous February, while being held at Fort Monroe, Phillips reportedly hallucinated that an army was after him and tried to kill himself by beating his head repeatedly on his cell wall. With his death sentence suspended, he was taken to Central State Hospital at Petersburg.

Phillips was a wily patient. On Jan. 29, 1904, the *Alexandria Gazette* reported that the "desperate lunatic" had escaped from Central State. He was recaptured near Richmond on Feb. 3, returned to Central State, and placed in solitary confinement.

In early April 1911, Phillips escaped again and made his way to Richmond, then to Washington D. C. to visit a sister. He then returned to the hospital voluntarily, "being satisfied with his trips."

A year later, during a blinding snowstorm, Phillips escaped a third time and remained free until January of 1915, when he was caught in Baltimore and returned to Petersburg.

Phillips behaved himself until 1930, when his sister, Gertrude Tuckson, appealed to Washington D.C. lawyer Goldie Paregol to investigate her brother's case. She was convinced her brother was no longer insane and was innocent of the 1900 murder. The case reopened, and a further investigation by state physicians corroborated Tuckson's assertion that Phillips was not insane.

The case drew the attention of Gov. John Garland Pollard, who contacted Phillips' original defense attorney Burdett Lewis, who by 1930 was a commonwealth's attorney. Lewis wrote the governor a letter stating that he clearly remembered the Phillips case because, in 1901, it was proven that Grant Watts had indeed killed Private Joseph New yet was still acquitted. Ballistic evidence concluded that Phillips' high-powered rifle bullets would have exited New's body at point-blank range. The evidence also showed that bullets from Watts' cheap pistol would not. The bullet that killed New did not exit his body.

Lewis told Pollard that he would have pursued the case further but that Phillips had been declared insane and institutionalized and was no longer in danger of being wrongfully executed.

Yet he was perfectly willing to let a guilty man walk free.

Gov. Pollard granted Richard Phillips an absolute pardon on Nov. 14, 1930. Central State Hospital released the 52-year-old Phillips two weeks later.

William Harper: "I couldn't lose my husband over this."

> I watched the white woman ... and for that day, she was queen in the courtroom. The judge, the prosecutor, her father who told of her fright – all rallied round to defend her honor ... It was only later that I realized the horror of what she was doing to herself ...
> -Anne Braden, excerpts from "A Letter to White Southern Women." Dec. 1972.

On the evening of Jan. 6, 1931, Portsmouth woman Dorothy Skaggs went drinking and dancing at Caroon's Dance Hall in Elizabeth City, North Carolina, with a man who was not her husband. Skaggs, in turn, made up a lie to keep her husband from finding out (and not to violate a sexist law that prohibited women from crossing state lines "to engage in illicit activities"). She went to Norfolk police and claimed that around 6:45 p.m., a Black man hit her over the head while walking to a guitar lesson. He then dragged her into an alley and knocked her unconscious. She also discovered that when she awakened four hours later, she had been raped.

The next day, on Jan. 7, William Harper, a 22-year-old Black Coca-Cola delivery driver, was arrested on a minor, unrelated charge. Harper appeared in a police line-up, and Skaggs almost immediately identified him as her rapist. Later that day, Harper admitted he was guilty and signed a written confession.

Harper's attorney Lester Parsons presented a strong case that mainly seemed to work. Harper pleaded insanity, but the prosecution trotted out doctors who testified that the defendant was not insane but merely "dull" and with a ten-year-old's intellectual functionality.

Harper's father took the stand and testified that he was with his son at home in Norfolk at the time of the crime. Also taking the stand in his defense, Harper withdrew his confession, claiming police had tortured him into signing. An Elizabeth City police officer testified he patrolled that alley two or three times between 6:30 p.m. and 10:30 p.m. the night of the alleged attack and never saw anyone there.

Despite the defense's strong case, Skaggs's "unmistakable" identification of Harper from the stand and her sobbing, tear-filled testimony "was enough to convince the jury that the negro was guilty." Harper was convicted and sentenced to death in the electric chair.

But Skaggs' lies soon began haunting her.

On Feb. 7, only days after the conviction, a man contacted Harper's attorney. He presented credible evidence that he had spoken with Skaggs in Elizabeth City minutes after the rape that allegedly occurred in Norfolk. The attorney took this news to the judge, who immediately ordered a new trial.

The heavily publicized second trial began on March 3. Skaggs again took the stand, described the attack in detail, and positively identified William Harper as her assailant. The defense countered that Skaggs was a drug user and invented her attack as cover. Then, the defense produced no fewer than nine witnesses who testified they saw Skaggs dancing with a married man in Elizabeth City on the evening of the attack.

Witness Catherine Ketchum testified that she spoke to Skaggs at the same club five days after Harper's conviction. When she asked Skaggs why she made up the rape story and railroaded an innocent Black man, Skaggs replied, "Oh, I couldn't lose my husband over this." Skaggs then told Ketchum that police described Harper in detail to her before she went to the line-up, then boasted that she identified him correctly on the first try.

On Friday, March 6, after 32 minutes of deliberation, the jury found Harper not guilty, and he walked out of jail.

But that was not the end of the case. Determined to find something with which to nail Harper, six weeks later, a grand jury indicted Harper for robbing Skaggs of her purse and $1.50. Police arrested Harper again. However, that grand jury also indicted Skaggs and her friend, Ketchum, for perjury.

Dorothy Skaggs went to trial, was found guilty of perjury, and sentenced to five years in prison. She was later acquitted at a retrial. Five days after Harper's indictment for robbery, a judge dismissed the charges against him. Harper was freed again and reinstated at his job with Coca-Cola.

No White Man Should Suffer Such Indignity: Abolition Efforts 1897 - 1964

> The death penalty is not necessary for the protection of society; that trial has proven it not to be the great preventive agent it was once considered; that instead of minimizing crime, as all punishment should do, it actually increases and inspires it, as it serves as an incentive to the morbid vanity of criminals; that it is a degrading relic of barbarism, and unworthy of any highly developed system of government.
>
> -Richmond attorney William E. Ross, *The Virginia Law Register,* Dec. 1905.

In this *Virginia Law Register* article, Ross advocated for a gradual abandonment of Virginia's death penalty through judicial and legislative actions, such as pardon reform, instead of an abrupt repeal. He closed with a bold prediction, but with the usual racist caveats:

> With all confidence, the writer ventures the expression that the end of the present century will not find the death penalty (except perhaps for treason or rape) upon the statute books of a single civilized country of the world. Deep-rooted prejudices and the morbid cry for revenge cannot stem the tide.

Origins of Abolition

The "Great Act" of William Penn in 1682 was the first in America to break with precedent by prescribing the death penalty for premeditated murder only. However, Pennsylvania officials were not impressed, and by 1718 the much harsher English penal code was adopted, which included 13 capital offenses. Still, Pennsylvania would go on to become a leader in penal reform.

Cesare Beccaria's 1767 essay "On Crimes and Punishment" impacted abolition efforts worldwide. His conjecture was simple: there was no justification for the state to take a life. The essay gave European abolitionists a commanding voice, and as a result, Austria and Tuscany abolished their death penalties.

In colonial America, Dr. Benjamin Rush, a signer of the Declaration of Independence who in 1787 founded the Pennsylvania Prison Society, challenged the theory that the death penalty was a deterrent. An early believer in the "brutalization effect," Rush boldly maintained that the use of the death penalty led to an increase in crime, a theory proven true in the nineteenth and twentieth centuries.

Rush also noted the hypocrisy of the application of the death penalty when he wrote in a collection of essays that "It seems to us that government is guilty of a wicked, stupid blunder, when it undertakes to illustrate the sacredness of human life, by murdering the criminal."

Rush successfully corralled Benjamin Franklin and Philadelphia Attorney General William Bradford into his corner, best described as abolition-with-few-exceptions. Bradford, who later became the U.S. Attorney General, worked with the Quakers to establish degrees of murder based on culpability – a first in Colonial America.

Bradford was revolutionary in that he, like Rush, also believed that capital punishment did not deter crime. He pointed out that in Virginia, for example, horse stealing was a capital crime but was also the most frequent crime committed in that state. However, because of the severity of the punishment, getting a conviction was almost impossible. Bradford concluded that a law was worse than useless if it could not be enforced. In 1869, Virginia reduced horse stealing from a capital crime to a felony and no longer eligible for death.

As early as 1838, some states, particularly in the northeast, either abandoned the death penalty for almost all crimes or ceased mandatory death sentencing, replacing those statutes with discretionary sentencing guidelines. Abolitionists perceived these steps as victories because those previous mandates applied death to anyone convicted of a capital crime, regardless of age, race, gender, or circumstances.

"Abolition with exceptions" was the rule mostly in northern states. Michigan abolished the death penalty in 1846 but retained it for treason only until 1963. Rhode Island abolished the death penalty in 1852, only to restore it in 1882 for any life-term convict who committed murder. In 1837 Maine passed a law that stated that no condemned person could be executed until one year after sentencing, and then only upon a warrant from the governor. Maine formally abolished the death penalty entirely in 1887.

In the American South, including post-Jefferson Virginia, the exact opposite was happening, with capital crimes overwhelmingly applied on a racial and classist basis. Tennessee flirted with abolition only for one year, from 1915 to 1916, but retained it for rape only to protect the virtues of their white woman from those "marauding" Black males.

Affluent White Men and Their 'Other Women'

Public dismay with the execution of whites was prevalent in Virginia, starting as early as 1887, when Thomas Cluverius hanged in Richmond for the murder of his adopted mother's niece, Fannie Lillie Madison, of Manquin. A romance had developed between Madison and Cluverius, a young lawyer from Centerville. In March 1885, when Madison discovered she was pregnant, she met Cluverius in Richmond to tell him that he would be a father. That evening, the distraught young attorney, who was already engaged to another woman, drove Madison to the water reservoir near Hollywood Cemetery, where he struck her over the head and drowned her.

Police quickly identified Cluverius as the assailant. He was convicted and then hanged for the murder on Jan. 14, 1887.

Almost immediately, newspapers and clergy members spoke out against the hanging of such a promising young (white) man who had so much to offer society. The Jan. 21, 1887, *Shenandoah Herald* reported that Rev. Royal Pallman of the Second Universalist Church preached that "the judicial killing of T. J. Cluverius was a mistake of the death penalty."

The article editorialized that "... the unhappy man has paid the penalty of his crime according to the criminal code ... the practical result of which must be the large reinforcement of the conviction that the death penalty is a sad and terrible mistake."

Three-Time Mayor was a Two-Timing Husband

As a respected attorney and popular Charlottesville Mayor, J. Samuel McCue enjoyed an abundant life with his wife Fannie and four children in the most fashionable section of town. In 1904 a young woman came to McCue to file for divorce, and soon she and McCue began an affair. Then, on Sept. 4, police were called to the McCue house, where they found Fannie dead in the bathtub, shot through the chest. Her husband lay nearby, with several abrasions and according to the press "feigning unconsciousness."

McCue claimed a burglar had assaulted them, but police found no evidence of entry. Loudly claiming innocence, McCue bought an ad in the *Daily Progress* offering $1,000 reward for information leading to the conviction of his wife's killer. He even curiously hired the Baldwin Detective Agency to investigate, but after one day they were convinced he was the killer. By Sept. 7, he was arrested and charged with murder when circumstantial evidence accumulated, including the Baldwin detectives discovering that he and Fannie frequently quarreled. At trial, enough evidence was presented to convince the jury, and after 26 minutes of deliberation found him guilty and sentenced him to death. He hanged in the Charlottesville jail yard on the frigid morning of Feb. 10, 1905.

This is not where this story ends. In a bizarre coda, a New York salesman traveling through Norfolk got off a train and noticed a suspicious man in a low hat with his coat pulled up as if to conceal himself. As the character boarded the train, his hat caught a woman's umbrella, knocking it and a wig off his head. The salesman recognized the wigless man as Samuel McCue, who ducked onto the train leaving the hat and wig on the platform.

Rumors circulated that the wealthy and prominent McCue had struck a deal to fake his execution so he could flee the country. Several newspapers pointed out numerous discrepancies in his hanging: McCue was hanged not at noon, as announced, but at 7:35 a.m. He was also hanged with his back to the few gathered spectators. The drop was not eight feet, which was standard, but three feet – not enough to break the neck. McCue was hanged not with the traditional black hood over his head, but in a full black robe which obscured his entire body. The deputy who adjusted the rope paused not once but twice to put his hand on McCue's shoulder while he corrected something under McCue's neck. Spectators also saw him whisper several times into McCue's ear.

McCue supposedly strangled to death since the neck was not broken, but he did not struggle. The body was cut down very quickly, and hustled away under much secrecy. There appeared to be no funeral, and he was supposedly buried at his family home, "Brookville," near Afton.

Later McCue's body was allegedly moved to Charlottesville's Riverview Cemetery, next to his wife Fannie. Only her name appears on the headstone. In 2003, cemetery officials confirmed to a reporter from *The Hook* magazine that a probe of the "husband" side of the plot contacted something that could be a burial vault or casket. However, short of disinterment, there is no way to tell if there is anything inside.

The Last Rich Socialite Executed in Virginia

Henry Clay Beattie Jr., of 1529 Porter Street in Richmond, went to his death in the electric chair on Nov. 24, 1911, for the July 18 murder of his wife, Louise Wellford Owen Beattie. the Richmond press blamed the Beattie murder on secular white decadence: "truly a pathetic picture of twentieth-century civilization, a sad commentary on the wild passions of the day, and a pitiable condition of human affairs .... "

In 1907, while dating Louise, 23-year-old Henry started dating a 13-year-old girl named Beulah Binford, who, according to the press, "had a reputation for being fast." She gave birth out of wedlock two years later and gave the child up to Mrs. Mary Trout of Roanoke. The little boy, named Henry C. Beattie Trout, died at age 11 months of infant cholera and was buried in Shockoe Hill Cemetery.

Never admitting paternity and still planning to marry Louise, Beattie convinced Binford to move to Raleigh, N.C., and made her promise to remain there.

Beattie's eventual marriage to Louise, a native of Dover, Delaware, pleased his father, whom the younger Beattie depended on for support. The marriage was not happy, yet they had a son, Henry Clay Beattie III.

Beattie continued to run around behind his wife and, by coincidence, ran into Binford at a baseball game in Norfolk. Falling for her again, he promised to buy her a house if she moved back to Richmond.

Beattie and Binford then met secretly at various hotels and resorts around the city. However, his father later learned of the affair and threatened to withdraw support of his son, placing Henry in an untenable financial situation.

In July 1911, Louise Beattie and the baby went on a multi-day visit to Thomas E. Owen, her uncle in South Richmond. On the 18th, Henry took her for an automobile ride. At 11:00 p.m. that night, he returned to Owens' home, driving with one hand, with the other cradling his bloody and lifeless wife. Beattie claimed to Owen that a tall man with a long beard stepped onto Midlothian Turnpike near a railroad crossing and stopped the car. He then shot and killed Louise with a shotgun.

After bloodhounds found nothing, and an investigation went nowhere, it dawned on the police that there had been no tall man with a beard at all but that Henry Beattie, telling lie after lie, must have pulled the trigger on his wife inside the car.

Police arrested and charged Beattie. On July 22, he never flinched while on the witness stand at a coroner's inquest for three and a half hours under a grueling cross-examination. Although wide discrepancies opened in his story, he never backed down.

During the lunch break, Henry's cousin Paul aggravated the case against Henry when he signed an affidavit swearing that he had purchased the single-barrel shotgun for his cousin at a Sixth Street pawn shop.

Richmond's society circles embraced the case, and it dominated the front page of the *Richmond Times-Dispatch* for days. On Aug. 6, while awaiting trial, an unperturbed Beattie posed in his jail cell in a white shirt for a portrait by Richmond photographers Homeler & Clark. "For ten minutes, he remained under the eye of a camera, and no artist ever found a subject so much at ease, so quiet, so still," reported the press.

But the evidence was overwhelming, and Beattie was found guilty of first-degree murder and sentenced to death.

Just days before Beattie's execution, after a fruitless appeal to the Supreme Court of Virginia, a prominent but unnamed physician tried to convince Gov. Horace Mann to not only commute Beattie's sentence to life imprisonment but abolish Virginia's death penalty altogether, at least for the remainder of his term. The Nov. 11, 1911, *Alexandria Gazette* reported that "The physician ... believed he would have the support of a majority among the ministers of the gospel in Richmond in advocating the abolition of capital punishment in Virginia ...."

"The physician further stated that he was convinced the movement for respite launched by him in the interests of Beattie would be taken up by a wide and sympathetic circle of citizens generally who advocated the speedy doing away with the infliction of capital punishment under the law."

The Nov. 17, 1911, *Clinch Valley News* echoed the sentiment, reporting that "There is considerable discussion now going on in the papers of the state as to abolishing the death penalty in this state, substituting life imprisonment therefore. The question came up and was precipitated in the newspapers by an effort now being made to have the sentence of Beattie, the wife murderer, commuted to life imprisonment ... We have thought and felt for years that capital punishment is wrong, first, last, and all the time."

But Beattie was executed, then buried in Richmond's Maury Cemetery beside the woman he so heartlessly murdered. Their shared headstone reads "Beyond the River."

The Conniving Doctor

Another notable white execution – in a story torn straight from the pages of a seedy dime store journal – was that of Dr. Wilmer Amos Hadley, a 36-year-old Richmond physician and Army Major. In 1913, he met and married Susan Kathleen Tinsley in Texas. Hadley, who was divorced, was looking for a wealthy wife this time, but after they married, he realized that his new wife was not wealthy, and he quickly lost interest.

In 1918, the University of Richmond Army hospital appointed Hadley as chief surgeon, while Susan remained in Texas. He had grown weary of the marriage and, while in Richmond, fell in love with one of his nurses, Grace Mercer. He even gave her a diamond, and they set an April 1919 wedding date.

In November 1918, Susan unexpectedly arrived in Richmond, surprising her scheming husband. He told her that spouses were not welcome at the army hospital, so he got her a room in a boarding house, where he mostly ignored her while running around with Mercer.

On Nov. 24, in a spirit of reconciliation but also in an ugly reprise of the Cluverius incident, Hadley asked Susan if she would like to take a ride in his canoe in the James River. She agreed, and while on the water, he offered her a sip of whiskey spiked with the sedative chloral. He then tied her unconscious body to the boat's anchor and dropped her overboard.

Over the next three weeks, Hadley concocted a web of lies, claiming that Susan was traveling out west, and after his discharge from the Army, he told friends he was going out to meet her.

But just after Hadley left Richmond, on Dec. 30, Susan's body somehow became untied from the anchor and turned up along the banks of the James. She was eventually identified, and not knowing Hadley's whereabouts, police contacted her sister in Cincinnati. She, in turn, showed them a telegram from Hadley telling her he was sorry, but Susan had died and was buried in San Juan, Puerto Rico. A check of burial records showed that a woman named Susan Hadley had been recently buried there.

Hadley later admitted he bribed a cemetery owner to put his wife's name on the register.

When police questioned Grace Mercer, she told them that the last letter she got from him was postmarked Dallas, Texas, and he had explained that Susan died in California.

With his picture posted in every metropolitan post office and police station in the country, Hadley was finally apprehended in August 1921, trying to buy a ranch in Falmouth, New Mexico.

Newsboys shouted on every downtown corner that Hadley had been arrested and returned to Richmond. Under questioning, he admitted to killing Susan, claiming he had done so because she cheated on him, a proven untrue charge. He was convicted, sentenced to death, and electrocuted on Dec. 9, 1921. Reportedly icy calm entering the chamber, he even leaned over and helped a fumbling corrections official secure his leg strap.

Hadley's story, along with fellow white condemned Virginians Thomas Cluverius, and Henry Clay Beattie Jr., received extended, detailed, and heavily sympathetic coverage in the white-owned press because of how extraordinary it was during this era for a prominent, wealthy white man to be not only sentenced to death but actually executed. White-on-white society crime resulting in executions ran completely counter to the state's propensity for executing impoverished Blacks, whose stories merited only the barest of press mentions and frequently in the most bestial of terms.

And these affluent, lovelorn, white defendants' stories persisted, sometimes for decades. Cluverius, Beattie, and Hadley were for years depicted as victims of conniving "other women" or unfair social or judicial circumstances. Beattie had two songs recorded about him. Hadley's story received extended life in the pages of numerous true detective magazines well into the 1950s.

Predictably, talk of abolition in the press only followed the execution of one of these prominent, cheating, white men.

The Hillsville Controversy

On March 14, 1912, after being sentenced to one year in the State Penitentiary for interfering with a police officer the previous January, Floyd Allen – a venerable and powerful white citizen of Carroll County – stood up inside the Hillsville Courthouse and announced, "Gentlemen, I ain't a-goin'." He pulled out a pistol, and the entire courtroom, packed with armed Allen family members and armed court officers, exploded in a barrage of gunfire. In the end, Judge Thornton Massie lay dead, as did Sheriff Lewis Webb and commonwealth's attorney William Foster. A juror, Augustus Fowler, died two days later, as did a spectator, Elizabeth Fowler. Clerk of court Dexter Goad was severely wounded, shot through the neck and legs. Also injured were Ridney Allen, brother of Floyd; two jurors; and three court spectators. Floyd was also injured after taking a bullet to the groin.

The elder Allen was convicted of first-degree murder on May 16, even though he was considered more a ringleader, and it was unclear whom he had shot, if anyone. His son, Claude Swanson Allen, was first convicted of second-degree murder for killing Judge Massie and first-degree murder for killing Sheriff Webb. Again, in the chaos, nothing could be definitively proven. Regardless, the courts sentenced father and son to die in the electric chair on March 28, 1913.

"Claude approached the death chair, silent and unafraid, like a young Greek god," stated a reporter of the stolidness of the condemned white prisoner. "He helped the executioners adjust the straps around his wrists."

Of the funeral and burial, the press announced:

> No scripture was read, no text announced. Three Baptist ministers made short talks of warning as the caskets waited in the mist. The procession formed to take one last look before the lids were closed, and for an hour, three old men with wavering voices sang familiar hymns as the spectators passed by. The privacy of a few last sad moments remained for the family
> ...

The actual truth of this story has been constantly re-interpreted by shifting political proclivities. However, the "Hillsville Massacre" at its core remains a tale of the political animosity between the Allen family's violent but affluent leadership in Carroll County's Democratic Party and the local Republicans, who in the preceding elections had finally voted out the Allen's dominance. Both men's executions (in a rare white-on-white crime) struck many as shameful at best and a travesty of justice at worst, triggering serious debates in Virginia newspapers around death penalty abolition.

Biased news articles that hinted at a Republican vendetta against the men, prompting the shootout and the eventual executions, added fuel to the argument.

Vivid and lengthy descriptions of the formerly powerful but now broken old white man, Floyd Allen, willingly limping into the death chamber, his head held high, to his ultimate fate in the chair after extended melodramatic goodbyes between him and his son, drawing tears from the attending pastors, convinced many that no white man should suffer such indignity. Subsequent histrionic stories told how the family had to sell their homes and farms to pay court costs. Floyd's widow died "far from her Carroll County hills," haunted and broken-hearted in a strange land, grieving for her husband and son.

The 1914 General Assembly actually voted to award $14,000 to Allen's estate to pay the condemned men's legal fees – a first in Virginia criminal justice history. The bill passed in the Senate by a single vote and passed through the house by five votes.

After a series of negative, anti-Allen articles in the *Newport News Daily Press*, Pastor C. B. Richards, minister of the 24th Street Church of Christ in Newport News, wrote a letter to the editor in April 1913. In it, he admonished the paper for their condemnations of the Allens and their portrayal of the family's supporters as radicals and cultists:

> You say the majority of people in Virginia desired their execution. This is but a mere assumption based upon the verdict of but twelve men, and one of them, like Judas Iscariot, filled with remorse and conscience-stricken, went out and committed suicide. We cannot say that the verdict of twelve men is necessarily the verdict of the majority of over one million citizens. Nor can we say confidently that the verdict of twelve men is infallibly true and that the law never makes a mistake.

He admitted that "I am one of the sympathizers of those men and their families, but prefer not to be classed with 'mobs' and 'fanatics.'" He closed his letter with an important PS: "This case may serve one good purpose for Virginia, that is, to abolish capital punishment."

The 1912 Allen case and the letter triggered a series of abolition columns, both for and against, in several Virginia newspapers well into the following year. In a column headlined "Do Away with Death Penalty," the May 29, 1913, *Virginia Gazette* ignored the Allens entirely, instead making a statistical argument for abolition by citing lower violent crime rates from the handful of states who had already abolished.

The article pointed out that from 1900 to 1909, the United States Bureau of Statistics reported a homicide average of 8.25 per 100,000 in states that actively used the death penalty. However, states that abolished the death penalty reported 3.82 homicides per 100,000 – an eye-popping decrease.

The report concluded that Hanover County Del. M. D. Hart planned to introduce a bill in the 1913 Assembly session supporting death penalty abolition in all cases except "for assault on women and desertion in time of war." While Hart did not follow through, Sen. G. Walter Mapp, of Princess Anne County did, with the strong approval of Hart. The bill unfortunately died in committee.

The "assault on women" caveat as suggested by Hart prevailed in all discussions regarding abolition in 1913, a hefty execution year, with 14 executed – nine Black and five white. Since Blacks were overwhelmingly accused, convicted, and executed for assaults on (white) women, there was no interest in sparing them from death for those crimes. Any discussions on abolition then seemed to be intended for whites only.

The Mar. 30, 1913 *Daily Press* (and other papers) opposed abolition for these reasons.

And, because of the specter of lynching, the editors were not at all shy about expressing their bigoted opinion that abolition would unleash an apocalyptic hellscape of predatory Black rapists, pursued by armies of revenge-obsessed lynch mobs:

> When the fear of death is taken from the negro criminal, no white woman in Virginia will be safe from the attacks of the fiend in human guise ... But, after capital punishment is abolished and the negro criminal begins his attacks, there will prevail a mob violence in Virginia such as no state has ever known, for Virginia men would never allow the punishment for such crimes to be mere incarceration of the guilty ones in the penitentiary, which is no punishment at all for them.

In stark contrast, the March 17, 1913 *Richmond Times-Dispatch* published a surprisingly progressive sermon on abolition and the then five-year-old electric chair by Leigh Street Baptist Church Pastor J. J. Wicker. "The electric chair belongs in the dark ages," Wicker announced from the pulpit. "It ought to be torn up and carried out and piled up with all the horrible death-dealing agents of heathenism and burned beneath the light of a cross from which we hear the prayer, 'Father forgive them, for they know not what they do.'"

Unfortunately, by Spring of that year, as memories of the Hillsville violence dimmed, abolition talk also faded from the page. The April 13 *Daily News* one last time expressed their bigotry of low expectations when they summed up what they considered the definitive position on capital punishment:

> Some citizens who are now talking so glibly about abolishing capital punishment would be among the first to join a mob to lynch a black beast for committing a nameless crime (rape), if there were no death penalty provided in the laws of Virginia ... The time may come when it will be safe for Virginia to abolish the death penalty. God speed the day. But it is not yet.

An Alternative is Introduced

In stark contrast to the attitudes expressed in some newspapers, in the 1914 General Assembly session, Shenandoah County Sen. Frederick Tavenner introduced Senate Bill 190. This bill amended Sec. 3663 of the criminal code by giving juries latitude to sentence first-degree murder convictions to either death or life in prison.

In an interview with the Mar. 10, 1914 *Roanoke World News*, Tavenner insisted that miscarriages of justice were too frequent in first-degree murder trials as a jury was legally bound to impose only death if the prisoner was found guilty. "A jury will often fail to find him guilty or will reduce the crime to second-degree murder to escape a sentence of death," he explained. Tavenner also feared that adverse publicity and heated courtroom passions improperly convinced juries to impose death when it was not warranted.

While he insisted his bill was not a gateway to death penalty abolition, the progressive senator expressed hope that future Assembly sessions would add to the bill, noting that "This is a time of reform and mending, not of retaliation."

"Men are coming more and more to believe in the exercise of firm human kindness and not quick retribution without a chance for betterment in the criminal."

The bill became law, and the numbers suggest it may have played a brief role in slowing the pace of executions. While there were 11 executions in 1915 and nine in 1916, they dropped sharply to five in 1917, then three in 1918, four in 1919, and only one in 1920.

Fear of Foreigners

America is under mob rule.
-Boston Symphony conductor Karl Muck, after being deported to Germany under the Federal Espionage Law, 1919.

Between 1907 and 1918, Kansas, Minnesota, Washington, Oregon, South Dakota, North Dakota, Arizona, and Missouri practiced that "firm kindness" Tavenner declared by abolishing their death penalties. Kansas Gov. Edward Hoch wrote on March 23, 1907, that "The fatal defect of the capital punishment theory is that it cheapens life instead of magnifying it as its votaries have believed. The criminal usually takes life hurriedly without much deliberation, but the law takes plenty of time and does it deliberately."

With such strong momentum and eight more states in consideration, 1917 was on track to be a banner year for abolition. However, after the Russian Revolution and America's entry into World War I that year, Americans became increasingly concerned about the possibility of a homeland revolution, as the fear of foreigners and escalating class conflicts with socialists posed significant challenges to the American way of life. In September 1920, a bomb exploded in a horse-drawn wagon on Wall Street, killing 40 people and injuring over 300, putting an exclamation point on the scare.

To temper the terror, the U.S. Congress in 1917 rushed two bills into law – the Espionage Act and the Trading with the Enemy Act.

The Espionage Law frantically and most unfairly targeted thousands of immigrants for arrest for treason using a meager standard of evidence. Orchestra conductor Karl Muck and 29 members of the Boston Symphony were held as enemy combatants under threat of lynching at Georgia's Fort Oglethorpe because the FBI mistook Muck's shorthand notations to Bach's "The Passion of St. Matthew" for some sort of spy code. They were ultimately deported.

Under the Trading with the Enemy Act, President Woodrow Wilson appointed A. Mitchell Palmer "Alien Property Custodian," to seize property that belonged to imprisoned immigrants that could potentially obstruct the war effort. "All aliens interned by the government are regarded as enemies," he wrote, "and their property is treated accordingly."

A Pennsylvania abolition bill sailed through the Senate in 1917 and was expected to pass the House "with votes to spare." Unfortunately, two days before the final vote, an explosion at a munitions factory in Chester was rumored to be the work of "spies of alien enemies." Panicky assembly members hedged their votes, and the bill died.

By 1920, six of those nine abolition states had nervously reinstated their death penalties. The reasons are numerous but mainly due to this pervasive, anti-socialist, anti-radical xenophobia. This hysteria culminated in the "crime of the century" convictions of anarchists Nicola Sacco and Bartolomeo Vanzetti for robbery and murder at the Slater and Morrill shoe factory in South Braintree. Massachusetts in 1921. They were executed in 1927.

In 1977, Massachusetts Gov. Michael Dukakis issued a proclamation pardoning Sacco and Vanzetti, stating that they had been treated with prejudice.

Of the 13 inmates executed by Virginia between 1917 and 1920, none were foreigners, but every one was Black.

Virginia's First Female Delegate Introduces an Abolition Bill

Another long-term drop in Virginia executions started in 1926 (with five, after eight in 1925), then continued for almost a decade. Juries hesitated to impose the ultimate punishment, instead choosing life terms or reduced convictions. And whether intentional or not, this jury reluctance coincided with another abolition bill sponsored by one of the first women elected to Virginia's House of Delegates, Sarah Lee Fain of Norfolk.

After the Nineteenth Amendment was ratified in 1920, Fain became involved in Democratic Party politics. In 1922, she was volunteer secretary for Claude Swanson's successful United States Senate reelection campaign committee. In 1923, she secured one of Norfolk's four House seat nominations. The following year, Fain and Helen Moore Timmons Henderson of Buchanan County became the first two women elected to Virginia's General Assembly.

Her career in the House of Delegates got off to a historically dubious start when she voted in favor of the Eugenical Sterilization Act, which authorized the involuntary sterilization of those deemed unfit to have children. Later that day, she voted for the Racial Integrity Act, making interracial marriage illegal. Still, she was popular with her constituents and emerged victorious in a 1925 primary.

In 1926 Fain introduced her death penalty abolition bill, which would have still preserved the death penalty only for assaults against women and acts of treason. The Jan. 12 *Richmond Times-Dispatch* was not a fan of the bill, lamenting the failures of the courts already in upholding the current laws:

> While Mrs. Fain will doubtless be ably supported in this measure, if introduced, it is a poor way to check the crime tide in America by making it any easier for the criminal than it now is, thanks to the unrelenting efforts of sobbing sentimentalists, emotional newspaper writers, women on State pardon boards, etc. When not more than one murderer in one hundred is executed for his crime in the Land of the Free and the Home of the Brave,

it impresses the casual observer that we have pretty nearly abolished capital punishment altogether.

We consider Mrs. Fain's proposed bill both ill-advised and undesirable.

When the bill went to committee, treason was removed, leaving assault, attempted criminal assault, and arson (again, offenses charged overwhelmingly to Blacks) as the sole death penalty-eligible crimes. Despite picking up 29 floor votes, the bill failed.

Still, after the 1926 General Assembly session, the *Times-Dispatch* reluctantly admitted that the writing was on the wall with capital punishment due to a growing public consensus against it. "Any judge of a criminal court will testify that the number of persons stricken off jury lists by reason of the fact that they express conscientious scruples against the extreme penalty is growing year by year," a March 18 editorial stated. "Revulsion against legal killings is an obvious sign of the times."

"The Times-Dispatch would hesitate to say that capital punishment should be abolished in Virginia, but it may point out here with assurance that the infliction of it is becoming more and more unpopular."

The last illegal lynching in Virginia was also in 1926, when a mob of white men broke a Black man, Raymond Bird, out of jail. He had been arrested and charged in Wytheville with having sex with a white woman. He was then shot multiple times and dragged for miles behind a truck. They hanged his dead body from a tree on a nearby road as a final indignity. Even though there was one arrest, there were no convictions

A National Abolition Group Forms

There is reason to believe that in the course of the present century, the use of the death penalty will finally pass away.
-Raymond T. Bye, *Journal of the American Institute of Criminal Law and Criminology*, Vol. XVII, Aug. 1926.

Del. Fain's bill coincided with the creation of the first national death penalty abolition group since 1845, called the American League to Abolish Capital Punishment. Organized by attorney Clarence Darrow, he in 1924 had successfully saved Nathan Leopold Jr. and Richard Loeb from execution in the thrill-killing of a 14-year-old boy. With his partner, former San Quentin Warden Lewis Lawes, the group ambitiously petitioned to stop the death penalty nationwide.

Lawes told the Oct. 11, 1928 *Los Angeles Post-Record* that he would first fight tooth-and-nail to end the death penalty in his home state of California. "I am willing to abandon my private interests during the next legislative session in Sacramento and devote my whole time to helping seek a repeal of capital punishment, that barbarous heritage of the dark ages."

The organization was novel in that it abandoned religious opinions and sentiments to focus on the pertinent impracticalities of the death penalty. Still, it saw no success, as no state abolished the death penalty between 1917 and 1957.

Back in Virginia, on Feb. 2, 1928, Del. Fain boldly announced she would again introduce a death penalty abolition bill in the upcoming General Assembly session, this time with no exceptions, making life in prison the "supreme penalty for conviction in any case."

"Two years ago, I fought this fight almost single-handed and my bill won twenty-nine votes," she told the *Times-Dispatch*, admitting that the exceptions in the 1926 bill did not represent her "true convictions." "This time I have secured several co-patrons, and I confidently believe this bill will be given mature consideration."

Her arguments for the passage of the bill ring hauntingly true 100 years later. She told the Associated Press that abolition would create "justice tempered with mercy and uncontaminated by wealth," explaining that capital punishment "is almost never administered to men with enough money to prove their insanity." She also argued that laws to "hang or electrocute criminals are really class legislation."

The House Courts of Justice Committee on Feb. 14 heard arguments supporting the bill. Justice J. Ricks, Judge of the Richmond Juvenile Courts, declared that "surety of detection, rather than the severity of punishment, is the greatest deterrent against the commission of crime."

Attorney Harry Smith Jr., who defended several capital cases, stated that revenge has no place in the law, and that individuals differ on what constitutes justice. "Murderers kill under abnormal emotional stress," he told the committee, "While the State by electrocution kills in cold-blooded fashion."

"Justice is not an exact science in its operations."

Fain's bill died in committee under fears it would lead to an increase in lynching – which, coincidentally, was outlawed the same session. This groundbreaking bill was the first in the nation to specifically define lynching as a state crime when signed into law by Gov. Harry F. Byrd Sr.

There were most likely behind-the-scenes negotiations between Byrd (who had been stung politically by the Raymond Bird lynching) and House and Senate leaders in killing Fain's abolition bill while elevating his anti-lynching bill. Byrd even admitted in his opening address to the 1928 General Assembly that the enforcement of "merciless capital punishment laws" negated the need for lynching. "There is no excuse for lynching in a State where the enforcement of the law in cases likely to provoke mob violence has been prompt and rigorous. Attempted rape in Virginia may be punished by death, and juries are quick to punish crimes that once incited men to take the law in their own hands."

In short, Byrd needed capital punishment to remain in effect to get his anti-lynching bill passed, thus Fain's abolition bill quietly died in committee.

Social Orders

The 1935 execution of two more white men, Walter Legenza and Robert Mais, again triggered sporadic news essays and columns favoring death penalty abolition, despite popular opinion that execution was an appropriate punishment for gangsters of that era.

The Aug. 5, 1936 *Richmond Times-Dispatch* mused that "The efficacy of capital punishment as a crime deterrent has been disputed with figures which at least give color to the argument against it." The article pointed out that the American League to Abolish Capital Punishment provided statistics that showed from 1919 to 1928, the homicide rate for death penalty states was 8.3 per 100,000. In contrast, the rate for non-death penalty states was 3.6 per 100,000 – numbers almost unchanged since 1909.

The report also listed Virginia – the most active death penalty state – with a jaw-dropping homicide rate of 18.3 per 100,000 during this period. Clearly, any deterrent effect in Virginia was not presenting itself.

"Regardless of any statistics ... an increasing number of Americans believe with a Chicago judge that "the life-for-a-life philosophy is a relic of feudalism," wrote the *Times-Dispatch*. "Or of a state of barbarism in which revenge was the motivating power."

Nationally, from the late 1920s to the 1940s, the death penalty surged nationwide due, in part, to criminologists who argued that the punishment was a necessary tool in maintaining social order as Americans suffered through Prohibition, the stock market crash, and the ensuing Great Depression. There was an average of 167 executions per year throughout the thirties – more than in any other decade in American history. Virginia alone executed 27 inmates between 1930 and 1939.

Fueling this fear of foreigners was the pro-fascist Bund movement, which promoted Nazism in the United States. The movement capped on Feb. 20, 1939, when 20,000 Nazi sympathizers, flanked by a stage decorated with twin banners of Hitler and George Washington, chanted "Heil Hitler" at a rally at Madison Square Garden. During the summer, Penn Station ran "Camp Siegfried Special" trains to Yaphank, Long Island, where Bund created training camps that taught marksmanship, camping, survivalism, and even eugenics classes.

During and following World War II, executions dropped off considerably in most states, with isolated pockets of activity. Thirty-three percent of the 135 executions nationwide in 1943 occurred in New York, North Carolina, and Georgia. And of these executions, 118 were for murder and 17 for rape. There were no executions for any other crimes.

In 1943 Virginia executed only two – James Mooring, a Black, for murder, and Harry Farris, a white, for a robbery-murder. However, for the entire decade, the Old Dominion led all other states with a total of 31 executions from 1941 to 1949. Nine were killed in 1946 alone, with three murderers – George Grissett, James Hough, and Arthur Johnson – executed consecutively on June 21.

World War II and the following Cold War certainly stopped any talk of abolition in Virginia.

Abolition talk, post-Martinsville

Less than one month after the February 1951 executions of the Martinsville Seven, Julius and Ethel Rosenberg were charged with federal conspiracy to commit espionage and went to trial in Ossining, NY. On April 5, both were sentenced to death for selling atomic bomb secrets to the soviets. After two years of appeals, New York's electric chair claimed them both on June 19, 1953. They were defendants in the nation's second "crime of the century" and the first espionage executions during peacetime in American history.

On July 8 of that year, the *Richmond Times-Dispatch* asked in an op-ed titled "An Old Question Is Up Again: Is Death Penalty Justified?" The article was not in response to the seven Black Martinsville men killed two years earlier several blocks up the street from their own offices. Instead, as the writer stated, because of lingering questions of the (white) Rosenbergs' possible innocence and "the wide publicity given the executions."

Of course, no case in Virginia history had generated as much international attention as the Martinsville case. Unlike the Rosenberg's, no one seemed to be questioning if any of the Black Martinsville men could have been innocent.

"Our own guess is that a poll of Americans now would show a majority opposed to complete abolition of the death penalty," the op-ed speculated. "But the number who have doubts about capital punishment seems to be growing, possibly at a rate large enough ultimately to tip the scales against such punishment."

The editorial was correct in that nationwide, and even worldwide, the death penalty was falling more and more out of favor as the decade progressed. Great Britain outlawed capital punishment for several types of crimes in 1957 before abolishing it entirely in 1965. Most European and Slavic countries had long abandoned the practice: Belgium executed its last prisoner in 1918; Portugal in 1852; the Netherlands in 1870; Switzerland in 1942; and Norway in 1905. Sweden abolished the death penalty in 1921, and Denmark did the same in 1930.

Almost all South American countries abolished their death penalties or declared moratoriums after a continental conference on the subject in 1941.

In the United States, after Michigan, Rhode Island, Wisconsin, and Maine abolished their death penalties, Minnesota followed in 1911, then Puerto Rico in 1929. Alaska and Hawaii had both abolished their death penalties in 1957, two years before gaining statehood.

"The More Bizarre and Horrible the Act, the Less Responsible the Actor is for the Act."

On Oct. 29, 1961, in Roanoke, Rev. Greta Crosby delivered a sermon titled "The Sequel to Punishment."

"I think that vengeance, like all evil, has its origin in good," Rev. Crosby told the congregation. "I think it began as a manifestation of the deep power of life found in all living creatures … I think it began as a part of the impulse to self-defense … But somehow, as man left animalhood and developed mind and memory and then machines, he twisted and exalted this aggressive tendency all out of proportion to the need of self-defense; he carefully nurtured within himself the cancer of vengeance and called it ennobling. What began in the power of life was bent back upon itself and became death-dealing."

"Let me then speak for myself and say that to my sorrow, I have often felt the unwelcome white heat of vengeful anger within me. It is my unwilled first reaction to various situations. It contradicts my knowledge and understanding, but there it is."

Rev. Crosby knew the penchant for vengeance, especially in the racist and segregated Virginia criminal justice system. So in 1964, at the height of the Thomas Wansley trial in Lynchburg, she created a local death penalty abolition organization called "Death to Death."

That misplaced theory of vengeance drove her opposition. "My first reaction to the report of a heinous act, one that outrages by horror, such as molesting and murdering a child – my first reaction is that boiling in oil is too good for the malefactor. And yet, I know better. I know that as a general rule, the more bizarre and horrible the act, the less responsible the actor is for the act."

While little is known of Death to Death, Rev. Crosby's daughter, Lara Pollock, said in 2021 that her 90-year-old mother "was a bit of a child protégé." She got her undergraduate degree from Ohio Wesleyan in 1951. When she expressed an interest in foreign service, she was told that having a law degree would be a good credential for this line of work. "She graduated from Harvard Law School with a degree in Jurisprudence in 1954," Pollock explained, "only the second year in which women were allowed to attend the University."

Death to Death seems to have dissolved around 1964 after something very unusual happened.

The Moratorium Years 1963 – 1981

Press Pause

> We bring good things to life!
>> - Former advertising slogan used by General Electric. Virginia's electric
>>   chair was re-wired and upgraded in 1962 with GE components.

In July 1961, Carroll Garland, a Black Lynchburg man, was arrested and convicted of robbing and murdering a gas station attendant, Jimmy Nuckols, when he thought Nuckols was reaching for a gun under the counter. He was executed less than eight months later, on Mar. 2, 1962.

This Virginia execution was the first a woman was allowed to witness. It unwittingly also became the last execution in the commonwealth for twenty years, marking the first intentional multi-year pause in executions since the practice began in 1608.

Virginia joined an informal, multi-state moratorium on executions in 1963 as part of a declining trend in jury-imposed death sentences that started in the 1950s. In 1962, only 18 of 44 nationwide jurisdictions with death penalty laws carried out executions. Despite California Gov. Edmund Brown's vigorous opposition, California, Texas, and Florida alone were responsible for more than half of the 47 executions that year. In 1961 there were only 41 executions across the country – the lowest in 31 years.

Just before March 1962, Virginia corrections officials had become concerned that the electric chair was no longer the "elegant" means of execution that it once was. Fifty-four years of heavy use was wearing on it, increasing the possibilities of malfunction.

Although the chair was about to go unused, North Side Electric Co. of Richmond won the contract to upgrade the electrical apparatus with a low bid of $19,058 and using General Electric components. They also replaced the original rheostat switch with a single pushbutton.

The pause in executions was not just for internal and technical reasons – many foreign countries expressed indignation at the United States over their wholesale and seemingly arbitrary use of capital punishment, especially in those cases where Blacks received death penalties for non-homicide crimes.

For example, in 1958, an Alabama Black man, Jimmy Wilson, was sentenced to death by an all-white jury for robbing a white woman, Estelle Baker, of $1.95. This sentence prompted various newspapers worldwide to question if the value of American life had been reduced to less than two dollars.

Wilson's attorney, Judson Locke, did not cross-examine Baker or any other witness at the trial. He did not call Wilson to testify in his defense or call any other defense witnesses. As a result of this inept and incomplete defense, the trial lasted just over four hours, and the all-white jury took less than an hour to convict Wilson. In turn, they sentenced him to death only on the robbery charge, making him only the fourth Black man sentenced to death for robbery in the history of Alabama.

According to the *Des Moines Register*, a court official suggested that the jury was angered that Barker testified that Wilson had spoken to her "in a disrespectful tone," persuading them to convict. Rubbing salt into the wound was the Alabama State Supreme Court, which justified the extreme penalty of death for the robbery of only $1.95 by stating that "the amount of the money or the value of the property taken is immaterial."

"A penny, as well as a pound, forcibly extorted constitutes a robbery, the gist of the offense being the force and terror."

The worldwide outcry was intense. Hundreds of shouting men and women carrying anti-American slogans marched to the consulate in protest in Jamaica. They also chanted as they marched, "If Jimmie Wilson goes to the electric chair, no American white man nor woman can remain in Jamaica."

The American ambassador to the Hague was threatened with death if the execution occurred. In Perth, Australia, demonstrators hanged a Black effigy from the flagpole in front of the American consulate under a sign that proclaimed "Guilty of theft of fourteen shillings."

Even the *Birmingham Post-Herald*, an ultra-right-wing, tough on crime newspaper, argued that clemency "would serve not only justice but the best interests of Alabama as well ... the sentence of death, if carried out, could never be satisfactorily explained much less justified before world opinion."

Mindful of the negative impact of this execution, Secretary of State John Foster Dulles requested that Alabama Gov. James Folsom commute the sentence to life imprisonment – which he did. Alabama paroled Wilson in 1973 after serving 16 years.

In Virginia, the Martinsville Seven case in 1951 had provoked a similar, equally intense international outcry. Unlike Gov. Folsom, who realized the potential public relations damage and properly acted to stop it, Virginia Gov. John Battle instead closed his ears and allowed the executions to proceed, and international reputation be damned.

The impact of the burgeoning civil rights movement also played a role in the decline of Virginia's death penalty, especially when it was revealed that of the 236 executions the Old Dominion carried out between 1908 and 1962, a startling 201 were of Blacks.

Still, despite the dwindling use of the chair and the building pressures from overseas, some states, including Virginia, hesitated to impose total abolition, choosing instead to sidestep it legislatively. In 1961, about 15 states considered measures to stop or limit death penalties. By 1965 20 states had limited their death penalties, with several such as New York, Iowa, Vermont, and West Virginia abolishing them entirely. New Mexico followed in 1969. More than 60 percent of Oregon's electorate had voted for abolition in a 1964 voter referendum.

The Massachusetts Senate approved an abolition bill, but the House deferred it. In response, Gov. Endicott Peabody announced he would commute any death sentence imposed while he was governor.

There were also a few setbacks. Delaware abolished its death penalty in 1958, only to bring it back two years later. After restoration, their average homicide rate increased by 3.7 persons per 100,000. They repealed it again in 2016.

Abolition efforts in Nebraska were stalled in 1959 by the murder spree and execution of Charles Starkweather. In Connecticut, the "mad dog" slayers Joseph Taborskey and Arthur Columbe killed seven people between 1950 and 1960, and any chances of death penalty repeal in that state – although Taborskey's execution was the last one in that state until 2005.

The inconsistent support for the death penalty throughout these states seemed to come primarily from corrections officers and prison wardens, who told legislators that the threat of executions kept capital convicts relatively safe. The point was valid, but for varying reasons – Charlottesville defense attorney Steven Rosenfield, who defended many capital cases, said in a June 2021 interview that death row inmates, with rare exceptions, were the most well-behaved in the prison system. "The guys on the row never hurt each other," he recalled. "... And you know why in particular that death row prisoners were the safest was because they ultimately wanted the governor to commute their sentence, and the last thing they wanted to do was to kill somebody or hurt somebody, especially a correctional officer."

Research buttressed Rosenfield's observations. Toni V. Bair, who took over as director of the notorious Mecklenburg Correctional Center in 1985 then later became regional warden, wrote in the June 1, 2016, *Washington & Lee Law Review* that "Research has shown that death row inmates are not more likely, and are frequently much less likely, to be violent while incarcerated than other inmates in general population who have committed murder."

It wasn't just northern states limiting the use of the death penalty throughout the 1960s – even the South, which had accounted for 65 percent of all executions nationwide in the late 1940s, saw executions plummet. After 105 executions in 1947, executions in southern states dropped precipitously to 48 in 1957, then down to 13 in 1963.

Gallup polling confirmed the falling popularity of the death penalty nationwide. In 1957, 47 percent of respondents favored capital punishment, 34 percent opposed it, and 18 percent had no opinion. By 1966 the numbers had flipped, with 42 percent supporting and a remarkable 47 percent opposed. From then until 1972, the responses leveled at around 50 percent favoring capital punishment, with 40 percent opposing it.

Of Virginia's declining use, the Aug. 5, 1963, *Richmond Times-Dispatch* wrote that "It is gratifying to see the death penalty being used sparingly. The snuffing out of a human life is an awesome thing, no matter what offense against society the person has committed."

But the editorial closed with a curious, hypothetical conclusion: "Yet, total elimination of capital punishment by law does not seem to be the answer ... What deterrent against murder would there be, for example, in the case of a prisoner already serving a life sentence? He certainly would have no fear of another life sentence."

In 1963, a University of Pennsylvania law professor, Anthony Amsterdam, began consulting with the NAACP Legal Defense Fund (LDF) to formulate better strategies to fight death sentences at the state and federal levels. One of the strategies pursued by Amsterdam and the LDF that had significance in Virginia was the recognition of the role of race in rape convictions and death sentences. Between 1900 and 1963, for example, Virginia executed 68 Black men for rape and attempted rape, but not one white.

This particular strategy at the time sadly went nowhere.

Then There Were Five

At the 1963 moratorium, there were five inmates on Virginia's death row. They were Clyde R. Near, convicted in 1959 of murder; Frank Jimmy Snider, one of the scarce few white Virginia men sentenced to death for the 1956 rape of a nine-year-old girl in Roanoke, and who legally eluded ten attempts to execute him during his 16 years on death row; Melvin Reese, who was convicted of murder; and Jay Timmons, convicted of murder in Norfolk. The fifth was Thomas Wansley.

Virginia's chair's slumping popular support and inelegance, coupled with the rejection of the death penalty among academics and political and legal elites as a suitable means of punishment, had been looming for years. In 1962, after ten years of work, a collective of lawyers and law professors with the American Law Institute published The Model Penal Code. In it, sentencing was based on the premise that retribution (death) was not sufficient justification for punishment. "It is inhumane and morally unacceptable."

During the 1950s and 1960s, several writers and politicians were vocal in their support of death penalty abolition, with almost no predictable and irrelevant "soft on crime" responses. A few governors, including Edmund Brown of California and North Carolina's Terry Sandford, outspokenly supported abolition. Ohio Gov. Michael DiSalle, who served from 1959 to 1963, constantly campaigned to abolish the death penalty and focus on rehabilitation. He even hired convicted murderers for his household staff. Hubert Humphrey made abolition a campaign theme in his unsuccessful 1960 Presidential run.

Virginia Gov. Albertis Harrison, however, was a strong supporter of the death penalty, declaring it a deterrent. He also admitted he had no facts to back up his opinion.

Nationwide support for the death penalty also eroded significantly after the 1966 exoneration of Dr. Sam Sheppard in Ohio for the murder of his wife, Marilyn. Sheppard was first convicted in 1954, with the prosecution initially seeking death. In a compromise verdict, Sheppard was convicted of second-degree murder and sentenced to life in prison. Twelve years later, as in the Thomas Wansley case, he was retried because unrelenting and adverse publicity against him had been declared prejudicial. He was then acquitted when bloodstain evidence proved he was not the murderer.

The Sheppard case became the basis of the 1963-1967 television show and the 1993 movie "The Fugitive."

One of the most visible and outspoken opponents of capital punishment from 1948 to 1960 was a California death row prisoner. Caryl Chessman, a small-time crook dubbed the "red light bandit," was convicted in 1948 of kidnapping for robbery and assault, not murder. Still, he received a death sentence due to California's "Little Lindbergh" law, which prescribed the death penalty for a kidnapping if the victim was physically harmed in any way.

During Chessman's 12-year appellate process, which appealed his conviction 42 times but never overturned it, he gave several erudite and consistent interviews concerning his plight, convincing many that he was innocent of the crime. He also wrote four books, including the wildly popular "Cell 2455, Death Row," published in 1954 and translated into Spanish, Italian, Japanese, and Greek. Others, however, saw him as a master manipulator and con man who was simply gaming the court system.

Chessman's trial – presided over by Judge Charles Fricke, who had sentenced more men to death than any other California judge – was ludicrously, almost criminally biased. Chessman, who defended himself, was denied access by Fricke to the daily transcript, which was riddled with over 2,000 errors because the court reporter died before transcribing his notes. Chessman was not allowed to attend the transcription certification hearing. The U.S. Supreme Court then denied his motion to invalidate the re-certification.

His May 2, 1960 execution provoked more bitter international criticism of the United States' capital punishment system and kept death and abolition on the front pages throughout the decade.

The Quiet Decade

> My personal feelings about the death sentence now is that it's used to satisfy people's Roman urges ... Like the arena, that's how it's used today. It's not used as a tool for justice. If it were, it would be absolute. Regardless if you were white, black, or poor, if you committed a certain offense, the death penalty would be automatic. It isn't.
> -Commuted death row inmate John C. Short, who had been sentenced to death by an all-white jury in 1967 for the murder of 85-year-old Edward Walker, a Richmond storekeeper, in a 1985 *Style Weekly* article.

The June 2, 1967 execution of Luis Monge in Colorado was the last in America for a full ten years, as all states put their death sentences on hold, waiting for more specific procedural guidance from the court systems. Colorado convicted Monga for the murder of his pregnant wife, Leonarda, and three of their ten children – Alan, age six; Vincent, age four; and Teresa, age eleven months. His execution pended for all of 1966 while Colorado voters considered then voted on a referendum on continuing the death penalty, which ultimately passed. After the referendum, in March 1967, Monge asked a Denver court to hang him at high noon on the front steps of the Denver City Building. The court denied his request, and he died instead in the state's gas chamber. Monge's surviving children joined him in his last meal.

Even though Virginia observed a moratorium on executions, and with widespread support plunging, some Virginia juries, primarily in Norfolk, Pittsylvania County, and Roanoke, continued as late as 1972 to impose death penalties. Three more Black men, Elvin Brickhouse, Bernard Fogg, and Cecil Wood, received death sentences for rape.

In sentencing Fogg and Brickhouse, Norfolk Judge H. Lawrence Bullock said,

"Something has got to be done to make this town safe for citizens to travel the streets peaceably ...."

Despite the pause, the death penalty curiously remained on Virginians' minds throughout the 1960s into the 1970s. In 1970, Fredericksburg Republican Del. Benjamin Woodbridge Jr. told a *Free-Lance Star* reporter that he was opposed to any moves to repeal the death penalty even though there had been no executions in eight years. "There are just some people who ought to be permanently removed from society," he insisted, adding that he was even in favor of expanding the death penalty to include "narcotics pushers" guilty of multiple offenses.

Virginia State Penitentiary Guard Captain Q. E. Mitchell told the same reporter that the death penalty was no deterrent in its current form. "It is cruel and unusual punishment to keep a man on the hook. A man should have every opportunity to appeal but not have to stay on death row for ten or 14 years."

By 1972, Virginia had 11 death penalty-eligible crimes on the books – more than any other state.

Cruel and Unusual Redux: the Furman Decision

> One searches our chronicles in vain for the execution of any member of the affluent strata of this society.
> -Supreme Court Justice William O. Douglas, writing in the *Furman* decision.

Two 1968 U.S. Supreme Court cases that directly affected the death penalty proved just how cumbersome and complex the management of capital punishment had become. In *U.S. v. Jackson,* the court held that a provision of the federal kidnapping statute requiring that the death penalty be imposed only upon a jury's recommendation was unconstitutional because it encouraged defendants to waive their right to a jury trial to ensure they would not receive a death sentence.

Another case, *Witherspoon v. Illinois,* maintained that potential jurors could be disqualified only if prosecutors could show that the juror's attitude toward capital punishment would prevent them from making an impartial decision.

The Supreme Court dealt the abolition movement a setback in May 1971 with *McGautha v. California*, ruling that the lack of legal standards by which juries imposed a death sentence was not an unconstitutional violation of the Eighth Amendment. Those states, in turn, were free to give juries unguided discretion in sentencing.

But then, on June 29, 1972, in a 5-4 decision, the U.S. Supreme Court reversed itself and surprised almost everyone by suddenly in the groundbreaking case *Furman v. Georgia* declaring the application of capital punishment cruel and unusual.

On Aug. 11, 1967, Savannah, Georgia resident William Micke Jr. surprised William Henry Furman, a 26-year-old Black man, as he burglarized his home. Furman claimed that as he fled, he tripped, and the gun he was carrying discharged, killing Micke, a father of five children, through a closed door. Furman was convicted of murder and sentenced to death by the Chatham County Superior Court in a one-day trial on Sept. 20, 1968.

Furman appealed the verdict to the Georgia Supreme Court, with the defense claiming that the death penalty, in this case, was "cruel and unusual." That court disagreed, tersely writing that "The statutes of this state authorizing capital punishment have repeatedly been held not to be cruel and unusual punishment in violation of the constitution. Hence there is no merit in this complaint." Furman then appealed to the U.S. Supreme Court.

On June 28, 1971, after reviewing almost 200 pending capital cases, the U.S. Supreme Court announced it would hear arguments in four death penalty cases, including *Furman*, lumped under the single heading *Furman v. Georgia*. Each was limited to a single question: "Does the imposition and carrying out of the death penalty, in this case, constitute cruel and unusual punishment in violation of the Eighth and Fourteenth Amendments?"

(The Eighth Amendment prohibits cruel and unusual punishments. The Fourteenth Amendment prohibits states from denying anyone equal protection of the laws or from depriving anyone of "life, liberty or property without due process of law.")

The other death penalty cases included *Jackson v. Georgia* and *Branch v. Texas*, both which concerned the constitutionality of the death sentence for rape convictions. *Aikens v. California* joined Furman as the other murder case.

Anthony Amsterdam and the NAACP Legal Defense Fund argued *Furman v. Georgia* in the U.S. Supreme Court on Jan. 17, 1972. Then, on June 29, the Court, in a 5-4 decision, declared in a *Per Curiam* opinion that capital punishment was cruel and unusual as it was employed on the state and federal levels. The Court stated that it was disproportionately applied to the "poor and despised, and lacking political clout, or if he is a member of a suspect or unpopular minority." The Court also ruled that the death penalty was too often imposed on the "constitutionally impermissible basis of race" and on those who had received poor legal representation.

All nine justices wrote separate opinions, and the majority held the application of the death penalty cruel and unusual for differing reasons. William Douglas stated that the practice was racially discriminatory in its application. William Brennan focused on the declining use of the death penalty due to public rejection. Thurgood Marshall maintained that the death penalty no longer served any legitimate purpose and that retribution was not a valid form of punishment. Potter Stewart and Byron White wrote that their concern was that death sentences were applied randomly to so few people as to have no deterrent effect. "These death sentences are cruel and unusual," Stewart wrote, "in the same way that being struck by lightning is cruel and unusual – they are capriciously, freakishly, and wantonly imposed."

While Stewart disagreed with the application of the death penalty, he did not believe it violated the Eighth Amendment, arguing that the death penalty could satisfy the public's desire for vengeance. "When people begin to believe that organized society is unwilling or unable to impose upon criminal offenders the punishment they 'deserve,'" he stated, "then there are sown the seeds of anarchy – of self-help, vigilante justice, and lynch law."

The statement echoed an old Jim Crow-era criminal justice trope that used lynching as a pretext to influence laws, manipulate courtroom procedures, guide and intimidate juries, and influence white-owned press coverage, all while speeding up executions.

"American citizens know almost nothing about capital punishment," Thurgood Marshall rightly observed, and was sure that if they only knew as much as he did, "the great mass of citizens would conclude ... that the death penalty is immoral and therefore unconstitutional."

The four dissenting Justices – Chief Justice Warren Burger, Harry Blackmun, Lewis Powell, and William Rehnquist – were all Nixon appointees, brought in for his tough-on-crime campaign promises. Burger wrote in his dissent that setting aside the death penalty was handing state legislatures "the opportunity and indeed unavoidable responsibility to make a thorough re-evaluation of the entire subject of capital punishment."

Ironically, in later years, Powell and Blackmun declared their opposition to the death penalty.

Furman voided forty state death penalty statutes, and 629 death row inmates in 32 states, including 12 in Virginia, had their death sentences commuted to life in prison.

Furman was the first time in American history that the Supreme Court had ruled against capital punishment. Still, the decision did not technically prohibit the death penalty – it instead required states to stop the arbitrary, racially-biased use of it. The court also suggested that new legislation – created and imposed by the states following specific mandates – could make the administration of death sentences constitutional again.

But for the time being, with this groundbreaking Supreme Court decision, the men on Virginia's death row were reportedly "elated" when they suddenly found their sentences commuted to life in prison, with even the possibility of parole. According to a June 30, 1972, Associated Press story, Mrs. Gloria Hanks, secretary to Rev. Charles Kramer, was visiting death row when the television news announced the decision. She said the prisoners were aware a decision was imminent, but all thought "it would go the other way."

The story also reported that the guards' reactions were mixed. One told the reporter there would "always be capital punishment" of one form or another. Another said, "they don't know what it's like in this prison ... they [the inmates] spit in your face. They wouldn't even make good punks."

12 Relieved Men

Henry Lee Clere was a white man convicted in the grisly 1970 dismemberment murder of Thomas McKown in Chesapeake. After his commutation, he became a model prisoner, journalist, and photographer at the Virginia State Penitentiary. The American Penal Press in 1976 awarded him "prison writer of the year," and he won an additional six national awards in prison journalism and photography. Clere and fellow inmate Ron Greenfield also recorded and produced a penitentiary radio program called *Encounters* which Richmond's WGOE radio aired every Saturday morning from 8:30 to 9:00 a.m.

Clere was routinely denied parole because of the brutality of his crime. He died in

March 2008.

In March 1972, Cecil Wood became the last Black man in Virginia sentenced to death for rape. According to *Wood v. Zahradnick*, the 27-year-old Wood broke into the Norfolk home of two older women he had known all his life. He allegedly raped one of them, severely beat them both, temporarily abducted both, and fled in their car after stealing their television and a sum of money. Police arrested him a few hours later while driving the automobile containing the stolen goods.

In his non-jury trial, Judge George Whitley said that he sentenced Wood to death due to the "heinous nature" of the crimes, adding in standard boilerplate that his example would serve as a deterrent to others.

An immediate appeal to the Supreme Court of Virginia left his conviction intact. Still, it nullified his death sentence per the *Furman* decision and sentenced him to life plus 60 years.

Then, another appeal in 1977 revealed a horrifically incompetent defense by his original attorney, Frank Watkins.

Watkins, who was deceased when the appeal was filed, had made zero pretrial preparations in 1972. He only visited Wood three times in prison and did not seek a mental examination of his client, who was well-known to be mentally unstable with a very low I.Q. Watkins did not attempt to interview defense witnesses, not even Wood's girlfriend, who was with him the night of the attack. He selected a non-jury trial fearing that "inflamed tensions" surrounding the case would taint a jury, then went to trial with only Wood's testimony as his defense.

The original trial thus had consisted solely of the victim and police recounting details of the crime and the arrest. Watkins did not cross-examine them. Taking the stand, Wood confessed that he was addicted to heroin, and on the night of the crime, he had taken "five to seven bags" of it and drank a large quantity of moonshine whiskey. He claimed that he remembered none of the events of that night.

The opinion noted that "What Wood had done was so senseless that any lawyer should have sought available expert assistance to explore the possibility that Wood was suffering with a transitory psychosis," exacerbated by substance abuse. But Watkins had done none of that.

Watkins truthfully seemed to despise his client. In response to an inquiry by the ACLU to take over the case, Watkins wrote, "I ... respectfully suggest that you petition the Court of Appeals to be made counsel of record. If the court is willing to grant your petition, I shall be delighted to turn over my entire file to you and withdraw from this case with joyful hosannas."

In his opinion, Judge Robert Merhige Jr. wrote that Watkin's incompetence violated Woods' Sixth Amendment right to a fair trial and ordered him released. Merhige also rejected an attempt to retry him in 1979.

Wood was one of four of the 12 former death row inmates to be later released, and none of them were re-arrested. "I think it shows that murder is often an inexplicable and random act and that people who commit murders are not necessarily beyond hope and can change their lives," Jenni Gainsborough of the ACLU's National Prison Project told

Richmond Times-Dispatch journalist Frank Green in June 1997.

"It was a special occasion," Cecil Wood later told Green in that same article of the *Furman* decision. "I was young, only 27 years old, right, and I was kind of dumb. I didn't go to school that much. I was only a kid ... I didn't know that much about the law, but now I know a lot about the law."

Possibly not one of the 12 commuted death row inmates from this era distinguished themselves as Claude Frizzell Bloodgood III, a white murderer, swindler, and chess genius convicted of killing his mother in Norfolk in 1970. After leaving a Delaware prison in 1967 for robbing a Stuckey's, Bloodgood returned to Norfolk and was promptly charged with forging his mother Margaret's signature on checks.

Troubled by bouts of mental illness aggravated by drug use, Bloodgood threatened his mother with death if she pressed charges. She did, and he was tried, convicted of forgery, and jailed for a year.

Then, only nine days after his release, on Nov. 19, 1969, Bloodgood and a man he had met in prison, Michael Quarick, surprised his mother on the porch of her East Ocean View home. Quarick testified he stood by "horrified" as Bloodgood beat, then strangled her.

After rolling her body up in a porch rug, they drove west into New Kent County, where he left her on the ground. Convicted and sentenced to death for the crime, Bloodgood managed to elude six execution dates before the 1972 *Furman* decision commuted his sentence to life.

While in prison, Bloodgood started playing chess by mail and with fellow inmates. At one point, he had over 3,000 certified games under his belt in prison and another 2,000 games going by correspondence. Bloodgood played and won so many games against inferior opponents that by August 1996, he suddenly found himself the No. 2 rated chess player in America, with a grandmaster-class rating of 2702, second only to New York's Gata Kamsky. In comparison, the highest-rated player ever was Russia's Garry Kasparov, at 2838.

And it happened like everything else in Bloodgood's life – through deceit and by gaming the system. He was a good player but hardly world-class. Years earlier, Bloodgood had even informed the U.S. Chess Federation of their flawed rating system that artificially inflated scores when a small group played many, many games in a closed pool (such as prison). But no one there wanted to listen to a former Virginia death row inmate.

Bloodgood was also unique in that he was a death row inmate who believed in capital punishment. "I'm probably at odds with most everybody who's been on death row," he told *Virginian-Pilot* reporter Marc Davis just before his death on Aug. 4, 2001. "I believe in it. I think that there's a place for it."

Bloodgood died of lung cancer at Powhatan Correctional Center while participating in the 15th U.S. Correspondence Championship. Today, the U.S. Chess Federation refuses to acknowledge Bloodgood's score or that he even played chess.

The remaining death row inmates commuted by *Furman* include:

Elly Joseph Huggins, white, was convicted and sentenced in 1971 for murdering an

11-year-old boy in Newport News. The child's stepmother hired Huggins for $200 to kill him. Huggins made parole in 1990.

Harry Junior Williams, Black, was convicted in 1967 of the murder of James Sarver and wounding his wife and two of their four children in a home invasion in Pittsylvania County.

Elvin Brickhouse Jr. and Bernard Ross Fogg, both Black, were sentenced to death for the July 1966 rape of a 19-year-old white woman in Norfolk. Re-sentenced to a breathtaking 650 years in prison, Brickhouse made parole in 1987 and was officially discharged in 1992. His whereabouts are unknown, as is Fogg's, who made parole in 1986.

Lawrence Wright Jr., Black, was sentenced to death for the Sept. 1971 murder of Norfolk City Police Sergeant Robert Bouchard. He was paroled in 1991 but went back to prison in 1992 for possession of cocaine.

Loren N. Duffield, a white sailor, was sentenced to death in 1963 in Norfolk for the abduction, rape, and murder of a 14-year-old girl whom he had promised a babysitting job. Duffield was one of the longest-serving inmates on Virginia's death row when *Furman* was decided, having been there eight years.

Sherman Brown, a Black Vietnam veteran, was convicted and sentenced to death by an all-white Albemarle County jury in 1970 for the slaying of a four-year-old Ivy boy, supposedly after raping the boy's mother. Still incarcerated in 2021, Brown is one of the longest surviving inmates in the Virginia system. The Innocence Project is also still on this case after the 2016 discovery of a vaginal swab at the University of Virginia Medical Center taken from the mother that proved Brown was not her rapist.

Barry C. Johnson was convicted and sentenced to death for the 1966 murder of Shirley Healey in a carjacking in Gloucester County. Corrections officials perceived him as a problem inmate and brutalized him numerous times, including tear-gassing him inside his cell. When taken to solitary confinement a third time in 1970, Johnson was punched by a Captain Baker with a tear gas gun and then chained to the cell bars at Baker's orders. He remained chained for five days, with his waist and arms secured to the bars so that he could not fully sit or recline. He was forced to urinate and defecate on the floor where he stood.

He made parole in 1995, and his family moved him out of state.

Arthur Hodges was convicted and sentenced to death for the August 1971 shooting deaths of two Roanoke County men, Warren Watson and Boyd Ferguson. He died in the State Penitentiary in 1977.

The twelfth man, Frank Jimmy Snider, had been released from death row in 1969 after almost 16 years as he awaited a new sentencing trial ordered for his 1956 rape conviction. He was held in the Richmond City Jail when the *Furman* decision was announced. In 1975 he was granted work release, and he died in 1997. He was the only inmate to dodge death by the 1963 moratorium and the 1972 *Furman* decision.

Slowly, the Engine of Death Roars to Life

On Jan. 12, 1974, a band played "Dixie" to a 19-gun salute as Virginia swore in Mills Godwin for the second time as governor, this time as a Republican. Godwin had served as governor from 1966 to 1970 as a Democrat but became concerned Virginia was becoming too liberal, so he switched parties and ran again, winning a tight race against Sen. Henry Howell.

In his first address to the 1974 General Assembly, Godwin announced that the resumption of the death penalty was high on his list of priorities, calling for it "for several serious crimes." He claimed that juries should have *the option* (emphasis added) to impose the ultimate punishment under three specific circumstances: conviction of murder of an enforcement officer in the line of duty; conviction of murder in the course of rape and arson; and the second conviction of first-degree murder.

University of Virginia political scientist Nancy Joyner wrote in her June 1974 report "The Death Penalty in Virginia: Its History and Prospects" that "By suggesting that the death penalty be 'optional' in these cases, Godwin's proposal appears to contradict the Supreme Court's ruling in the *Furman* case, which cited discretion as being potentially discriminating,"

A study by the capital punishment advisory committee of the State Crime Commission also disagreed with Godwin, writing that "the unsigned majority opinion emphasized that a legislative decision to reinstate the death penalty might be both unwise and counterproductive." The report added there was no link between the punishment and the prevention of serious criminal acts in states that did not have a death penalty and those that did.

The study's majority report emphasized that the Assembly's three primary reasons for reinstating the death penalty – retribution, deterrence of potential criminals, and the prevention of repetitive criminal acts by inmates – could introduce the real possibility of it being used on innocent people, as well as re-introduce a "brutalizing effect" to Virginia's criminal justice system. The majority recommended that the General Assembly create a more effective parole system instead of pursuing more severe penalties.

In the 1974 Assembly session, a Senate bill nonetheless responded to Godwin's request with eight inclusive capital crimes. A House bill prepared by the Courts of Justice Committee fell far short of what Godwin or the Senate wanted, offering only three capital crimes that were death penalty-eligible: murder in the commission of abduction with the intent to extort money (including kidnapping and skyjacking); killing for hire; and murder by an inmate in a penal institution.

Leading the charge against the resumption of capital punishment in the Assembly session was ACLU attorney Philip Hirschkop. After a graphic description of how in the electric chair a man's eyes sizzle, his hair falls out or catches on fire, and his skin turns black, he asked the members of the Senate and House Courts of Justice Committees, "Which of you would want to pull the switch?"

Hirschkop contended that capital punishment most often victimized the poor, marginalized, and Black communities and that Virginia had most likely executed many innocent persons. "If we pass this now," he warned, "we'll get into wholesale killing very quickly."

He had no idea how true his words would become in the assembly-line execution model of the 1990s.

In April 1974, a month after the Assembly dispersed without acting on the death penalty, the Supreme Court of Virginia stepped into the fray by unanimously upholding Virginia's mandatory death penalty for the murder of a corrections officer by an inmate. The previous February, V. Cassell Adamson, attorney for inmate Malcolm Jefferson, argued that the *Furman* decision invalidated Virginia's only mandatory death sentence. However, the high court ruled that the federal court determined that the death penalty *per se* was not constitutional and was banned only in instances where state laws allowed for its discretionary use.

Jefferson and another inmate had killed State Farm guard Raul Monte in November 1971 in an escape attempt. Jefferson was never executed.

Despite the low level of support for the death penalty over the previous two decades, the *Furman* decision seemed to galvanize nationwide support, according to Joyner. Her report found that 21 states had reenacted capital punishment statutes at the beginning of 1974, and 14 others were expected to do so by mid-year.

"Public sentiment appears to favor the 'modified resurrection' of the death penalty in Virginia," she wrote. Although those favoring abolition may have prematurely celebrated the *Furman* decision, she reminded that three of the majority justices indicated that it was the arbitrary application of the death penalty that was an unconstitutional violation of the Eighth Amendment's provision against "cruel and unusual."

Back in the Killing Business

> The present return to the practice of the death ritual demonstrates clearly the extent to which the people of our country are in the grip of this atavistic pre-civilized pattern of social behavior. We have the means of successfully treating the social deviant without resort to ritual killing.
> -James Rogers, in the booklet "Human Sacrifice U.S.A.," 1984.

At the start of Virginia's 1975 General Assembly session, death penalty reinstatement seemed to lack traction, possibly because hardcore supporters still wanted to significantly expand the number of death penalty-eligible crimes, scaring off potential, more moderate supporters. Regardless, identical bills gained momentum and passed both the House and the Senate, and on Feb. 14, 1975, Godwin signed the death penalty back into Virginia law.

These bills, effective Oct. 1, mandated a death sentence for first-degree murder when committed under one of six specific circumstances. Three made murder death penalty eligible when committed during a robbery, rape, or abduction. The remaining three circumstances were murder for hire, murder by a prison inmate, and murder of a police officer. "I think we here recognize the rights of a victim of a crime," Godwin pronounced at the signing. "We don't want to put emphasis on rehabilitation all the time. I'm for rehabilitation, of course, but I think we have to recognize a balance."

Even as Godwin signed the bill, the Senate was not giving up on their expansion bill, which at the time was in the House Courts of Justice Committee awaiting a vote. This proposal greatly expanded death penalty-eligible crimes to include the murder of subpoenaed witnesses, the murder of an on-duty firefighter, and killing by torture or starvation. Finally – in a disturbing throwback to the class, gender, and race-biased patterns of the Jim Crow past –committing or *attempting to commit* (emphasis added) the non-homicide crimes of rape, arson, robbery, and burglary were proposed. There was also talk of adding the murder of a judge to the list after the fatal shooting of Louisa County General District Court Judge Stewart A. Cunningham by Curtis D. Poindexter, a radical Muslim convert.

The House committee voted down the death penalty expansion on an overwhelming 14-5 vote. After a mistrial in Louisa, Poindexter was convicted of murder in an Augusta County court and sentenced to life in the penitentiary.

Gregg v. Georgia

Like *Furman* in 1972, on Mar. 31, 1976, another Georgia case went before the U.S. Supreme Court but with very different results. On Nov. 21, 1973, Fred Simmons and Bob Moore picked up hitchhikers Troy Gregg and Floyd Allen in Florida. The car later broke down as they drove north, but Simmons bought another car with a large amount of cash he carried with him. Simmons later picked up another hitchhiker, Dennis Weaver, and dropped him off in Atlanta. Sometime after midnight, the four men pulled into a rest stop to sleep. The following day, the bodies of Simmons and Moore were discovered in a nearby ditch, both dead with gunshot wounds to the head.

On Nov. 23, Weaver read of the killing in the *Atlanta Journal-Constitution* newspaper and promptly called the Gwinnett County police. He relayed information about the victims, the suspects, and the car's description. The next day, Gregg and Allen were arrested in Simmons' car near Asheville, North Carolina. A .25-caliber pistol, later proven to be the one used to kill Simmons and Moore, was found in Gregg's pocket.

Gregg pleaded that the killings were in self-defense, but Allen testified that Gregg shot them in a robbery. The first trial found Gregg guilty of two counts of armed robbery and two counts of murder.

At the second penalty trial, the judge instructed the jury that it "would not be authorized to consider [imposing] the penalty of death" unless it first found beyond a reasonable doubt one of three aggravating circumstances: that murder was committed while the offender was engaged in the commission of two other capital felonies, meaning, the armed robbery of Simmons and Moore; that the offender committed the offense of murder to steal money and Simmons' automobile; and that the crime of murder was outrageously and wantonly vile, horrible and inhuman, in that they involved the "depravity of mind of the defendant."

The jury returned death verdicts after finding the first and second of these circumstances valid on each count. The Supreme Court of Georgia affirmed the convictions for murder and the death sentences, concluding that the rulings had resulted from no prejudice or any other arbitrary factor and were not disproportionate to the crime.

Gregg v. Georgia was one of five "July 2" cases before the U.S. Supreme Court, *Roberts v. Louisiana, Proffitt v. Florida, Woodson v. North Carolina,* and *Jurek v. Texas.* The *Gregg* case questioned "Whether the imposition and carrying out of the sentence of death for the crime of murder under the law of Georgia violates the Eighth or Fourteenth Amendment to the Constitution of the United States."

In these cases, the court set two guidelines to which these state legislatures must adhere to apply constitutional capital punishment: they had to provide objective criteria to limit death sentencing discretion, and the objectiveness of these criteria must be ensured by appropriate appellate review.

Secondly, the sentencing had to allow the judge or the jury to consider mitigating factors, including the age, history, background, character, and record of the accused defendant.

In *Gregg, Proffitt,* and *Jurek,* the court, in 7-2 decisions (Brennan and Marshall dissenting), found that the capital sentencing processes of Georgia, Florida, and Texas met these criteria. In *Woodson* and *Roberts,* the court, in identical 5-4 votes, found that the mandatory sentencing processes of North Carolina and Louisiana were unconstitutional.

"The punishment of death ... is no longer morally acceptable in our society," Brennan wrote in his dissent, "and it serves no penal purpose more effectively than a less severe punishment."

In short, *Gregg* reinstated the death penalty to states for murder convictions only under specified conditions. The opinion maintained that the death penalty did not offend "evolving standards of decency which mark the progress of a maturing society" as first described in *Trop v. Dulles* in 1958.

(Although *Trop v. Dulles* was not a capital case, abolitionists seized the court's logic and applied it to capital punishment, maintaining that the United States had matured to the point that its "standards of decency" no longer supported or tolerated the death penalty.)

The moratorium of *Furman* was officially over, and many states – especially in the South – started to resume executions.

Gregg was the first of several cases that defined, expanded, then tangled and confused the nation's use of the death penalty. Henry Schwarzschild, director of the ACLU Capital Punishment Project, wrote in Michael Radelet's 1989 book "Facing the Death Penalty: Essays on Cruel and Unusual Punishment" that *Gregg* and its "seemingly endless series" of companion cases "... are dense and contradictory rationalizations of constitutional doctrine, statutory texts, social objectives, criminological analysis, moral theory, psychological assumptions, and political judgments."

Indeed, as Radelet pointed out in his 2001 paper "Twenty-Five Years after *Gregg,*" although the Supreme Court claimed the death penalty did not offend evolving standards of American decency, the death penalty "clearly violates the evolving moral standards of most other countries with whom the United States shares its human rights commitments, and it clearly violates the evolving moral standards of most religious organizations."

By 1976, however, states such as Virginia were incensed at the idea that Washington should be telling them what they could or could not do regarding capital punishment. A mere four years after *Furman*, 37 of the 50 states had re-introduced death penalty laws.

Florida ramrodded new death penalty statutes through their legislature in 14 days, but Utah was the first to resume executions. Gary Gilmore, who had been found guilty of first-degree murder in October 1976 for killing gas station employee Max Jensen and Provo motel manager Ben Bushnell, chose not to appeal his death sentence. He fired his lawyers and after being given the choice of a volunteer firing squad or hanging, chose the firing squad. He was executed on Jan. 17, 1977.

In his 1979 novel "The Executioner's Song," Norman Mailer wrote that after the gunshots, "Gary never raised a finger. Didn't quiver at all. His left hand never moved, and then, after he was shot, his head went forward, but the strap held his head up, and then the right hand slowly rose in the air and slowly went down as if to say, 'That did it, gentlemen' ... the blood started to flow through the black shirt and came out onto the white pants and started to drop on the floor between Gary's legs, and the smell of gunpowder was everywhere."

The Impact of *Gregg* in Virginia

> We kill humanely not out of concern for the condemned but rather to vividly establish a hierarchy between the law-abiding and the lawless. It may be death we are doing, but it is death whose savagery law insists it can, and will, control.
>
> -Legal scholar Alan Hyde.

As the 1977 Virginia General Assembly session took up the death penalty question in light of the *Gregg* decision, 18 Episcopal and Catholic Bishops, Priests, and Lay Leaders issued a statement voicing opposition. They cited four distinct reasons: one, "It is wrong for the state as well as the criminal to take the life of a human being;" second, "the official sanctioning of violence by the state in the death penalty sets a tone for the citizenry;" third, "enacting the death penalty can be a smokescreen for not creatively addressing violence and crime;" and fourth, "through the state, society needs not to be about vengeance, but about the protection of its citizenry, regardless of how bizarre their behavior may be."

On Jan. 30, 1977, the House Courts of Justice Committee brushed aside faith leaders' concerns and began discussions to bring Virginia's death penalty into compliance with the Supreme Court's *Gregg* guidelines. For example, the bill restructured capital crime trials into two segments so juries could weigh aggravating and mitigating circumstances, giving the jury latitude to impose death or life imprisonment. The bill also required automatic review by the Supreme Court of Virginia, which would have the power to overrule a death sentence and order a life term.

Also, the Assembly added more and more death penalty-eligible crimes to the bill, including mass murder, killing by planting a bomb and murdering a witness under subpoena.

After the Supreme Court rejected the constitutionality of the mandatory sentences Godwin had signed into law in 1975, the Virginia General Assembly instead amended these sentences – including murder in the commission of abduction with intent to extort money, murder for hire, and murder by one incarcerated – to make death optional.

Kids in a Candy Store

Restarting Virginia's machinery of death and tacking on more death-eligible crimes seemed to become a giddy contest among House Courts of Justice Committee members. Finally, in one hearing, a frustrated observer from the Quaker Friends community announced that she was "shocked and appalled" that members were cavalierly laughing and joking about new ways to kill people. Suddenly chastened, several members apologized, claiming that while there may have been some levity during discussions, it by no means meant that they failed to take the death penalty seriously.

On Feb. 8, the Courts of Justice Committee passed the bill and sent it up the chain. A Harris survey conducted on Feb.12 showed that Americans supported the death penalty nationwide by a 67 to 25 percent majority. A 46 to 40 percent plurality opted for the death penalty even if it were proven "not more effective than long prison sentences in keeping people from committing murder."

By Mar. 1, the bill was revised with the "broad brush" amendment, which included making any premeditated murder eligible for the death penalty. This amendment prompted a caution by Del. A.L. Philpott that the U.S. Supreme Court would immediately overturn such far-reaching legislation. "You know, and I know that the first time you come up with an emotional situation, you're going to get the death penalty," Philpott told the committee. "That's exactly what the Supreme Court is waiting for – for the death penalty to be imposed in an emotional situation, and then they're going to strike it down."

Accordingly, that summer, the U.S. Supreme Court ruled on several capital cases, making implementing the death penalty a moving target for those states itching to reinstate it. On June 6, the court ruled in a sharply divided 5-4 decision that the death penalty could not be mandatory for persons convicted of killing police officers. Then, on June 29, 1977, another Georgia case, *Coker v. Georgia*, struck down the death penalty in a 7-2 decision for the rape of adult women. Not because it had been notoriously racially biased against Blacks, but because it was determined to be "grossly disproportionate" to the crime.

Final Preparations

The deliberate, institutionalized taking of human life by the state is the greatest conceivable degradation to the dignity of the human personality.
-Former Supreme Court Justice Arthur Goldberg reported in the *Boston Globe*, Aug. 16, 1976.

Eventually, the Virginia legislature's death penalty statute was determined to comply with *Gregg* and all the companion cases and was signed into law by Gov. Godwin. The law allowed for the death penalty in capital cases when there was a finding of one of two aggravated circumstances, vileness or future dangerousness. The judge or jury also examined all mitigating circumstances, including those not enumerated in the statute. The Supreme Court of Virginia automatically reviewed all death sentences.

The Virginia Court also upheld the constitutionality of *Gregg* in the 1977 case *Smith v. Commonwealth*, interpreting the aggravating circumstances' "vileness" standard as "a degree of moral turpitude and psychical debasement surpassing that inherent in the definition of ordinary legal malice and premeditation." The court also maintained in a "future dangerousness" standard that the commonwealth "must prove beyond a reasonable doubt that there is a 'probability' that the defendant would commit 'criminal acts of violence' such as would pose a 'continuing serious threat to society.'"

Despite the florid and academic descriptions, the "vileness" standard left open floodgates of abuses. The U.S. Supreme Court ruled that Virginia could no longer have a mandatory death penalty; therefore, vileness could facilitate prosecution to twist aggravating circumstances into fitting the definition. They merely had to convince a jury to find one of three factors: torture, depravity of mind, or aggravated battery. The jury also did not have to agree on which of these applied.

Defense attorney Gerald Zerkin said in a 2021 interview that "this ridiculous vileness statute [was] interpreted down to nothingness. All you had to prove was that you used more than the minimal force necessary to accomplish the killing. So, if you shot somebody twice, you satisfied the vileness predicate. It had been reduced to meaninglessness."

Zerkin is a Queens, New York native and Boston College-educated attorney who started practicing as a legal aid in 1976. Beginning in 1981, he represented 13 death row inmates in post-conviction proceedings.

"It did strike me that the capital murder law that applies to crimes that are especially 'vile' is a bit vague," wrote then-penitentiary inmate Evans Hopkins in the Aug. 22, 1982 *Washington Post*. "What is the determining factor of a 'vile' murder? Being reminded by this week's protests of the 'vile' atomic bombardment of Nagasaki and Hiroshima, and seeing telecasts of the continuing 'vile' bombardment of a civilian population in Beirut, I wonder what's really 'vile.'"

The same held with "future dangerousness," which, according to Zerkin, was "farcical" in that there were no scientific standards to measure or predict it. "You had no way to determine whether somebody would be a future danger or not ... the issue was some theoretical dangerousness; in case they somehow were ever released that they could be a danger out in public."

Virginia was one of only three death penalty states that recognized three "future dangerousness" inquiries – the defendant's prior history, criminal record, and facts of the offense that led to a conviction. The American Psychiatric Association maintained that predictions of future dangerousness had been proven wrong in two of every three cases. They claimed those predictions were so unreliable that they considered it a breach of professional ethics even to speculate whether an individual would be a future danger.

It would have been a moot point – clinical diagnostic risk assessments to predict the defendant's actual future dangerousness, however, were unbelievably inadmissible in Virginia courts, making them the only courts in the country to predict future dangerousness without providing or allowing clinical evidence.

Attorney Rob Lee noted in a 2022 interview that the most simplistic argument was that if someone murdered somebody in the past, that was the best predictor of how they would act in the future. "I think that some people, certainly a lot of prosecutors, latched on to that," he explained. "But the truth is, that's not true, particularly in prison. You might think this guy is a danger, but if you put him in prison, that's a different environment, and you need to be assessing how he's going to behave in that environment."

Some inexperienced court-appointed attorneys had no clue how to object to these and other violations of due process that Virginia allowed that the federal courts recognized as invalidating death sentences.

In her 2016 paper "Nothing Is Certain but Death: Why Future Dangerousness Mandates Abolition of the Death Penalty," Louisiana attorney Carla Edmonson wrote that "in limiting the defendant's opportunity to put forth mitigating evidence and to rebut evidence of future dangerousness, Virginia ensures that jurors are likely to base their penalty-phase decisions on speculative, incomplete, and inaccurate information."

(To compound the confusion and introduce a terrible realization, in 2003, The Capital Jury Project, a national consortium of studies, interviewed jurors in capital cases to determine their decision-making and understanding of determining verdicts. The study found that a shocking 53 percent of Virginia's capital jurors mistakenly believed that a death sentence was required (not just authorized) if they saw the murder as vile. Forty-one percent mistakenly thought that a death sentence was required (again, not just authorized) if they found that the defendant posed a future danger. In short, they confused *requiring* a death sentence with *authorizing* one, a confusion that may have sent capital defendants to death based on a juror's simple misunderstanding of the rules.)

In its final form, the bill rolled in even more crimes as qualifiers for capital murder: murder in the commission of a robbery while armed with a deadly weapon; murder in the commission of rape; and murder of a state or local police officer for the purpose of interfering with his official duties. In 1981, the murder of more than one person in the same act or transaction became a capital crime.

While the legislature hammered out the legal details, the Virginia Department of Corrections started preparing for the resumption of executions. Electrocutions would continue as they had since 1908 in the dank east basement of the Virginia State Penitentiary's "A" Building. However, death row moved to the newly-opened Mecklenburg Correctional Center, the state's newest maximum-security facility, about 90 minutes south of Richmond. At the penitentiary, officials unpacked the electric chair, cleaned, varnished, repaired some water damage, and placed it back into working order.

Picking a Death Team

As the electric chair was refurbished, a corrections supervisor at the penitentiary approached a young officer, Jerry Givens, and asked if he would like to volunteer for execution duty as a member of the newly formed "death team."

A former Philip Morris employee, Givens, had just lost his job in 1974 when he passed the penitentiary on Belvidere Street one afternoon. He stopped to apply for a job as a corrections officer. He was hired, and shortly after starting work, an inmate took a swing at him. Givens dropped him with a single punch, earning him the nickname "Stun Gun Givens."

"I gave it a whole lot of thought," Givens said in a 2016 *Richmond Magazine* interview of his invitation to be part of the execution squad. "I thought, 'Why did he come to me? Why me of all people?' But I also had some flashbacks to what I saw as a teenager."

When Givens was 14, he went to a neighborhood house party where he witnessed a young partygoer, a girl he had wanted to ask to dance, get shot in the head. She later died.

"A person has to be stupid, downright stupid to go out there and kill someone knowing that Virginia has the death penalty," he recalled saying. "Why would you take someone's life, knowing you could be executed? You might as well commit suicide. I put a lot of blame on the condemned."

In a Friday evening meeting in "A" Basement, he and eight other officers ultimately volunteered for death duty, assuming vows of secrecy for what they were going to do there. "We agreed to take the job and agreed that what was said down there stayed there."

With the legislation settled and signed, the electric chair repaired, and the hand-picked death team on standby, all that was needed was a condemned inmate to execute.

Almost Executed: Silas Rogers

> The death penalty is imposed not upon those who commit the worst crimes, but upon those who have the misfortune to be assigned the worst lawyers.
>
> -Attributed to attorney Stephen Bright

It was 9:40 a.m. on July 18, 1943. Silas Rogers, a 21-year-old Black man, stood on the Appomattox River Bridge between Petersburg and Colonial Heights, holding a bag containing personal belongings and hitchhiking north to Richmond. Suddenly a Petersburg police car skidded to a stop beside him. Two furious policemen leaped from the car, drew their revolvers, and ordered Rogers to drop the bag and lay on the ground.

A world war was on, and Rogers, a former shoe shiner in a Miami barbershop, had received his draft notice. He was on his way to a New York selective service board when a conductor on the Seaboard Coastline Railroad Silver Meteor train asked him to disembark at the Petersburg station for being a stowaway in the baggage car.

The two policemen shoved him into the car and, as they drove him to the Petersburg station, accused him of murdering a fellow officer, Robert. B. Hatchell.

A Murdered Policeman

The night before, Officers Hatchell and W. M. Jolly were on a routine patrol when they spotted a Studebaker with North Carolina plates reported stolen. They U-turned in pursuit, and the car sped down West Washington Street, reaching speeds over 70 mph before it wrecked near the Petersburg Hospital. The driver jumped out and ran around the back of the building. Two passengers in military uniforms, named Jordan and Stephens, remained in the car and were taken into custody by Jolly, while Hatchell took off on foot in pursuit of the driver.

Thirty-five minutes later, two shots rang out from a ravine behind the hospital, and Hatchell was found shot dead. His gun, and the shooter, were nowhere to be found.

These revelations dumbfounded Rogers – he had been on the train the entire time. While in police custody, he insisted they had the wrong man. He steadfastly denied any knowledge of the stolen car, the two soldiers in the back seat, or shooting officer Hatchell. But the police were undeterred and, knowing they had their man, began forcibly extracting a confession.

Waterboarding at the Hands of the Police

Hustings Court record 2855, *Silas Rogers v. Commonwealth of Virginia* (1943) graphically described the brutal Jim Crow-style treatment Rogers endured at the hands of the Petersburg police:

He was there severely beaten by the members of the Petersburg Police Force. He was struck over his head by a blackjack which inflicted a severe gash and a knot on his head. He was also hit with hard fist blows about the body and face which caused him to bleed profusely from the head and nose. Three glasses of water were poured up his nose as he was pinned to the floor on his back by several police officers. A police officer pointed a gun in his face and threatened to kill him. His hair was pulled, he was slapped down, and his hands were bent backwards to the near-breaking point. All of this was done to the defendant by the police officers in an attempt to coerce from him a confession that he shot and killed Officer Hatchell.

Finally, Rogers could take no more, and he confessed under such duress that the commonwealth's attorney could not stomach its description at the trial. The actions were so revolting that they merited a rare admonishment from the Supreme Court of Virginia: "The record does disclose that when the defendant was first arrested [Rogers] was inhumanly assaulted by the police officers who had him in charge," stated *Rogers v. Commonwealth.* "Such conduct upon the part of the officers of the law merits our utter disapproval. The assault made upon the defendant was a cowardly one, uncalled for and beyond the realm of justification."

Just after the torture, the two AWOL soldiers, Jordan and Stephens, were brought in to identify the beaten and bloodied Rogers. They claimed he was not the driver. In addition, at about 1:30 on the same day, police forced Rogers to sign a curious statement typewritten by someone else that stated that he came to Petersburg from Raleigh on a red truck.

While police confined Rogers in a cell at headquarters, they and the city manager, who claimed never to doubt Rogers' guilt, strangely continued to search with bloodhounds for two days around the Petersburg Hospital and Lee Park area. They pulled fingerprints from the Studebaker, but none matched Rogers'. Also, no paraffin test was conducted on Rogers to determine if he had recently fired a gun.

On Trial

Silas Rogers was indicted in the Hustings Court of the city of Petersburg on Aug. 6, 1943, for the murder of Robert B. Hatchell. The prosecution told their version of the story: on the night of July 17, or early the following day, a Studebaker owned by Leslie Cook was stolen from his residence in Raleigh, North Carolina. The driver, who the Commonwealth claimed was Rogers, picked up two soldiers, James Jordan and Charles Stephens, outside Raleigh and gave them a ride to Petersburg.

Hatchell and Jolly saw the car, then pursued it until it crashed. Hatchell died from a bullet entering his left hip and exiting his abdomen. Neither the bullet nor the gun was introduced at trial.

While Jordan and Stephens testified that Rogers was the Studebaker driver, they also admitted that they were AWOL from the army. In addition, they claimed that it was dark when they got into the car and informed the police they were stationed at Camp Pickett when they were stationed at Jackson Barracks in New Orleans.

A patient in Petersburg Hospital, Leonard Bain, testified he saw Rogers run by his window, followed several minutes later by Hatchell, who stopped and talked with him for several minutes before resuming his chase. A neighbor testified that she saw the driver wearing a white sailor hat and a tan shirt torn on the shoulder. However, she stated further that she could not identify Rogers as the driver.

Officer Jolly testified that Rogers was the driver of the Studebaker. However, he admitted that he did not get a front view of his face, only a side view. Not one witness could identify Rogers or anyone resembling him in the hospital's vicinity within at least 20 minutes before the shooting and at no time afterward.

Two witnesses for the Commonwealth were permitted to testify that the defendant signed a statement that he came from Raleigh to Petersburg on a red truck, an obvious ploy to portray Rogers as a liar. Rogers testified that he signed that statement under duress after being beaten and waterboarded by the police. Also, the clothes Rogers wore on the day of his arrest were introduced as evidence, but police had cleaned them to wash out the bloodstains they received during the beating.

Testimony for the defense, including that of a Seaboard employee in Hamlet, North Carolina, buttressed Rogers' story – that he saw Rogers get on the train near Raleigh, where he stowed away in the baggage car. A conductor who discovered him just before the train stopped in Petersburg and ordered him off testified that the space where he was riding was dark, and he did not get a good look at his face.

Despite all the holes in the story and the complete lack of forensic evidence, the jury found Rogers guilty of first-degree murder and sentenced him to death.

An out-of-town Black man charged with murdering a white Virginia police officer with his own weapon simply had no chance in 1944 of being found not guilty.

Three writs of error were submitted for review by the Supreme Court of Virginia in October 1944, but they upheld the verdict, with an execution date set for Nov. 24.

An Incredible Coincidence

But one week later, on October 17, a Seaboard diesel supervisor named Murray was chatting with a road foreman, A.L. Foxworth, about the problem of hoboes on the trains. Murray mentioned that he had once found a "colored boy" stowing away on the Silver Meteor, and he had ordered him off in Petersburg. Foxworth was aware of the case against Rogers and told Murray he should go to the authorities. On Oct. 24, Murray met with Rogers and his attorneys on death row at the penitentiary. After the meeting, Murray told death row supervisor Capt. Penn "that is the boy."

Murray signed an affidavit attesting to Rogers' presence on that train, including details only the two could know. However, Rogers' court term had concluded, making it too late to introduce this eyewitness evidence in a new trial. But once Murray's affidavit became public, the commonwealth started backpedaling, claiming that maybe Rogers did come to Petersburg by train after all – but that admission threw out any motivation for the Washington Street car chase and the testimony of the two deserters.

While Rogers still managed to elude three more execution dates, the only real hope at this point lay with the brand-new Virginia Pardons Board or the governor.

A Commutation and a Strange Ally

In October 1945, the Pardons Board, citing reasonable doubt, commuted Rogers' death sentence to life in prison. As inmate number 51111, Rogers got a job in the penitentiary as a sewing machine operator, and that is where his case paused for five full years.

Then, on Dec. 29, 1950, Silas Rogers acquired an unlikely supporter – the *Richmond News Leader* and its firebrand editor, James J. Kilpatrick.

It may have been the most unlikely union in journalism history. During his years as editorial page editor of the *News Leader*, from 1950 until 1966, Kilpatrick blasted court-ordered integration. He supported the "massive resistance" movement created by Virginia's white ruling class and did much to damage Virginia's reputation during a period of critical social and racial change. He invented arguments as "interposition," interpreted as a states' rights gambit that would allow state officials to ignore federal laws they simply didn't like.

Kilpatrick, however, believed that the courts had unfairly convicted Rogers and presented his case in a series of editorials titled "The Curious Case of Silas Rogers."

At the same time, *Argosy* magazine also took up the case. They found a man in Florida named Robert Carroll who swore he loaned Rogers a "light brown jitterbug coat." But the coat seen in the Studebaker was described at the trial as black. They also found out that Rogers had never learned how to drive and that the soldiers in the car, who by then had disappeared, perjured themselves. In light of these developments, Rogers' attorney, Robert Cooley Jr., and civil rights attorneys Spottswood Robinson and Martin A. Martin also continued to pursue his case diligently.

After Kilpatrick's series ran, and after the conclusion of the 1952 special session of the General Assembly, Gov. John S. Battle – perhaps smarting from the negative publicity surrounding the Martinsville Seven case the previous year – ordered an independent study of the Rogers case. He even traveled to Petersburg to study the crime scene. Then, on Dec. 23, Kilpatrick got a call from Battle saying, "You'll be glad to hear this – Silas Rogers is coming out tomorrow."

"Silas, Get that Suit Ready."

Confident he would be released, Rogers months earlier asked his supervisor in the tailor shop if he could make a suit to wear out of the penitentiary. With his approval, he sewed a dark blue suit that remained on a hanger for nine months until a "trusty" from the Superintendent's office walked by his cell one day and told him, "Silas, get that suit ready."

Dressed in his homemade suit, Silas Rogers walked out of the penitentiary gate on Dec. 24, 1952, smiling broadly while holding an unconditional pardon signed by Gov.

Battle. Battle granted the pardon based on "a mass of evidence" accumulated over the ten years Rogers spent on death row and as a "lifer."

"I never lost hope," he told *News Leader* reporter Charles McDowell over lunch at Byrd Field (now Richmond International Airport) while waiting to travel to his sister's home in Newark, N.J. "I still had my hope when there was only two days left before that electric chair."

During his two years on death row, he watched eight men walk past his cell on their way to the chair – Ray Woodall, Howard Walker, William Clatterbuck, Willie Jones, Holman Thomas, Raymond McDaniel, Mancy Christian, and Lonnie Pearson. "I saw some fellows go to that electric chair smiling, and some that weren't smiling," he recalled.

Rogers remained in New Jersey for the rest of his life. He, unfortunately, got in more trouble – in Dec. 1954, he received a two-year sentence for assault. In Oct. 1956, he received a six-year sentence for assaulting a woman. He was paroled in 1960 and died in 1983.

1982: Virginia Resumes Executions

The death penalty may or may not be "cruel and unusual," the Virginia death sentence and execution of Frank Coppola may or may not be constitutional, he may or may not have been guilty. But he and Muriel Hatchell are dead, and both died horrible and unnecessary deaths, and all the posturing by lawyers, journalists, judges, and prison officials isn't going to change that. All I can understand is that our lives as people and as a society have been cheapened and debased by the deaths of these two individuals. The only regret that I have is that it won't stop here.

-Ned Scott Jr., on the resumption of executions in Virginia after a 19-year moratorium, *ThroTTle* Magazine, Richmond, Va. Sept. 1, 1982.

Earl Clanton was initially supposed to be Virginia's first execution since 1963.

Clanton, a Black man, was convicted and sentenced to death for the strangulation and stabbing murder of Wilhelmina Smith in Petersburg in November 1980. Virginia bulldozed him through the judicial system in a breathtaking 22 months in a Jim Crow-style "Virginia way" screw you to the Supreme Court and its mandates. He was one week away from electrocution in August 1982 when he received a stay from a state judge.

When Clanton went to the back of the line, Frank Coppola went to the front.

A Murder in Newport News

In early April of 1978, Coppola, with his wife, Karen, and acquaintances Joseph Miltier and Donna Mills, drove to the Newport News home of Peyton and Muriel Hatchell. The plan was for Coppola, disguised as a priest, to get inside the house and for Miltier to follow him to rob the Hatchells. Peyton was a car dealer, and it was rumored they had a large amount of cash inside. Hatchell refused to let Coppola in, however, and the group left.

Frank Coppola had been a local high school basketball star and even received a scholarship to Old Dominion College (now University), but got thrown off the team for disciplinary reasons. He was also briefly a Roman Catholic Seminarian.

As a Portsmouth policeman, he reportedly ate live spiders and chewed razor blades in front of rookies to show how tough he was. He was temporarily suspended from the force in 1966 for falsifying a police report. Although reinstated in October of that year, he resigned on June 30, 1967. He and Karen had two teenage children.

A week later, on the night of April 22, Muriel Hatchell again opened her front door to a woman delivering flowers. She refused to let the woman inside, and as an altercation ensued, Coppola and Miltier burst in and demanded money.

They allegedly beat Muriel unmercifully for hours, smashing her head repeatedly against the bathroom floor, then tying her to a chair with a Venetian blind cord. Coppola was in a rage, constantly screaming, "Where's the money, give us the money," as he punched and choked his victim.

When Peyton Hatchell arrived home, he was repeatedly beaten with a pistol, his face pushed into the floor as a man's voice demanded money. He was tied up and dragged across the floor until he could see his bound wife on her knees on the bathroom floor.

"Honey," he said to her, "if there's any money in the house, tell the people where it is."

Muriel never had a chance to respond. She was pronounced dead at the scene of "blunt force injuries complicated by aspiration."

Robbed of $3,100, his watch, and his car, Peyton survived emergency surgery that placed a metal plate in his head and testified against the defendants. Since he could not positively identify Coppola as his or his wife's attacker, Donna Mills entered into a plea bargain in which the Commonwealth agreed to recommend life in prison for her. She testified first against Miltier, who was found guilty of capital murder and sentenced to life in prison for delivering the fatal blows to Muriel Hatchell. Mills then testified against Coppola, who received the death penalty due to the "atrociousness" of the crime. Karen Coppola received a 21-year prison sentence.

Transcripts of Coppola's 1979 appeal to the Supreme Court of Virginia (*Coppola v. Commonwealth*) showed that Miltier delivered the fatal blow to Muriel Hatchell. However, the court concluded that Coppola's role as ringleader and that the evidence indicated he had "repeatedly beat[en] [the victim's] head against the floor" was sufficient to constitute the "aggravated battery" condition that justified the death penalty:

> The evidence leads to the conclusion that Coppola was not only a joint murderer of Mrs. Hatchell but that he was also the leader in organizing and directing the group to commit the armed robbery. His conduct towards Mrs. Hatchell, however, culminating in her death, appears from Mills's testimony to have been more violent and vicious than that of Miltier ...
>
> ... After reviewing the records, and considering the crime and the defendant, we hold that the atrociousness of Coppola's conduct exceeded that of Miltier and that the sentence of death is not excessive or disproportionate to death sentences generally imposed by Virginia juries in horrifying crimes of a similar nature.

Not Geared for Living

> It doesn't strike me as strange that a white ex-cop might be less fearful of two 55-second cycles of high voltage than of being dogged for years in captivity by a vindictive administration and an inimical population, especially since he would still probably have to suffer in solitary confinement, with death-row doubt, for an extensive period.
>
> -Author and former penitentiary inmate Evans Hopkins, "Notes from a

Prison Cell on the Coppola Execution." *Washington Post*, Aug. 22, 1982.

Frank Coppola became the fifth person nationwide to be executed since the *Gregg* decision. He was also the fourth to refuse further appeals and pursue his execution. Of the five, only John Spenkelink was executed against his will by Florida in May 1979 after exhausting 22 unsuccessful appeals. The others – Gary Gilmore in Utah (executed in January 1977); Jesse W. Bishop in Nevada (executed in October 1979); and Steven Judy in Indiana (executed in March 1981) – all, like Coppola, voluntarily stopped their appellate process to pursue state-assisted suicide.

In firing his attorneys, Coppola said, "further incarceration for these charges that I have maintained my innocence of can only lead to my being stripped of all personal dignity and continue to induce tremendous hardship on my family."

"I had it with the courts dangling my life in front of me, holding the death penalty over me," he told a reporter. "I felt I owed it to myself total control of my own destiny. They've said to me, 'We're going to take your life.' I say back to them, 'Come on, do it.' It's my decision. What the hell, we all have to die. At least I can say when."

Joe Ingle, Director of the Southern Coalition on Jails and Prisons, told the *Richmond Times-Dispatch* that Coppola "is in control of the situation and is very clear about what he wants to do and why he wants to do it."

Despite his outside reputation as a swaggering tough guy, inside prison, Coppola was more of a mentor for other inmates and kept many of them out of trouble. These included Joe Giarratano, on the row for a murder and rape that he did not commit. "I was fighting the guards every day," he recalled in a 2022 interview. "I'd make them come in my cell. And we did it, like, 30 days straight, and Frank snatched me up and said, 'You can't beat them like that.' And he gave me a copy of the original 'Prisoner Self-Help Litigation Manual,' written by Daniel Potts. He said, 'This is how you fight them.'"

In a last-ditch effort to save his former client's life, attorney J. Gary Lawrence filed a mental incompetence suit in the U.S. District Court. Coppola wrote to Judge D. Dortch Warriner that "No one can relate to death, but people don't understand that I have been on death row for four years. I'm not geared for living ...." Judge John D. Butzner Jr. of the U.S. Fourth District Court of Appeals granted a last-minute stay at the lawyers' request acting in defiance of Coppola's wishes. They claimed that the years spent on death row in Mecklenburg's "horrid conditions" might have robbed Coppola of the capacity to decide the question rationally. In addition, they cited a constitutional review of Virginia's death penalty still pending in the case of Charles Stamper.

Coppola had other reasons for stopping his appeals. His kids were being taunted at school. Plus, he had kidney failure and did not want to face a lifetime of dialysis.

Gov. Charles Robb ordered an immediate appeal of the stay. In response, Attorney General Gerald Baliles dispatched two prosecuting attorneys, James Kulp and Jerry Slonaker, to Washington to overturn the stay. They rushed to the Supreme Court and, finding the main door locked, finally got in through a side door and submitted their request for a reversal at 7:25 p.m.

Civil liberties advocates were shocked and surprised that Virginia would pursue an execution so aggressively, but the U.S. Supreme Court seemed neither shocked nor surprised. After a brief discussion, Chief Justice Warren Burger and four others voted at 10:25 p.m. in an unprecedented telephone conference call to overturn the Fourth District Court stay. Apparently, they never considered the arguments of defense attorneys George Kendall, Stephen Bright, and William Walsh, who arrived with their papers at 10:22. Bright had written his motion for a stay of execution by hand in the car as they raced through the late-night, almost-empty serpentine D.C. streets.

It was logged as received by the Court at 11:05 p.m.

"I Wonder Who's Afraid of Virginia's Chair"

> I don't care if the man is a white cop. He's a convict like us now, and the dudes here ought to realize that if they kill one convict they'll kill us all."
> -Unnamed penitentiary inmate, quoted by Evans Hopkins. "Notes From a Prison Cell on the Coppola Execution."

About 45 minutes later, news of the overturned stay reached Coppola at the penitentiary in Richmond. At 11:18 p.m., three guards escorted him 10 feet from holding cell #1 into the death chamber. With an unnerving calm, he sat down in the oak electric chair modeled after the chair in Sing-Sing and built by inmates 74 years earlier. Del. Samuel Glasscock, a witness, told the UPI that Coppola said nothing but looked the six citizen witnesses "right in the eye" after being strapped into the chair

At 11:21, Corrections Department Director Raymond Procunier announced, "Fire it up!" An unnamed executioner keyed and started the generator with a loud whine. At his signal, Coppola's body lurched violently against the restraints when hit with a 2500-volt burst of electricity.

> They're killing him now. Everyone thought that nothing was going to happen. A reporter interrupted "Hart to Hart" a few minutes ago and said that the court said to fry him. Spoiled my chess game. I went out on the tier, saw a few men crowded around the TV, others playing cards as usual. I am back in my cell now, thinking about it. I picture Coppola as seen last week exercising, a tall man, Kojak bald head, and a Fu Manchu mustache. I imagine what is happening in the building I'm in, less than 100 feet away ...
> -Evans Hopkins

Jerry Givens acted as an alternate executioner for Coppola, and he recalled how nervous he and his team were. "We had not had an execution in 20 years," he explained. "We hadn't practiced on a real person, of course, and that basement was hot and covered wall to wall with people."

Whether because of nerves or faulty preparation, the Death Penalty Information Center listed Coppola's execution as botched. After the first jolt, Coppola was still alive, so a second jolt was ordered. Although no press representatives witnessed the electrocution, and the Virginia DOC released no details, an attorney who was present verified that it took two 55-second jolts to kill Coppola. The second produced a crackling sound as Coppola's head and leg caught on fire, filling the chamber with acrid smoke and the rancid odor of burning flesh.

Givens explained that an officer did not roll Coppola's pants leg far enough to clear the electrode, catching it on fire.

"No one wants to be burned alive," wrote Hopkins. "The horrible end of electrocution is viewed with fear by many, but quite often this fear is superseded by rage at the sanctioning of such violence by the state."

"If you could imagine a rather big, older [machine] – like a big air conditioner – turning on and then sitting on a concrete slab," wrote prison rights advocate Marie Deans of being nearby the electrocution apparatus in the 1980s. "You're on the same slab. You can feel the vibrations. ... it's that kind of revving up and then this sort of loud grinding [sound]. Then it's done twice ... it feels like it's inside you ... it feels like it's in your chest, and it's pushing against the chest like your chest is going to burst."

Procunier, who was new to Virginia and badly wished to project a tough-guy image, announced that death occurred at 11:27 p.m.

"I wonder how the crowd outside feels at catching sight of the body," wrote Hopkins. "I wonder if the men now locked in their cells on the street side of the building can see what's happening out there. I wonder if others wonder how we feel in here. I wonder if they care."

"I wonder who's afraid of Virginia's chair."

From the comfort of Virginia's governor's mansion, Charles Robb noted, "The decision not to interfere with the order of the circuit court of Newport News was the most difficult and emotionally draining decision I have had to make as governor of Virginia."

"If all of Virginia could have witnessed that as I did, they would agree there has to be a better way," Del. Glasscock claimed after the execution.

Moving Forward in Reverse

> They went to pull him up out of the electric chair; they couldn't get him out
> of the chair. I grabbed one side, [two corrections officers] grabbed on the
> other side, and we put him back on the stretcher. I'll never forget it. He was
> laying back on the stretcher with his arms and legs locked up.
> - Corrections technician Michael Morton, describing removing Frank Cop-
> pola's locked body from the electric chair after his execution to *Richmond
> Times-Dispatch* journalist Frank Green, May 24, 1998.

Throughout the warm, muggy August evening, about 100 curiosity seekers and some who said they came to pray for Coppola's soul talked quietly in an informal vigil against a wall across from the penitentiary. Many were members of the Interfaith Task Force of Virginia, who opposed the death penalty. "I just came out because it's something I feel strongly about," a stocky construction worker named James Fralin told United Press International reporter Jim Norvelle. "This sign says all you can say about it," he continued, pointing to a homemade sign, "Thou Shalt Not Kill. There are no exceptions."

Sally Winston, a self-described evangelist, said she came because "a soul is at stake." Another abolitionist, Dorothea Hoffheins, claimed she had been fasting for four days protesting the scheduled execution.

Walter Sullivan, Bishop of the Catholic Diocese of Richmond and staunch death penalty opponent, lamented that "I feel it is a very tragic moment in the history of our state. It's a tragic response, an act of violence in the face of violence."

The plight of Frank Coppola and the conditions at Mecklenburg Correctional Center's death row that prompted Coppola's wish to be executed raised the eyebrows of Tennessee minister Rev. Joe Ingle, who had received numerous letters from Joe Giarratano. Since Virginia provided no post-conviction legal counsel to death row inmates, Giarratano had mailed over 30 letters to lawyers and charitable organizations seeking counsel for Coppola, and Ingle was the sole respondent.

Traveling to Virginia to meet Coppola, Ingle was shocked at the "barbarity" of conditions at MCC and the Virginia State Penitentiary and the lack of organized grassroots opposition to the death penalty.

Clearly, Virginia had not adequately prepared to resume the death penalty, and abolitionists had not prepared to vigorously oppose it.

Problem at Mecklenburg

When the Virginia State Penitentiary first opened on April 1, 1800, problems quickly became apparent. There was no perimeter security, and outsiders frequently passed contraband through the first-floor cell windows. The solid oak cell doors had no windows, so guards had to open them to check on the prisoners. There was also no area for a night security guard to walk past the cells "for the purpose of preventing evil communication" between the prisoners. Guards and trustys carried water from the nearby James River since there was no well or spring-fed water source. Inmates emptied their toilet buckets through a trough to a holding pond near the river, and the drifting stench was unbearable in the summer.

Architect and construction supervisor Benjamin Latrobe underestimated Richmond winters, so prisoners spent their time shivering in unheated cells under thin blankets as cold winds, freezing rain, and sometimes snow howled through open, barred windows.

Similarly, Mecklenburg Correctional Center, or MCC, suffered its own deficiencies and problems when it opened in Boydton in April 1977 as a model of "escape-proof" maximum-security prisons and as a badly-needed source of employment in economically depressed Southside Virginia.

There were more contemptuous reasons why the state built MCC far from any urban centers: there was no public transportation there, so the distance proved daunting to families and Richmond and D.C.-based attorneys, who sometimes had to travel hundreds of miles round-trip for short visits and meetings.

Two modern supermax prisons, Wallens Ridge and Red Onion are similarly squirreled away in the coalfields of far southwestern Virginia, a six- to eight-hour drive from Richmond. Wallens Ridge is also the largest Black community in Southwest Virginia.

Constructed at the cost of just under $20 million, MCC and its five matched buildings, each with a capacity of 72, was described in the 1978 *Mecklenburg Ledger-Star* as a new home for "Virginia's most dangerous and disruptive." One of those was Thomas Penn, known by fellow inmates as T.P., who with his brother William became Richmond's first serial killers in 1966 when they murdered six people over seven weeks. William received two concurrent 20-year sentences, but Thomas received four life sentences. He received a fifth life sentence in 1974 when he killed a fellow inmate. In 1987, T.P.'s life of violence abruptly ended when he was stabbed to death by another fellow inmate, Jesse Hale Jr.

By 1978, MCC rose as the strict, modern-day remedy to a disintegrating Virginia penal system plagued by escapes, work stoppages, and riots. The courts had also battered Gov. Godwin and prison officials in many recent legal cases that exposed cruel conditions and brutal behavior by poorly-trained guards and sadistic administrators.

Only four months after MCC opened, 300 inmates at the penitentiary handed the warden a list of 32 demands before staging a sit-down strike. The strike quickly escalated into a near-riot until a violent thunderstorm cleared the yard. A subsequent cell-to-cell sweep by guards turned up over 100 homemade weapons, proving how primitive and ineffective the Virginia penitentiary system had become.

In his opening remarks at the MCC ribbon-cutting, Godwin predicted that the prison would remedy the recent failures of the state correctional system, promising "a firm and lasting and unbreakable connection between crime and punishment."

By 1979, the moldering penitentiary in Richmond was still open, and MCC – both as a facility and a modern penal concept – groaned under the burdens of exorbitant operational costs, stringent, biased, and vindictive regulations, inadequate inmate medical and psychiatric care, and a host of hiring and training deficiencies.

Inmates admitted to MCC came under one of two criteria: the Special Management Unit, or SMU, reserved for very disruptive inmates who would likely remain in solitary confinement permanently. The alternative was the "Phase Program," which (in theory) would allow inmates a chance to progress through phases of incarceration, earning privileges along the way and eventually earning their way into general population.

The Phase Program quickly failed because the MCC staff had too much discretion to rescind privileges if the inmate did not comply with either of two narrowly-defined behavioral categories. According to a 2019 ACLU report by Senior Staff Attorney Vishal Agraharkar, a Board of Corrections member wondered "whether it is better not to attempt the Phase Program at all than to do it wrong."

Complicating matters were undertrained corrections officers, who, at $12,644 per year, were among the lowest paid in America and worked with few protocols and almost no supervision. MCC was also the most expensive prison in Virginia to operate, spending over $29,000 per prisoner per year by 1983-84, nearly double that of other facilities.

The ACLU reported in 2019 that a 1984 state Board of Corrections investigation revealed that MCC and DOC officials had cold-called other Virginia prisons begging for transfers to keep the facility full so they could justify its jaw-dropping operating costs.

It became apparent that Virginia spent too much money on security bells and whistles and not enough on basic job training and paychecks. In 1981, three females sneaked cash, a revolver, rounds of ammunition, and a pound of marijuana past two security guards into a temporary mobile visitation facility while visiting James Briley and Earl Clanton.

While chatting with the women, Briley and Clanton began cutting a hole through the plywood wall for the exchange to occur. "They had double-wide trailers that we visited in," Giarratano recalled. "They had the visiting room, the glass, and the plyboard underneath where you're sitting. And they were just actually cutting it out."

Giarratano said another inmate, Michael Marnell Smith foiled the plan. "Mike terminated his visit and on the way back, told the guards, 'Man, they're getting a gun in and smokes or something.' And they ran over, and sure enough, they see the pistol and a pound of weed."

The officers received a suspension.

"Most of your officers are honest and dedicated," death row inmate Dennis Stockton wrote to Warden Sherman Townley in 1983, "but you do have a few crooks working here."

Stockton, a 43-year-old North Carolina native, was convicted in March 1983 of the murder for hire of 17-year-old North Carolina boy Kenny Arnder in Patrick County, a crime in which he unwaveringly maintained his innocence. Stockton also kept a death row diary while at MCC in which he extensively described long days of brutal heat, mind-numbing tedium, homosexual affairs, extensive drug use, and incompetent corrections officers who simply turned their heads amid repeated violations of the rules.

The publication of Stockton's "Death Row Diaries" in the Sept. 16, 1984, Norfolk *Virginian-Pilot* newspaper enraged Virginia's DOC and took prompt revenge. They moved Stockton into horrific conditions at Powhatan Correctional Center, known at the time as one of the most inhuman in the entire country. While there, Stockton eventually gave up on his appeals, despite the real possibility that he never executed the murder-for-hire and lingering doubt that the murder had occurred in Virginia.

Compounding MCC's toxic mix of confusing procedures and lax ineptitude was a preponderance of building design flaws that inmates frequently exploited. These included stairwell hiding places, blocked lines of sight, prison-yard obstructions, and even concealed cell air vents, which allowed inmates to grow pot plants and hold conversations.

Death row inmates discovered that they could confuse the head counts when returning from recreation if not ordered to go directly to their cells. They could mill around a common day room, move from cell to cell, or duck unnoticed into an unlocked bathroom door adjacent to the control room.

"It was just sort of weird," Fr. James Griffin recalled of MCC in a 2021 interview. Griffin was a death row minister at the facility in the 1980s and got to know all the inmates there. "It was just a weird place. It wasn't scary. I was only scared a couple of times, and that was when the door closed, and I'd be in someone's cell, and it's the Brileys or someone else. I said, 'If this guy's a murderer, he can murder me right now.' But they never did."

Griffin added that, like Coppola, everyone he counseled there would choose execution rather than remain on death row for 20 years. "The ones that lived on death row for 13 or 14 years, like Lem Tuggle, for them, it must've been hell."

Out of Control

Hailed at its opening as state-of-the-art and "escape-proof," MCC by 1981 was more a Hollywood backlot set of a prison than a real one. Based on punishment and warehousing rather than education and rehabilitation, policies and procedures had reverted to the darkest nineteenth-century days of the State Penitentiary. Politicians and prison design experts described it as procedurally archaic. Alvin Bronstein, head of the ACLU's National Prison Project, claimed conditions at MCC were the worst he had seen, and procedures were "out of control." Gov. Godwin's declarations that the facility would rehabilitate Virginia's penal system had spiraled into meaningless propaganda.

Then, on Aug. 1 of that year, MCC inmates had enough of the dehumanizing, slipshod conditions that they believed forced Frank Coppola to choose death over life and filed a class-action lawsuit against the DOC in the U.S. District Court for the Eastern District of Virginia. The suit, *Brown v. Hutto*, alleged that MCC conditions fell "beneath the standards of human decency" and inflicted needless suffering in violation of inmates' constitutional rights. The suit listed unsupervised and poorly trained staff, the lack of activities, and derisory medical and psychiatric care. The lawsuit also claimed violence permeated the facility, with inmates suffering injuries during excessive and frequent physical confrontations with guards. A jury had awarded one inmate $18,000 in damages after a brutal beating by a guard.

During shakedowns and cell searches, when guards entered the cell, one would pin the reclining inmate to his bunk with his body weight behind his clear shield while the others shackled his wrists and feet. According to one anonymous report, they would slide a pole through the shackles and carry the inmate out "like a hunting trophy."

Two unnamed guards in 1980 admitted to this author that while the inmate was in this vulnerable and humiliating position, they sometimes, for a laugh, slammed his head into the opposite wall "accidentally on purpose."

Brown v. Hutto settled on April 8, 1983, with MCC agreeing to numerous concessions. These included simple everyday matters like attaching desks and stools inside the cells. A written policy outlining when the toilets in the isolation units would be turned off to keep an inmate from deliberately flooding his cell assured that no inmate had to eat a meal beside an unflushable toilet. MCC also agreed to new physical restraint policies, not establishing a death row segregation section, and using only ordinary disciplinary procedures against death row inmates.

MCC also agreed to form an Institutional Classification Committee (ICC) to classify inmates when they entered the facility, taking into account security risk, mental and physical health, prior record, and specialty designations as hearing impaired, protective custody, and transitional, among others.

The settlement agreement also covered telephones, visitation, outdoor recreation, grievance procedures, staff training and rotation, background checks for staff members, access to the law and general reading library, mail, newspapers, religious programming, educational opportunities, and several others.

The suit drew criticisms from corrections officials, who complained of being hamstrung in their interactions with death row inmates. A retired former head of security at MCC, Harold Catron, a strict disciplinarian nicknamed "crooked neck Catron" by inmates, told *Richmond Times-Dispatch* reporter Bill McElway in 2009 that prison rights advocates, including those in *Brown v. Hutto*, shouldered much of the blame for MCC's failures. He claimed, for example, that it was "unbelievable ... that we were in a position of having to allow death-row inmates to congregate with one another up until 10, 11 p.m. at night in the dayroom."

"That's how the Brileys were able to operate, to gain control of what was going on."

While the concessions of *Brown v. Hutto* improved the lives of death row inmates at MCC, corrections officials claimed that in 1984, that decision led to a humiliating international debacle that, despite a year of warnings, seemed to catch everyone but the inmates off-guard.

Death Row Breakout

> This place is run on corruption.
> -Death row inmate Dennis Stockton on Mecklenburg Correctional Center,
> in "Death Row Diary." The *Virginian-Pilot*, Sept. 16, 1984

MCC's much-ballyhooed reputation as escape-proof was ironically a contributing factor to May 31, 1984, when six condemned prisoners walked out the front door, with no shots fired and no one injured, in the largest death row escape in American history.

Concerned inmates repeatedly revealed the breakout in advance to prison authorities and to J. Lloyd Snook, a Charlottesville defense attorney who had defended many of the inmates on the row. Snook was a young, struggling lawyer but was well-known on death row, as he had taken the first five capital defendants, free of charge, on their habeas petitions as Virginia prepared to resume executions. He warned prison officials that an escape plan was in progress, down to the minutest detail, including where the weapons were hidden, that a bomb threat would be called, and how the inmates would trick the guards.

Authorities scoffed at the warnings because after all, the prison was escape-proof.

Dennis Stockton's diary, hand-written between 1983 and 1985, evolved in 1999 into a book by Joe Jackson and William Burke Jr. entitled "Dead Run." The diary and the book described a facility and a system by 1984 in absolute chaos. In the weeks before the escape, an assistant warden sent the DOC a list of suggested security improvements to compensate for the recent court decision and the building design flaws. Death row was located in "C" pod on the second floor of Building 1. The facility's maintenance department was on the first floor, which the list proposed relocating because of the risk that inmates could get in and steal saw blades, tools, and scrap metal.

While MCC implemented none of these changes, Jay Cochran Jr., director of the Virginia State Police's Bureau of Criminal Investigations, claimed in a post-breakout report and to the *Virginian-Pilot* that none of the suggestions would have prevented the escape. Because of the prison's supposed airtight construction, he, like Catron, blamed "a simple thing like headcount."

Cochran also divulged those warnings of an escape, with the locations of weapons to be used, had been received from an unnamed inmate (later revealed as Stockton) by the state attorney general's office in April, an entire month before the actual breakout. Cochran said a search based on the unsigned note failed to turn up the hidden weapons listed.

The attorney general's office blamed the note on the inmate's unhappiness with MCC conditions and wanting a transfer to the State Penitentiary in Richmond.

Corrections officials, psychiatrists, and attorneys considered Dennis Stockton a killer but a reliable chronicler of life on death row. State psychiatrist Dr. Miller Ryans told the *Virginian-Pilot* that he read portions of Stockton's diary, observing that "the man keeps specific notes ... it's fascinating. [On one page], he mentioned something that had been mentioned to me by another inmate. It was word for word what this inmate had said to me. It had to be the exact truth. He was very, very meticulous in putting down entries. It's amazing. It was just like a stenographer."

Martinsville lawyer Philip Gardner, who initially represented Stockton, told the paper that his client "has as good an ability to recall facts as anybody I've ever seen. He has a remarkable ability to recall minute details from distant memory ... his intellectual capacity is high."

Joe Giarratano, however, scoffed at the accuracy of Stockton's diary in a 2022 interview. "It's bullshit," he divulged before clarifying himself. "Pieces of what he said were true. But a lot of it was just shit he made up on the fly. And a lot of the information he was given wasn't true because it was intentionally not true. It's what we told him."

In addition to the observations on the guards, Stockton kept obsessive notes on his fellow death row inmates and how they constantly observed, schemed, and gamed the system. The use of marijuana among them, for example, was pervasive, and many grew plants inside their cells. Stockton himself grew a plant inside his concealed air vent. One guard pleaded guilty to smuggling pot into the prison in 1983, and an October 1984 shakedown revealed 75 joints inside James Briley's cell. County prosecutors, however, declined to press charges because of Briley's death row status. It wasn't until July 1984 – two months after the breakout – that Gov. Robb finally acknowledged the drug problem there. "[smuggling] is done with such frequency; it's devastating that it continues on the scale that it does."

In a letter to Warden Townley, Stockton claimed he heard several guards claim they made more money selling pot every year than they made in pay from MCC.

Giarratano recalled that marijuana frequently came into the prison inside VHS videotapes through the assistant warden's office, who had no clue what was passing over his desk. "It's a miracle they never got busted because I saw one of the packages that came in from the assistant warden's office," he related. "He said, 'Oh, your videotapes are in there.' I went in there and got the videotapes, and the box was open. And we pulled them out. And two of the videotapes, you can see half of a plastic bag hanging out. Each bag had about an ounce of weed."

Stockton recorded how inmates saved fruit off the meal trays to make "homebrew" in trash cans, which kept many of them shit-faced. "Everybody has been falling down drunk on all that 'homebrew,' plus all the dope," Stockton wrote of a raucous Christmas Day party in 1983. "The guards are all turning their heads ... I wish I had a movie camera to make movies of this drunk bunch and show them later."

Guards most likely ignored the drunkenness because, unlike other portions of the prison where drinking led to fights, the homebrew tended to keep the inmates on the row jovial and quiet. Many former employees, a counselor, and a former medical officer all told the *Virginian-Pilot* that it was common knowledge that death row inmates made wine.

A former nurse, Frances Wilson, also told the *Virginian-Pilot* that one of the demands made by inmates in August 1984 was less pork and more fruit to make homebrew.

Homebrew was not the only drink the row inmates concocted on death row. According to Fr. Griffin, inmates would also make "washing machine coffee."

"They have granules like a Keurig," Griffin recalled, "you just put it under the hot water of the washing machine and make coffee."

Many death row inmates also inexplicably had large amounts of cash. Stockton recalled James Briley handing him a roll of bills estimated at $3,000 to hold while Briley played basketball. According to Stockton, the money was smuggled in the mail and from Greensboro N.C. via a guard. One mailroom employee in early 1984 discovered $160 sandwiched between some polaroid pictures mailed to the Brileys.

Stockton also described homosexual trysts (between "punks") on death row that were routinely ignored by the guards but which sometimes led to arguments, fights, and security issues. "Homosexual relationships of some standing" occurred among the inmates, claimed Cochran, who admitted that he knew only one gay relationship on death row.

One of those "punks" was John Joseph LeVasseur, known as "Little John" or "Little one" due to his diminutive stature. He was born Tran Quang Vu Tuan in a Vietnamese orphanage and was Virginia's first adopted Southeast Asian orphan. Yet he was sentenced to die on Nov. 5, 1982, for the grisly murder of Pamela Brenner of Woodbridge. LeVasseur told police that he had taken LSD, smoked marijuana, and drank two beers on the day of Brenner's death. He claimed to have no memory of the killing.

When LeVasseur landed on death row at MCC, the slight, bespectacled immigrant was reportedly raped by another inmate, then "sold" to James Briley for two cartons of cigarettes to be his personal punk. Giarratano, however, disputed the rape, claiming in a 1983 letter to William Menza at Amnesty International that "the guy wasn't raped, I don't know what kind of game he is playing. He consented, and I know this for a fact ... Nobody here is stupid enough to try a stunt like that."

Giarratano clarified that LeVasseur was intimidated into submission. And he was a punk for Linwood, not James. James Briley used Timothy Bunch as his punk.

Giarratano also recalled saving Linwood's life one day when the more volatile James caught his brother messing with Bunch. "[James] caught him in the act. He had a knife up and was going to hit his brother in the back. The knife was coming down. And I hit him like a linebacker."

Planning for E-day

The way Mecklenburg was set up, they were so dependent on physical security. Well, it's not the physical security that's ever a problem. We can always find a way around that. Escapes happen because of human error.

-Joe Giarratano, interview, Jan. 23, 2022.

While James Briley claimed the escape planning took two years, Stockton noted in his diary that the first talks of an escape started in September and October 1983. "General discussions," he wrote, "just informational."

Giarratano reported that he and the others watched the guards for over a year. "We kept meticulous notes, counted times which guards work which shifts, when they come around, when they took their breaks, bathrooms, what the lieutenants were doing, which female officers they were screwing around with. We knew what was going on."

On March 5, 1984, nine inmates – Linwood and James Briley, Earl Clanton, Alton Waye, Willie Lloyd Turner, Derick Peterson, Timothy Bunch, Willie Evans, and Dennis Stockton – pushed two tables together on the right side of "C" pod. They surrounded themselves with law books to make it look like they were discussing appeals, and while a guard sat with his back to them watching television less than 35 feet away, they hatched a plan to break out.

Stockton noted that at this meeting, responsibilities were assigned. James "JB" Briley would take hostages, give instructions, and monitor phones. His brother Linwood would also help take hostages, observe the process and do what was needed. Earl "Goldie" Clanton would hide in the guard bathroom between the right and left pod, then rush the control room to open the pod doors. Stockton would keep lookout at the windows, plan an escape route south, then drive the getaway vehicle. Alton Waye would help take hostages. Willie Turner would make and stash weapons, then help secure the left side of the pod. Joe "Joe G" Giarratano would help take over the control room, secure the left side, and coordinate the telephones. Derick Peterson would help take hostages and take control of the downstairs. Willie Evans would help with hostages, ensure all were securely locked up, and get their keys. Timothy "Tim Bo" Bunch would do whatever was needed.

Willie Lloyd Turner was a natural to be in charge of weapons. "Turner was so intelligent," attorney Julie McConnell said in a 2021 interview. "He had supposedly figured out how to get out of his cell at night. I never saw this, but he wrote that he could get in and out of his cell and visit other people. He was quite ingenious."

In a 1994 telephone interview, Turner told *Virginian-Pilot* journalist Laura LaFay that he took great pride in his ability to make and stash contraband. In addition to fake guns, saw blades, and knives, he fashioned a 3-foot Samurai sword from part of his bed frame.

Most impressively, he made keys that opened his cell door and those of other cells. As guards let him in and out of his cell, he memorized the key's design. Then, he stripped a piece of aluminum from his toilet and bent it into the shape of the key. He claimed the aluminum was soft enough to bend and shape but strong enough to open the cell door.

Turner claimed that if the key didn't work the first time, he would just "fiddle with it'" until it did. He said he could usually make a key in a single day.

While Turner had experience with keys and weapons, Earl Clanton had some escape experience. On April 28, 1980, while on trial for malicious wounding after hitting a 17-year-old with brass knuckles, he simply walked out of the courtroom during a lunch recess and was still a fugitive when he was arrested for the murder of Wilhelmina Smith.

About 12 of the 24 death row inmates were initially in on the plan, but within days several began dropping out, especially after two security shakedowns in one week spooked them. Stockton recalled one shakedown rumor on March 7, just after one of two Tennessee escapees was shot and killed in Marion, N.C. He wrote of how James Briley asked him to retrieve a shank (homemade knife) that he had hidden above cell 67's doorway in preparation for the shakedown:

> JB told me to go over there and get a knife that was up there. But I couldn't reach it. Guard [name redacted] came in. He got a chair, reached up there and got the knife. He brought it to JB's cell. JB had him take it and put it in his sock. When the shakedown never came, the officer gave it back to JB. Guard [name redacted] also brought pot (at other times) to JB.

On March 20, after a 3-hour meeting about 'the plan," Charles Stamper, Alton Waye, and Timothy Bunch backed out. Stockton noted that they pored over logistical information gathered over 45 days, including details of prison security, building maps, and interoffice phone numbers. All of these were procured from corrections officers.

One anonymous death row inmate was quoted after the escape that if he had as much information about the facility that those six had, all 300 prisoners could have walked right out of there. "That's how secure it was."

On March 24, Willie Evans went to Stockton with an alternate plan to break out and form a "combat unit" to commit armed robberies. "He claimed he had somebody who could bring [guns] in," he wrote. "There were no takers."

Also on March 24, a new inmate, Lem Tuggle, was brought to the row. Tuggle, or "Tug," had been convicted and sentenced to death for the murder of 52-year-old Jessie Havens. He killed Havens only 104 days after being paroled for the 1971 rape and murder of a 17-year-old. After only one day on the row, Tug told the inmates he was fully committed to the plan.

"We planned, and we talked, and we discussed," Tuggle narrated in an undated recording made on a smuggled tape recorder. "We had escape committees. We had a little committee that any kind of problem popped up. You had to clear it through the committee before you could take any kind of action at all because the escape overrode everything here. There was nothing more important than the escape. So, that's the way we had it set up. And no personal conflicts. Nothing overrode the escape."

Tug also had a history of breakouts and had gone AWOL numerous times in the military. Before his first murder trial, he had fled Smyth County Jail by sticking a sharpened plastic spoon in the back of a guard, telling him it was a knife.

Tuggle was 5-ft 9-inches, 350 pounds, with massive arms and a visible tattoo that read "Born to Die." Corrections officials claimed he simply looked like a killer.

"He was a big guy, just a real big, physical specimen," Fr. Griffin recalled. "And he was sort of unkempt [with a] big beard, like a country boy. He liked to talk and be a blowhard, so to speak. But we became friends [and he] asked me to be there for his execution."

A False Start

The original date for the escape was April 15, 1984, but it had to be pushed back because the inmates had not yet made enough knives and files. They were stashed inside a false wall in Turner's cell, #68, and in a hollow table column as they were completed.

Other inmates at MCC assisted in making weapons. According to the book "Dead Run," inmates doing landscaping would drop homemade knives in piles of leaves left under the windows to the row, then tie them to fishing line lowered from the windows. After dark, the inmates would retrieve the weapons from the leaf piles.

"We had a guard bring us all the codes to the radio," Tuggle claimed in the audio recording, "call letters, you know, everything that they used, like, what a 10-52, 10-33. 10-33 means the officer needs assistance, and 52 means someone's sick and needs the nurse to come there. We had all of them. And, like I said, that came from one of the guards. He was paid off, and he brought it over."

On April 16, after a two-hour meeting the previous day, Stockton decided to back out of the plan after discussing it with Turner and Giarratano because he believed the hostage-taking was too dangerous. Also, a rumor circulated that Stockton tipped off the guards, forcing Giarratano and Turner to warn him that JB, Linwood, and Clanton were "going to take care" of him and anyone else who backed out. This development created mistrust, with some inmates fearing the escape would dissolve into a futile blood bath.

More paranoia gripped the inmates after another cell-to-cell shakedown on April 18. Information had reached the guards about the plan, and while the Brileys suspected Stockton, Stockton, in turn, suspected it was Willie Evans who leaked. No weapons were found, but the inmates remained on lockdown.

This situation escalated on April 20 when the entire pod went into "General Detention" because, according to a memo from Assistant Warden W. A. Crenshaw, "the administration has received reliable information that the security of the institution may be jeopardized." Guards beat on the walls and ransacked the cells in searches for contraband and again found nothing.

The information indicated that the inmates were plotting to cause serious property damage and personal injury to the staff and other inmates. An investigation into this situation has been conducted and appropriate security measures have been taken to ensure that the pod area has been rid of all weapons ... the results of the investigation are inconclusive and will continue until such time as the institution is assured of being able to operate in a safe, secure manner.

-Institutional Classification Committee report, Mecklenburg Correctional Center death row, reported by the *Virginian-Pilot*, April 24, 1984.

"They had a road map that would have taken them right to it," Stockton claimed of the shakedowns and weapons searches. "But they still didn't find it."

Giarratano explained that the shakedowns resulted from misinformation Stockton was providing the prison. "He'd give it to the warden, whoever he was giving it to. And they'd come in like gangbusters and tear the place up, couldn't find anything. And then, after about five or six times doing that, they just quit listening to him. He didn't know what he was talking about."

On April 27, the MCC administration terminated the lockdown over Catron's objections. He told the *Times-Dispatch* that it was a mistake, that death-row inmates were hardened people who assessed your strengths and weaknesses for years. "They will learn exactly who you are, and if they sense any willingness to cut corners, they will take advantage of that."

On May 7, Stockton received news that the Supreme Court of Virginia found no errors in his Patrick County Circuit Court trial and that his execution date had been set for July 27, 1984. He reportedly shrugged and placed the notice in his pile of legal papers.

On May 13, Stockton sent an anonymous letter to Catron with a map of cells 63, 65, and 68 showing where the weapons were hidden. Jay Cochran told the *Virginian-Pilot* that a search based on this note failed to discover any concealed weapons. Still, Cochran admitted that an investigation conducted after the breakout turned up those weapons and more, with many inside a table column in which a hole had been filed, then patched with a plaster made of chewed paper and paint chips painted over.

"The hiding places were so obvious it looked like a child had done them," wrote Lt. James Lettner, head of general investigations for the state police's Bureau of Criminal Investigation.

Giarratano disputed Cochran's version of the story of the discovered weapons. "We gave them everything," he admitted. "I remember it was Lt. Hawkings, he was one of those lieutenants that we took [hostage]. I let everybody out when it was over. And I took all the weapons, gathered everything up, and brought them to him."

"I took the handcuffs off of him. I said, 'Here you go. Here are all the weapons.' He looked at me and said, 'What are you giving them to me for? What do you want me to do with them?' I said, 'Well, you don't want to leave them lying around in here.' I mean, they weren't little pieces of metal. There were long blades made into machetes."

Stockton was frustrated by the guards' incompetence. "I wrote the letter because [the Brileys and Clanton] thought I was informing," he wrote in his diary. "The letter was to inform the administration of what was happening ...Tuggle told me they were going to kill all those who knew of the plan and didn't go along."

Tuggle frequently talked of killing – for instance, he bragged to many that he killed an inmate named Jones in Marion Correctional and successfully made it look like a suicide. He also said on May 26 that if they successfully got outside the wall but could not get out the gate, they would come back inside and "kill a bunch of hostages." Stockton didn't know to believe him or not.

Stockton's letter forced yet another shakedown. A supposed explosives-sniffing dog was taken cell-to-cell but accomplished little other than licking the inmates' candy bars and knocking over personal items while the bemused inmate stood handcuffed outside his cell. Each cell search took only about 45 seconds.

E-Day

At 6:00 p.m. on "E-Day" (Escape Day), May 31, the inmates – some of them clean-shaven for the first time, with their hair combed, which should have raised suspicions, but did not – went outside for two hours recreation. A beardless Tuggle told Stockton that they were leaving later that night and, since he had once been a moonshine runner, asked which roads he should take to get south. At 7:00 p.m., Turner returned to his cell, retrieved the concealed knife blades and handles, and assembled them. At this time, Turner asked a guard to give him a roll of tape, later used to tape hostages' mouths shut. The guard handed it to him.

When the inmates came back in at 8:00 p.m., there was a single guard in both the left and right day rooms and one in the control room, each armed only with a stun gun. There were no security cameras in the entire prison at this time. As the inmates came up the stairs, Earl Clanton ducked into the guard's bathroom, locking the door. The other inmates mingled in the right day room, and since there was no headcount, Clanton's absence was not noticed.

At 8:30 p.m., a nurse administering medicine found the bathroom door locked, a development for which the inmates had failed to account. JB quickly explained that the bathroom was out of order. The nurse believed him and went to "B" Pod to get water.

Just before 9:00 p.m., JB asked the control room guard, named Holmes, to retrieve a book from the left side room. Against procedure, the guard left the room, leaving the door open. Briley yelled to Clanton, who rushed into the control room from the bathroom.

Two guards checking on an intentionally plugged toilet in cell #67 were simultaneously taken hostage by Linwood Briley, Peterson, Tuggle, and Turner and forced to strip. Seeing what was happening, Officer Holmes ran back to the control room and had almost wrestled Clanton out, but JB rushed in with a shank and took the guard hostage.

"[Holmes] had [Clanton] pinned against the counter of the control room trying to hold him still," Giarratano recalled of the incident. "And Clanton was just taking blows from the guard, but he was trying to reach around him so he could hit the buttons. And then JB came in, and Clanton managed to hit the button. The doors came open."

Inmates ordered guards to the area on the phone then took them hostage as they arrived, oblivious to what was happening. Inmates, many armed with homemade shanks, overpowered all the guards in both day rooms, stripped them of their uniforms, and tied their hands. They started to tape their mouths, but this became too time-consuming, so they gave up.

In contrast to what Stockton claimed, Tuggle insisted that the group had decided that no one would get hurt in the escape. "Absolutely no one was going to get hurt in this escape," he admitted in his recording. "We had done made our minds up to that. We was not going to let anybody participate in the escape that was going to hurt anyone, and that was an absolute fact. I mean, if we got out, we got out, if we didn't, we didn't, but nobody was going to get hurt on account of it."

Shift commander Hawkings told WRIC News in 2019 that "When I got up to the top of the stairway, I saw an inmate I knew, and he had an officer uniform on. So, as I turned to go back [to] the steps, that's when I met James Briley coming up the steps. He had a shank, put it to my neck, said if I tried anything, he would kill me. I thought my time had come, you know?"

Officer Prince Thomas remembered in that same interview coming face-to-face with Linwood Briley, wielding a lawnmower blade with a rag wrapped around the end of it.

By 10:30 p.m., the inmates held 13 guards and three nurses hostage. "So, we just called them over one at a time," Tuggle said, "and we got everyone on the compound, a whole bunch of them. We took them hostage as we got them in, tied them up, took their clothes from them."

An anonymous inmate later told the *Virginian-Pilot* that nine inmates on the left side of the pod had also been taken hostage when in fact, they were locked in their cells.

A nurse later reported that most of the inmates were smoking marijuana as they locked them in a water closet behind the shower room. Many were repeating the Lord's Prayer.

Turner and Giarratano changed their minds about escaping at this time and elected to stay in the pod. They locked Evans in his cell during the escape for his own safety because the Brileys wanted to kill him.

"Willie Lloyd Turner and Joe G. realized that things would go badly because of the Brileys," recalled Julie McConnell. "I mean, I talked to T[urner] about it a lot, and he was just like, 'People were going to get killed, and I didn't want that to happen.' Like those nurses didn't deserve to be raped or killed. He just decided he and Joe were not going to let that happen. So, they locked them in a cell to protect them, and basically orchestrated the Brileys and them leaving, and they're staying behind and making sure nobody got hurt."

"[Giarratano] didn't think the escape was a good idea, but he couldn't stop them," recalled defense attorney and future VADP Board chair Steve Northup. "I mean, at that point, Joe had come out of the drug and mental illness fog that he was in when he got convicted. And in the first few years of being on death row ... he was beginning to think maybe he could establish his innocence and get himself off of death row, which is what happened. So he didn't want to jeopardize that."

While Willie Evans got most of the credit for no one getting hurt, raped, or killed, many credit Turner and Giarratano.

First, the watch commander was forced at knifepoint to call the first-floor control room, which operated Building 1's entrance gates. He told the first-floor guard, Coraleen Epps, that a replacement was on the way, and she was to report to administration to take a phone call. Her replacement – unknown to her – was Derick Peterson in a guard's uniform. Again, against policy, the control room guard opened the door. She was taken hostage and forced to show how to open the gates before she was locked in a bathroom.

Terrified she was going to be raped or killed or both, Epps claimed in that interview that it was Earl Clanton who vowed to protect her. "He said, 'I'm not going to let anyone come in here and hurt you. You have my word,' and he didn't. He stayed right there in front of the door. I think Earl Clanton saved my life."

A "white-shirt" (a captain) was captured when he arrived at "C" Pod and was ordered with a knife to his throat to help secure a van. Giarratano then made the call. "The guard on the gate that night was a guy named Batillio, a really nice guy. I'm pretending to be a guard. I said, 'listen, we found the bomb on death row.' He's panicking. I said, 'no need to panic. We got it.' We had planted the seed that we had the bomb earlier, so the ATF came looking for it. And they couldn't find anything. So now they get a call. All the guards are convinced we got it."

"We brought the captain up here, told him ... we had to really convince him that he would be seriously hurt if we didn't get out of here," Tuggle explained. "And, of course, he was convinced, and he was scared to death. So, he helped us get out of there. As a matter of fact, we had made a mistake in calling the back guard, and he corrected this real quick. He said, 'Hold up, you can't tell her that,' he said, 'If you tell her that, you won't get out.' So, he made the call himself."

"And Batillio, he's freaking out," Giarratano continued. "He said, 'What do you want us to do?' I said, 'Okay, I need you to open both sally port gates and bring a van in. We're going to carry the bomb out and drive it off the compound.' And nobody's thinking, you don't do that with a bomb. You're going to leave it sitting there and call the bomb squad."

"It was like the Keystone Cops."

The six escapees quickly dressed in riot gear, including full-face helmets, shields, and gas masks found in a nearby storage closet. They grabbed two fire extinguishers, ripped the day room 19-inch RCA television from the table, placed it on a stretcher, and draped a sheet over it. They then ran about 150 yards to a waiting van near the sally port, a double-doored structure designed to isolate vehicles between two gates so the personnel and contents can be checked, just inside the prison's main vehicle entrance. They yelled they had a bomb and to clear the way as they doused the covered television with fire extinguishers.

"I was on the back end of the stretcher, and somebody else was on the front, then we had two people shooting the blankets with the fire extinguisher, like, to give it more realism," Tuggle explained.

Julie McConnell claimed that the television was Turner's idea. "He came up with putting a TV under a blanket and saying it was a bomb."

"What I saw particularly with Turner ... was [a person] who grew up in abject poverty, had very difficult life, made terrible decisions, and took someone's life. There's no making up for that, but they were more than just that one terrible thing they did."

"Turner," she added, "could have been a valuable contributor to society in a different circumstance."

Back upstairs, Turner and Giarratano, in ill-fitting found uniforms, staffed the control room and started releasing hostages. "I'm manning the phones, sick calls, and doors," Giarratano recalled. "Keeping knuckleheads from trying to kill each other, trying to get into cells. You know, because I controlled all the doors, they couldn't get to the guys like Evans if they wanted to kill him. The Brileys intended to kill [Evans] before they left. and they wanted to get Larry Hawkings, the lieutenant, because he was a mean son of a bitch."

Stockton noted that it would have been morning before anyone knew what was happening if they had not done this. Even the inmates on the first floor had no clue what was transpiring right over their heads.

Tuggle recalled that the van sat at the gate, equipped with two-way radios, just as the Captain ordered. "There was the guard standing beside the van, and Derick [Peterson] hollered at him, 'Take off running! Run, we got a bomb!' And boy, just as soon as he said that, the guard took off running. We never did see him no more."

The six inmates hustled across the prison yard with their identities concealed in the darkness and beneath darkened riot helmets. Then, according to Giarratano, they "chunked" the "bomb" into the back of the van.

They ordered the tower guard by radio to open both gates immediately. She hesitated, as it was a policy violation, but relented and opened the gates.

"The funniest thing about it, there'd been rumors that there was going to be an escape," Tuggle narrated on his tape. "So, the administration had placed an extra guard in a truck, back behind the building, outside the fence, where he could view the backside of the building. They thought if any kind of escape came to happen, they'd be coming out the back of the building. They never expected what we did."

"To this day, they still don't know how they made an escape, and nobody got hurt," explained Giarratano. "There was no way they could explain it. If they could have come in and said, 'Yeah, they killed this guard, they killed that one, they raped this one, they did this, they did that. It was a bloody massacre. That's how they got out.' No, they walked whistling dixie out the door."

At 10:47 p.m., an older model prison van containing James and Linwood Briley, Earl Clanton, Derick Peterson, Lem Tuggle, Willie Leroy Jones, $758 in cash taken from the guards, changes of clothing, and hundreds of marijuana joints disappeared into the pitch-dark countryside of southside Virginia.

Fear and Lockdowns

After the escape, they came in and locked us down, tore everything up.

Destroyed the place. Destroyed all of our property, smashed typewriters, TVs, I mean, they just trashed everything. Everything was in a big pile either out on the tier or the pod floor somewhere. And they kept us locked down, and they were dogging us. Didn't want to feed us. We couldn't get to medical, couldn't get out of our cells for showers, all that stuff.

-Joe Giarratano, interview, Jan. 23, 2022.

The search for the escaped death row inmates was dubbed the most expensive manhunt in United States History. People saw the Brileys everywhere – in Virginia, North Carolina, New York, New Jersey, even Canada – and police had to pursue every lead.

Police picked up Earl Clanton and Derick Peterson in a Warrenton Laundromat, enjoying wine and cheese the day after the escape. Their prison-issued shoes gave them away. The others, especially the Briley's, remained far more elusive.

The six escapees made a fundamental mistake in Warrenton that police picked up quickly. After ditching the van in a dark corner in a school parking lot, the men walked for hours in the early morning darkness to find a vehicle with keys. "We found one car that had the keys in it," Tuggle said. "We turned the key ... you know how the dash lights come on when you turn the key? We did that, and the lights came on and we thought we had one. We pushed it out to the road and got in it, and then it wouldn't crank. And so we wound up having to push it right back where we found it."

The men left one of the prison 2-way radios in that car.

The escape, unfortunately, produced collateral damage that never got reported. *Richmond News Leader* journalist Rex Springston recalled that while he and his wife Kathy were in Roanoke Rapids, North Carolina to visit a relative, a news story reported that a man and woman left a loaded gun out. "It was to protect themselves against the Brileys, and their kid [accidentally] shot them. Probably just a young baby was playing with it or something."

"They were like working-class or lower, and the [newspapers] didn't want to touch it."

When news of the escape reached Richmond, the city went into lockdown. Homicide detective and future Richmond Sheriff C.T. Woody Jr. remarked, "Even the thugs went into hiding," fearing the Brileys would return to Richmond and resume the random and perverse mayhem they had inflicted in 1979.

Anyone involved in the Briley trials, including judges, attorneys, and witnesses, received police protection. Police advised Briley gang member Duncan Meekins' family to seek protection or leave town. Everyone locked their doors and windows. Many started carrying concealed weapons. Handbills appeared on utility poles in the Virginia Commonwealth University area, imploring students to limit their nighttime walking and do so in groups.

Before the escape from MCC, Richmond had begun healing from the Briley experiences. But the news on May 31 brought all the pain, heartbreak, and terror roaring back.

"I think what concerned me the most was that I had seen firsthand what they were capable of doing," Woody told the *Richmond Times-Dispatch* in 2009. "I knew their determination to seek revenge. You never forget the smell of death and the smell of blood from what they did,"

The three Briley brothers – Linwood, James, and Anthony – grew up in Richmond's Highland Park neighborhood. In 1978 and '79, they became a notorious gang of sadistic murderers who, along with a 15-year-old named Duncan Meekins, terrorized Richmond for an entire year, violently killing eleven people and possibly as many as twenty. Their victims during that eight-month spree were white, Black, rich, and poor. Richmond Circuit Court Judge James B. Wilkinson called the Briley violence "the vilest rampage of rape, murder, and robbery" he had seen in his 30-year career.

Sensationalized stories of their childhood proliferated – that they raised poisonous snakes and spiders and delighted in dropping mice into the cages. Their divorced father kept his bedroom door padlocked at night for protection against his sons.

Linwood, the oldest, had served a year in reform school at age 16 for shooting to death their 57-year-old neighbor, Orline Christian, in January 1971. The crime almost went undetected – relatives at Christian's viewing noticed a small wound under her arm and alerted the funeral director. A subsequent check revealed she had been shot. When questioned about the murder, Linwood shrugged, commenting that "I heard she had heart problems. She would have died soon anyway."

In 1972 James was convicted of firing at a police officer also at age 16 and served time. He had only been free a few months when he and the others began their crime spree. Anthony was the youngest of the brothers and is not believed to have killed anyone. As of 2021, he was still in prison and reportedly has an upcoming parole hearing.

Duncan Meekins took a plea deal in return for testifying against the Brileys. He received life plus 80 years.

When Detective Leroy Morgan assisted with the interrogation of Linwood Briley in October 1979, he nor anyone else knew that the Brileys were allegedly responsible for killing popular Richmond D.J. Johnny "Johnny G" Gallaher. Gallaher had been kidnapped randomly behind a local nightclub called the Log Cabin. His bullet-ripped body was found Sept. 15, partially submerged in the James River. Morgan and Gallaher had been good friends, and Morgan had taken Gallaher's death personally.

At the interrogation, Morgan noticed a turquoise ring on Linwood's hand. His heart stopped—he recognized it as belonging to Gallaher. He had been with Gallaher when he bought it. That ring led to Linwood's death sentence for Gallaher's murder.

James Briley received two death sentences for the horrifying murders of North Richmond resident Judith Barton, who was five months pregnant, and her five-year-old son, Harvey.

"He put a gun to the head of a 5-year-old child and blew his brains out," Assistant Commonwealth's Attorney Warren Von Schuch told the Richmond Times-Dispatch in 1985.

Neighbors of the Brileys painted a far different picture of the family than prosecutors and the press. They described Linwood, or "Lin," as a thoughtful neighbor who mowed lawns for elderly neighbors and helped his friends fix their cars. They said he spent many hours with his young son and his girlfriend, the child's mother, taking them to the

Virginia State Fair and other family outings.

The Briley trials attracted large crowds to the Richmond courthouse. Prosecutors said one of the reasons for the notoriety was their seemingly random crimes struck fear in every corner of the city, and curiosity drove residents to see justice served in person.

Von Schuch told the April 19, 1985, *Washington Post* that James Briley had been "the more volatile, less predictable" of the two brothers. "What Linwood did, Linwood thought about. James would do whatever occurred to him."

Death penalty abolitionists feared that the Briley cases could set their cause back possibly decades and would only expedite the executions of the other 24 men on death row. "Linwood Briley happens to be one of the worst, but most of the cases on death row are horrible," Chan Kendrick, chair of the Virginia Chapter of the ACLU, told the Aug. 16, 1984 *Washington Post*.

Even the ordinarily outspoken NAACP, fully aware of the racial disparities of Virginia's death penalty, tempered their opinion of the execution of Linwood. "People in Richmond feel that crimes committed by this individual to be so heinous and so vicious and so violent, I just think it has quelled the voices that would speak out," admitted State Director Jack W. Gravely in that same *Post* article. "The crimes reeked of a kind of mentality that we feel the community, especially the Black community, could not condone."

Murder Groupies

Sometimes with high-profile crimes (and escapes), serial killers take on a mythic, almost heroic status, especially when they go to death row. Their deaths at the hands of the state become, to some, a perverse martyrdom. "Because when it comes to serial killers, the myth is what matters," Julie Beck wrote in the Oct. 21, 2014, edition of *The Atlantic*.

The tradition of the mythic killer hearkened back to 1927 when Grayson County native Kelly Harrell recorded for the Victor Talking Machine Company "The Ballad of Henry Clay Beattie." It was a bouncy folk tune about the infamous Richmond socialite wife-killer whose salacious trial had been front-page news for weeks before he was executed on Nov. 24, 1911. Floyd and Claude Allen created similar hero-worship as "political prisoners" after their 1912 courtroom shootout and subsequent executions.

The Briley brothers were no exceptions. Dozens of pornographic Polaroids plastered the inside of Linwood's cell at MCC, mailed to him along with many marriage proposals by women dubbed "murder groupies" and "murder freaks," labels that emerged during the Ted Bundy trials.

Researcher Sheila Isenberg reported in her 2000 book "Women Who Love Men Who Kill" that these women, who hailed from all walks of life but mostly from loveless or abusive backgrounds, seemed to crave the seemingly endless amount of attention the inmate gave them. Also, she claimed for once they appeared to control the relationship.

The 24-hour media attention around the Brileys also spawned the creation of a set of baseball-style bubblegum cards created by Richmond artist and writer F. T. Rea. Rea's idea hatched when he saw a group of kids in the Carytown section of Richmond playing and pretending to be the Brileys.

Rea related in a Nov. 7, 2007, entry in his online blog *Slantblog* that he ran the idea by some friends, then designed the series to parody the international media craze around the breakout rather than as a money-making scheme. "I was trying to use the blackest of humor to try and deglamorize them," Rea told the Aug. 24, 1984 *Washington Post*, "To get people to remember who they really are." Within days, he sold 150 sets and soon made the cards available on a consignment basis in a half-dozen stores.

"Finding myself in a position to goose a story lampooning the overkill presentation of the same press corps that was interviewing me was delicious fun," he admitted of the attention he got from the press.

However, Rea reported that his project began to sour along the way. A woman whose husband was on a crew that cleaned crime scenes confronted him about the conditions at those scenes. After selling about 600 of the 14-card sets, he withdrew the cards and walked away from the project.

"Like it or not," Rea wrote, "I had become a part of what I had been mocking in the first place."

In addition to the cards, two Lynchburg radio station employees composed a song titled "The Ballad of the Briley Brothers," which they played on the air early in the summer of 1984:

> *Now the death row in Mecklenburg ain't the nicest place for sure;*
> *You won't find it in a travelogue or auto club brochure.*
> *The rooms are small, the food ain't great, and the guards are big and burly.*
> *So Lin and James and four more guests checked out a little bit early.*
> *... Well the local folks and the FBI are getting mad at you,*
> *You're never where you're supposed to be, come on, you know it's true ...*

The ACLU's Henry Schwarzschild was not amused. "That kind of stuff strikes me as pretty obscene," he told the *Post*. "Whatever your views on the issue, one can't make fun of it. That seems outrageous human conduct."

David Bruck, at the time a capital defense attorney in South Carolina, told the *Post* that these death penalty novelties sometimes had the ironic effect its advocates least desired – "It inevitably focuses attention and public sympathy on the murderer."

Recapture

> ... The fact is, their so-called-max-security has been a bluff all along. Because of the Virginia General Assembly's budget cuts against the prison system, the cost of all back up systems were out of reach. So it was a bluff that they were ever in place.
>
> -Dennis Stockton's diary.

After the MCC death row escapes, the key to the water closet where the hostages were held disappeared, so inmate Dana Edmonds – who was incredibly strong – bent up the bottom of the steel door so another inmate could slither in and begin removing handcuffs. As the hostages crawled out one by one, they were greeted by Willie Evans, who shook their hands and announced "I'm Wilbert Evans, and I kept people from getting killed!"

The day room was a shambles as the first of many guards rushed to the scene. Stockton recalled laughing at the flailing, stumbling guards pointing fingers amid excuses and recriminations while inmates like Evans extolled their heroism.

Investigations into the escape revealed the startling lack of protocol and the bungled communications between administration, corrections officers, and local law enforcement. MCC's command didn't learn of the escape until 11:15 p.m., over 25 minutes after the stolen van exited the gate and headed south. The inmates were halfway to North Carolina before nearby law enforcement agencies were notified. State Police were not informed of the breakout until after 11:30 p.m., and Gov. Charles Robb did not learn of the escape until 2:00 a.m.

In South Hill, the acting police chief did not receive descriptions of the escaped inmates until 16 hours after the breakout, and he was informed there were five escapees, not six.

With Clanton and Peterson in custody after only one day of freedom, the van discovered nearby, and a blue Ford Ranger pickup truck reported stolen, Warrenton, North Carolina, was sealed off by police over fears that the escapees were still around. Sightings came in from Portsmouth, Norfolk, and various locations in North Carolina.

Virginia State Police, however, believed the four inmates were heading north on I-95, so they focused on contacting the all-night gas stations north of Richmond based on the gas mileage of the stolen vehicle.

Riding in the stolen pickup, the two Brileys, Turner, and Tuggle turned north, almost retracing their route right back by MCC, hidden in plain sight. "We were just a few hundred yards from the prison, and that's something they would have never expected," Tuggle narrated into his recorder. "And we saw all these cars and all these cop cars and everything going up into the prison. We just drove right on through them, kept right on going."

A gas station attendant in Thornburg verified to police that a blue pickup stopped there, containing three Black men in the cab and a heavyset white man seated in the back, facing backward. Tuggle later told reporters that he could not describe the escape route from Warrenton to Philadelphia because he only saw the backs of the road signs.

The Brileys exited the vehicle in Philadelphia, leaving Tuggle and Jones to continue north. In New Jersey, Tuggle claimed they got lost, and he could not get back onto the turnpike. He decided to ask a state police officer for directions in front of a convenience mart. "So, I walked up to the car just as pretty as you please and asked him directions on how to get back on the turnpike, and he told me," he boasted. "And I thanked him and went off on my way. And sure enough, he gave me the right directions, and I got on the turnpike."

As they drove, they listened to news reports of their escape. Tuggle laughed that a guy in Arizona who looked just like him got picked up and interrogated before they let him go.

After selling almost everything in the truck for gas money, including the jack and spare tire, Jones and Tuggle reached Vermont on their way to Canada. Jones got out in the northern part of the state, near the Canadian border. He called his mother, and she persuaded him to surrender, which he did.

After dropping off Jones, Tuggle turned south and made the mistake of robbing a souvenir store clerk at knifepoint. He was arrested on June 8 in the southern corner of Vermont when he wrecked the truck trying to outrun a local sheriff. "I think you'll find I'm wanted pretty bad by the people back in Virginia," he shouted to the deputy who approached him, gun drawn.

The Brileys had also made a mistake by seeking out an uncle of theirs, Johnnie Lee Council, in a North Philadelphia neighborhood called Fairmont. They got jobs as hand-ymen at Dan's Custom Car Factory. A traced phone call led to their arrest on June 19 at 9:00 p.m. as they barbecued chicken over a charcoal fire in an alley. Neighbors had nick-named Linwood "Lucky." James was known as "Slim."

Once the Brileys were arrested, Jay Cochran called the Executive Mansion. When Gov. Robb warily picked up the phone, Cochran told him that the 20-day siege was over – the Brileys were in custody.

MCC, Richmond, and Warrenton breathed a collective sigh of relief.

"Kill the Negro"

> To be honest, up till that time, I had not given the death penalty a lot of thought. I kind of had a vague intellectual opposition to it but it wasn't well thought out by any means. But in that moment, it became crystal clear to me that if the death penalty produces this kind of an outcome in the popu-lace of Virginia, there's something profoundly wrong with the institution. And so, I became an ardent opponent of the death penalty from that day forward.
>
> -Former Virginians for Alternatives to the Death Penalty (VADP) Execu-tive Director Michael Stone, of the 1984 Linwood Briley execution, in a 2021 interview.

Four months after the great escape, on Oct. 12, 1984, Linwood Briley died in the elec-tric chair in the basement of "A" Building at the State Penitentiary in Richmond. His seemingly expedited execution date was not a result of the escape – Virginia set his date before that.

This execution was the one that seemed to galvanize and separate anti-death penalty protestors and those pro-death into two unmistakably defined groups. This execution was the one that highlighted the Jim Crow-style racial antagonism that accompanied the implementation of the death penalty process, especially against a Black man in 1984 Virginia. This execution was the one that finally gave a resounding voice to the anti-death penalty movement in Virginia, jump-starting a nascent, organized abolition movement.

On the night of Linwood's execution, about 100 death penalty abolitionists, including Stone and several others who would later emerge as abolition leaders in Virginia, gathered solemnly on the east side of Belvidere Street to hold a candlelight vigil protesting state-sponsored killing. As they sang "Amazing Grace," another group almost 250 strong – described as a "drunken" lynch mob, more reminiscent of 1904 than 1984 – gathered on the west side of Belvidere Street at the edge of a working-class neighborhood called Oregon Hill, making the execution a street party.

These people waved signs, but there was no peace in their messages. A middle-aged man in a windbreaker and a younger woman beside him held up pieces of cardboard that said, "Kill the Negro" in blocky hand lettering. Another sign read, "Fry Coon Fry." In a swipe to the praying group across the road, one man's sign read, "Those against the death penalty hold Linwood's hand when they throw the switch."

Although no weapons were visible, many carried long sticks. One man tied a heavy rope into a hangman's noose while many in the crowd began chanting "burn n*gger burn," "kill the n*gger," and other grotesquely racist mantras.

Surprisingly, several Black men were in this crowd. "You know he deserves to die," a white man explained to them. The Black men only nodded.

"If you had any doubt whether there were racist aspects of the death penalty, that kind of experience would eliminate it," explained Steve Northup, who was on the abolition side with his wife, Wendy. Both of them were early leaders in Virginia's abolition movement.

Local D.J. and abolition advocate Richard Yates spent most of the evening with fellow abolitionists, offering encouragement and handing out cans of beer from a paper bag. He called those across the road "fascists."

"As a bouncer who has worked Grace Street and beat up so many people, all I have to say is this is fucked," he almost shouted in frustration to *ThroTTle* magazine editor Jeff Lindholm. "Do you think violence does any good, hurting somebody? The anger doesn't help."

At the front of the mob, two men unfurled a six-foot Confederate flag. One of them told Lindholm that they were "supporting the confederate way of earlier times."

"We think justice today is screwed, nobody should get appeals," one of them explained, advocating not just their warped version of white supremacy but monumental ignorance of the criminal justice system. "The Confederate flag was back when we had segregation, not all this integration we have now."

It is important to recall that there was almost none of this same race-baiting protest at the execution of Frank Coppola two years earlier because Coppola, of course, was a white man.

One resident, John Miska, said he wanted to see Briley killed because "he's proven his depredations. He's shown the state's inabilities to keep him locked up. He's the ninth victim of his own crimes."

Prosecutor Warren von Schuch echoed Miska's opinion, justifying the execution by telling the Oct. 14, 1984 *Washington Post* that "Killing was part of Briley's lifestyle. He would have done it again. He showed us that. If his killing prevents further murders, then it's the morally sound position."

Unlike the public frontier justice of the past, there was a distance between the crowd and the event. The secrecy laws instituted by the Virginia legislature in 1879, 1908, and 1976 were working as intended. No one was really sure what was going on in the "A" Basement and when, and that was precisely how the state wanted it.

And since no one could see the execution, rumors coursed through the mob. One man walked among them, claiming that Linwood was dead and that it took 28 seconds. Many claimed that they saw the streetlights surrounding the penitentiary briefly dim, signaling a successful electrocution and starting a bogus rumor that persists today. One elderly Oregon Hill woman told this writer that she turned off all her lights and even unplugged her refrigerator "so more electricity could get to the penitentiary."

Michael Stone had just moved to Richmond to take the position of associate director of the Office of Justice and Peace for the Catholic Diocese of Richmond. One of Bishop Walter Sullivan's issues was prison reform, especially the death penalty.

"A couple of months after I had moved here, there was an execution scheduled," Stone recalled in a 2021 interview. "And Bishop Sullivan encouraged his staff to participate in the execution vigil outside the old penitentiary, less than a mile from the State Capitol."

Stone added that the Briley debacle "was a very visceral experience" and explained that his opposition to the death penalty that emerged on this night was not based on the seriousness of the Brileys' crimes but the behavior of society towards it. "Heinousness in a sense is irrelevant ... the death penalty isn't about what they did; it's about who we are as a people," he said. "And so, no matter how heinous the crime and how horrid the details are, this is not about them. This is about us. What are we going to do about it? And I think dealing death is not the way to deal with the problem of violent crime."

In 2015 Stone was hired as VADP Executive Director, serving until his retirement in September 2021.

Just before 11:00 p.m., several people emerged from the penitentiary and got into a nearby sedan. Many of the pro-death crowd pushed past police and surrounded the car, with some beating on the hood. Officers with German Shepherds pushed them back, warning they would unleash the dogs.

Inside the death chamber, the execution was nerve-wracking for recently-promoted Virginia State chief executioner Jerry Givens, not just because it was his first job but because high-profile executions came with lots of publicity.

Givens, a profoundly religious African-American Baptist, explained that as he shaved Linwood's head for execution, he asked him – as he asked all 62 men he prepared to execute – if he wanted to pray with him. Briley had been baptized in the penitentiary chapel a few days earlier, but he did not respond.

Givens prayed anyway. "I prayed to forgive the condemned man and for God to bless the victim's family. I said a prayer for all people and prayed that things would be better for [the prisoner]."

By law, Linwood arrived at the state penitentiary 15 days before his execution date and was placed in a cell 40 feet from the chamber in an area referred to by corrections officials as "Space E." After a complete physical, the death row team spent two weeks prepping him to die.

"We prepared that man for his last day on earth," Givens explained. "[That] was the key. That process was slow to us, but it was fast to him because he was counting down the days. And on that last day, 99% of them were ready."

Most of them, he said, were exhausted by the stress of losing appeal after appeal and were already "emotionally dead."

Like most defense attorneys and death row chaplains, Givens claimed he never saw Linwood or any of the condemned as the monsters that prosecutors, society, and the press frequently portrayed them. "Maybe it was because he realized this was the last of everything, and he wanted to be on his best behavior. I could not treat him like a monster; I had to treat him like a human being."

Fr. Griffin clearly remembered meeting both Brileys. "They used to come to Mass. They weren't Catholic, and I didn't know whether they liked the Mass or the wine. So, they probably liked the wine."

Griffin added the brothers always seemed "a step away from being there." "Like their mind was somewhere else or something. I'm not a psychologist, but that's what it seemed like to me. Maybe it's because they were famous ... I don't know. They just never seemed grounded to me."

Witnesses reported that Linwood Briley was "very, very calm" as the execution team led him into the chamber. His last words were that he was not guilty.

The guards seated him in the chair, then methodically strapped his legs, arms, and chest. One pulled a mask over his head, covering all but his nose and the top of his head. Another team member put a metal cap containing a sea sponge soaked in brine on his head. The brine was the proper salinity when a fresh egg, provided by the penitentiary kitchen, floated in it. An electrode was screwed on the head cap, and another screwed around his ankle.

Givens pushed a button at the warden's signal that delivered a first, then a second 2,500-volt jolt of electricity. Witnesses noticed the stink of burning flesh, accompanied by a slight wisp of smoke from his ankle, but his death seemed swift. Richmond attorney B. Randolph Wellford told the *Post* that "His fingers ... kind of tightened up almost in a fist, but in a deranged manner."

"I thought I'd probably get a queasy feeling in my stomach," Wellford added, "but I didn't. It didn't bother me at all. I don't think it bothered anybody at all ...."

Briley was declared dead by a prison doctor ironically named Dr. Robert Fry. His body was removed from the chair, frozen in a seated position, and taken to the cool-down room adjacent to the death chamber. A guard stood on Linwood's chest to press his torso flat, while another lowered heavy sandbags onto his chest and joints to crush them straight. Exposed hot skin adhered to the cool steel table and had to be peeled off.

At 11:05 p.m., a barely-heard announcement outside the penitentiary wall stated that

Linwood Briley was dead. The abolitionists blew out their candles and removed tags on their shirts that contained the name of a death row inmate and their victim(s). Meanwhile, middle fingers, drunken shouts, and vile, racist epithets accompanied by the crackle of firecrackers spewed from across the road before the mob dispersed to attend a neighborhood barbecue. "He's gone, brother," one man shouted amongst the bloodlust. "He's gone to hell and got burned."

Wedding Bells

> He says he's innocent, and I'd as soon believe him as racist authorities.
> -Evangeline Grant Redding Briley, shortly after marrying James Briley on
> death row, March 1985.

On March 28, 1985, Ronald Reagan was the U.S. President, Phil Collins' "One More Night" was the top song, and convicted killer James Briley, 28, married Evangeline Grant Redding, 44. They married 20 feet from the electric chair scheduled to take his life less than one month later.

Reporters were not allowed at the ceremony at the State Penitentiary cell, with Briley inside and his new bride standing outside. They held hands through the bars. Present for the double-ring ceremony, officiated by prison chaplain Marjorie Bailey, was a corrections officer and Briley's father, James D. Briley.

Briley Sr. and Redding were both strip-searched before entering the chamber.

"He's a fantastic person," Redding told the *Times-Dispatch* of her new husband. "He's gorgeous, charming, and intelligent. He lights up my life ... imagine a woman my age marrying someone like that."

Redding, a divorced mother of four, was far from being another of the Briley "murder groupies." In 1969, after several years as a social worker for the Halifax County, N.C. School System, she became the first African American in that state to produce and host a television show, "Together with Evangeline," which aired on WNCT-TV in Greenville. In 1971, she became the first woman and the first African American to produce and host a series for North Carolina public television. Her series on school integration, called "Thursday's Child (has far to go)," was an award-winning ten-episode series shown statewide. She and her brother, Gary, also established a media production and publishing company called Evan-Redd Productions, Inc.

An outspoken criminal justice activist, she was also a vocal supporter of the "Wilmington Ten," nine Black men and a woman who were falsely convicted and sentenced to 29 years in prison for arson and conspiracy. After serving ten years, their convictions were overturned, and they were released.

Redding stated that she took an interest in the Brileys in 1979, then began writing to James after Linwood's execution. She told reporters that she had fallen in love with JB in January and married him to "add credibility" to her efforts to get him released from prison. Redding also insisted that all three Brileys were victims of a police conspiracy because they had previous criminal records, and police could easily pin unsolved crimes on them.

"We're going to free this man because he is innocent," she claimed. "He is not going to be executed."

But He Was

James "JB" Briley was executed on April 19, 1985, at 11:07 p.m. for the murder of Judith Barton and her son Harvey. Corrections officials claimed he made no final statement but "just smiled."

Penitentiary chaplain Russ Ford's memory of Briley's execution differs vastly from the sanitized DOC version. "James Briley goes in, sits in the chair, and fights it. And [the electrocution] tore up his body and stunk up the chamber and everything. And that's according to the guards – the death squad members told me how bad it was."

The next day, corrections officials made sure Willie Lloyd Turner got a good look – and a good smell – of a box containing Briley's burned and soiled clothing.

The mother of one of Briley's victims, Shirley Barton Hayes, did not want to see him executed for the murder of her daughter Judy and her grandson. "I don't believe in taking another life," she told *Richmond News Leader* journalist Rex Springston. "I wish James Briley would confess that he did it, so his soul would be right with God."

At around 7:45 a.m. that day, four inmates attempting to delay the execution put pillowcases over their heads and, armed with screwdrivers and clubs, tried to force a guard into a cell. Seventeen maximum security inmates then started a melee in which nine guards and one inmate were injured. Guards quelled the disruption after about 30 minutes.

A report released by a special grand jury blamed the disturbance on "assaultive, anti-social" inmates transferred from MCC "who took advantage of lax regulations at the penitentiary" to launch a riot.

JB's attorney, Gerald Zerkin, recalled the last-minute legal maneuvers on the day of the execution. "We had a hearing in front of Judge D. Dortch Warriner on the day of the execution. And there was all this press amassed outside the federal courthouse. Judge Warriner was a very difficult judge, but he arranged for us to leave the courthouse through a backway with the help of the marshals. We came out on Bank Street instead of Main Street, where the press was waiting for us so that we could leave in peace and go to the penitentiary."

If Bigots Wore Signs

As with Linwood's execution the previous October, an estimated 250 prayerful death penalty opponents gathered on the east side of Belvidere Street, and a similar raucous group of an estimated 350 death penalty supporters gathered on the west side, drunk and shouting racial taunts. Police reported no significant incidents other than a handful of disorderly conduct arrests.

Especially noticeable was a group of whites among the death penalty supporters wearing Nazi armbands, saluting and shouting such supremacist slogans as "white power" and "Sieg Heil." In response, the Sept. 7 *Richmond Times-Dispatch* posed the question, "Were the cheers for the executions of two Black brothers an example of racism in the state that, without safeguards, could poison Virginia's justice system? Or were the demonstrations more a reply to executions of two criminals notorious for one of Richmond's bloodiest crime sprees?"

The drunken racism was the same old story, but the Nazi-inspired white supremacy display was a new and alarming development. Charlottesville capital defense attorney Lloyd Snook saw the display as a symbol of a recently addressed problem, which concluded that racism was widespread in Virginia's criminal justice system. The problem was so pervasive that he asked the Supreme Court of Virginia to rule that Blacks tried for the murders of whites should have the right to quiz potential jurors about personal racial bias.

Snook pointed out correctly that Virginia's history was littered with death sentences disproportionately given to Blacks, especially those who killed whites. He reminded them that 201 of the 236 people executed in Virginia from 1908 to 1962 were Black, and insisted that existing bigotry affected the imposition of the death penalty.

Virginia Attorney General William Broaddus scoffed at the suggestion, replying in a brief that regardless of someone's knowledge of the checkered history of Virginia's capital punishment system, the capital murder laws that took effect in 1977 were "constitutional and fair."

On the contrary, Snook countered. His brief cited a five-state study that proved that a suspect accused of killing a white person was almost five times more likely to receive a death sentence than one who kills a Black. A separate 1984 Virginia ACLU study found that a Black who killed a white had an 8.2 percent chance of receiving a death sentence, while a Black who killed a Black had a 0.6 percent chance of receiving a death sentence.

Snook pointed to the demonstrators outside the penitentiary during the Brileys' executions as further evidence of his contention, proving the absolute need to keep racists off capital juries.

"If bigots wore signs, *voir dire* (questioning) on racial prejudice would be unnecessary," he said.

One of Snook's clients, Willie Lloyd Turner, was sentenced to die for the 1978 murder of W. Jack Smith Jr., the white owner of a jewelry store in downtown Franklin, Virginia. Six months before the murder, Turner had been paroled from prison, where he had fatally stabbed a fellow inmate. Due to negative pre-trial publicity, his trial moved out of Franklin to Northampton County on the Eastern Shore.

During jury selection in Northampton, Snook suggested that Judge James Godwin ask potential jurors whether they would harbor prejudice because Turner was Black and Smith was white. While Judge Godwin refused to do that, he did ask the potential jurors whether there were any reasons they "could not be impartial." The jury convicted him and recommended a death sentence. Judge Godwin affirmed the sentence.

Snook asked the Supreme Court to give Turner a new trial on the grounds that Godwin's refusal to confirm juror bias was unconstitutional. Unbelievably, he won a review,

Attorney General Broaddus replied that Judge Godwin handled the questioning of potential jurors correctly and that no racial bias was apparent. "That race did not infect the jury's deliberations is borne out by the fact that four jurors, including the foreman, were black," Broaddus said.

In 1986 the U.S. Supreme Court, in *Turner v. Murray*, at least acknowledged the unique susceptibility of racial prejudice in capital sentencing. A year later, in *McClesky v. Kemp*, the Court majority ruled that damning statistical evidence was not applicable and that a defendant had to prove individualized racial hostility. This ruling allowed the racially disproportionate imposition of the death penalty to continue with no constitutional checks or balances. This decision dealt a staggering blow to challenging racial discrimination in applying the death penalty.

Joseph O'Dell: Destroy the Evidence

On Feb. 6, 1985, police officers in Virginia Beach arrested Joseph Roger O'Dell for the rape and murder of Helen Schartner, whose body was found in a field adjacent to a bar O'Dell was known to frequent. In 1987, after representing himself, he was convicted and sentenced to death, mainly on blood evidence and the word of a prison snitch.

O'Dell appealed unsuccessfully to the Supreme Court of Virginia, Federal District Court, and even the U.S. Supreme Court. Justice Harry Blackmun wrote he had "serious questions as to whether O'Dell committed the crime" and warned of what a "gross injustice" would result "if an innocent man were sentenced to death."

In a letter to the Virginia Beach Circuit Court, O'Dell petitioned to DNA test an extant sperm sample held by them. The evidence was tested in 1990 but was too small to yield conclusive results. In June 1997, with O'Dell's guilt still seriously questioned, the Circuit Court rejected a petition filed on his behalf to release the evidence for more advanced testing. The Italian government and Pope John Paul II took up his case, asking that his life be spared.

Two months later, the U.S. Supreme Court also rejected his last appeal. With his guilt still doubted, and with his case attracting worldwide attention thanks to the untiring work of his new wife, Lori Urs, O'Dell was executed in July 1997. Urs reportedly married O'Dell before his execution to gain access to the evidence in his case.

Death penalty opponents and Urs, a third-year law student, would not give up as long as the court held that evidence. In late 1997, the Catholic Diocese of Richmond petitioned the Virginia Beach Circuit Court to release the evidence for more testing. The court denied the request, suggesting that since the defendant was dead, the evidence should be destroyed as required by law.

In a 1999 law review article on the DNA Controversy, titled "Truth and Justice or Confuse the Courts?", Urs argued that the courts relied on inaccurate early reports of blood matching and flatly disregarded the importance of subsequent, more advanced testing.

Nothing worked. In March of 2000, the DNA evidence in the O'Dell case stored in a Virginia Beach circuit court file was burned without further testing.

Urs believed the DNA destruction was nothing more than a cover-up. In the March

16, 1997 *Richmond Times-Dispatch*, she said, "It would undermine the public confidence in the application of the death penalty in the state of Virginia if, in fact, the officials admit they made a mistake."

In granting the request to burn the evidence, Circuit Court Judge Edward Hanson Jr. said, "This case has been ruled on and ruled on and ruled on."

O'Dell was buried in a 600-year-old cemetery in Palermo, Sicily.

A Very Arbitrary Manner

> All the evidence suggests that our system would be among the least reliable. We require the prosecution to provide only minimal pretrial discovery to defendants, rarely require a witness list, and never require the disclosure of witness statements. We make it difficult for indigent defendants to obtain experts or even an investigator. In short, Virginia uses trial by ambush, a system designed with convictions, not reliability, in mind.
> -Capital Defense Attorney Gerald Zerkin, in an undated online *Style Weekly* editorial.

By 1984, a disturbing number of Virginia attorneys, especially those with experience, had removed their names from court lists of those willing to defend indigent clients, citing Virginia's lack of a public defender system and reliance on court-appointed attorneys. State Bar President William Dolan told the June 25, 1984 *Washington Post* that the defections had caused a state court crisis that "grows worse by the hour."

As a result, the quality of counsel in capital cases plummeted. "Of the first ten guys who received the death penalty (since 1976), at least 5 of them had lawyers who would later be disbarred," recalled defense attorney Steven Rosenfield. "[There was an] extremely high disbarment rate for lawyers who at one time have done these criminal cases. The obvious conclusion was that judges picked lawyers who would not spend weeks at trial. They would not file endless motions, and only do the bare minimum to get through the process. The money was deplorable. So, they found cronies who would undertake to represent the first dozen, two dozen people who ultimately got death sentences."

Alexandria attorneys George West and James Clark knew the money problem all too well – they were paid $573 each for spending hundreds of hours defending George Alec Robinson in a capital robbery-murder case. Neither of them had been involved in a death penalty case before, and they felt victimized by Virginia's court-appointed lawyer system. Some lawyers were even forced to borrow money to keep the lights on in their offices while slogging through the endless hearings, delays, and changes of venues while dealing with the crushing emotional toll of capital cases.

After getting only 20 minutes of sleep the night before, Clark said the verdict was guilty, but the recommended sentence was four life terms, not death.

West told the *Post*, "I could not afford to do this more than once."

Steven Rosenfield recalled working with Zerkin on his first capital case around 1988. "My first capital involvement was when Gerry, who after Lloyd Snook, became truly the most knowledgeable and most skilled practitioner in Virginia at all phases of capital cases. He asked me to help him with one of the guys who would later be [executed], but I was a minor player. After he got executed, I decided that I needed to get involved as best I could."

Rosenfield recalled his second capital case was defending a 16-year-old Black youth named Russell Tross who had killed a white Harrisonburg storekeeper trying to stop him from shoplifting. "There was a local lawyer who had never done a capital case, and I was asked to co-counsel with him. I didn't have much criminal defense experience, so I did what I thought was conscientious. I contacted people who had a lot of, even early on, capital experience, Gerry being the main one, and got motions from him to file. We brought in experts. In the [Shenandoah] Valley, it was unheard of. We litigated the hell out of that case, and no Black people were on our jury pool."

Like Zerkin, Rosenfield soon got a reputation as a talented, aggressive attorney, filing motions and making judges think and even worry about what would happen on appeal if they didn't grant a motion. He got results – out of nine capital cases that went to trial, eight of the defendants received life sentences, with only three of them going to the jury. One was not guilty by reason of insanity.

"Virginia Executes Retarded Man"

-*New York Times* headline, June 27, 1985.

In May 1978, Morris Odell Mason committed ghastly and horrifying crimes. His spree began with the May 2 murder of 86-year-old Ursula Stevenson in the town of Birdsnest only a month after being paroled on an arson charge. Then, during a described "alcoholic rampage," Mason entered the Northampton County home of 71-year-old Margaret Hand. After ordering her to close the drapes, he beat her with an ax before sodomizing her. Mason then sat her in a chair and reportedly nailed her left wrist to the armrest before tying her up, then set the room on fire. He fled but returned to retrieve an item he feared would identify him.

The next day, Mason set another house on fire, then went to yet another homeplace, where he maimed a 13-year-old girl and sodomized and abducted her 12-year-old sister before setting the girl on fire. The girls survived..

"I am the killer for the Eastern Shore," he boasted after pleading guilty to the rape, arson, and murder of Ms. Hand. "I'm the only killer they ever had around here. I made the Eastern Shore popular." He received a death sentence, plus seven life sentences plus 100 years for his crimes.

Something wasn't right with Mason, and the other death row prisoners at MCC knew it as soon as he arrived there to await his execution. On Dec. 31, 1983, Dennis Stockton wrote in his diary that "Morris Mason can be summed up in one word – CRAZY."

In a letter to Joe Ingle of Mason, Joe Giarratano wrote that "living with him is like living with a hyperactive eight-year-old. He could never sit still, and would never stop talking."

Morris Mason's case would have been yet another example of a Black man executed for killing a white person, but mental illness and intellectual disabilities complicated by substance abuse muddled his situation. Mason had been diagnosed as "mentally retarded" years earlier and had an I.Q. of 66. The state diagnosed him on three separate occasions as a paranoid schizophrenic, and he spent time in Central State Hospital. As a child, he complained of hearing voices ordering him to destroy things, and neighbors described him from an early age as a bomb waiting to go off. Also, his lawyer, Lloyd Snook, stated that just days before his murder spree, Mason vainly begged his parole officer to take him off the streets and put him back in custody because he was sure something terrible would happen. Virginia, however, had no halfway houses, and his pleadings went unheeded.

Other inmates at the penitentiary and at the Bland Farm who knew Mason told Evans Hopkins it was evident that "the man ain't responsible" and that he acted "just like a big baby."

"He couldn't stand to be by hisself [sic]," a penitentiary inmate said. "He would pay dudes with his VA (Veterans Administration) money to keep him company, write letters for him and stuff."

However, the Virginia Attorney General's office clinically countered that Mason had received an "adequate psychiatric evaluation" before sentencing, and subsequent mental health examinations found no mitigating factors to present to the judge.

In a television news interview with Mason taped just after his conviction in 1978, he grinned into the camera. "It don't worry me," he said of his most certain impending execution. "Why should it worry me? I did wrong, right? So I get electrocuted."

Rex Springston recalled a short interview with Mason for the *Richmond News Leader* but regretted the chance he almost had to do a longer one. "[Marie Deans] arranged for me to have a phone interview with Morris Mason, and an editor didn't want me to do the interview. He said, 'the guy is retarded. He can't even express himself.' And that was the story, Virginia was executing a disabled guy."

"Instead, the day of his execution, Mason called me at 10:00 in the morning," Springston continued. "I talked to him, typed up his comments, and put them in the story for that day. It was previewing the execution because it occurred late at night. And those comments were read on NPR and appeared in other news media, so we should've done that fuller, longer interview earlier."

Mason's appeals ran out when the U.S. Supreme Court voted 7-2 not to interfere in the sentencing.

For his last meal before his June 25, 1985 electrocution, Mason ordered two Big Macs, two large fries, two apple pies, two large soft drinks, and two hot fudge sundaes. Executioner Jerry Givens, who was with Mason during his final hours, realized that Mason "had no idea" what was happening to him when he only ate a few bites of the second sundae.

"Guys like that, something is wrong with their mind," Givens said. "He ordered

McDonald's ... and he ate so much he said, 'Givens, I can't eat all this, put it in the freezer for tomorrow.' He was not kidding or being sarcastic; I knew that he wasn't ready."

Of the 62 executions Givens performed for the Commonwealth of Virginia from 1984 to 1999, Mason was the only one who did not seem to grasp his fate.

Before he went to the chair, Mason asked Marie Deans what he should wear to the funeral.

"Burn – Damn you!"

> In the basement below me on this 25th of June, Morris Odell Mason's head and calf are being carefully shaved by men who will, with the same strange care, soon attach to the bare patches of skin the electrodes that will kill him. They give him a shirt and pants that have Velcro fasteners that will not conduct electricity or retain heat and burn the hands of the doctor who will check the silenced heart ...."
>
> -Evans Hopkins, "My life Above Virginia's Electric Chair." *Washington Post*, July 21, 1985.

The execution of Mason at the Virginia State Penitentiary drew the same strictly segregated crowds of death penalty abolitionists and supporters, although the numbers of both dwindled considerably since the execution of James Briley two months earlier. Perhaps Mason was not high-profile enough, or maybe the "imbruting effect" (later called the "brutalizing effect") of executions, first warned by Richmond author W. Asbury Christian in 1912, was creeping into society.

Earlier the previous day, death penalty opponents, led by Dr. Jerome Gorman and his wife Donna, placed two white homemade coffins against the west fences of the state capital to protest not just the execution but the dramatic increases in murder rates following them. "To kill people is not the way of civilized society," Gorman told a UPI reporter. "Extra murders are occurring because of this [state sanctioned] violence."

That night, on the west side of Belvidere Street, the stereotype white rednecks, boozers, and brawlers gathered to cheer the death of yet another Black man. "It's Miller time!" one man shouted. Another held a sign that read, "How does it feel to burn in a chair – burn damn you – Koon!" Inside the penitentiary, the inmates had been on lockdown for days to avoid a repeat of the inmate violence that accompanied the execution of James Briley.

Across Spring Street, about 100 abolition supporters gathered, having marched from an earlier church service. Gorman expressed much bitterness toward the execution of Mason and the recent resurgences of executions in particular.

"It's highly unusual," he angrily told the *Richmond Times-Dispatch*, "executing a guy who is a [moron]." Gorman found out later that evening that Allyn Sielaff, who was the new head of Virginia's DOC, had indicated to a reporter that they were considering moving the electric chair out of the penitentiary to MCC. "They ought to move it to the Capital steps, or Gov. Robb's living room if they like it so much," he responded bitterly.

On the day of Morris' execution, Gov. Robb agreed to meet with eight members of Richmond's clergy. One of those clergy members, Fr. James Griffin, recalled that conversation:

"Gov. Rob says, 'Well, I'm a Christian man too, and I hate what I have to do, but I'm also the governor of Virginia, and I have to carry out the laws of the State of Virginia. I don't think any of you would like to make that decision tonight.' I said, 'Well, I would. I'll make the decision.' He said, 'No, you know what I mean, Father.' And I said, 'Well, yes, I do. I know what you mean, but I disagree. Is there any way you can let justice and mercy reside in the same place?' And he said, 'Well, I think I'm going to have to go through with the execution tonight.'"

According to a July 3, 1985 letter written to the *Richmond Times-Dispatch* by Griffin, Robb concluded the meeting by telling the group, "You all are making a difficult situation more difficult."

"No, Mr. Robb," Griffin countered in a post-execution missive, "we are presenting to you an opportunity to show your rightfully tough stance on crime, act justly, and spare the life of a mentally retarded man. We were seeking to make a difficult decision easier. Gov. Robb, [an] opportunity to be for life, show good faith to the remaining men on death row, and act courageously sat right in your lap. You missed that opportunity."

Mason had no chance of a commutation with Gov. Robb. The recent public pummeling Robb had endured over the Mecklenburg escape, coupled with the prisons' crumbling infrastructure and the never-ending court cases alleging sadistic and incompetent behavior by corrections guards, leaders, and administrators, made him fear he would be painted as soft on crime. On the national political stage, where Robb had his eye, that was a fate worse than death.

In Mason's case, the U.S. Supreme Court may have reprieved him under a ruling that stated that a defendant with psychological disorders had the right to an examination by an independent psychiatrist in their defense. Mason, however, pleaded guilty, losing that opportunity.

After Mason's electrocution, corrections officials had to let his body sit for about 30 minutes before taking him to the cool-down room and cracking his fused joints straight again. Exhaust fans hummed as guards smeared Vicks ointment under their nostrils to blunt the odor of seared flesh.

The state vigorously pursuing the execution of a "mentally retarded" man had a chilling effect on the inmates on the row. Fr. Griffin wrote a letter to incoming MCC Warden Toni Bair stating he was "genuinely concerned about the remaining men on death row in Mecklenburg."

"I felt the men are taking the attitude that 'if Morris' case didn't get commuted to life in prison with no parole, then none of us has a chance,'" he wrote, concluding with "... I do fear trouble."

"You Have to Forgive Them."

After the electrocution of Morris Mason, there were four more executions in the

1980s. They were Michael Smith (Black), executed for rape and murder, July 31, 1986; Richard L. Whitley (white), executed for rape and murder, July 6, 1987; Earl Clanton Jr. (Black), executed for robbery and murder, April 14, 1988; and Alton Waye (Black), executed for the murder, Aug. 30, 1989.

Men on death row have only each other for companionship, so as awkward as it seems to an outsider, cloistered friendships emerged, with each having the surreal understanding that the friendship was temporary. In an essay in Michael Radelet's 1989 book "Facing the Death Penalty" titled "The Pains of life," Joe Giarratano recollected his last phone conversation with his row friend Michael Smith just before his execution. Smith was the inmate who informed guards at MCC in 1981 that female visitors were attempting to pass a gun and weed to James Briley and Earl Clanton. Based on that act, Smith's attorney, Lloyd Snook, unsuccessfully appealed to Gov. Gerald Baliles to commute his sentence to life in prison. Baliles did delay the execution for about 40 minutes while attorneys carried a request for a stay to the U.S. Supreme Court but ultimately let it proceed.

In his final conversation with Smith, Giarratano wrote:

> Other than quick hellos, our conversation consisted of a few scattered questions tied together with long silences. I could feel the tears leaking from my eyes as the hopelessness overwhelmed me. I wanted to tell Mike to fight the guards until the last second – to take some of them down with him – but all I could say was, "I love you, my friend. I'm sorry I can't stop this." Mike's reply still rings in my ear: "I'll be fine Joe, you know that I'm going home. Please don't do anything you might regret later.
> You have to forgive them."

Smith received a death sentence for the 1977 rape and murder of 35-year-old Audrey Jean Weiler of York County. The night Smith was executed, he requested that he be able to hold his Bible in his lap. The attorney general's office denied the request for the fear the Bible would burst into flames.

They may have worried less about the lapse in protocol and more of the symbolism of an execution causing a Bible to explode in flames.

"Michael was so scared. He was in terror that night," recalled Russ Ford. "The most terror I've ever seen in any of the men that I worked with, Michael experienced. And what if it did burn the Bible? What did it matter? But I wasn't surprised when they denied it."

Michael Smith's appellate lawyer was a University of Virginia-educated attorney named Richard Bonnie. The first thing Bonnie did for his first capital defendant was file a brief on behalf of the UVA Law School's Post-Conviction Assistance Project challenging the constitutionality of Virginia's "aggravating circumstances" statute. He also urged the court to more specifically interpret the statute's vagueness. In addition, he argued that the psychiatric testimony that the prosecutors had introduced violated Smith's Fifth Amendment right against self-incrimination. The Supreme Court of Virginia threw out this argument for the simple reason Smith's original attorney, in defiance of Bonnie's suggestion, failed to raise it on appeal.

"This 'freakishness' of the legal process is one of the factors that ultimately doomed the death penalty," Bonnie explained in the April 4, 2021 University of Virginia Law School News. "Should whether or not a defendant is executed turn on an attorney's un-intended failure to raise a meritorious claim on appeal – even though he raised it at trial and even though an amicus party brought it to the attention of the state Supreme Court?"

Bonnie's work in the early 1980s provided casebook information on death penalty laws and processes that were still being established. His research helped establish a unique law and psychiatry program in the Schools of Law and Medicine, which included forensic evaluations of capital defendants under the Forensic Psychiatry Clinic.

You Got a Gun Right Behind You

"I was appalled at what was going on," Toni Bair, deputy warden at the Utah State Prison in Salt Lake City, told the *Washington Post* in January 1985 when he became the new warden at the troubled MCC. His appointment was part of an administrative shakeup following the notorious death row escape. "The filth, the disruption, the disor-der, the ranting and raving, the inmates treated like caged animals."

"I want to get rid of the mystique that Mecklenburg is such an infamous place," he continued. "I want it to go from being the worst prison in the nation to the best."

Sweeping changes occurred – and according to Bair, new controls and protocols pre-vented a repeat of the 1984 escape. At 11:00 a.m. on Nov. 28, 1985, Officer William S. Reese picked up the phone in the C Pod control room and heard someone (later revealed as Joe Giarratano) say, "Reese, you got a gun right behind you. You do what you're told, and you won't get hurt, and if you don't believe it, just turn around and look."

Reese told the *Richmond Times-Dispatch* he turned and saw what he said looked like a "cannon barrel" pointed at him.

It was a cardboard fake. But what was not fake was the homemade bomb Willie Lloyd Turner had made from a table leg and match heads. It suddenly detonated, cracking the control room glass.

In the ensuing commotion, inmates wielding chair legs and homemade knives at-tacked, trying to break out the glass windows in the control room as Reese sent out an SOS on the prison phone system. Twenty armed guards arrived and quickly quelled the disturbance.

"It looks like our procedures worked, and nothing needs changing," Bair told the *Times-Dispatch*.

Joe Giarratano was later honest, if cautious, in describing his role and intent in a letter to Bishop Sullivan:

> Bishop, is it wrong for me to try and escape those who wish to murder me or assist those others who are awaiting death in the state's chair? ...When we saw that our ruse wouldn't work, we surrendered peacefully rather than

hurt anyone; and our surrender came long before the show of "deadly force." We did have some real weapons in our possession, but they were only for effect to give the guard a legitimate excuse for his superiors. We never had any intention of ever using them to harm anyone.

A Professional Death Squad

Almost a year after James Briley's execution, his widow, Evangeline Grant Briley, showed up in Richmond and called for a human chain around the entire six-acre penitentiary property on April 18 to protest capital punishment.

Dressed in a black cape and a gold turban, she threatened to set fire to the American flag she carried, calling it "a symbol of slavery and war and aggression."

She told reporters that she still communicated with her late husband. "He and I do communicate, but it's not talking like you and I," she told Jim Mason at the *Richmond Times-Dispatch*. "But we do have a spiritual communication with each other, I at his gravesite and he at my home ... He urges me on. Whenever I'm discouraged is when I feel his presence, and he gives me signals."

Accompanying this spiritual admission was a more pragmatic eight-page anti-death penalty essay. In it, Briley argued that the death penalty served as no deterrent to murderers and that, in its current form, was wielded as an instrument of genocide against "the black race."

Briley's "ring around the prison" protest did not materialize.

Befriended then Banned

So, their thoughts about the two things that I did were, "You've got contraband unauthorized from a music store, and you laundered money." And so, basically, they said, "You're getting too close to the inmates, and they're using you. And for your own good, we're going to ask you not to come to the death row anymore."

- Father James Griffin, on his 1987 ban from ministering to death row prisoners at MCC, in a 2021 interview.

Starting in late 1984, Fr. Griffin and a former Sisters of Charity nun, Marcelline Niemann, became familiar and trusted fixtures to the death row inmates at MCC.

"At the time, I worked at St. Mary's Richmond as a priest, where [Marcelline and I] got to know each other," recalled Griffin. "It was, at the time, surprisingly open for visitors on death row. I couldn't believe they let us bring pepperoni, cheese, Ritz crackers, and stuff like that. And then we would have Mass, and they let us bring wine. And anyone could go to Mass. You didn't have to be Catholic, technically. Whether they go to communion, that's up to them, but they were surprisingly open to our ministry on death row."

But these ideal conditions abruptly changed for Griffin when one day in early 1987, an inmate asked him to transfer $70 from his account to Lem Tuggle's account to supposedly pay a gambling debt. Even though the money cleared with no problems, Griffin was called on the carpet by assistant warden David Smith, who reminded him that such transfers were forbidden because it "encourages gambling and extortion."

A few weeks later, Giarratano asked Griffin to go to B. Dalton Bookstore and purchase a Janis Joplin tape. Griffin bought the tape and then mailed it to Giarratano from St. Catherine's Church in Clarksville.

At his next visit to the row, Smith again called him into his office, where he threw the cassette on his desk before announcing, "Father Jim, you are no longer welcome here. The inmates are just using you." Griffin asked what his options were. Smith answered, "None" before ordering him to turn in his ID badge.

On April 6, 1987, a stunned Griffin wrote in a letter to the inmates on the row that because he had been banned from MCC, he was regretfully stepping down from the Virginia Coalition on Jails and Prisons and would no longer be seeing them.

These events triggered a sudden and somewhat strange series of circumstances from the MCC administration. They abruptly transferred Willie Lloyd Turner to Powhatan Correctional Center's maximum-security building, followed by a massive shakedown on death row that lasted over three days.

Officers stripped all of the death row cells of every item. Inmates' personal articles, legal papers, and attorney correspondence were removed and examined outside of their presence in blatant violation of specific federal court orders. These papers were returned, some overnight, with pages missing or destroyed. Televisions, radios, typewriters, and stamps were destroyed or rendered useless.

The entire incident made no sense to Bishop Sullivan, Deans, or especially to Griffin, as he had gone through the proper channels to procure the tape. Giarratano even showed now-regional administrative warden Toni Bair the pre-approval form, signed by Lt. Jones, who admitted doing so.

A Death Row Suicide ... or a Murder

Fr. Griffin noted that just after MCC banned him from death row, he received a heartfelt letter from death row inmate John LeVasseur, who claimed that Griffin was "forsaking" him by leaving, claiming that "I don't know if I can go on."

Then, on April 20, 1987, guards found LeVasseur dead, hanging from a strip of bedsheet in the shower at the end of the upper-level death row cells. Warden Charles Thompson claimed an investigation indicated LeVasseur hanged himself.

It seemed to be the first death row suicide since "Cocky" Joe Robinson in 1954.

"I heard going to death row that might not have been what happened," Griffin recalled of the incident. "There might've been someone else involved, but I don't know who. But I remember Bishop Sullivan writing me a letter saying, 'Do you think your being banned from death row had anything to do with his suicide?' Then his mother wrote me a letter saying, 'Thank you for ministering, etc etc.' So, if he committed suicide, it makes me sad. If he didn't commit suicide, then they got it all wrong."

Marie Deans also suspected foul play. In a May 5 letter to coalition members, she wrote, "On April 20, John LeVasseur was found dead in the shower. The administration report about how John was found and what had been going on at the time was inaccurate."

Maybe, as Deans and Fr. Griffin suggested, they absolutely got it wrong. "I'm probably the only one that knows this," Giarratano confided. "Joe Payne knew as well. Lem Tuggle killed John LeVasseur."

He described how he was on the phone in his cell talking to Deans when Payne approached and asked, "Man, who are you talking to?"

"I said, 'I'm talking to Marie." [Payne] said, 'Can you get off the phone? I need you to come down here.' So I get out. I go out in the pod and walk down to Tuggle's cell. And LeVasseur is laying on the floor dead."

Giarratano claimed that apparently, Tuggle tried to punk out LeVasseur to someone, and LeVasseur punched him in the face. "I don't think Tuggle meant to kill him. He actually sat on him. He was trying to hold him down. And didn't realize ... he was so fucking big. He sat on his head. And John suffocated. He was foaming at the mouth. He was dead."

Payne and Tuggle then carried LeVasseur's body to the shower. They tied a sheet to the showerhead, then sat him down on the floor, lifted him with his feet outstretched, then put the noose around his neck, where they left him. They closed the curtain.

"Nobody said anything," Giarratano said. "The guard came around to make rounds, and he went down and moved the shower curtain and saw him."

"And the crazy thing was, they moved the body, but they left his glasses. John's glasses were still laying on the floor in [Tuggle's] cell. The guards didn't see it."

Asking for a Riot

In an April 27, 1987 letter to Bishop Sullivan, Deans claimed she feared that the bogus reasons used to ban Fr. Griffin from MCC would lead them to ban all Catholic clergy and lay ministries from Virginia prisons. "They consider your ministers arrogant, uncooperative, and unprofessional (high praise in my book) because they insist on treating prisoners as human beings."

Bishop Sullivan told the May 5 *Richmond Times-Dispatch* that "[Griffin's] forced resignation from Mecklenburg is another dehumanization of inmates and a further denial of their opportunity to practice their faith."

Griffin knew he had rubbed corrections officials the wrong way in the past, handing out crucifixes or writing paper, but that these actions, according to him, were all part of being a Priest. He saw nothing improper or unlawful in what he had done, yet he found himself a pariah with DOC, unable to return and minister to the men who needed him so much.

While Deans worried in a letter to coalition members that these actions were "asking for a riot," eleven of the inmates on the row elected on midnight, May 1, to protest differently – by going on a hunger strike.

According to a statement from the inmates, the strike was intended as a peaceful protest against MCC policies that included barring Fr. Griffin, along with several complaints concerning confiscated legal papers and routinely ignored inmate grievance procedures. Lem Tuggle and Derick Peterson, two of the six death row inmates who escaped and later recaptured, were among the strikers.

The inmates ended the hunger strike 4-1/2-days later when Warden Thompson promised that he would investigate their complaints.

It Will be More Comfortable for Everybody

On June 1, 1987, the DOC finally installed central air conditioning in the death chamber at the State Penitentiary. A noisy, dripping window unit failed to make the sweltering basement even remotely comfortable when electrocutions occurred.

"It's like an oven down there," Gerald Zerkin told the *Richmond Times-Dispatch* of the conditions in the airless, windowless "A" basement chamber. "It's a godforsaken place."

"It's just a matter of having it ready when we need to use it," penitentiary operations officer Dwight Perry said in the same story. "It will be more comfortable for everybody."

The condemned inmate most likely disagreed.

During the July 6, 1987 execution of Richard Lee Whitley for the rape and murder of 63-year-old Phebe Parsons of Fairfax County, witnesses requested that the newly installed air-conditioning be turned off moments before the execution. They claimed the blower would have prevented them from hearing any last words.

Whitley had no last words.

Germany Can Go to Hell: the Jens Soering Incident

A large swath of Virginia saw these [defense attorneys] as probably pinko communist do-gooder bleeding hearts, but they were performing a public service. Everybody deserves a defense, right?

-Retired *Richmond News Leader* journalist Rex Springston, in a 2021 interview.

In 1989, Virginia's inhuman prison conditions and liberal use of the death penalty caught the eyes of the 19 judges of the European Court of Human Rights. Four years earlier, in 1985, University of Virginia Echols Scholar Jens Soering (also spelled Söring), a wealthy West German citizen, was charged with the vicious murder of a Bedford County couple, Derek and Nancy Haysom. They were the parents of Soering's girlfriend, Elizabeth Haysom, a UVA honors student.

After the double-murder, Soering and Haysom fled to Britain, where they were later arrested and detained after writing fraudulent checks. During interrogation by police, Soering confessed to the murders, later claiming that he believed he had diplomatic immunity and could shield Haysom from prosecution. Haysom was extradited to Bedford County, where she was convicted of being an accessory to murder and sentenced to 90 years in prison.

While in Britain, the European Court refused to extradite Soering to Virginia, ruling unanimously in a landmark decision that if Soering were found guilty of capital murder in Virginia, he would "suffer inhuman and degrading treatment or punishment," including the death penalty, which Britain had abolished.

Adrian Butler, a spokesman for the court, told the July 8, 1989 *Richmond Times-Dispatch* that it was not just Virginia's death penalty that was a human rights concern, but the treatment Soering could receive while in prison, both from fellow inmates and corrections officials. "The court took the view that the extradition would be a breach of the human rights convention ... the court was very clear. It was a clear ruling to the British government not to extradite."

The court summary stated that "decision by a contracting state to extradite a fugitive may give rise to issue under article 3 where substantial grounds shown for believing that person concerned faces real risk of being subjected to torture or to inhuman or degrading treatment or punishment in the requesting country."

Butler said that he expected Soering to be extradited and tried in West Germany, where he would face a maximum sentence of 10 to 15 years in prison.

Many in Virginia did not know at the time that at the request of Soering's lawyers, Joe Giarratano had submitted an affidavit to the European Court of Human Rights graphically describing the violent and chaotic conditions of MCC's death row. Many of the court's summaries were Giarratano's descriptions almost word-for-word.

The court's decision provoked a 30-minute tirade by Bedford County commonwealth's attorney James Updike Jr. in front of the county courthouse. "It is without question outrageous, lacking in any sound legal basis and lacking any logic," he hyperbolically howled, acting as judge, jury, and executioner. "This is one of the most ridiculous decisions recorded by a tribunal in the history of mankind. They may very well turn him loose."

European Court President Judge Rolf Ryssdal told the Associated Press that sending Soering to be tried in his home country "would remove the danger of a fugitive criminal going unpunished as well as the risk of intense and protracted suffering on death row."

When asked if he would assist the West Germans in prosecuting Soering, Updike said he may change his mind, "but right now, Germany can go to hell."

Ultimately, Soering was not extradited to Germany but back to Virginia, where prosecutors had to promise not to seek the death penalty. He pleaded not guilty, but his case stumbled because of his recanted confession and inadequate counsel against a raging prosecutor hell-bent on a conviction. Soering was found guilty and sentenced to 90 years in prison in a problem-plagued, farcical trial that threw genuine doubt on his guilt.

"[Haysom] was the brains behind the operation," recalled Rex Springston, who covered the trial for the *Richmond News Leader*. "He was infatuated with her ... I saw her on that show 'Virginia Current' several years ago, and they weren't using names, but I said, 'That's Elizabeth Haysom.' They just said Elizabeth, ... But it was a fascinating trial."

In the following years, Soering's original lawyer was disbarred and admitted he had a mental impairment during the trial. Then in 2009, 42 existing pieces of evidence from the Haysom crime scene were DNA tested. Of those, 31 were too degraded to produce a conclusive result, but the 11 good samples excluded Soering and Elizabeth Haysom. Also, in 2009, Gov. Tim Kaine approved Soering's transfer to a German prison, where he would have served about two more years. Facing a "soft on crime" uproar, Kaine's successor, Robert McDonnell, rejected the approval.

In 2016, investigator Chuck Reid admitted long-standing doubts of Soering's guilt. In 2017, Albemarle County Sheriff J. E Harding released a report at a press conference urging Gov. Terry McAuliffe to release Soering after three forensic scientists agreed that blood found at the crime scene did not match Soering's. Also, in 2017, Soering's new attorney, Steven Rosenfield, announced that the University of Richmond's Institute for Actual Innocence supported Soering's pardon petition based on DNA evidence that excluded him.

Rosenfield is convinced Soering was innocent.

In November 2019, the Virginia Parole Board recommended to Gov. Ralph Northam that both Haysom and Soering – both model prisoners – be released into U.S. Immigration and Customs Enforcement custody for deportation to their home countries of Canada and Germany. Under the terms of the deportation, they may not return to the United States.

The Penitentiary's Final Gasps

Earl "Goldie" Clanton, one of the original death row escapees from MCC and who was originally the first scheduled execution since the reimposition of the death penalty, had another execution date set for March 17, 1988. However, a judge decided that Virginia should not execute a man on St. Patrick's Day.

Instead, Clanton was electrocuted at the State Penitentiary on April 14, the Feast Day of St. Lidwina of Schiedam, who the Catholic Church calls "a prodigy of human suffering and heroic patience." That day was also Yom HaShoah or Holocaust Remembrance Day. Dr. Jerome Gorman, speaking on behalf of a small band of volunteers called People Against the Death Penalty, acridly noted that the state was not okay with executing a man on a holiday that people celebrated by drinking profuse amounts of green beer, but Holocaust Remembrance Day was perfectly acceptable.

Clanton had been condemned to death for a November 1980 murder. He was one week away from execution in August of 1982 (after a truncated two-year appellate process) when he received a stay of execution from a state judge.

Citing incompetent counsel, Judge Robert R. Merhige Jr. voided Clanton's death sentence in July 1986. According to Merhige, the attorney should have brought out Clanton's history of childhood abuse. When the Fourth U.S. Circuit Court of Appeals reversed Merhige's decision, Clanton's date was set for March 17, 1988. But in early February, his date was changed again to April 14.

While Clanton was living in legal limbo at the penitentiary, Jay North, the former child actor and star of the 1960s television show "Dennis the Menace" interviewed Clanton while researching the MCC escape for a possible movie. He delayed the project when

Clanton's death sentence was reinstated. Although North worked briefly with Deans and the SCJP, the project ultimately went nowhere.

"The constant thought of death is like your angel," Clanton told journalist Ben Cleary in a March 15, 1988 *Style Weekly* interview conducted in the MCC visiting room. "He or she professes to be a good angel – and tries to lure you into suicidal thoughts. 'Why don't you just kill yourself and get it over with? Take the pleasure away from them.'"

Alton Waye was the final inmate put to death by Virginia before the dawn of 1990. A 34-year-old army veteran, Waye was convicted of the 1977 brutal rape and murder of 61-year-old Lavergne Marshall in Lunenburg County.

According to trial testimony, shortly after the killing, a man identifying himself as Alton Waye called the police to tell them he had killed a woman and then turned himself in. Police later claimed he would not have been a suspect because nothing linked him to the Marshall murder. His lawyer, Lloyd Snook, argued that brain damage, borderline mental disabilities, alcoholism, and drug use threw real doubt on his confession. The June 27, 1994 *Virginian-Pilot* reported that they had discovered suppressed evidence that dismantled the prosecution, including solid evidence that Waye's cousin, Len Gooden, was also inside the house during the murder.

Nonetheless, it took the jury ten minutes to reach a guilty verdict.

"I think by the time it got to the jury, they were so mad at Alton Waye because they saw the bloody photographs that they wanted to put him away," said Snook. "For whatever it's worth, you had a young Black man accused of raping and killing an elderly white woman."

Outside the penitentiary and across Belvidere Street, only a handful of death penalty supporters shouted and carried signs – a far cry from the hate-filled mobs inspired by the executions of the Briley brothers just a few years earlier. Holding aloft a sign that read "Fry the Murderer," Mary Jones told a UPI reporter, "I feel sorry for his mother because you can't help what your children do."

Simultaneously across the street, several dozen death penalty abolitionists held yet another candlelight vigil. Henry Gerrard Sr., director of the Virginia Association to Abolish the Death Penalty (VAADP), said this was "a sad day for the commonwealth."

For unknown reasons, the State Penitentiary documented the 1987 execution of Richard Whitley, the 1989 execution of Alton Waye, and the 1990 executions of Richard Boggs and Wilbert Evans on audio cassette. They are reportedly real-time narrations by an anonymous corrections official as the executions occur. They are stored at the Library of Virginia and have 50-year privacy restrictions.

Two Convictions by DNA, Two Very Different Outcomes

On Jan. 22, 1988, in Great Britain, Colin Pitchfork was the first person anywhere to be convicted of a violent crime by DNA evidence. He was sentenced to life in prison, with a minimum of 30 years to serve, for the rapes and murders of two 15-year-old girls, Lynda Mann and Dawn Ashworth, in neighboring Leicestershire towns almost three years apart.

Alec Jeffries, Peter Gill, and David Werrett developed the DNA extraction techniques which compared semen samples taken from the bodies of both girls with blood from an initial suspect, Richard Buckland, which conclusively ruled him out.

Pitchfork was picked up and questioned after an overheard conversation in a bakery. He eventually pleaded guilty to the attacks.

In Virginia, similar crimes were unfolding, which like Pitchfork, led to a conviction based on DNA and coincidentally also cleared the name of an innocent person.

Timothy Spencer, who became known as the southside strangler, committed three rapes and murders in Richmond and one in Arlington in the fall of 1987. He is believed to have committed at least one other murder in 1984, that of Carol Hamm.

At the time, Spencer had been released after a three-year prison sentence for burglary and lived in a Richmond halfway house when he raped and killed all five of his victims. He committed the murders on the weekends after signing out of the facility.

The attacks were vicious. Debbie D. Davis, a 35-year-old account executive with *Style Weekly* magazine, was murdered in her South Richmond apartment on Sept. 18, 1987. She had been strangled with a sock around her neck tightened with a short length of vacuum cleaner pipe. Her cause of death was ligature strangulation.

Dr. Susan Hellams, a neurosurgery resident at the Medical College of Virginia (now VCU Health) in Richmond, was murdered in her home the night of Oct. 2, 1987. Her husband discovered her partially clothed body on the floor of their bedroom closet. Like Davis, the cause of Hellams' death was ligature strangulation, caused by two belts tied around her neck.

On Nov. 22, 1987, 15-year-old Diane Cho was found in her family's Chesterfield County apartment. She, too, was raped and strangled in a situation similar to the Davis and Hellams murders.

Finally, Susan Tucker, age 44, was raped and murdered in her condominium in Arlington, Virginia, around Nov. 27, 1987. Her body was not discovered until Dec. 1.

Arlington police arrested Spencer on Jan. 20, 1988, for the rape and murder of Tucker when they established he had traveled from Richmond to spend Thanksgiving with his mother, who lived only about a mile from the victim. After being charged with the Richmond murders, he was tried in Arlington first on July 11 and found guilty.

Lifecodes Corp. performed the DNA tests in the Spencer case. Their specialists testified that the DNA pattern found in Spencer's blood was identical to that found in semen at the attack scene. They also affirmed that the odds against such a match in Black North Americans was one in 705 million.

"There is no mistake. There is no room for error," stated Jack Driscoll, an assistant commonwealth's attorney.

Criminal justice consultant Lee Lofland was one of the witnesses to Spencer's April 27, 1994 execution. "After glancing around the brightly lit surroundings, Spencer took a seat in the oak chair and calmly allowed the death squad to carry out their business of fastening straps, belts, and electrodes," he wrote in an April 2020 entry in his online blog "The Graveyard Shift." "As they secured his arms and legs tightly to the oak chair, he looked on, seemingly uninterested in what they were doing."

Lofland recalled sitting directly in front of Spencer, separated only by a partial glass wall. "His gaze met mine, and that's where his focus remained for the next minute or so. Not even a remote sign of sadness, regret, or fear. Either he was brave, heavily sedated, or stark-raving mad."

Lofland recalled that after the execution, an eerie calm filled the chamber. "The woman beside me cried softly. I realized that I'd been holding my breath and exhaled slowly. No one moved for five long minutes. I later learned that this wait time was to allow the body to cool down. The hot flesh would have burned anyone who touched it."

Early VAADP director Julie McConnell recalled meeting Spencer's mother, Thelma Spencer, while her son was still on death row. "One of the first meetings I had in Northern Virginia, [Spencer's mother] came. She was just a sad, tired, hard-working woman. And she just looked so broken. I'm sure just living the rest of her life with everyone knowing that her son was the notorious Timothy Spencer must have been horrific."

"She just ... she seemed devastated."

In 2018, journalist, former *Style Weekly* contributor, and *Virginia Business* Editor Richard Foster created the "Southside Strangler" book and podcast. "*Style* [*Weekly*] wanted to partner with me on a true-crime podcast, and we all realized very quickly that it was the 30th anniversary of the southside strangler case, and of course, Style had a strong connection to that. Debbie was friends with a lot of the people I knew there," Foster explained in an Aug. 31, 2021 email. "Many of Debbie's coworkers were still there when I worked there. In fact, one of them still is a coworker of mine today."

While the conviction of Colin Pitchfork in Britain exonerated Richard Buckland, the conviction of Timothy Spencer in Virginia also acquitted David Vasquez. Vasquez was an intellectually disabled young man who had confessed and pleaded guilty in early 1985 for the murder of Carol Hamm after police recorded themselves spoon-feeding him details of the crime. While the standard of the DNA evidence was inconclusive, the FBI concluded that Spencer, not Vasquez, most likely was responsible for the Hamm murder.

The wrongfully convicted Vasquez was granted an unconditional pardon on Jan. 4, 1989, after serving five years of a 35-year prison sentence.

The Prison Lawyer and the Expendable Man

Being on death row saved my life.

-Joe Giarratano.

Joseph M. Giarratano Jr. may not know if he was born in 1957 or 1958, but he does know he was raised in a harsh, loveless environment. In New York, then Florida, his father was out of his life while shuttling in and out of prisons. His mother was physically and psychologically abusive and brought known drug traffickers into the house. His stepfather, his first trusted male role model, betrayed that trust by sexually abusing him from age seven to 12.

Giarratano continually ran away to escape his abusive home, only to be picked up by law enforcement and social services and returned. Since running was impossible, around age 11, he began self-medicating with drugs and alcohol. He dropped out of school in the ninth grade and, as a young teenager, attempted suicide many times.

When he was about seventeen, he was convicted of auto theft and sent to the Florida Department of Corrections. Inside the prison, he ran into his father for the first time since he was a child.

By age 21, Giarratano's drug and alcohol abuse had permanently damaged his liver. "The first blood test they did in prison, they said I had the liver of a 73-year-old man," he said in a 2021 interview.

Murders in Norfolk

During the summer of 1978, Giarratano and two others arrived in Norfolk to work on scallop boats. It certainly was not a rehabilitative environment, as his fellow watermen were a rough crowd who, like him, were heavy abusers of drugs and alcohol.

One of Giarratano's co-workers introduced him to Barbara "Toni" Kline, who lived in a duplex apartment in a house located in a bad Norfolk neighborhood. Kline's adjoining apartment was a drug hangout with abusers and addicts coming and going. Soon afterward, Giarratano moved in with Kline and her daughter, Michelle.

On Feb. 5, 1979, the unthinkable happened. Norfolk police discovered the murdered bodies of Michelle and Barbara Kline inside the apartment. Michelle had been raped and strangled in a bedroom. Barbara's fully dressed body was found in a bathroom, still wearing her coat. A brand new 8-pack of beer lay beside her. She had been stabbed multiple times.

With his mind clouded by alcohol and drugs, a mortified Giarratano thought he must have committed the murders but had no memory. In a panic, he boarded a Florida-bound bus, and the next day, in Jacksonville, he approached a police officer and confessed to the murders. When Norfolk police found out about the confession in Jacksonville, two detectives went there and interviewed him while the commonwealth's attorney indicted him for capital murder.

There was no forensic evidence linking Giarratano to the crime. The crime lab examiner identified 14 hairs on and near Michelle's body that did not match his in any way. In addition, the police found and photographed bloody footprints on the floor leading away from Barbara Kline's body. Long after Giarratano's conviction, his lawyers discovered that June Browne Tillman, the crime lab analyst, had microscopically and chemically examined his boots (which the prosecution claimed were the ones he wore during the crime and which supposedly contained blood from one of the victims). Testing found two drops of blood, but the type did not match the crime scene.

Norfolk police also found inside the Klines' apartment a driver's license belonging to an undisclosed male. The attorney general's office later confirmed this exculpatory evidence, but they conveniently failed to disclose it to the defense before the trial.

Giarratano's multiple, contradictory statements and confessions did not match any physical evidence and conflicted with the crime scene's condition and the victims' bodies on critical specifics. His confessions also radically changed over time, see-sawing back and forth on the motive, timing, and order of the murders and other fundamental details. Subsequently, Giarratano's five confessions were unsubstantiated and lacked any credibility.

Finally, it was determined that the killer was right-handed. Giarratano is left-handed and suffers from a neurological deficit in his right hand. In fact, the State Medical Examiner told Marie Deans that there was nothing in the file that tied Giarratano to the crime.

These troubling details didn't seem to matter.

Suffering from drug and alcohol withdrawal, Giarratano was a physical and emotional disaster when Virginia extradited him from Florida. Tortured by his belief that he murdered his friends, he attempted suicide. Corrections officials sent him to Central State Hospital in Petersburg, where they medicated him with high doses of Thorazine. Despite his suicidal tendencies and Thorazine fog, the commonwealth's psychiatrists concluded that he was competent to stand trial.

At trial, his inexperienced court-appointed attorney unsuccessfully lobbed a half-serious insanity defense. However, his still-suicidal client rejected that and a plea deal that would have spared him a death sentence, thinking that if he did not kill himself, then the state would do it for him. In May 1979, only 90 days after the crime, and in a non-jury trial that lasted less than one day, a Norfolk circuit court judge convicted him of capital murder.

After his conviction, a probation officer interviewed Giarratano's mother while preparing a court-ordered pre-sentencing investigation. She let him down once again – instead of trying to save her son, whom she had abused and neglected his whole life, she falsely portrayed herself as a loving, nurturing parent while depicting him as a complicated, violent, and rebellious child. At the same time, Giarratano asked the judge to sentence him to death and twice asked the court to set an execution date.

Imposition of his death penalty hinged on a single aggravating factor: his troublesome juvenile record coupled with his hostile court behavior created "a probability that the defendant would commit criminal acts of violence that would constitute a continuing, serious threat to society."

On Aug. l7, 1979, Judge Thomas McNamara sentenced Giarratano to death and sent him to death row at Mecklenburg Correctional Center.

Unbelievably, on Oct. 1, 1979, before the Supreme Court of Virginia even issued its decision on Giarratano's direct appeal, one of the two lead detectives in the case authorized that all of the physical evidence held by the Norfolk Police be destroyed. Neither Giarratano nor his attorneys were informed of the destruction, so they had no opportunity to object. This evidence included clothing, hairs, saliva samples, even Giarratano's boots – all items that later could have been DNA tested.

In addition to the destroyed evidence, other critical evidence simply went missing. "They just couldn't find it," Steve Northup recalled. "There was a thorough search done through the state lab and any other possible place where it would be, and they could never find it. So, if we're right that Joe's innocent, that evidence should have exonerated him. But he was deprived of the opportunity to do that." That evidence included a videotape of the crime scene.

For seven years after sentencing, Giarratano's attorneys went all in to prove his innocence and save his life. They hired expert investigators who traveled across the country, following leads and interviewing every available witness.

They uncovered some incredible facts. They discovered that the police had found the unidentified driver's license at the crime scene. They found information about suspects who may have had motives to commit the crime. They tracked down the Commonwealth's forensic analyst who worked on the case and discovered that her analysis showed that Joe's boots could not have made the bloody footprint found. They also found that Michelle Kline had not been raped, but the prosecution withheld this fact.

Virginia's ironclad "finality over fairness" protocols prevented Giarratano's lawyers from getting a hearing where they could present this evidence that raised substantial questions about their client's guilt. They were thus unsuccessful in overturning his conviction and death sentence in the courts, which procedurally evaded all constitutional error claims.

Meanwhile, by 1984 Giarratano, at the urging of Marie Deans, emerged from his drug and alcohol haze and started believing he was innocent. Still, his chances of escaping the electric chair at this point were bleak indeed.

With all of this stress, including his execution hanging over him, he was willing to take up the case of another young man who arrived on death row in 1984.

Earl Washington Jr.: The Expendable Man

On June 4, 1982, while returning home to her apartment in Culpeper, 19-year-old Rebecca Lynn Williams was raped and stabbed. She could do no more than identify her assailant as a black man acting alone and died a few hours later, leaving a husband and three young children.

At trial, her husband testified, "I asked her who did it, and the only thing she replied to me was a Black man, and that was about it." Before she died, she also told Culpeper Investigator Kenneth Buraker that she did not know her attacker, only that it was a single

Black man.

Almost a year later, in late May 1983, Earl Washington, Jr., a 22-year-old Black man, was drinking heavily with family members near Warrenton when a dispute broke out. Angered, Washington left and broke into a neighbor's house to steal a pistol he knew was kept in the kitchen. After finding the gun, the homeowner, Hazel Weeks, walked in and caught him. He hit her over the head with a chair, injuring her, then went back to the party. As he entered the house, the gun accidentally discharged, hitting his brother in the foot. Washington fled into the woods, where Fauquier County police found and arrested him a few hours later.

Washington had an I.Q. of 69 and a habit of compensating for his disability by politely deferring to and agreeing with authority figures. This trait was his undoing, as under police custody on May 21, 1983, he confessed to five different unsolved crimes, including rape, two attempted rapes, and breaking & entering. The fifth confession was raping and murdering Rebecca Williams.

Handwritten police notes of the interrogation stated that:

> Because I (the interrogator) felt that he was still hiding something, being nervous, and due to the nature of his crimes that he was already charged with and would be charged with, we decided to ask him about the murder which occurred in Culpeper in 1982. Earl didn't look at us, but was still very nervous. Asked Earl if he knew anything about it. Earl sat there and didn't reply, just as he did in the other cases prior to admitting them. At this time I asked Earl – 'Earl did you kill that girl in Culpeper?' Earl sat there silent for about five seconds and then shook his head yes and started crying.

Ruth Luckasson, a professor of special education at the University of New Mexico, maintained in a later clemency petition that saying yes is a coping mechanism for the intellectually disabled. "His seriously limited intellectual abilities have had grave effects on his life, and have clearly disadvantaged him during his contacts with the criminal justice system."

The Fauquier officers called the Culpeper police and invited them to participate in an interrogation the next day. The following morning, Washington talked again with the Fauquier police, followed by questioning from Culpeper police officers. There was no lawyer present for any of these interrogations.

While this questioning was not recorded, the interrogating officer later testified that Washington initially wrongly identified Rebecca Williams as Black, then corrected the statement when re-asked the question. This pattern became common throughout the interrogation, with police asking leading and non-leading questions multiple times until they got the answer they wanted. For example, he described Williams as short when she was 5'8". He also confessed that he stabbed her two to three times. She had been stabbed 38 times.

That afternoon, as Washington's "confession" was being prepared by police, officers drove him past numerous Culpeper apartment buildings to get him to identify Williams' apartment. It wasn't until the third time they went through the William's complex that Washington pointed to an apartment on the opposite end from where Williams was killed when asked to point out the crime scene. A frustrated officer then pointed to the Williams apartment and asked him directly, "Is that the one?"

Washington said yes.

Also, the Williams family had turned over to police a shirt that they did not recognize and thought may have belonged to the killer. They showed the shirt to Washington and asked if it was his. Again, Washington said yes.

The Trial

In November 1983, a clinical evaluation at Central State Hospital found that Washington's I.Q. of 69 placed him in "mild mental retardation." He was right at Virginia's minimum standard; therefore, the Culpeper Circuit Court Judge ruled that his confessions were correctly recorded and he was competent to stand trial.

During the first, or "guilt or innocence" trial, despite calling 14 witnesses, the only objective evidence the prosecutor, John Bennett, offered to link Washington to the murder was his "confessions" and identification of the shirt. Defending his first capital case, Washington's attorney, John Scott, failed to show the leading process of suggestion the police officers used to get the confessions admitted as evidence. He and his partner, Gary Hicks, also failed to show that Washington was incapable of understanding Miranda warnings and that his entire adaptive strategy for living consisted of attempting to please people by telling them what they wanted to hear. They only called two witnesses, Washington, and his sister. Washington's appearance was a disaster, and the prosecutor shredded him on the stand.

Most critically, Washington's counsel failed to present the obvious problems with seminal fluid found on a blanket at the scene. The commonwealth's serologic analysis showed that it could not have come from Washington. Even more incredibly, the semen type matched that of the initial suspect in the case, who was never charged.

On Jan. 20, 1984, Washington was found guilty and sentenced to death. James Grayson, who was Washington's second cousin and was in the courtroom when the verdict was read, told the Culpeper News in 2000 that attorney Scott warned the family not to react in any way as the police "had orders to shoot."

"And they put four policemen in front of us with their hands on their guns when they read the guilty verdict," he said. Alfreda Pendleton, Washington's sister, verified the story.

Then, between January and May of 1985, the Supreme Court of Virginia and the U.S. Supreme Court upheld Washington's conviction. Due to Virginia's arcane rules, he had no lawyer anymore. The Culpeper Circuit Court set a Sept. 5 execution date.

In the words of Margaret Edds in her 2003 book, Washington became "an expendable man."

A Meeting on Death Row

Earl Washington Jr. landed on MCC's death row just three weeks before the infamous May 9, 1984 breakout. He was in no way the stereotype scheming death row monster, and on that fateful day, he could only sit petrified, glued to the television in the dayroom, as chaos erupted all around him.

Joe Giarratano saw Washington and felt pity for him. He and Washington had only met briefly since his arrival, so Giarratano walked over to him and told him that maybe he should go back to his cell. In Edds' book "An Expendable Man," Giarratano said, "Poor Earl couldn't move. He literally was paralyzed with fear ... his whole body began to shake, and he couldn't move. I spent a couple of fast minutes trying to calm him. I lit a smoke for him, and after ... the first couple of drags, I was able to walk him to his cell."

Giarratano became Washington's friend, mentor, and eventually, his lawyer.

"He couldn't read, so he gave me his letter and asked me what it said," Giarratano reported of a letter that notified Washington that his direct appeal had been denied. It also warned him that the attorney general's office would set an execution date if he did not file a habeas petition by a specific date.

The only way to put a speedbump in front of Washington's execution would be for him to file state and federal habeas claims. With his original attorney Scott gone, and his family too poor to pay for another, it unbelievably was up to a man functioning at the level of a 10-year-old to use the prison law library and set his habeas appeals in motion.

As she had done many times before, Marie Deans got on the phone to lawyers up and down the east coast, trying to find one who would take Washington's case.

Mostly as a result of Washington's dilemma, in July 1985, Giarratano – who admitted he could not do simple math but could grasp complex and scholarly legal concepts – filed *Giarratano v. Murray* in the U.S. District Court for the Eastern District of Virginia as a class action lawsuit *pro se* (without attorney). The suit alleged that Virginia's failure to provide death row inmates legal counsel during habeas appeals was unconstitutional.

Giarratano even wrote to Judge Robert Merhige, who would be presiding over his class action suit, to explain the seriousness of the Washington case:

> It appears to me that if Mr. Washington is executed, that fundamental principles of Due Process and Equal Protection would, literally, be thrown out of the window. I have spent the majority of the past 24 hours doing general research in this area and have located fairly strong precedent that would support my basic proposition .... There is also precedent which indicates that some provision must be made to ensure that prisoners' [*sic*] have the assistance necessary to file petitions and complaints which will in fact be fully considered by the court ....

Giarratano explained that Merhige did not want to turn this case into a lawsuit because he would not be allowed to hear it, and he could not issue a stay of execution. Merhige converted it into a preliminary injunction; then, he personally made a claimed 200 phone calls trying to find a lawyer for Washington, with no luck. Giarratano instead turned it into a right to counsel case.

A prestigious New York law firm, Paul, Weiss, Rifkin, Wharton & Garrison, agreed to provide legal support for *Giarratano v. Murray*. When they sent to Virginia an associate named Marty Geer, Giarratano greeted her not with a "hello" but with "Earl Washington has an I.Q. of 69, an execution date three weeks away, and no lawyer. What the hell are you going to do about it?"

He had a lot of good reasons for saving Washington because if he were executed, there would be no *Giarratano v. Murray*. Giarratano said he told Geer, "I'll let y'all take it as long as y'all do it the way I want it done."

Geer returned to New York, telling her associates that the lawsuit and the upcoming death sentence of "the mentally retarded" Washington needed immediate addressing, and urged them to take his case in addition to the class-action suit.

When representatives from Paul, Weiss, Rifkin, *et al.* arrived, Giarratano told them, "We need to get Earl Washington a stay. They're going to kill him. And Merhige can't issue a stay." They responded, "Oh, we're not doing that. We're only here for [the lawsuit]."

Giarratano felt his blood pressure rising. "I said, 'Wait a second – do you realize that [Washington] is the lead plaintiff in this case? If they kill him, we don't have a [lawsuit]."

The lawyers responded, "Well, we have you." The exasperated Giarratano replied that he a straw plaintiff and had only put his name on the case so he could file the pleadings because Washington could not.

Giarratano fired the firm. Afterward, he told another attorney, Jack Boger, "I know I'm right. And they're not getting this case. We have to stop Earl's execution." After speaking with Eric Freedman, Giarratano and the firm compromised with a habeas petition to delay Washington's execution.

In August, as Washington was transferred from MCC to the State Penitentiary to await his Sept. 5 execution, the New York attorneys worked 23-hour days to get the petition filed to save Washington's life. While poring over attorney John Scott's original trial records, they were stunned to see the level of corruption by police in coercing Washington's confessions.

Nine days before Washington's execution, a paralegal hand-delivered two bound volumes, each four inches thick, to the Virginia attorney general's office, who signed off on them. The petition then went to Charlottesville to be signed off by Lloyd Snook, the attorney of record. Then, the petition went to Judge Sullenberger's office in Culpeper, arriving at 4:00 p.m.

Anticipating that Sullenberger would quickly reject the petition, he shocked them by signing a stay, temporarily stopping Washington's execution a mere nine days away.

Everyone briefly exhaled in relief. But there was far more work to do.

Giarratano v. Murray: Why it Mattered

> Picture yourself in this situation. You've been convicted of capital murder and sentenced to death. You are indigent, functionally illiterate, and mildly

retarded. Your court-appointed lawyer tells you that you have a right to appeal your conviction and sentence but that he will no longer represent you .... You've been moved into the death house. Your only choice is for you to represent yourself. You must file something with the court or be executed in less than 14 days. You have the right to file a petition for certiorari and a petition for habeas corpus, and a motion for a stay of execution. But before you can file, you must learn to read, write, overcome your retardation, obtain your trial transcript, understand the science of law, learn how to conduct legal research, analyze vast amounts of case law, formulate your issues, learn all the procedures, learn all the various court rules, understand civil procedure, constitutional law, criminal law and acquire the art of legal writing. You must do all of this and much more in less than 14 days.

-Alice McGill, quoting Joe Giarratano, in "Murray v. Giarratano: Right to Counsel in Postconviction Proceedings in Death Penalty Cases." *Hastings Constitutional Law Quarterly*, Fall, 1990

This class-action suit brought before U.S. District Court Judge Robert Merhige Jr. painted a broad picture of the sloppy inadequacy of inmate counsel. At the time, only seven private lawyers worked part-time for over 2,000 inmates, including those on death row, assisting in complex habeas appeals.

"Merhige treated you with respect," Giarratano said of the Judge. "He didn't tolerate nonsense in his courtroom. I had Earl Washington on the stand. The AGs were trying to mess Earl up because he was slow. They figured they could talk around him. And [Merhige] stopped it. He said, 'No, that's not happening to my courtroom. In fact, I'll ask the questions.' Then he got what he wanted out of Earl."

Since Judge Merhige sided with Giarratano in the two-day trial, the attorney general's office appealed to the U.S. Supreme Court, which struck down the lower court ruling 5-4. In a telling statement, Justice Anthony Kennedy revealed that he only voted with the majority because no death row inmate had been executed without a lawyer. But that if anyone had, he would vote the other way.

Giarratano insisted that even though he technically lost at the highest court, Justice Kennedy made an intelligent move. "It tells Virginia, 'Okay, we're not going to interfere with your process. But if you kill somebody without an attorney, then we will.'"

The message was received, and soon afterward, Virginia began appointing attorneys for the habeas appeals of indigent death row inmates.

Curious Discoveries

Looking for an attorney to tackle Earl Washington's absurdly complex habeas arguments, Marie Deans turned to Fairfax attorney Robert Hall, who agreed to look into the case. After reviewing the documentation, he realized something terrible was going on. For example, no forensic evidence linking Washington to the crime was presented at the trial. Even stranger, a May 1983 state forensics lab report stated that Washington's finger and handprints did not match any found at the scene. Also, the information made no note of hair samples collected from Washington, even though samples were compared to other suspects.

Electrophoresis testing was done on a vaginal swab and on seminal fluid found on a blanket at the crime scene. This testing excluded Washington and the victim's husband, Clifford Williams.

Bottom line, it appeared Culpeper Commonwealth's Attorney Bennett had withheld these results from the defense at the original trial, and Virginia's 21-day-rule prohibited their introduction in the habeas proceedings.

But Hall was not deterred – on Nov. 29, 1985, an updated habeas petition laid out all the discrepancies and omissions, including the newly-found forensic evidence, the inconsistencies in Washington's confession(s), the lack of testing on the shirt found at the scene, and the failure of Washington's original attorney to get an independent third-party psychiatric evaluation.

But, it was business as usual in the Virginia courts. First Culpepper Circuit Court Judge Sullenberger shot down the motion for a hearing. Then in February 1988, the Supreme Court of Virginia rejected the appeal in two sentences: "Upon review of the records in this case and consideration of the arguments submitted in support of and in opposition to the granting of an appeal, the Court is of opinion there is no reversible error in the judgment complained of. Accordingly, the court refuses the petition to appeal."

The appeal was dismissed at the federal district court level without a hearing.

Eric Freedman took the case before the Fourth U.S. Circuit Court of Appeals, where after an 18-month wait, they received the good news that the Court ordered the case sent back for an evidentiary hearing.

The hearing convened in April 1992, with Robert Hall joined by Gerald Zerkin. Unfortunately, despite prolonged discussions and arguments as to whom the semen samples belonged, Judge Hilton ruled that the forensic evidence was inconclusive, and ineffective counsel assistance in the original trial was not proved. Then, on Sept. 17, 1993, the Fourth Circuit Court's three-judge panel upheld Judge Hilton's decision in a 2-1 decision that Washington had not been harmed by his attorney's performance.

"Unindicted Co-ejaculator"

On Dec. 20, 1993, Washington's lawyers threw a Hail Mary by filing a petition for a pardon to Gov. Douglas Wilder, who was completing his term in just two weeks. Then, on Jan. 14, 1994, Wilder commuted Washington's death sentence to life with the possibility of parole, citing his confession as the reason for not imposing a full pardon.

Wilder allegedly knew the results of two DNA tests performed by the state forensics lab in Richmond. The first was from the swab taken from the victim. A 1.1 allele genetic marker in the sample completely excluded Washington and Clifford Williams.

The Virginia attorney general's office – never willing to admit they had incarcerated and almost executed an innocent man – then concocted a (defense-named) "unindicted co-ejaculator" theory. They maintained that some of the semen could have theoretically come from Washington if there were two attackers. This preposterous theory was contrary to all the evidence, including the words of the victim Williams, who maintained with her dying breath to three different people that a single Black male had attacked her.

"Bob [Hall] and I hit the roof," explained Gerald Zerkin of this sudden unsupported disclosure. Slonaker, acting Attorney General Steve Rosenthal, and a state lab technician then had a press conference in which they announced it still could be Washington because the results didn't exclude the possibility that it was him and someone else.

"So we had our own DNA expert because we worked with the Innocence Project in New York," Zerkin said. "And we called our guy, and he said, 'It could be a million people. None of them is Earl.'"

Washington's defense team also believed that Gov. Wilder intentionally withheld the results of the second DNA test performed on the blanket, which were consistent with the earlier test and matched the first vaginal swab test. The telling report, signed Jan. 14, 1994, concluded that "... Earl Washington Jr. [is] eliminated as a possible suspect."

Not aware of these test results, the defense team had only two hours to accept Wilder's offer of life imprisonment, which canceled any further opportunities for appealing through the courts. Unfortunately, the only alternative was for Wilder to do nothing, which would have resulted in Washington's execution.

Barry Weinstein and Marie Deans drove to Mecklenburg to inform Washington of his choices – either take Wilder's conditional pardon, which could leave him in prison for decades, or refuse it, which could get him executed.

Washington chose to live.

There was no movement on the Washington case for five years as the innocent inmate transferred from one facility to another. Then, one Spring Day in 1999, a documentary filmmaker named Ofra Bikel walked into the Virginia Division of Forensic Science and asked the director, Dr. Paul Ferrara, for the 1994 Washington DNA test results. He curiously handed them over, and Bikel saw for herself the results that had been withheld from the defense.

In early 2000, the PBS show Frontline aired "The Case for Innocence." On the show, Bikel showed Bob Hall those results. "The power of the press ..." he softly said as he pored over the report for the first time.

Hall was circumspect of Wilder's willingness to let an innocent man languish behind bars. "I couldn't get beyond the deeply-seated feeling that the reason Earl didn't get pardoned, conditional or otherwise, had a political component to it, that when the governor left the office ... he had other ambitions, that he wanted to run for the United States Senate, and he was afraid that Earl Washington, if pardoned, would be out on the street and commit some crime ... and Earl Washington would become Willie Horton to Gov. Wilder's Senate campaign."

Bikel also confronted former Gov. Wilder on-camera with the question of why the defense was never informed of the blue blanket DNA test. Wilder stumbled, alternating between anger and feigned ignorance, stammering that he was unaware of that fact, and besides, Washington was alive because of him. Two years later, he was still angry, calling the show a "butcherous job."

Carry Out the Order

Virginia Senior Assistant Attorney General (and "death squad" member) James Kulp testified in *Giarratano v. Murray* that the state absolutely would have followed through with Washington's execution had Giarratano not filed the lawsuit on his behalf. In an exchange with attorney Jon Sasser, Sasser asked Kulp, "If you didn't hear from Mr. Washington, you were going to execute him whether he had a lawyer or not, isn't that correct?"

Kulp responded, "The order would have been carried out I am sure."

Sasser asked, "The order of execution?"

Kulp: "That is correct."

New Testing

By June 1, 2000, Earl Washington Jr. had been in prison 17 years for a crime in which there was no evidence he had committed. In 1995 his parents died, and the DOC refused to allow him to attend their funerals, saying that his presence would "be disruptive" to the family.

He was incarcerated at Keen Mountain Correctional when he was informed that Gov. Jim Gilmore – at the behest of Washington's legal team, Robert Hall, Eric Freedman, Gerald Zerkin, and Barry Weinstein – had ordered further, more advanced DNA testing called "Short Tandem Repeaters" (STR) on the samples from the scene.

It did not come easily. Gilmore dragged his feet in ordering the STR testing, which compared 13 genetic markers instead of only one as the earlier test. Even the conservative editorial pages of the *Richmond Times-Dispatch* urged Gilmore to order the tests. "A refusal by the governor to order a new test would amount to a horrible admission: that the state prefers to accept the possibility of having stolen a man's life over admitting it made a mistake."

The testing cleared Washington, and Gilmore eventually granted Washington a clinical, non-apologetic pardon for the capital murder conviction. But there was a caveat – the pardon was partial, only in that a jury would not have convicted him based on the evidence as it was known at the time. Also, Gilmore reminded everyone that Washington was still technically serving time for the Hazel Weeks assault – a crime for which he would have long been out of prison had it not been for the capital conviction.

Finally, he was released from prison to parole supervision in February 2001. Even then, an embarrassed and petulant Virginia robbed Washington and his supporters of the symbolism of seeing him walk out of prison by driving him out a back gate straight to Support Services Inc. in Virginia Beach as his friends and the press waited out front.

In 2002, Washington filed a civil rights suit in federal court against investigators and officials who prosecuted him. As part of the preparation for this trial in 2004, they subpoenaed biological evidence from the state forensic laboratory. They discovered the earlier testing had consumed all of the evidence from the original swab. Luckily, the state medical examiner held ten more slides containing testable material. It was all turned over to Dr. Edward Blake of Forensic Science Associates in Richmond, California. Blake discovered the DNA matched another inmate, Kenneth Tinsley, who was already serving a life sentence for a 1984 rape in Albemarle County.

In 2006, Washington was awarded $2.25 million from the estate of deceased state investigator Curtis R. Wilmore, who had coerced the false confession from him. In 2007, the Commonwealth of Virginia and Wilmore's estate agreed in an appeal to a settlement whereby Washington was to receive $1.9 million from Virginia for his wrongful conviction.

In 2007, Tinsley pleaded guilty to raping and murdering Rebecca Lynn Williams. Also, that same year, then Gov. Tim Kaine issued Washington an absolute pardon.

In light of the dozens of people who worked diligently to free Earl Washington, attorney Eric Freedman insisted in the Jan. 31, 2021 *Times-Dispatch* that, "The hero of that story is absolutely Joe Giarratano."

In 2004, the American Association on Intellectual and Developmental Disabilities awarded inmate Joe Giarratano and others an award for their work saving Earl Washington Jr.

With One Life Saved, the Jailhouse Attorney Works to Save His Own.

With Joe Giarratano effectively barred from getting another hearing by a Gordian knot of esoteric procedures and rules, his attorneys, like those of Earl Washington Jr., threw a Hail Mary to Gov. Douglas Wilder seeking clemency. They filed a thorough and convincing request for a conditional pardon detailing the problems in his case, including the unreliability of his confessions, the missing evidence, and the other deficits that cast substantial doubt on his guilt. The request was unprecedented, as it did not ask Gov. Wilder to grant him a full pardon but instead entreated that Wilder grant Giarratano a new trial to give him a chance to prove his innocence.

The clemency petition reaped unprecedented support from Democrats and Republicans, conservatives and liberals, opponents and even supporters of the death penalty. Support for Giarratano was international, and he became the most famous death row inmate in the world. Virginia newspapers whose editorial boards traversed the political spectrum all called for his death sentence commuted.

Meanwhile, per the execution order, Giarratano was moved into an "A" basement holding cell at the State Penitentiary to wait.

He was the only inmate there. That decrepit facility was finally closing after operating 191 years, and all the inmates had been taken to other facilities around the state. However, since the new death chamber was not yet completed at Greensville Correctional Center, state law mandated that the electric chair remain on standby.

Gerald Zerkin clearly remembered visiting Giarratano in the basement of that dark and decaying fortress. "The spookiest thing I think I've ever seen in my life ... The penitentiary had been emptied, so there was nobody in there except him. And the death house was in a basement. But you had to walk into the yard before you walked down the steps into it. And when you walked out, there was not a light to be seen, there was not a sound to be heard. I mean, it was just spooky beyond belief."

Gov. Wilder seemed genuinely troubled by the doubts surrounding Giarratano's guilt, so he tried threading a needle while still trying to appear tough on crime as he aspired to higher office. Stating that he believed he did not have the power to grant a new trial (echoing a statement made by Gov. Gerald Baliles to William Menza two years earlier), in February 1991, less than two days before Giarratano's scheduled execution, he granted him a conditional pardon. He commuted his death sentence to life in prison with the possibility of parole only after serving 25 years. So while there was not enough evidence to execute Giarratano, Wilder believed somehow there was enough evidence to keep him in prison for a minimum of 25 years.

He then authorized Attorney General Mary Sue Terry to seek a new trial.

Terry, a Democrat, who once notoriously said that "evidence of innocence is irrelevant" in rejecting new evidence in habeas trials, also had vigorously opposed any move to stop Giarratano's execution. She then turned down the new trial request without consulting Giarratano's attorneys. On Feb. 20, 1991, Terry – who was planning a run for governor and also wanted to appear tough on crime – stated in part, "He is not entitled to a new trial, and I shall initiate no further legal proceedings."

This decision crushed any chance of Giarratano receiving a new trial and relegated him to decades in prison.

This seriously misguided move torpedoed Mary Sue Terry's political aspirations. She soon vanished from Virginia's political scene altogether.

Too Smart for Virginia's DOC

While in prison, Joe Giarratano put his mind to work helping an estimated 30 fellow inmates with their legal issues. He assisted by writing requests for stays of execution and petitions for post-conviction relief in Virginia courts, federal courts, and even the U.S. Supreme Court. He was a one-man prison law firm.

In addition to assisting fellow inmates, Giarratano consistently provided accurate and objective information to outside lawyers investigating and even litigating prison condition cases to ensure that prison officials followed the law in how they treated inmates.

From the mid-1980s to the mid-1990s, Washington Post writer Colman McCarthy took students participating in his peace studies courses at local high schools, colleges, and law schools in the Washington D.C. area to prison to meet Giarratano. They heard his thoughts and theories on violence prevention, his advocacy for humane prison conditions, as well as learning about his case and about his efforts to find a lawyer for Earl Washington Jr.

"He's smart as hell," Steve Northup said of the former death row prisoner. "He's one of the best lawyers I know, even though he's not a lawyer."

Following McCarthy's lead, Giarratano also became interested in restorative justice, the concept that inmates must take responsibility for their actions as a pathway to redemption. After his transfer to Augusta Correctional Center in Craigsville, Giarratano conceived an inmate-run alternatives to violence course to teach inmates not to view themselves as victims but instead understand that their actions put them in prison. He called his idea the Alternatives to Violence/Peace Studies Program.

With Colman McCarthy and Marie Deans' help and Augusta Warden Lonnie Saunders' approval, the Peace Studies program soon became an independent, 50l(c)(3) nonprofit corporation with an outside board of directors and an inmate advisory board. Participants in the program had to be convicted of violent crimes, have extensive histories of prison violence, yet demonstrate a willingness to change their behavior.

The Peace Studies program was an overwhelming success. By the spring of 1995, 120 of Augusta Correctional Center's 1000 inmates had graduated from the program, 160 were enrolled in classes, and 300 more were on the waiting list.

Assistant Warden Stuart Taylor observed in April 1995, "Since the program started, there have been no incidents involving injury to anyone by anyone in the program."

But new leadership in Virginia's DOC and the governor's office thought Giarratano was becoming too big for his britches. They were afraid the attention his program attracted made them look soft on criminals, so in July 1995, new DOC director Ron Angelone ordered the Peace Studies program disbanded. A prison spokesman even alluded to alleged financial misconduct within the programs but never substantiated those allegations.

With the Peace Studies program terminated, the DOC transferred Giarratano to Buckingham Correctional Center, then started the rumor that he was a prison snitch. He had to be placed in protective custody when another inmate stabbed him.

We Have a Hot One

On Sept. 4, 1996, with no warning, DOC officials abruptly and inexplicably placed Giarratano on the governor's plane and flew him out of Virginia through a supposed "interstate agreement" to serve his sentence in Utah. A Utah DOC spokesman explained at the time that Virginia "called us and said, 'We've got this politically hot inmate; we would like to get rid of him.'" Virginia also dubiously claimed that they were transferring Giarratano because "Other inmates resent him. He was in danger. For his safety, we felt it best to put him in a state where he had no enemies."

Not to mention that he had the unmitigated audacity to show humanity and teach inmates that they could change their behavior – concepts counter to the DOC at the time.

When *Richmond Times-Dispatch* journalist Frank Green asked the governor's spokesperson why they were resorting to the outrageous expense of using the governor's jet to fly a single inmate across the country, he responded that Joe Giarratano had a big following on the outside, and they were concerned of a "Con Air incident."

("Con Air" was a 1997 movie starring Nicholas Cage and John Malkovich that depicted an airplane hijacked in mid-flight by prison inmates.)

In Utah, Giarratano was intentionally placed in total isolation for a week in the cell that once held the notorious Gary Gilmore. Later, he was locked in a cell nearly twenty-four hours per day, and whenever corrections officers moved him, he was handcuffed, shackled, and led by a dog leash.

While on a hunger strike to protest his treatment, Giarratano observed Utah DOC officials using a form of corporal punishment called "the devil's chair." With this device, officials would strip mentally ill inmates naked and strap them into the chair, where they would leave them for up to nine consecutive days.

As a result of his first-hand observations, Giarratano provided crucial information to the Utah ACLU attorneys investigating the use of the devil's chair, complete with the names of inmates on whom it had been used. Prison personnel had purposefully taken many mentally ill inmates off their medication before subjecting them to the chair, so they could not provide coherent accounts of their experiences. Unfortunately, on March 20, 1997, during a three-month investigation, a mentally disabled inmate, Michael Valent, died of a blood clot after 16 hours in the chair. This death finally forced Utah to stop using the chair and paid a $200,000 wrongful death settlement to Valent's family.

With his hunger strike entering its second month, Giarratano continued to mail ten letters a day to his supporters worldwide describing the abuses. Weary of the troublesome inmate and sick of enduring constant scrutiny of their practices, the Utah DOC had enough of Joe Giarratano and insisted Virginia take him back.

Virginia said no.

On to Chicago

With Virginia refusing to take back the problematic Giarratano, Utah instead sent him to Joliet Prison near Chicago, a facility known for its gang problems. However, he managed to avoid the violence as his in-house legal services were highly demanded. Still, Giarratano insisted that his incarceration outside Virginia was illegally retaliatory and filed a 32-page federal lawsuit on behalf of himself and another Virginia inmate held there, alleging various constitutional rights violations. He also alleged that Illinois failed to honor the contract it signed with Virginia in accepting the two of them.

After a transfer to Stateville, they placed him in disciplinary segregation for six months on a bogus infraction. He began another hunger strike that lasted for two months until mid-September 1998, when Virginia corrections officials announced that the "too hot" inmate, starving and hooked to IVs, was returning to Virginia.

The DOC also announced that Giarratano, for unexplained reasons, would not return to his former level 3, medium-security status but would be sequestered in Southwest Virginia's recently opened Red Onion Correctional Center, a "supermax" level 5 facility.

"Threw Me in the Hole"

It was nothing but revenge. Red Onion was a maximum-security lock-down facility located in Pound with no law library, no job training programs, and no education classes. General population inmates at Red Onion spent 23 hours per day in their concrete cells, behind solid steel doors with small, narrow holes for food trays. The cells were designed so that inmates could not see or communicate with one another. Guards carried shotguns filled with non-lethal pellets and electronic tasers and used them liberally.

During contact visits with their attorneys, inmates had to wear shock collars capable of delivering a 50,000-volt stun.

Giarratano noted in a letter written while at Wallens Ridge that when at Red Onion, "Anytime you had to leave the cell, you were cuffed from behind. Then [you] get on your knees until you were shackled (for the first four years, you would also have a Taser pressed to the back of your neck until you were shackled and leashed). Once you were standing, you had two guards escort you (one with a Taser pressed to your kidney area, the other holding the leash)."

"It's not a nice place," Ron Angelone said of Red Onion. "And I designed it not to be a nice place." In language similar to that used decades earlier in describing the ill-fated embarrassment of Mecklenburg Correctional, the Virginia DOC claimed that Red Onion was a prison designed for "the worst of the worst, inmates so dangerous that it's better to forget about rehabilitation and simply warehouse them."

In a December 1998 letter to the *Roanoke Times*, Giarratano described Red Onion as "another expensive house of pain and dehumanization." "People get shot and zapped for verbal insolence," he said. "Excessive force is the rule."

Giarratano pointed out in 2021 that Red Onion and its companion supermax facility Wallens Ridge in Big Stone Gap were built for economic reasons, not penological ones. "They built those because the coal industry was going under," he explained. "They wanted to create jobs. They didn't need Wallens Ridge or Red Onion. It was stimulus for the local economy."

"But they didn't have enough [inmates] to fill [them]," he continued. "Where are they going to get the worst of the worst? They started renting space out to other states. Guys coming directly from receiving and never broke a rule went directly to Red Onion. We had guys there from Mexico, Connecticut, Texas ... Had prisoners everywhere. Virginia was in the business of renting out cell space to pay the bills."

You Were Supposed to Die

Shortly after arriving at Red Onion in 1996, Giarratano got up one day and immediately fell. "My legs didn't work," he explained. "Immediate pain. They took me to the local hospital in Norton."

There, doctors found acute deep-vein thrombosis. "They said, 'We can't handle this. You need to life-flight him to MCV (Medical College of Virginia) immediately, or he's going to die.'"

Five hours later, Giarratano still waited in blistering pain inside the Norton Hospital as Red Onion officials decided that instead of a two-hour med-flight, they would take him to Richmond in an ambulance – an 8-hour drive.

After the torturous ride, the ambulance finally arrived at MCV. Giarratano recalled that a young guard named Mullins told him, "Giarratano, you're one tough son of a bitch."

"I said to him, 'What do you mean?'"

"He said, 'You were supposed to die en route.'"

Once inside the hospital, doctors told him they would have to amputate both legs.

One Leg and a Parole Hearing

Fortunately, doctors saved one of Giarratano's legs, and he was provided a prosthetic for the other. When he returned to Southwest Virginia, he went into general population at Wallens Ridge, where he found that eight years in solitary confinement at Red Onion made him hate crowds. "I get extremely uncomfortable being around or in groups of people," he wrote, "I have experienced panic attacks in these situations."

In 2001, just as Earl Washington Jr. was released from prison, rallying calls to grant Joe Giarratano a new trial started again. Hundreds of voices, including conservative editor James J. Kilpatrick, former California Gov. Edmund "Pat" Brown, actors Jack Lemmon and Mike Farrell, director Oliver Stone and numerous others, coalesced under the "Justice for Joe Giarratano" banner. The movement continued to build momentum until he became eligible for parole on Feb. 4, 2004.

At the hearing, his lawyers asked for any remaining evidence in the case to be DNA tested; however, since no evidence could be located, no testing could be done, and parole was denied. In fact, parole was denied another 11 times.

In December 2017, Virginia finally released Joe Giarratano from Deerfield Correctional, 38 years after being sent to death row. However, there was a catch; he was released for time served and not pardoned, which meant that he would be on parole, and, unbelievably, he had to register as a sex offender. That odious designation barred him from using a computer, working online, or having any contact with convicted felons, all of which his job as a paralegal demanded. His parole also mandated that he attend a weekly sex offender therapy for pedophiles group at $100 a pop.

"I went to one meeting, and it was a fucking joke. But I had to go," he said. After a few weeks, the psychologist told his parole officer that he was not participating in his treatment and was released from the program.

In 2018, Giarratano married his wife, Denise, in the Charlottesville Sheriff's office. Upon finding this out, his parole officer showed up at their house in a bullet-proof vest and informed him that he did not ask permission to marry, nor did he tell him his wife was Black.

One of his long-time attorneys hired him as a paralegal despite these ridiculous requests and obstacles. He also went to work with the University of Virginia School of Law Innocence Project.

Unfortunately, Giarratano's incarceration days were not yet behind him. In October 2018, after he was released from the sex offender therapy for pedophiles group for not participating, he was arrested for violating the terms of his parole. After 20 days in a Charlottesville jail, he was finally released. Then, after discovering that he had never been a pedophile and should not have been ordered to participate in that group therapy, the parole board lifted most of the restrictions. Although, under state law, he still had to register as a sex offender because his capital murder trial judge found him guilty of rape based solely on one of the five conflicting confessions – a rape proven by a forensic scientist never to have happened.

Giarratano returned to the local jail again when his parole officer trolled Denise's Facebook page and saw a picture of him posing in front of a polling station. Since there was a children's playground in the background, he was arrested again for violating parole.

Luckily, the case was quickly thrown out.

Where Are They Now: Earl Washington Jr.

After Earl Washington left prison in 2001, he settled into a quiet life with his wife Pam in Southside, Virginia, not too far from the former location of Mecklenburg Correctional Center. The now 60-year-old has put the past behind him and does no interviews.

Some simplistically tried to argue that Washington's release showed the system worked. "He wasn't executed," David Botkins, former Attorney General Mark Earley's spokesman crowed in 2001. "Ultimately, at the end of the day, the right thing was done."

"We still need to have closure," he added of his desire to retain the death penalty. "We still need to have deference to crime victims and their families, and we still need to have finality."

"Sheer dumb luck is not proof that the system works," countered Eric Freedman, the New York lawyer and professor of law at Hofstra University, in a Jan. 31, 2021 *Richmond Times-Dispatch* story. "It is a warning story of how the system almost failed."

Where Are They Now: Joe Giarratano

Today, Joe Giarratano has been fully released from parole by a new officer, and he and Denise live in West Richmond. He is employed by Premier Jury Consulting Services, LLC, a company owned by Sen. Joe Morrissey.

Despite his almost 40 years of hell at the hands of the DOC, he is not bitter and carries no grudges. When asked how he kept from being angry and vengeful, he pointed to Denise. "A lot of it has to do with her."

Perhaps too, he still recalls the final words of his friend Michael Marnell Smith just before he was executed. "You have to forgive them."

He may have a scarred liver and a prosthetic leg, but he is healthy and takes no medications – "not even an aspirin," he said.

"Not even an aspirin," Denise repeated.

The Well-Oiled Machinery of Death

The Financial and Human Costs of Making Virginia's Death Penalty the Fastest and Most Efficient in the Nation

> The law is a mighty machine. Woe to the unfortunate man who, wholly or in part innocent, becomes entangled in its mighty wheels, unless his innocence is patent or his rescue planned and executed by able counsel. The machine will grind on relentlessly and ruthlessly, and blindfolded justice does not see that the grist is sometimes stained with blood.
> -Edward Johnes, from "The Pardoning Power from a Philosophical Standpoint," 1893.

In Virginia, those convicted of capital murder faced one of two sentences, life in prison or death. The decision to seek death was made solely by an elected prosecutor in the jurisdiction or county where the murder took place. There were no standards to inform or guide these prosecutors, other than general state statutes, nor were there any administrative checks and balances to review or affirm this decision. Thus, in any case, the decision to seek death was solely left up to the discretion of the individual prosecutor, creating wide disparities from county to county or jurisdiction to jurisdiction.

These disparities became unsettling even when compared to neighboring counties. Thanks to commonwealth's attorney Paul Ebert, who served for 51 years, Prince William County led Virginia with 14 death sentences and nine executions between 1976 and 2018. Fauquier County next door, however, had not one execution since 1947. Loudoun County to the north similarly had no executions since 1944. Stafford County, Prince William's southern neighbor, had not had an execution since 1805.

No statistics proved that capital murders committed in aggressive jurisdictions such as Prince William County were more vile than those committed in jurisdictions that never imposed a death sentence. In fact, ten years after the last death sentence in Prince William, the county overall showed a lower violent crime rate than the rest of Virginia. The message, therefore, was clear – a crime that would get someone executed in Prince William would not get them executed in Fauquier, Stafford or Loudoun, or dozens of other jurisdictions statewide because of the discretion of one person. Therefore, Virginia's death penalty administration appeared to be based on geographical regions unrelated to the vileness of the crime or the defendant's future dangerousness. This is the very arbitrariness the *Gregg* decision and various other Supreme Court actions sought to stop, to little avail.

In the 2011 *Ohio State Journal of Criminal Law*, Professor James Liebman stated, "A given defendant's likelihood of receiving a sentence of death depends greatly on the county in which he was tried."

Still, Virginia death penalty advocates always prided themselves on how fair, swift and efficient the system worked. Former Attorney General Mark Earley's spokesman David Botkins told the April 15, 1999, *Richmond Times-Dispatch* that "Virginia has the most fair, balanced and carefully implemented death penalty system in the country."

Attorney General Evolution

From 1987 to 2001, Mark Earley Sr. was an avid supporter of Virginia's death penalty, first as a Virginia state senator, then as attorney general, finally as a Republican candidate for governor – but he later experienced a change in heart. In a 2015 paper published in the *University of Richmond Law Review* titled "A Pink Cadillac, an I.Q. of 63, and a Four-teen-Year-Old from South Carolina: Why I can no Longer Support the Death Penalty," Earley explained his evolution on the subject:

> I supported the death penalty for all of my public life spanning from 1987 to 2001 .... Today, I can still make a conceptual argument as to why it should be a tool in the arsenal of a prosecutor – but it is just an argument. And, to me, the argument is tired, strained, and no longer defensible.
> In the years I served the Commonwealth of Virginia, if you wanted to run for office, to oppose the death penalty was to be saddled with an albatross. Politically, it was safer and easier to support the death penalty for the most heinous of crimes.
> ...While serving in the Senate of Virginia for ten years, I am fairly certain that I voted for just about every bill that expanded the death penalty. I also did not hesitate to support initiatives that made it more difficult for a de-fendant to challenge their death penalty conviction on appeal—we were 'streamlining the process.'

Earley explained that his first capital case (which was thrown out), the case of the wrongly-convicted Earl Washington Jr., and the horrific case of George Stinney, the 14-year-old who in 1944 was wrongfully convicted and executed for murder in South Carolina, turned him against the death penalty for good.

"Sadly, George Stinney was not the first, and he will not be the last, to be put to death without a fair trial," Earley concluded. "The electrocution and subsequent exoneration of fourteen-year-old George Stinney has broken my heart. For me, it was the tipping point. I can no longer support the imposition of a penalty so final in nature, yet so fraught with failures. Now, like an obnoxious reformed smoker, I do not think anyone else should either."

As deputy attorney general, then as attorney general from 1985 to 1986, William Broaddus unwaveringly supported the death penalty. He contended that it was "consti-tutional and fair" and even litigated five condemned men into Virginia's electric chair. Yet a decade later, he too experienced a change of heart about capital punishment. In April 1996, U.S. District Court Judge Richard Williams tapped Broaddus and his partner, Alex Slaughter, to represent Angel Francisco Breard, who received a death sentence for the 1992 attempted rape and murder of an Arlington woman.

As part of their defense, the two gathered information on death sentences and life imprisonments of defendants who, like Breard, were charged between 1985 and 1996 with sex-related crimes and capital murder. The results shocked Broaddus – nine received life sentences, and 14 received death. He found no rhyme or reason for who got life and who got death, as many of those sentenced to life committed crimes just as atrocious as those sentenced to death.

"There's just no way I can conclude that the way we do this makes any sense," he told the May 24, 1996 *Virginian-Pilot*. "I have come to conclude that, in fact, we apply the death penalty in a very arbitrary manner."

"What are we trying to accomplish through the death penalty? Is it to prevent others from committing murder? If so, it is a drastic failure. Is it for retribution? Spite? An eye for an eye? If so, I've come to conclude that's not something I want to subscribe to. If it's to protect society, I think society can be protected just as well by keeping the person behind bars."

The Breard case had international repercussions. Just before his execution in April 1998, the United Nations' highest judicial court, the fifteen-judge International Court of Justice, unanimously ruled that the execution of Angel Francisco Breard, a native of Paraguay, should be stayed. Paraguay claimed Virginia police violated the Vienna Convention on Consular Relations by not informing Breard that after his arrest for murder, he had a right to consult with Paraguayan officials. The court ruled that "the United States should take all measures at its disposal to ensure that Angel Francisco Breard is not executed pending the final decision in these proceedings."

In addition, Broaddus and Slaughter were convinced that Breard had turned his life around in prison and fought tooth and nail to save his life. When the U.S. Supreme Court refused to stop the execution, they filed a new petition in Richmond's U.S. District Court, which turned them down. As he waited for his petition to be heard by the Fourth U.S. Circuit Court of Appeals, Broaddus received notice that Breard was dead.

Celebrating Death

> This is Linwood.
> -A handmade sign taped to a Halloween skeleton displayed by children
> outside the State Penitentiary on the night of Linwood's Briley's execu-
> tion, Oct. 12, 1984.

In his article, Earley described how as attorney general, he was in charge of a highly efficient group of five prosecuting attorneys known as the Capital Litigation Unit. They were also known derisively and, in his opinion, "unfairly" by some death penalty opponents as the "death squad," or sometimes the "electric squad."

The group, which formed in the 1980s, was known for their merciless proficiency in pursuing any legal means whatsoever, including sometimes little-known or arcane technical issues, to defeat the appeals of death row inmates. For example, in 1997, the office claimed that lawyers for Roger Coleman filed his petition for appeal to the Supreme Court of Virginia one day late. The death squad pounced, the petition was discarded, and Coleman was executed.

According to Joe Giarratano, the petition was filed in time, but the judge signed it the next day, making it only appear to be a day late.

In a 1997 Associated Press story, Washington & Lee law professor William Geimer called the death squad's work "death by technicality."

The group was so ruthlessly efficient that it could secure 12 executions in 18 months, compared to 26 executions it once took 13 years to achieve. One of those lawyers, Katherine Baldwin, proudly told the Associated Press how rewarding it was to be on the "side of right." "It's a privilege to be able to do this," she boasted. "There's just no doubt about the justice involved. The jury has already decided what the truth is."

"I don't understand the crazed aggressiveness," attorney Steven Rosenfield said of the group in that same story. "There's no way to really soften this – their exuberance to kill people can only be equated to (that of) totalitarian governments."

"[We] had a very aggressive attorney general's office that set execution dates as soon as they could," explained Gerald Zerkin. "They didn't even wait for cert[iorari] to be denied in the Supreme Court. They set execution dates anticipating the denial coming out of the federal habeas."

"I've thought of it like this kind of bureaucratic, methodical, inhuman 'just doing our job' kind of thing," Rob Lee recalled of this group and their processes. "It's like, 'I'm shutting down the human part of it and feeling justified to do this.' Maybe that's self-preservation. But they were, I think, very good at not allowing any kind of humanity to come into an execution chamber."

Some attorneys still recall the shocking habit that the infamous group allegedly had of partying the night of executions. "I was told they did things like celebrate executions and things like that." explained Steve Northup. "It was really macabre."

"They fought tooth and nail to uphold the convictions and see that the defenders got executed as quickly as possible," Northup continued. "That was their mission. And they were very dedicated. They worked very hard. And of course, they had unlimited resources."

In a 1987 "Penny Resistance" newsletter, Dr. Jerome Gorman wrote that after the execution of Linwood Briley in 1984, "the infamous 'electric squad' of the Virginia Attorney General's office held a party. Some on the electric squad wore shower caps to mock James Briley, who had been photographed wearing such a cap ... At this party, some toasted marshmallows 'real black' in celebration of the burning of Linwood and in anticipation of the subsequent burning of James in April 1985."

While Gorman's descriptions could not be independently verified, Julie McConnell echoed the rumors of celebrations on the night of an execution. "I heard about that. One of the judges who used to go to all of the executions was in the attorney general's office for a long time. I've never witnessed one. But they got cake, and they celebrated at the end of the case."

While the death squad attorneys had access to generous funds for quashing appeals with some left over for celebratory cake and toasted marshmallows, Northup explained that the situation was the exact opposite for death row defense attorneys. "We had no resources. At my firm, we did not have, at the time, a very active *pro bono* program. So there was no source of funds to pay for expenses."

An email query to the Virginia attorney general's office in November 2021 asking to confirm or deny these celebrations went unanswered.

The administration at Greensville Correctional Center also held a celebratory luncheon the day after a successful execution. Shawn Weneta, who at the time was serving a term for embezzlement, recalled these luncheons after the executions of Ricky Gray and Will Morva. "They would have a congratulations lunch the next day. And they'd have all this special food cooked to celebrate a successful execution. I remember feeling really sick about that. It's one thing to celebrate, like, a successful inspection ... I mean, there are lots of other things that you can pat yourself on the back for."

Since Gray's execution was reportedly mishandled, it is a mystery why the DOC considered it worth celebrating.

Because of the almost unlimited resources of the death squad, the nearly non-existent indigent defense, and an accelerated appellate process, the Death Penalty Information Center reported that by 1999, Virginia's rate of "fair, balanced and carefully implemented" executions per 10,000 people was highest among states with populations of more than 1 million.

More reasons to celebrate.

The Hidden Toll of Death Sentencing

> There is absolutely no way to conduct a well-run execution without causing at least one person to lose a little bit of their humanity, or to start at least one person on the cumulative path to post-traumatic stress.
> - Oregon State Penitentiary Superintendent Frank Thompson, 2017.

The attorney general's "death squad" and those legislators who supported the mechanical processes driving the death penalty possibly had no idea or did not care what their actions – performed in the venerable marble halls of the Virginia State Capitol far away from the death chamber – were doing not just to the inmates condemned to death but to the corrections officers, technicians, nurses, and even the executioner who carried out their gruesome edicts.

"It is not just the members of the execution team who experience feelings of guilt, shame, and mental torment," wrote Allen L. Ault in the July 31, 2019, *Washington Post*. "The trauma extends through the many correctional staff who interact every day with death row prisoners, often forming meaningful bonds over the course of many years and, in many cases, witnessing their changed mindsets and profound remorse. In my experience, the damage spills over into the larger prison community, causing depression, anxiety, and other mental and physical impacts even among correctional workers who do not work directly with those on death row."

Ault was chief for the U.S. Justice Department's National Institute of Corrections from 1996 to 2003. He was also commissioner of corrections in Georgia, Mississippi, and Colorado and chairman of the Florida Department of Corrections.

A 2005 Stanford study found that "Individuals must morally disengage in order to perform actions .... that are counter to personal moral standards. Capital punishment is a real-world example of this type of moral dilemma where everyday people are forced to perform a legal and state-sanctioned action of ending the life of another human being, which poses an inherent moral conflict to human values."

Post-Traumatic Stress

Michael S. Morton, a nurse-technician at the Virginia State Penitentiary when executions resumed in 1982, claimed that participating in the execution of Frank Coppola sent him into a spiral of PTSD-induced drug and alcohol abuse. In the late 1980s, he landed in Brunswick Correctional for 21 years after being sentenced for grand larceny, forgery, and statutory burglary.

After the Coppola execution, Morton claimed that when he went home that night, he couldn't sleep. "I just couldn't believe what had happened," he told the May 24, 1998, *Richmond Times-Dispatch*. "The next morning, I told them I couldn't come to work. I hadn't been asleep at all, and they said to take as much off as you need. I came in about three days later."

"They didn't give me no counseling, they didn't give me anything," he lamented. "This was the first one. They didn't know anything. Nobody talked to us how we felt about it – no nothing."

Authorities kept the identities of the 18 members of the Virginia execution team secret ostensibly to preserve their privacy, protect them from inmate retribution, and avoid potential lawsuits. They wore no name tags when functioning in their execution capacity. Morton was the first of only two team members to go public.

Death row chaplain Russ Ford wondered aloud in that same *Times-Dispatch* story that "Doesn't the average person think that if somebody went out and hooked up electricity to another person and then watched them cook – I mean, smelled their body and then handled that body, you know, put it in a body bag, take and put it in a hearse and then drive it out of the facility – that somehow, they'd be affected by doing that?"

Ford confided that some team members medicated their execution experiences with prescription drugs. Many experienced family troubles.

On April 3, 1994, Dr. Balvir Kapil, a physician employed by the DOC, admitted on National Public Radio that his participation in Virginia executions violated his Hippocratic oath and that he would no longer participate in them. His decision followed a ruling by the American Medical Association that a physician's participation in executions violated medical ethics. Kapil had been present at 12 electrocutions, checking inmates' bodies in the chair, indicating if more electricity was needed, and declaring the prisoner dead. As a result, a substitute, Dr. Alvin Harris, had to be brought in for the execution of Timothy Spencer.

"The AMA has no authority in the Commonwealth of Virginia," Harris told the Associated Press from his office in Franklin. "The AMA is not great God almighty."

A spokeswoman from the AMA said they had no problem with doctors certifying death outside the death chamber. But, she clarified, if a doctor checked an inmate after the first jolt of electricity and found that he was still alive, it put the doctor in an untenable position to "tell the executioner to take further steps to kill the inmate."

Jerry Givens was another execution team member who experienced a similar change of heart after executing 62 men. His final execution was the March 9, 1999, lethal injection of George Quesinberry.

"I was a good executioner; I was upholding the law," Givens claimed. "The responsibility was on the inmate. You make bad choices, you came to me."

Some thought Givens was too good at his job and pursued it with inappropriate enthusiasm. "Jerry really enjoyed the hell out of doing executions," reported Russ Ford. He added that Givens sincerely believed that the state of Virginia was "doing the right thing by executing these guys for the types of crimes they committed."

Ford recalled being at Joe Giarratano's press conference, and correspondent Chris Wallace, who is now with CNN, got a tour of the death house with Givens. "When Wallace came out, he was visibly shaken ... he said he had never seen anything like Jerry anywhere he's ever been about these kinds of things."

"I wanted a perfect execution," Givens claimed of the responsibility of his job, "because if the machine acted bad or the body caught on fire, it would come back on me."

Attorney and VADP board chair Jon Sheldon recalled that in his first meetings with Givens at a Doswell Burger King in 1999, he sincerely believed he was doing the condemned inmates a favor by killing them. "He talked to me about his role as an executioner and how it was really good for these guys. It was good because they didn't have anything in their future. It was good for them that they were being executed ... It was good for them because prison sucked. It was a fine thing for them."

Givens once claimed his goal was to get to a "century mark" – 100 executions. "Jerry had every reason in the world to do what he did," Sheldon concluded. "He thought it was compassion. These people had been ordered by wise judges to be killed."

Givens admitted in 2016 that maybe he got too eager to execute. "I was doing so many executions at the time, I was sort of addicted to executing – not that I enjoyed it, but you get into a certain mindset."

In 1995, Virginia transitioned from the electric chair to lethal injection with the execution of Dana Edmonds, who was convicted and sentenced for robbing and murdering a Danville grocer. Instead of pushing a button to send current into a man's body, Givens pushed a plunger and watched toxic amounts of chemicals enter a man's bloodstream – a process he found uncomfortably personal. "I had this syringe in my hand, and [I was] pushing the chemicals into that man's arm, and I started to feel more attached than I did just pushing that button. I could actually see the chemical going down the line and into the arm and see its effects." Givens was also concerned about barely-qualified prison medical personnel doing "cut-downs" if they could not find a vein in an inmate's arm. He also worried about the possibility of AIDS.

The Executioner Goes to Prison

In 1999, amid a flurry of seven planned executions, Givens went before a grand jury about receiving money for a truck from a former Richmond friend who had a previous drug-dealing conviction. The man asked Givens to buy the vehicle for him in his name to avoid paying excessive insurance premiums because of his poor driving record. "My friend offered me $10,000 cash for it, and I took it," Givens explained. He later discovered the man was still dealing, and he was charged with receiving known drug money.

The man testified that he had given Givens the cash to buy the vehicles, but Givens lied, telling a grand jury that he purchased the truck for Booker with money he won gambling in Atlantic City. He claimed his planning for the upcoming executions made him lie.

After conviction, Givens asked Sheldon if anything could be done in his case. "I did a lot of post-conviction work," Sheldon said of the case. "I investigated it. It seemed like a very unfair prosecution from the start. It seemed like a very interesting defense, but not one that would have any chance in post-conviction. None."

The jury found Givens guilty of one count of money laundering and three counts of perjury. He was sentenced to 57 months at a medium-security federal facility in Lewisburg, Pennsylvania.

"This is how God removed me from a situation I could not on my own get out of," he said in 2016. "I once told God that after I do 100 executions, I would stop, but God said no, I'm going to stop you now."

His stint in prison, the Washington case, and the switch to lethal injection forced Givens to realize the death penalty was wrong. Within a few months of his release, he decided to go public with his opposition and soon appeared on television and other media outlets in France, Spain, and Australia to tell of his work as an executioner. His role was a topic of great interest in countries where the death penalty had long been abolished. "In Spain, I was treated like a king!" he recalled.

Privately, Givens wrestled with his role in killing 62 men. After sitting with him in three separate interviews in 2016 and getting to know him as a friend, the emotional toll of his actions slowly became apparent. Still, he devoted the remainder of his life to abolition until his death of Covid-19 on April 13, 2020.

The JLARC Study

On Nov. 13, 2000, concerns over arbitrariness, bias and fairness persuaded the Joint Legislative Audit and Review Commission (JLARC) to approve a study of Virginia's capital punishment system. Perhaps legislators had also been humiliated by the April 2000 release of the ACLU report "Unequal, Unfair and Irreversible: The Death Penalty in Virginia" and decided to see what was going on.

Two principal concerns guided the report: the first was the role of prosecutorial discretion or the fairness with which local prosecutors applied the statutes that defined a capital crime. Abolition advocates argued that when a person was arrested for a crime that could legally be charged as capital murder, some prosecutors – such as in Prince William County or Danville – were far more likely to indict the accused for capital murder and pursue the death penalty.

The second concern was over the fairness of Virginia's appellate process. Many legal experts contended that Virginia's judicial review of capital cases had become a pointless process that rubber-stamped lower court decisions and routinely dismissed appeals on primarily technical reasons. Virginia's higher Court, in fact, had an 18 percent rate of reversal for death sentences compared to a national average of 68 percent.

The study was timely and landed in the middle of modern history's most active executing period. Between 1976 and 2004, Virginia politicians had chipped away at the appeals of death row prisoners because state and federal judges took a hands-off approach after death verdicts. The Supreme Court of Virginia never granted an evidentiary hearing or appointed an expert or an investigator to a death penalty case. Additionally, Virginia had cut the appeals process to less than six years, with at least two cases streamlined to less than two years. This was a fraction of the time of the second-fastest state, Delaware, which averaged twelve years.

Scott Sundby, a law professor at Washington & Lee University, told the April 4, 1999, *Washington Post* that "All three branches are in tune with each other in moving the death sentences along."

Stephen Bright, founder and director of the Southern Center for Human Rights in Atlanta, was far more blunt. "Virginia and Texas are absolutely the bottom of the barrel. There's no due process in either state. In other places, there's still some basic concern for fairness."

Historically, the study found that while exact numbers were not available, given the broad scope of Virginia's capital punishment laws, it was apparent that from 1908 to 1962, juries were returning a sentence of death for only a small number of the death-eligible cases. Death penalty supporters pointed to this limited use as a positive indicator that juries reserved the punishment only for the most egregious crimes. Opponents argued that the few eligible cases that received death were indistinguishable from the thousands that did not.

One answer may be found in the blatant racial disparities in the system from 1908 to 1963, with 86 percent of those executed during that period Black men and one Black woman. Executions for rape, attempted rape, and armed robbery were reserved exclusively for Blacks. Not one of the 41 men executed for rape was white, and each of the 14 persons executed for attempted rape was Black. All five armed robbery cases that resulted in executions were Black men.

During the modern era, 1977 to 1999, the study noted several distinguishing factors in seeking the death penalty. Claiming race was rarely, if ever, a factor during that 22-year window, Virginia commonwealth's attorneys were still more likely to seek a capital murder indictment when the murder victim was a female (hearkening to the old Jim Crow patriarchy of the past) and if the crime was committed in a rural jurisdiction.

The JLARC study softly concluded that Virginia's capital punishment system was a mixed bag. While the survey indicated that race no longer played a role in the decisions of local prosecutors to seek the death penalty, the findings were equally clear that the decision to seek the death penalty was more linked to where in the state the crime was committed than the actual circumstances of the crime. "Location, more than any other factor," the study concluded, "is most strongly associated with the decision by commonwealth's attorneys to seek the death penalty."

The study also dispassionately concluded that inconsistencies were evident in Virginia's statewide application of capital punishment. Judicial review "was characterized by narrowly-defined sentence reviews at direct appeal and adherence to procedural restrictions during post-conviction."

The study also found that the executive clemency process (gubernatorial pardons) needed more structure and public scrutiny.

Judicial review of Death Sentences

> Federal Habeas Courts sit to ensure that individuals are not imprisoned in violation of the Constitution, not to correct errors of fact ... "actual innocence" is not itself a constitutional claim.
> -U.S. Supreme Court Chief Justice William Rehnquist, in *Herrera v. Collins*,
> 1993.

By Virginia law, anyone who received a death sentence also received an automatic direct review to the Supreme Court of Virginia. The Court, however, looked only at objected-to trial errors, the proportionality of the punishment to the crime, and factors such as passion, prejudice, and arbitrariness. It is important to reiterate that appellate courts, such as the Supreme Court of Virginia, did not re-consider whether the defendant was guilty or innocent; they assumed that a constitutionally fair trial produced the correct verdict – an assumption that in the opinion of some came far too quickly with that "adherence to procedural restrictions" so casually mentioned in the JLARC study. If a defense attorney at trial did not realize an error was occurring and object at that time, the higher court would not consider the error, no matter how egregious.

Even if a death sentence had been passed unconstitutionally by the lower court, if at the time an unqualified or inattentive defense did not object, the Supreme Court of Virginia let the sentence stand.

Gerald Zerkin saw that adherence as excessively punishing. "The Virginia Supreme Court was totally hostile to capital defendants, just denied everything that came along," he claimed. "And you had no relief on direct appeal. You had a statute that was well-crafted quite frankly to avoid litigation problems with a non-weighing statute. So you didn't have these problems with aggravating factors being held unconstitutional."

According to the U.S. Supreme Court decision *Strickland v. Washington*, appellate courts could overturn a conviction only if they were convinced that the trial lawyer's performance was ineffective, including a reasonable probability that the trial's outcome would have been different had the lawyer been effective. As a result, challenging a conviction based on ineffective assistance of counsel was genuinely arduous.

Once the Supreme Court of Virginia completed its "proportionality review," the court could affirm the death sentence, commute the sentence of death to life imprisonment, or remand the case to the circuit court for a new trial or sentencing hearing. In the entire modern era (1976-2021), Virginia did not reverse a single death sentence on proportionality review. In comparison, Florida reversed 37 death sentences on proportionality review just between 1989-2003.

"I think it's fair to say the Supreme Court of Virginia strictly adhered to the procedural default rules," explained Rob Lee.

After the Supreme Court of Virginia review, a defendant could seek relief through the U.S. Supreme Court.

Defendants could also seek relief through writs of habeas corpus in both state and federal courts. The purpose of a habeas review was to protect inmates against unlawful confinement. A habeas petition initiated a civil proceeding against a law enforcement official, usually the prison superintendent or warden, to determine whether the prisoner's incarceration violated due process. These reviews looked at such factors as ineffective counsel, prosecutorial misconduct, and constitutional violations. From there, the case could go to the Fourth U.S. Circuit Court of Appeals and again to the U.S. Supreme Court.

Zerkin was equally critical of the role of the Fourth U.S. Circuit Court of Appeals in this "rocket docket" process. "[We] had a Fourth Circuit that rubber-stamped every habeas denial. So, there was nowhere, really, that you could go. You had a trial, and that was the end."

Cornell University law professor John Blum, who also represented capital cases, referred to the extremely conservative Fourth U.S. Circuit Court as "the black hole of capital litigation," adding "you lose cases you would win in any other court."

Federal courts such as the Fourth Circuit would not rectify the sentences of even severely flawed state trials unless excessively complicated procedures were followed from the trial level throughout the appeals. Death sentences were thus again frequently imposed through error and carried out.

In their study "A Broken System: Error Rates in Capital Cases, 1973-1995," James Liebman, Jeffrey Fagan, and Valerie West found outcomes in Virginia "highly anomalous, given the State's high execution rate, which was almost double that of the next nearest state, and five times the national average." Not only did the Fourth U.S. Circuit Court rarely grant habeas relief in capital cases, but it frequently reversed lower courts that did grant relief. Subsequently, several of those convicted and sentenced to death in Virginia would have had their death sentence overturned had they been tried in another state.

The Liebman study also found that of the 111 federal habeas petitions filed in Virginia capital cases between 1977 and 2001, federal district courts denied relief in 96 of them, leaving only 15 that granted a new trial or sentencing. Of those 15 cases, the Fourth U.S. Circuit Court of Appeals upheld the district court's ruling in just two.

Virginia, unlike other states, also viewed habeas petitions not as a right but a privilege; therefore, those sentenced to death were only appointed legal counsel in the first two steps of a potential nine-step process. Since 97 percent of Virginia's condemned prisoners were impoverished and could not afford to hire their own attorney, a volunteer attorney had to be located to study their case and prepare the proper motions and briefs before the 60-day deadline following their Supreme Court affirmance. They could be (and were) executed without the same opportunities other inmates across the country received to appeal their sentences. In capital murder cases, Virginia ranked 49th or 50th of states in providing funding for court-appointed attorneys.

A statute allowed "reasonable fees" to defense attorneys in direct appeals to the Supreme Court of Virginia, but those fees were a joke. Attorney David Heilberg represented Steve Roach on direct appeal of the death sentence imposed against him. After enduring soul-crushing hours of legal work, Heilberg submitted his timesheets to the Supreme Court to get paid. The "reasonable fee" selected by the Court was $6.00 per hour. Despite two appeals for a higher award, the Court said they would not change the award but offered to look into improving the system.

Ron Shreckengost, who received $550 to represent Syvasky Poyner's appeal, told the July 14, 1985 *Richmond News Leader* that was about $200 less than he would charge to argue a traffic case.

"It's appalling," Richmond lawyer Dennis Dohnal told the *Fredericksburg Free Lance-Star* in 1985 as he handled Charles Stamper's appeal *pro bono*.

21 Days Later

> Virginia has this incredible 21-day rule that says if you don't present evidence in 21 days, they'll let an innocent guy die. That's just atrocious when you think of it.
>
> -Sister Helen Prejean

Every state with a death penalty had a judicial exception in capital cases that allowed claims of innocence after the state's time restriction for the introduction of new evidence had lapsed. Thus newly-discovered evidence at any point in the appellate process could be introduced and weighed as a mitigating factor. This exception has undoubtedly saved many nationwide from a sentence of death.

Every state except Virginia. The commonwealth's notorious 21-day rule was the jet fuel behind her engine of death. After a final verdict was rendered, the law stated that the defense had only 21 days to introduce any new evidence of factual innocence that a reasonable person would accept as valid. With this rule, which was by far the strictest in the entire nation, someone could confess on day 22 to committing a crime for which someone else had been sentenced to death, and the confession would be inadmissible.

This rule contributed to Virginia governors granting clemency in more cases than any in the entire nation, with 12 commutations between 1976 and 2017. These commutations always had to correct something wrong within that accelerated system that

Botkins highly praised as fair and balanced.

A prevailing public misperception is that the appeals process would hear late confessions and tardy evidence. Still, in Virginia, they could not – the appeals process was designed only to find objected-to errors in the original trial, not to introduce new evidence.

One narrow exception to the rule was carved out in 2001, which provided that a defendant could file a writ of actual innocence. This exception specified admissible any new biological evidence (DNA, for example) that could not have possibly been discovered before the 21-day limit expired. When considered with the other evidence, this new evidence had to prove "that no rational trier of fact could have found proof of guilt beyond a reasonable doubt."

This exception expanded again in 2004 to include claims constructed on non-biological evidence under certain still-narrow conditions.

The 21-day rule, like most, was created with the noblest of intentions. The rationale was to motivate the defense to present their best case at trial. The rule assumed, however, that defense attorneys – many of them court-appointed, profoundly inexperienced, and paid a grand total of about $684 ($577 before 1984) for the most complex life-or-death case of their life – had the time, the resources, and the personnel to investigate and locate all existing evidence. This process proved to be an impossibility in Virginia's expeditious death penalty trials.

In several cases, the Virginia attorney general's office displayed dogged adherence to this technical rule in place of fundamental human rights as part of their "death squad" methodologies. Joe Giarratano, Earl Washington, Herbert Bassette, and Joseph Payne all had their death sentences commuted to decades or even life in prison, with serious reservations about their guilt. Even with enough evidence of their innocence to induce a gubernatorial pardon from death row, all four men remained in prison serving long sentences because the 21-day rule blocked any new trials or the introduction of newly-discovered exculpatory evidence.

Several other Virginia death row inmates were not so privileged and went to the electric chair or the lethal injection gurney because of the state's relentless dedication to the 21-day rule. Roger Coleman's legal team in 1992 found and introduced DNA evidence after 21 days that they claimed would at least raise a reasonable doubt of his guilt or maybe even exonerate him from the rape and murder of his sister-in-law. The Supreme Court of Virginia in 2002 denied a request by several newspapers and New Jersey-based Centurian Ministries, who investigated claims of innocence, for new DNA testing. Coleman was then executed.

However, because of the advocacy work of VADP and others, Gov. Mark Warner, in a unique and unprecedented decision, agreed in 2006 to test the sample. "This is an extraordinarily unique circumstance, where technology has advanced significantly and can be applied in the case of someone who consistently maintained his innocence until execution," Warner stated. "I believe we must always follow the available facts to a more complete picture of guilt or innocence."

Unfortunately, the sample proved Coleman was the killer, provoking howls of "I-told-you-so" from gleeful death penalty supporters in newspaper letters across Virginia.

The Death Penalty Information Center (DPIC) lists several other examples. "Death Row Diary" author Dennis Stockton was executed in 1995 despite the prosecution's key witness admitting to a reporter after 21 days that he had lied on the stand. There was also late evidence found that the murder of the victim, Kenny Arnder, may not have occurred in Virginia.

Ronald Bennett was executed in 1996 after his ex-wife recanted her testimony against him after 21 days and instead implicated herself and his cousin.

Michael Satcher was executed in 1997 even though a later, more advanced method of DNA testing directly conflicted with an earlier state DNA test. The later test, performed after 21 days, found that Satcher's DNA could not have matched any of the DNA evidence from the crime scene.

Roanoke Democrat Del. Clifton Woodrum first introduced a bill in the 1994 General Assembly to ease the 21-day rule. Some referred to it as the "Earl Washington bill," and Gov. Wilder lobbied for the bill even after he left office.

Woodrum was a death penalty supporter who believed the system was flawed and vulnerable to executing an innocent person. "I thought if you had evidence of actual innocence, you should be able to introduce it as a matter of right rather than leave it up to the uncertain fate of the executive," he explained. "There's no such thing as a perfect system ... but when we're administering the supreme penalty, we have an obligation to make it as close to perfect as we can."

But the bill died in the Senate, the first of many annual legislative failures to reform the draconian rule.

From 1997 to 2001, Arlington Democrat Del. James Almand sponsored a measure to extend the 21-day rule. In 2000, the House of Delegates set a three-year limit to introduce new evidence. But the Senate reduced it to 45 days. Disappointed, Almand pulled the bill from consideration.

Virginia was so strict with their 21-day rule that former Attorney General Mary Sue Terry famously said around 1992 that "Evidence of innocence is irrelevant" if the 21-day cut-off was missed.

Marie Deans' response to this comment was that inmates barred from introducing new evidence after 21 days were "the fatted calves being sacrificed on the altar of a legal technicality."

Incinerate the Evidence

DPIC has found that since 1973, 186 persons nationwide wrongfully sentenced to death have been released from death row because they were innocent. Florida leads with 30 pardons, acquittals, or dismissed charges. Illinois had released 20 from death row, and Texas has released 16.

"We now know for every 8.3 executions, there's an exoneration," DPIC Director Robert Dunham told the Dec. 16, 2021 *Washington Post*. "That's an appalling failure rate. If we read that about any other public policy, it would not be tolerated."

North Carolina wrongfully held Charles Finch, a Black man, on death row for 43 years. Charges against him were dismissed in 2019 when it was determined he had been sentenced in 1976 because of false forensic evidence, prosecutorial misconduct, mistaken eyewitness identification, and perjury. Florida similarly dismissed charges against Clifford Williams in 2019 after he also wrongfully served 43 years.

With the possibility of innocence nationwide so pronounced, the question begging to be asked is, has Virginia ever executed an innocent person?

Virginia more than likely executed innocent people between 1608 and 1962. Del. Mike Mullin, who in 2021 sponsored the death penalty abolition bill in the House of Delegates, wrote in the Feb. 2, 2021, *Washington Post* that historically, "...the commonwealth shamefully failed to provide even a modicum of due process to the men and women who were facing death sentences, predominantly to the overwhelming number of Black Virginians who were eventually executed."

Virginia death penalty supporters frequently pointed out that the system worked because, since 1976, only one person on death row had been found innocent and released. But this simplistic statement ignored the measures Virginia implemented to ensure their dogged emphasis on finality over fairness, making post-execution innocence almost impossible to prove.

Prosecutors and state officials, usually under political pressure to reduce crime, including those possessed with Virginia's belief in absolute closure, destroyed evidence, usually by incineration, as soon as the appeals process was exhausted or the execution performed. In addition, courts would not entertain innocence claims after the defendant's execution. In addition, the introduction of any newly-discovered evidence could theoretically be stymied by prosecutors citing the 21-day rule.

Convincing a partisan state official who may be politically or professionally invested in the conviction also made the motion extremely unlikely to succeed.

There are also examples in Virginia history where evidence was destroyed or "went missing" prematurely. Robin Lovitt was scheduled to be executed on July 11, 2005, for the Arlington murder of Clayton Dicks. In April 2001, however, Robert McCarthy, the Chief Deputy Clerk of the Circuit Court of Arlington County, ordered the evidence destroyed, despite being told by two other clerks to preserve it because the case was a capital one. McCarthy responded that he was authorized to destroy the evidence after the Supreme Court of Virginia affirmed Lovitt's convictions.

In addition to the Supreme Court of Virginia, the U.S. District Court for the Eastern District of Virginia upheld Lovitt's conviction and sentence, who claimed no harm, no foul. Then, in a statement, the Fourth U.S. Circuit Court of Appeals said they would only overturn the conviction if it could be shown that McCarthy destroyed the evidence "in bad faith."

When the U.S. Supreme Court refused to hear the case, Virginia set a new execution date for Nov. 30. Then, less than 24 hours before the execution, Gov. Mark Warner, citing the wrongful destruction of evidence, stepped in and commuted Lovitt's death sentence to life in prison.

In 2001, attorneys for Joe Giarratano requested from the Norfolk police numerous pieces of evidence from the 1979 Michelle Kline murder scene. These included a man's driver's license that was not Giarratano's, a crime scene videotape, and, most importantly, vaginal swabs and fingernail clippings known to contain sperm samples that could be DNA tested to prove Giarratano's innocence. An exhaustive search never located this evidence.

The problem of missing and prematurely destroyed evidence was not peculiar to Virginia. A 2007 *Denver Post* investigation revealed that since 1987, the destruction of DNA evidence in 28 states weakened or eliminated efforts by an estimated 141 inmates to prove their innocence.

The National Registry of Exonerations lists 53 Virginians who since 1989 have been wrongfully convicted of serious but non-capital crimes, including charges of rape, robbery, child sexual abuse, and assault. Eighteen were convicted of murder. These men and women spent 739 years in Virginia prisons for crimes proven they did not commit. More than half of these exonerated individuals were Black.

While post-mortem evidence examination could theoretically exonerate an executed individual, it cannot bring them back from the dead. Trying to prove that an innocent person had been wrongfully executed was never considered a prudent use of resources that could be better suited to releasing other innocents from prison, or stopping yet another execution.

PART II: LIFE

Death Row Mom: Marie Deans and The Virginia Coalition on Jails and Prisons

> VCJP is aware that Virginians, like all Americans, are angry about legal technicalities that allow the guilty to go free, but if our anger has driven us to the point that we are willing to use legal technicalities to punish the innocent ... then it is time for us to admit that we do not have a system of justice ... it is nothing more than a system of gratuitous punishment.
> - Marie Deans, Program report, The Virginia Coalition on Jails and Prisons (VCJP), 1992.

Since the nineteenth century, researchers and social scientists have noted an increase in crime and homicide rates surrounding executions. They called it the "Brutalization Factor." In the 1840s, for example, pickpockets brazenly worked the crowds surrounding the executions of men sentenced to death for pickpocketing. W. Asbury Christian wrote in his 1912 book "Richmond: Her Past and Present" of the "morbid people" who gathered in 1852 for the last public executions of two pirates, named Reid and Clements, and for the Oct. 22 hanging of a Black man, John Williams, for the murder of Mrs. V. B. Winston and her child.

Christian concluded the passage by observing that "Public opinion was slow to protest against the imbruting effect of public executions."

In their 1980 New York study "Deterrence or Brutalization - What Is the Effect of Executions," researchers W. Bowers and G.L. Pierce found that, on average, homicides increased by two or three in the months immediately following an execution, and by one incident two months after an execution. The rate decreased insignificantly in the third month.

The study concluded that the effect of executions "has been to increase homicides, not to deter them."

"These findings," the authors concluded, "represent a direct challenge to the constitutionality of the death penalty regarding its negative impact on the victims of homicides sparked by executions."

Florida noted similar increases in homicides in the early 1990s, and homicide rates began dramatically increasing in Texas at the same time when that state began a disturbingly aggressive succession of executions.

Death penalty supporters argued that executing a human being demonstrates how deeply they value human life by sending what they believe is a strong deterrent message. Abolitionists, in turn, argued that executions showed that society's reliance on violence to solve its problems drove the brutalization factor.

"This One's Boring"

> Each execution causes the blood lust to rise, the ugliness in us to take over. You even see priests, chaplains, and attorneys becoming desensitized to the state taking a life.
>
> -Marie Deans, "A Survivor's View of Murder," c. 1985.

Researchers and even death penalty observers have noted that as executions increase, they become more accepted, then largely ignored. While over 300 people showed up to protest for and against Linwood Briley's execution in 1984, less than nine years and 15 executions later, only four people demonstrated against the execution of Syvasky Poyner in 1993. About a dozen traveled to Greensville Correctional Center in July 2017 to participate in a vigil during the execution of William Morva, Virginia's last execution.

Execution news stories in heavy death penalty states as Virginia became routine and soon fell from the front pages to small mentions elsewhere in the paper, it at all. At best, the populace became accustomed to the event and frequently expressed tired indifference.

In 1992, a group of local teenagers gathered at Greensville Correctional to gawk at a small handful of vigil attendees protesting the execution of Timothy Bunch. Many of them expressed disappointment at the gathering, noting how other executions had been more interesting.

"This is my third or fourth one," 15-year-old Chris Gay told a reporter for the *Potomac News*. "This one's boring. I've been to them where hundreds of people are around."

Another Greensville County High School student, Jaime Parker, explained he was only there to take notes for a sociology class report.

In his 1991 book, "Death in Life: Survivors of Hiroshima," psychiatrist and researcher Robert J. Lifton warned of "psychic numbing" – a growing indifference to suffering and death which is personified by the growing, then casual acceptance of violence, including executions.

The fear of brutalization and psychic numbing to the use of death was the impetus behind the creation of Virginia's first modern-day organized abolition movements, which began between the re-imposition of the death penalty in 1977 and when Virginia resumed executions in 1982.

The Southern Coalition on Jails and Prisons

In early 1982, just as the first variant of VADP emerged, Tennessee minister Joe Ingle, who was director of the Southern Coalition on Jails and Prisons (SCJP), received a letter from Joe Giarratano pleading for legal help for Frank Coppola. Coppola had given up on his appeals and wanted to be executed rather than live in the horrors of Mecklenburg Correctional Center.

Formed in 1974, the SCJP initially focused on general prisoners' rights, including healthcare and visitation, in North and South Carolina, Georgia, Alabama, Mississippi, Tennessee, Arkansas, Florida, Louisiana, and Kentucky. However, after the 1976 *Gregg* decision, the coalition members focused more specifically on death penalty abolition in those states. In addition, they lobbied heavily for alternatives to incarceration to reduce the growing southern prison population.

Ingle visited Coppola several times at MCC and was mortified at what he witnessed there and by what Coppola told him. After several visits, he called his friend and associate, Marie Deans, who was working in South Carolina for Amnesty International and volunteering for the SCJP while recovering from injuries she received in a train accident on her way to a conference in Seattle

A Charleston, S.C. native, Deans was a social activist from an early age, joining protesters who tried to integrate Deep South lunch counters. She took an interest in death penalty abolition after an escaped convict murdered her mother-in-law, Penny, in 1972. Between 1973 and 1979, Deans served on the National Coalition to Abolish the Death Penalty. In 1976 she founded Murder Victim's Families for Reconciliation, a national organization of over 110 families of murder victims who worked in various capacities to assist other murder victim families and abolish the death penalty.

As a volunteer for SCJP, she worked in four states recruiting lawyers for death row prisoners, doing crisis intervention and death row mitigation interviews. In South Carolina, she acted as liaison between death row inmates and the DOC in a substantial prison conditions suit. By any measure, an impressive amount of work for a single person.

Ingle knew that if anyone could clean up the mess in Virginia while helping death row inmates, it was Deans. Just days after the Coppola execution, in August 1982, Deans and two Amnesty International volunteers, William Menza and Pat Murray visited MCC's death row. They spent three hours speaking directly to Joe Giarratano, Earl Clanton, Buddy Justus, and Willie Lloyd Turner under the piercing eyes of a furious guard, who was not amused when the tough-as-nails Deans ordered him to remove the men's shackles.

It was the first time MCC had removed shackles for a non-lawyer visit – a testament to Deans' no-nonsense attitude. Deans loved to recall corrections officials' unspoken rule about her: "Thou shall not fuck with Marie Deans."

During the meeting, Deans realized Frank Coppola had not been exaggerating the conditions at MCC's row. The inmates described in lurid detail the lack of access to the law library and to attorneys. They protested the inedible food, the guard-on-inmate violence, and the almost non-existent recreation time.

Deans was especially stunned that corrections and even MCC itself were so disorganized and indifferent that no one – including the Supreme Court of Virginia – could tell her with any accuracy precisely who was on death row. And because of the conditions, she learned that seven more men, like Coppola, were planning to drop appeals and be executed to get the hell out of MCC.

Giarratano was impressed by Deans and the meeting. "She actually treated me like a human being ... I got a sense that, okay, this is a person who cares."

Deans had experience with death row inmates wanting to drop appeals. In 1976, she visited South Carolina's death row to meet with J.C. Shaw, who was to be the first inmate executed in that state after the *Gregg* decision. "I was stunned at myself for being stunned by him because I didn't know you could murder someone and look so human," Deans recalled of her initial meeting with Shaw. "I had all the prejudices that everybody else had that don't know any better."

After several more visits, she convinced Shaw to restart his appeals. A year later, she served as a liaison between the South Carolina death row inmates and the state prison system. She gained so much confidence from the warden and prison staff that she was allowed to meet the inmates with no corrections officers present – an unheard-of practice.

After her meeting in Virginia, Deans returned to South Carolina, called Joe Ingle, and told him she wanted to open a coalition office in Virginia. "[Virginia's death row] was so awful. The whole death penalty scene was so awful here," she told Roanoke College Professor Todd Peppers, which he later recounted in his 2017 book "A Courageous Fool." "I'm not trying to sound like a martyr or a do-gooder, but the need was so great." J. Lloyd Snook agreed to be president of the coalition.

In a 10-page position statement and funding proposal, Deans and John Vodicka wrote that:

> A Virginia Prison Project would operate with the belief that it is important to involve community people in making decisions about corrections and the death penalty. We do not think experts are needed to run departments of corrections because crime is a community problem, and when properly informed, the community is able to make just decisions about what needs to be done. We feel this method would result in meaningful coalitions for effective work on criminal justice issues.

When the VCJP started, one inmate had stopped his appeals and was executed, another had recently stopped his appeals, and eight others had told their families or attorneys they were stopping theirs. Deans claimed their will to live was drained by the system and by the effect they saw their sentences were having on their families.

Once the Coalition began counseling these men and their families, all nine resumed their appeals.

A Rabbit Hole of Inhumanity

> One of the saddest facts about the people on death row is that once you know their true – and almost always hidden – stories, the wonder becomes, not that they murdered, but that they didn't murder sooner and more often.
> -Marie Deans, in an address to the Illinois Synod of the American Lutheran Church, Springfield, Illinois, May 31, 1986.

Deans moved to Richmond in January 1983 and soon found herself spiraling into the vortex of corruption, violence, and inhumanity within the Virginia DOC and especially on death row at MCC. She teamed up with Lloyd Snook for client visits, where she found out officials routinely opened legal mail, cut short or denied attorney visits, and shackled inmates during visits. Sometimes she was allowed only to speak to inmates through their cell door food slot.

In her opinion, she found more humanity in the inmates than she found in Virginia's antiquated legal processes and corrections personnel. Virginia had long denied capital defendants due process. Attorneys with no experience in criminal cases (dubbed "real estate attorneys" by Steven Rosenfield) frequently found themselves appointed to a death penalty case. Courts were negligent in providing capital witnesses or pre-trial investigations. Judges rushed through the trials, and verdicts came quickly, with little deliberation.

Capital defendants in Virginia went to "trial by ambush" without knowing who the witnesses were against them. They also had no right to know who the police interviewed and no right to know what those witnesses told police unless it was exculpatory.

With a death sentence hanging over a recently-sentenced inmate and with no attorney provided, Deans and even fellow inmates like Giarratano scrambled to find a lawyer willing to take the case on a *pro bono* (unpaid) basis.

"I started having to go further and further afield," Deans testified in *Giarratano v. Murray*. She also said she frequently had to make telephone inquiries up and down the East Coast to find any lawyer who would take a death row appeal.

In a 1985 letter "to whom it may concern," Roger Coleman wrote that he found himself on death row a year earlier without an attorney and an imminent court filing deadline. "Mrs. Deans, in a 30-day period, ran up a $500 phone bill in a successful effort to locate attorneys for myself and two other death row prisoners who were without attorneys. When all others refused to help us it was VCJP that came forward to assist us."

"[Deans] was like the death row mom," Laura LaFay explained. "And she'd be the one to come around and say, 'Now you need to file an order for state review representation,' 'Now you need to file an order for U.S. District Court.' None of these guys would have known anything, but Marie made sure that happened."

Fr. Griffin recalled meeting Deans around 1984. "She would have us try to raise funds for the VADP at the time when it was just a fledgling," he said. "She would meet me out of prison and come up with an idea about what to do. Then I'd see her on death row when we go do mass with Bishop Sullivan, and she'd be there for that. There was no one like her, and she really gave her life to the movement."

Many lawyers were resistant to Deans' requests, as death row appeals were considered the "ulcer-producing" side of the practice because of the enormous work involved with a human life in the balance. Richmond lawyer Dennis W. Dohnal told the July 11, 1986, *Richmond Times-Dispatch* that he spent 250 futile hours on the appeal of death row inmate Charles Stamper. In that class-action suit, other lawyers testified that they spent a similar number of hours working on death row appeal cases.

Steve Northup recalled how Deans approached him to become involved in death penalty habeas work. "I was a corporate attorney representing corporate and business clients. But not too long after we went down to [the 1984 Linwood Briley] protest, I volunteered to take on a habeas corpus case. Marie Deans needed somebody in Virginia because Virginia was getting ready to execute a lot of people. And there were no lawyers for these guys that were on death row to challenge their convictions."

"[Since] they had no right to get court-appointed counsel, the only way was through volunteer attorneys. And Marie was recruiting attorneys to represent these guys. And at the time, it was all guys on death row starting in the late 1980s, somewhere around in there. We lost the case, and eventually, our client was executed."

Smear and Discredit

The VCJP was sponsored and funded until 1985 by Lutheran Social Services (LSS) of Greater Washington D.C.'s Department of Advocacy and Education. After 1985, LSS disbanded, and the coalition was incorporated. The VCJP's board of directors included appellate attorneys, clergy, a death row inmate, a non-death row inmate, and those involved with prison reform, counseling, and abolition. The coalition also had excellent working relationships with the NAACP Legal Defense Fund and had credibility with clerks of courts from Virginia Circuit Court up to the U.S. Supreme Court.

Deans brought humanity and order where there was none. She designated older, more reliable inmates to be monitors to watch and ensure nothing happened to the newer and younger inmates in the death row pods. She also convinced some of the more trustworthy guards to look after them or face the consequences directly from her.

Inmates who misbehaved or broke the rules faced the real threat of losing her support, which they sorely needed. When Wayne DeLong beat up Charles Stamper, leaving him paralyzed from the waist down, he received the full brunt of Deans' anger. "I'm out here living on a pauper's wage and trying to raise my son and working like 120 hours a week to prove that ya'll are not a future danger, and you just go out and prove that you are," she shouted at him. "I'm trying to keep your ass out of the electric chair, and you're trying to put everybody's in it."

DeLong heard loud and clear, and he became one of Deans' most trusted death row monitors until his 1993 suicide.

Virginia DOC did not submit its prisons to inspection, audit, or accreditation by the American Correctional Association, so officials who had mostly been free to treat death row inmates as severely as they pleased had no idea how to deal with Deans and her coalition. After conceding numerous treatment and legal rights issues in a 1984 federal court case, in which Judge Robert Merhige Jr. ordered the DOC to "stop their games," the department instead resorted to scurrilous slanders and insults to attack Deans, the VCJP, and their relationships with the men on the row. One assistant warden, obsessed with the long hours Deans spent with Joe Giarratano, told Giarratano's attorney that Marie and Joe were having an affair, citing phone calls and "love letters" as evidence.

After hearing of this, Deans got up in the warden's face at her next visit and reminded him that since she was working as a paralegal, any calls and letters between her and her clients were confidential and that he violated the law by making them public.

Still, the rumors persisted until the FBI, at the behest of the DOC, opened an investigation into Deans' relationships with the men on the row to assess her likelihood to "harbor death row inmates." Someone in the DOC told the FBI that Deans was likely to conceal an escaped South Carolina death row inmate named Fred Kornahrens due to her "extreme viewpoint" on the death penalty.

When questioned by the FBI about harboring Kornahrens and a possible romantic relationship with one Virginia death row inmate, Deans reportedly snapped, "What, only one? I would have thought rumor mongers would have had it up to at least ten by now."

The final report failed to recognize Dean's sarcasm and painted her not as a hard-working paralegal but another death row murder groupie, stating that she, by her admission, was romantically linked to at least "ten or eleven" death row inmates in Virginia and South Carolina.

In the book "A Courageous Fool," Deans was blunt in her assessment of the Virginia DOC, the FBI, and the "Virginia way" during those early years. "The thing about these people that drove me crazy was their pettiness ... and this fucking good ol' boy shit."

"Marie is supposed to have a cantankerous kind of personality, but we never had words," penitentiary chaplain Russ Ford recalled his relationship with Deans. "We got along great. I loved her. She loved me. We were out all hours of the night together, working with capital punishment issues. So, yeah, I'm a fan, and I think she was a fan of mine. And I guess in many ways, we were the only ones that could understand each other."

Threats and Intimidation

Marie Deans' actions humanized the death row inmates, which sat badly with the DOC, leading the anger against her to escalate. Counseling death row inmates had always been disapproved in the penal system, as it disrupted a process designed to drain the men of their will to live so they would go quietly to their execution.

One morning in 1983, Deans found a realistically stuffed body bag by her front door. Several months later, a chalk outline of a body was in her parking space. She had to replace six slashed tires on her car in one eight-month period – something she could ill-afford on her salary. "I have received more threatening remarks, letters, and telephone calls than I could begin to count," she wrote in a Nov. 11, 1983 letter to her friends on death row. "I've been threatened with every known torture and told I should be put in your laps when you go to the chair."

While there was never any definitive proof these actions originated within the DOC, Deans knew they had.

The $35,000 taxpayer-financed heart operation

One death row case Deans took up was that of Manuel Quintana, a Cuban refugee convicted and sentenced to death for the 1981 murder of an Arlington woman. Quintana reportedly knew only three words of English, with two of them "electric chair." Deans found out that Quintana had been a doctor in Cuba and that the Castro regime had murdered his father.

As she investigated his case, Quintana had a heart attack on the row. Though he survived, Medical College of Virginia doctors determined that only major open-heart surgery would save his life. The DOC refused the operation and transported Quintana back to MCC. Once back on the row, Quintana suffered a second heart attack, and he was rushed again to Richmond. This time the DOC relented, authorizing the $35,000 procedure. Quintana, however, refused the surgery, and he died a fews days later. Deans was with him when he died of cardiac arrest.

Bishop Sullivan personally celebrated his funeral Mass.

A Lawsuit Ends the Coalition

In the months leading up to the May 20, 1992 execution of Roger Coleman, his law firm issued press releases attesting to his innocence, going so far as naming who they believed was the real killer.

Deans was shocked that they also added her name on the releases, despite warning them not to. Then, as could be expected, that man later filed a $5 million lawsuit against the attorneys and Deans.

Washington lawyer David Kendall agreed to represent a panicky Deans in the suit, and he was successful in getting her name released from it – but the damage was done. Foundations and major donors who had earlier agreed to give her coalition grant money refused to do so until the suit got settled. Worse, money promised to her by the firm for working hundreds of hours with Coleman was never paid.

Out of money, the VCJP permanently closed its doors on Aug. 31, 1993, after 12 years. Deans, who never made more than $13,000 a year as the director, drew no salary in that last year of existence.

Refusing to slow down and living on donations, she became a self-taught mitigation expert and with Charlottesville attorney Denise Lunsford founded the Virginia Mitigation Project (VMP). She also continued to bring fundamental human rights to the inmates on death row through lectures, debates, and sharing her mitigation expertise. She was a natural-born storyteller and could weave facts and statistics into a compelling narrative presented to juries weighing life or death. Because of her diligence, only two of the 200 men she helped defend during their sentencing hearings ultimately received a death sentence.

"I'm more frustrated than discouraged. It seems like as we moved closer and closer to the public finally saying, 'Get this off our backs,' then the money [ran] out," Deans told the *Richmond Times-Dispatch*. "What this [election] has displayed very prominently is that fear is really a political commodity, and that's what politicians are using."

She still had a fight inside – she jumped into the Earl Washington case and stayed with it until October 2000, when Gov. Jim Gilmore, after a year-long delay, finally granted Washington a pardon.

Deans released a press release to counterpoint Gilmore's bland announcement of Washington's innocence. "We have kept a man-child on our death row for almost ten years and came within days of killing him because the State has placed finality over truth," she seethed. "Because our laws and rules address procedure and technicalities over justice, and because we simply refuse to recognize that our system is far from perfect. It is time for us to change the laws and rules and attitudes that allow for stories like Earl's to happen."

"One More Turn of the Screw"

> When proponents of the death penalty ask me what I would do with all of these "misfits," or "monsters," or "animals" on death row, I ask them if they have ever wondered why our society produces so many murderers. The usual response is either a blank look or intense anger.
> -Marie Deans, Illinois Synod address, May 31, 1986.

With Washington freed and the Coalition shuttered, Deans believed her days as a death penalty activist were likely over. She hunkered inside her Charlottesville townhouse, her health failing most likely due to PTSD, scraping by doing medical transcription work and wondering why the world seemed to have turned its back on her. In 2002 she started writing her memoir and even applied for a fellowship with the Virginia Foundation for the Humanities. Despite spending months "praying to the fellowship gods," her application was rejected, and she was devastated.

As Deans finished chapters of her memoir, she became more and more frustrated that no literary agents or publishers were interested. When one friend suggested she send it to a smaller academic press for less money, she snapped, "I can't afford to [be paid] in prestige."

By 2005 her health had worsened. She was bedridden with a severely broken ankle, and then she was diagnosed with lung cancer. Bouts of nervous exhaustion and depression complicated her excruciating back and leg pain and kept her on a cocktail of medicines, leaving her confused, angry, and frequently child-like. She still shared letters with her old friend Joe Giarratano at Deerfield Correctional and sometimes expressed guilt of bemoaning her situation while Joe sat for decades in prison, wrongfully convicted.

Two weeks before Deans died, she moved into a Charlottesville Rehabilitation clinic and rekindled her friendship with Denise Lundsford, the attorney who had worked with her at the Virginia Mitigation Project. Lundsford visited daily, bringing food and ensuring she was getting proper care.

Marie Deans died at age 70 on April 15, 2011 in Lundford's arms. She was buried in North Carolina.

Yet another victim of Virginia's death penalty.

Abolition Efforts 1976 - 1990

VADP, VAADP, then VADP Again

Why do we kill people who kill people to show that killing people is wrong?
                                                                    -Early VADP slogan.

In January 1985, Pizza Hut ran a nationwide commercial humorously depicting a death row inmate facing imminent execution ordering a pizza for his last meal. When he received news of a gubernatorial pardon, he was saddened because he would not get his pizza. The ad closed with, "After all, you only live once."

The commercial created controversy in Virginia and the Deep South but especially in South Carolina, where the ad was uncomfortably similar to the execution of J.C. Shaw. He ordered a pizza for his last meal. Pizza Hut pulled the ad.

"That such an advertisement could be conceived, produced, and used is a sign of serious moral sickness," stated a story in the February 1985 issue of *Life Lines*, the newsletter of the National Coalition Against the Death Penalty. "That such an abomination sparked spontaneous outrage sufficient to bring it to an end is an encouraging sign of health."

Being Proactive

Another "encouraging sign of health" in Virginia was a vigil on Jan. 16, 1977, sponsored by the Roman Catholic Office of Social Ministry and held outside the State Penitentiary for the imminent execution in Utah of Gary Gilmore. Also attending was a brand-new group of about a dozen proactive, faith-based volunteer advocates calling themselves Virginians Against the Death Penalty (VADP).

At a December 1976 press conference, Deborah Leavy, head of the ACLU national movement against capital punishment, and Rev. Emmett Cocke, Pastor of Pace Memorial United Methodist Church (now Pace Center for Campus and Community Ministries) at Virginia Commonwealth University, claimed that "unfounded myths along with ignorance of the facts" surrounding the death penalty were driving legislators to "embrace the ultimate punishment once again."

Leavy explained that proponents of capital punishment were under the delusion that it was an "easy answer" as an effective crime fighter and that it saved taxpayers money by eliminating the cost of housing criminals who receive life sentences.

The country was going through a significant reckoning in the mid-and late-1970s. Society seemed to be unraveling; inner cities were crumbling, and drug use and violent crime were skyrocketing. Interest rates climbed to stratospheric highs, keeping many out of new homes, and the price of fuels such as gasoline and heating oil crept higher. America was also embarrassed by failures in Vietnam and Iran, when embassy workers were taken hostage and held for 444 days.

Consequently, politicians found in this dreary environment that crime could pay for them by becoming tougher on it. Law and order became the rallying cry, from presidential to county sheriff elections, candidates all vied to prove who was toughest on crime. As a result, nationwide, the death penalty was extended to dozens of new crimes, and appeals and other protections for capital defendants were dramatically cut back and, in some cases, eliminated.

Rev. Cocke said that it was "urgent for Virginians to speak out now against the death penalty before laws of the state make it legal and killing by the state is a reality."

Cocke, who claimed to oppose the death penalty on both moral and practical grounds, was one of the first protestors to publicly acknowledge that capital punishment, as administered before the 1972 *Furman* decision, was discriminatory in that it was imposed more often on the poor and minorities. He used Gary Gilmore to point out that his desire to drop appeals and face a firing squad "dramatizes that the commonwealth can be put in the position of granting a death wish – a suicide wish."

Leavy characterized Gilmore as a "loser who is having the only victory in his life, and the state of Utah is providing it."

"We need to keep people off the streets," she agreed, "but I think we can do that without inflicting the death penalty – becoming murderers ourselves."

The May 25, 1979, execution of John Spenkelink in Florida invoked partisans on both sides of the death penalty controversy to argue that other states, especially Virginia, would be encouraged to follow Florida's lead. Unlike Gilmore, who chose to be executed, Spenkelink went unwillingly to his death after exhausting years of appeals for the murder of an ex-convict named Joe Szymankiewicz.

Prison officials across the United States reported that the Spenkelink execution had a chilling effect on condemned prisoners in death row cells. Henry Schwarzschild told reporters, "First Utah, now Florida. The state role of bloody dishonor is growing ... the question is how many lives will be taken by American executioners before the death penalty is abolished."

On the day of the Spenkelink execution, members of VADP – who were trying to form chapters in Richmond, Charlottesville, and Tidewater – again stood vigil outside the penitentiary. Rev. Cocke said they were protesting "the kind of society that produces criminals then executes them."

But not all members of the faith community were entirely on board with abolition, at least in Spenkelink's case. The Rev. Calvin Eaves of Richmond's Clover Hill Baptist Church said that a day of mourning for victims of violent crime was more appropriate. Of Spenkelink, he said, "I can't shed too many crocodile tears over this."

Records of this early adaptation of VADP are almost non-existent, and any other abolition efforts by them are unknown. Rev. Cocke left Richmond in 1979 to serve as pastor in churches in Alexandria until his death of cancer in 1992.

Virginians Against the Death Penalty

In October 1981, after the resumption of the death penalty but before the state resumed executions, another volunteer group called Virginians Against the Death Penalty formed within the Virginia ACLU under the leadership of Chan Kendrick and Bruce Cruser, of the Citizens for Humane and effective Corrections. It billed itself as a "statewide membership organization working specifically to halt all executions in Virginia; to educate the public regarding the myths surrounding capital punishment; to monitor cases in the commonwealth with the potential to be capital cases; and develop an organized lobby to oppose the expansion of death sentences."

"Seventy-one percent of all prisoners under sentence of death are in Southern prisons and jails," an Oct. 29, 1981 mission statement/letter stated. "There has never been a more pressing need for a broadly based organization concerned about the states increasing and misguided tendency to use death as an instrument of public policy."

At the time, Virginia was the only southern state without a cohesive coalition of individuals laser-focused on opposing the death penalty, despite 17 men already on death row and with executions getting ready to start again after an almost 20-year hiatus.

Stop, Regroup, Restart

After two years of being unable to get off the ground due to the lack of funding, a specific plan, or a prepared structure, Virginians Against the Death Penalty (VADP) emerged again in 1983, this time as a member of the Southern Coalition of Jails and Prisons, and led unofficially by Donna and Jerome Gorman. A handout stated the group worked through "education, advocacy, legislative monitoring, and public witness" to oppose capital punishment. Like the previous incarnation, the group also expressed plans to expand in other cities as awareness grew.

One of the group's annual activities was holding interfaith press conferences at the State Capitol in honor of President Reagan's National Day of Prayer. "We affirm our concern for law and justice in society," a May 3, 1984 statement read in part. "The arbitrary and capricious imposition of the death sentence mocks justice. The factor of human error renders capital punishment an immoral act because it negates the possibility of restitution and correction of inadvertent errors."

During the 1984 National Day of Prayer, Norfolk Del. J. Samuel Glasscock, an ardent death penalty opponent who had witnessed the execution of Frank Coppola, joined the group at the podium. "Executing criminals is a killing," Glasscock told the small crowd at the Capitol. "It is a premeditated killing." Other speakers included Fr. James Griffin, Rabbi Beverly Lerner, and Rev. James Payne.

This variant of VADP succeeded in establishing chapters in Richmond, Norfolk, Charlottesville, and Northern Virginia, but again, as an all-volunteer organization, struggled with proactive organizing and advocacy in the pro-execution headwinds.

More Than Attending Vigils

In 1986, BJ Brown Devlin was instrumental in organizing a coalition including members of the Catholic Diocese, the Virginia Interfaith Center for Public Policy, and the

ACLU into the first formal statewide abolition organization called the Virginia Association Against the Death Penalty (VAADP). A Campaign for Human Development (CHD) grant from the U.S. Conference of Catholic Bishops provided funding for two years, and the ACLU donated a basement office space at Six N. 16th Street in Richmond among several other non-profits.

The Gormans did not join this effort, as they concentrated their efforts on their abolition group, People for Abolishing Legal Murder (PALM).

Devlin explained that since the CHD typically funded grassroots organizations, she had to make the case that VAADP, while rooted in the faith community, was still a "collaborative effort to enact social change" in which the grassroots had not yet formed.

A Proposal Narrative noted that the board of directors included veterans from previous abolition attempts, "all of which were short-lived due to a lack of organizational focus, start-up funds, and a statewide orientation." The narrative also described that "VAADP differs from previous efforts in its experience, specific focus, organizational linkages and commitment to hire full-time staff to ensure continuity and implementation of a cohesive anti-death penalty strategy." Devlin also stressed that their work complimented, not replaced, the diligent work of Marie Deans, who functioned then as much as a death row paralegal and counselor than just an abolitionist.

The announcement of the formation of VAADP rankled some members of the four existing chapters of VADP, as they had not been consulted or made aware of a "statewide" abolition organization. But as VAADP noted in their mission statement, pre-1985 opposition to the death penalty had been sporadic and primarily limited to crisis response in the form of letter writing, church services, and vigils at the penitentiary during executions. These were generally followed by a period of inactivity until the announcement of the next execution.

A Dec. 17, 1985 letter from Rev. David Lee in Charlottesville to ACLU Director Chan Hendrick stated that he knew members in Charlottesville "were not satisfied with just attending vigils on execution dates," or with the organization's lack of focus and a general plan.

"I have evidence that others in other chapters are also ready to do something more than just attend vigils," he continued. "The energy is out here and ready. It is therefore unfortunate and awkward that a breach appears between grassroots chapters and your board. We do need to get our act together, all of us ...."

George Ricketts, executive director of the Chaplain Service and the first president of VAADP, responded for Kendrick on Dec. 23 that they had unsuccessfully tried to involve the various scattered members of the VADP chapter with the formation of VAADP. Ricketts said the group selected the name VAADP as distinct and different from VADP after that group refused to meet with them.

Ricketts closed his response on a conciliatory note. "I appreciate your interest in fighting the death penalty and hope the Charlottesville group will want to be a part of this new effort."

For the first two years, veteran activists and representatives from statewide organizations who shared opposition to the death penalty primarily comprised VAADP. In addition to Ricketts, Kendrick, and Devlin, others included Bruce Cruser; Dena Joy of the Richmond Friends; ACLU Board member Stephen Retherford; Attorneys Richard Taylor and Gerald Zerkin; and former death row inmate Clyde Near. In January 1987, a 15-member board elected by the membership replaced the interim board of directors at the first annual meeting.

The organization set ambitious goals for the tough road they were traveling. They planned to build opposition to capital punishment with citizen legislative advocacy and educate the public about Virginia's death penalty's "discriminatory peculiarities." They set a goal to fashion a statewide coalition that better reflected Virginia's racial and economic diversity by creating six chapters in various regions. They finally stated they would "fight for laws that would restrict the use of and ultimately abolish the death penalty in Virginia."

The 1980s were a challenging time for abolition work. "I ran VAADP for a few years," explained Julie McConnell, who became executive director in 1989 and continued until the money ran out in early 1991. "My main job as director was community organizing and lobbying. We couldn't abolish the death penalty at the time, but we could try to keep further expansion from being enacted, and we could also try to work around the edges."

When the original CHD grant ended, money got tight. "We raised some money. We kept going for a while, but eventually, it just became very difficult. We worked hard and did great stuff, but it was on a shoestring, and we were in this tiny little basement office with no windows."

Because funding was such a problem, McConnell said that she had to split her time between VAADP and the Virginia Interfaith Center for Public Policy to pay her bills. Then, when VAADP folded, she moved to Wyoming. "I had been doing all this anti-death penalty work, going to death row, organizing vigils, and working at the county assembly. And it was so intense, and I decided maybe working with kids made more sense. Perhaps I could intervene in such a way that they wouldn't end up on death row."

There were some VAADP successes in that short time. McConnell introduced standards of counsel that eventually were adopted, maintaining that no attorney could be appointed to a capital case without meeting those standards.

"They were certainly never as rigorous as we would like," she recalled, "but they were better than nothing. They had to have experience as a first chair who had done capital cases, and they had to have gone to the training at the capital case clearinghouse. So that was one of the initiatives that we succeeded in getting passed."

VAADP also lobbied with the ACLU to get mitigation added to jury instruction. "Before that, the jury was not required nor instructed to consider mitigation. So that was huge to add intellectual disability, for example, to the mitigation that juries had to consider."

These mitigation guidelines, expanded in 2003 and again in 2008, stated that a mitigation investigation should begin immediately upon legal counsel's entry into a case. This investigation would delve into family history and court, school, social service, and other government agency records. Consulted experts would determine the defendant's competency to stand trial, looking at any insanity, intellectual disability, or other aberrational background issues. They also sometimes reached out to the victim's family, clergy, and anyone else closely associated with them to gather facts.

After VAADP folded in early 1991, it wasn't long before another organization rose to take its place.

Behind Closed Doors and Curtains: Virginia's Legacy of Death Penalty Secrecy

In 1984 or '85 ... I put in a bill to reinstitute public hangings. I was completely serious. I was in the old city hall and saw this picture of the old scaffolds, right on Capitol Square. In the old days, everybody saw the executions, but now we put executions so far out of sight they don't have any effect. I voted against lethal injection the same way ... [With LI], execution became a very casual thing: you just gave them an injection and they slipped away. It made it comfortable for the public. I don't think it makes any difference how you execute somebody — hanging, firing squad, or lethal injection. It's all execution, isn't it?

-Former Republican Hanover County Del. Frank D. Hargrove Sr., *Style Weekly*, Jan. 31, 2001.

Change of Heart

Elected to the Legislature in 1982, Del. Frank D. Hargrove Sr. quantified his law-and-order agenda with his 1984 bill to resume public hangings. His reasoning was to display the punishment as a deterrent.

It was not the first time a legislator raised the specter of public execution in the Virginia General Assembly since the re-introduction of the death penalty in 1976. That same year, Virginia Beach Republican Sen. Joseph Canada said he would introduce a bill to permit executions, probably not in the town square but in a public place, to deter crime. "The press, the public, and anyone who wants to go to [an execution] should be able to do so," he told a UPI reporter. He predicted offering the legislation in the 1977 Assembly session.

Charlottesville Democrat Sen. J. Harry Michael was also in favor of a public execution bill. He admitted that there were no figures to prove that capital punishment deterred crime, but he insisted, "there is no statistical proof that it doesn't deter crime."

A lawyer, Michael claimed he spoke to numerous individuals charged with felonious assault who admitted to him that "I would have killed the so and so, but I didn't want to fry."

It is unknown if any other public execution bills were ever introduced.

By 2000, however, the very conservative Hargrove displayed a new attitude about the death penalty that he said evolved just after ending parole five years earlier. That year he unsuccessfully introduced a bill to abolish the death penalty entirely. He then re-introduced the bill every General Assembly session for several years afterward, only to see it laughed out of committee on the first day.

"Execution is a permanent, irreversible action, even though evidence may occur later that it was wrong to do that," he told the *Washington Post*. "Life without parole provides the same service without the same finality."

Both Sen. Canada's point in 1976 and Sen. Hargrove's eight years later contended that executions conducted behind closed doors defeated the purpose – making it public would, as in colonial Jamestown days, induce fear and disgust then, ultimately, deterrence.

Of course, his public hanging bill – like his abolition bills – went nowhere.

Unsavory Spectacles

For over 280 years, starting in 1622 and continuing until 1909, hangings were public and sometimes attended by hundreds or even thousands of people. Public executions in the communities where the crimes occurred were believed to have virtue and be a crime deterrent.

In 1849 England, author Charles Dickens felt otherwise. In November of that year, Dickens witnessed the public hanging of husband-and-wife murderers. He shared his experience in a letter to the editor of the *London Times*, where he described the gathered 30,000 revelers as "so inconceivably awful as the wickedness and levity of the immense crowd collected at that execution this morning could be imagined by no man."

The bacchanal circus of singing and dancing spectators he witnessed celebrated the state killings. Nobody left deterred or swearing off lives of future crime.

In Virginia's Black communities, public executions also evolved into something unanticipated. Hundreds or even thousands sometimes showed up at public hangings of mostly young Black men. They brought picnic lunches, sang, and prayed aloud with the prisoner. Food stands and patent medicine sellers began popping up.

Virginia's white ruling classes were shocked that those public and predominantly Black executions, like those in Britain, were infused with evangelical fervor until they more resembled carnivals or tent revivals than executions.

A frustrated Virginia General Assembly, on March 29, 1879, abruptly passed a law banning public hangings following a bizarre spectacle that occurred only four days earlier at the New Kent County Courthouse, just a few miles east of Richmond.

The Gallows Ball

On March 25, two young Black men, 21-year-old Julius Christian and 20-year-old Patrick Smith hanged for robbery and murder in the courthouse yard. Their executions were attended by about a thousand people, almost exclusively Blacks. News stories reported that the field resembled a country fair. Food and beverage booths were erected. An "educated pig" and itinerant musicians "enlivened the occasion." One enterprising northerner even set up a sideshow of some kind.

After the hangings and the burials, the few whites drifted away, but the Blacks reportedly hung around the shallow graves of the recently deceased felons until dark, supposedly determined to have a celebration but not wanting to begin until midnight due to local superstition.

Then, the announcement surged among the crowd that a "Grand Gallows Ball" would commence at midnight inside a nearby tobacco barn. As the clock struck midnight, about 500 people gathered inside the barn, waiting for the signal to begin.

An unnamed reporter who covered the hangings also attended the ball. "It was a weird scene," he wrote in a dispatch to the *Cincinnati Enquirer*, "the building was lighted by pine torches held by negro boys stationed in the corners," casting the barn in a spooky, smoky haze. He also reported the odd ethnic mix of the attendees, including not just "young Black men and maidens," but also "a dozen beautiful quadroons (people one-fourth Black) from Richmond, and in the center of the building stood seven or eight Indians, belonging to the tribe from Indian Town nearby." A band consisted of three banjo players and a fiddler set up in a corner.

Crank up the Band!

Days were hard, road got rough
Turned in his papers, and he'd had enough
But late at night all alone
Those old times shone – through the Mississippi Sawyer.
- "The Mississippi Sawyer," lyrics by The Hill Billies, music traditional,
recorded 1926.

At midnight, a "burley tobacco hand" named Isaiah Peterson, introduced as "the boss negro," stood on a salt barrel and announced, "The hour for rejoicing is at hand! Let the musicians take notice, and all others! Choose your partners!" The band then struck up a traditional instrumental called "The Mississippi Sawyer." Everyone began dancing with wild abandon in a surprisingly integrated fashion. "The Indians danced with quadroons, negro men danced with colored girls, and all went merry as a marriage-ball," wrote the astonished reporter. "As the music went on, the musicians and dancers grew wilder and wilder, as though possessed by the devil."

The festivities continued until 2:00 a.m., when Lucina Macon, a local woman considered a "Voudou Negress," appeared in the center of the ballroom, wearing a blue and white checkered dress. She waved her hand, and the music stopped. Then, she took out slivers of hemp rope from a red bag, sprinkled them with something from an old jug, and started a series of incantations, reported as "... in what the negroes say here is an African dialect." She claimed in a loud voice that it was the rope cut from the Smith and Christian gallows and that if the dancers purchased a piece of the rope for 50 cents, they would live 90 years and be safe from all evil, even from those who may trick or poison them.

There was such a rush to purchase the rope pieces that a fight broke out, and those who could not get a piece "acted like fiends" and begged others for even a thread. The woman then announced that for those who did not get a bit of rope, only an article of clothing of the recently deceased would "affect the charm" and save them.

A hundred people reportedly rushed to the graves of Smith and Christian, only to flee back to the barn in horror, claiming the ghosts of the two men were seen walking around their burial sites. Lucina informed them that Smith and Christian had not died because she had given them "the charm." Several women reportedly fainted at the news.

Later, the reporter determined that the dancers had interrupted two resurrectionists (grave robbers), most likely Chris Baker and his partner, Ceaser Roane. They stole freshly-buried corpses for student dissection at Richmond's Medical College of Virginia (now VCU School of Medicine).

Most of the agitated crowd hurried home, but a few stayed until 5:00 a.m. to sing a doxology, concluding the Gallows Ball. Lucina announced that all who danced at the Gallows Ball would be able to dance for the rest of their lives, "even if they lived until ninety."

When the General Assembly rushed through their bill prohibiting public executions, the April 2 *Petersburg Progress-Index* smugly reported, "this shall put an end to all such gallows picnics and jollifications as was witnessed at New Kent Court-house."

Or, maybe not. "The Gallows Ball in New Kent was such a success that the darkies are talking about getting one up in Chesterfield [April 25]," stated the April 3, 1879 *Alexandria Gazette.* "The passage of the bill by the Legislature prohibiting public executions, while [keeping] the crowds from watching the dying of the poor wretches, will not prevent the gallows ball – the new departure in colored circles."

The article added that Henry Lewis, "a comely looking negro youth," would be hung because he was convicted of killing his grandmother with an ax when she refused to give him a piece of ginger cake. Lucina, the "old Virginia negro Voudou doctress," would also attend.

Gov. Claude Swanson, however, commuted Henry Lewis's sentence to life in the penitentiary, so there was no Chesterfield Gallows Ball.

The secrecy law had no discernable effect on limiting crowds at hangings, as all it did was specify that localities build a wall or hang a curtain around the scaffold. Thousands still sometimes gathered for hangings, only to stand on nearby hills or, in some cases, scale the wall then sit and watch. It wasn't until 1908, when the General Assembly considered the switch from hanging to the electric chair, that they effectively ended public executions.

Somber White Witnesses

> If there is anything that awes a negro, it is that which is mysterious and inexplicable, and the methods of death which we have described would have greater restraining influence on intending criminals than any form of punishment now in vogue.
> -The *Richmond Virginian* newspaper, after describing alternative execution methods as adding cyanide to an inmate's food, March 22, 1910.

Legislators and newspapers around the commonwealth overwhelmingly approved the 1908 law, which moved executions from open-air hangings accompanied by long speeches and parties to an electric chair in a grim basement in front of a handful of somber white witnesses. The Oct. 14, 1908 edition of the *Richmond Times-Dispatch* explained that "The publicity, the excitement and the general hurrah-and-holiday air attending the old-time hanging were a positive allurement to the negro ... The electric execution wholly does away with that ... the whole affair is conducted with secrecy and mystery, well calculated to inspire terror in the heart of the superstitious African."

The new statute also prohibited newspapers from publishing any details of electrocutions – laws remaining in effect until 2021. Photographs, illustrations, and films of actual electrocutions were expressly forbidden. There was no penalty for violation, but the press "observed the spirit of the law, if not the letter, ... For the wholesome effect it will unquestionably have in Virginia."

As a result, there are very few eyewitness descriptions of actual electrocutions from this period. The ones that exist are purposefully vague to comply with the "spirit" of the execution law.

The removal of public executions to a private basement was considered a victory for both progressive reformers, who desired a more humane form of execution, and Jim Crow segregationists, who wanted to stop large groups of Blacks from congregating and partying in public. Surrounding the execution process in awe and mystery was a white win-win.

Rat Poison: The Switch to Lethal Injection

> States have circumvented this carefully and extensively regulated supply chain to acquire drugs for use in lethal injection. They use overseas sellers, unlicensed middlemen, and secret compounding pharmacies. The result is twofold: it undermines federal laws that protect the public health, and it circumvents pharmaceutical companies' ability to ensure the safety and effectiveness of drugs in the supply chain.
> -Amicus Brief of Pharmacy, Medicine, and Health Policy Experts in *Bucklew v. Precythe.*

Virginia first considered switching away from electric chair executions to lethal injection (LI) in 1988. Bill sponsor Sen. John H. Chichester, a Republican from Stafford County, cited the method's popularity in other states as either a singular execution method or an option. Chichester also truthfully exhorted that LI was designed not to be more humane to the condemned inmate but to the inmate's family members, who were handed a battered and blistered body with cooked organs and crushed joints after an electrocution.

A coalition of religious and medical professionals and death penalty opponents helped kill the measure by arguing vehemently against it. Frederick H. Gretenhart, director of the newly formed VAADP, said Chichester's bill merely put a sugar coating on state-sanctioned killing. "Lethal injection may be more obscene," he told the House Courts of Justice Committee, "because it provides the illusion of humaneness in the killing."

In the December 1988 *Virginia Medical Journal*, Drs. Jerome Gorman, Dieter Groeschel, and Richard Keenan agreed that lethal injection "looks more like therapy than punishment ... The only difference is that the 'patient,' once 'put to sleep,' is not recovered. By wrapping punishment in a therapeutic cloak, the whole process leading to that final moment feels less aversive to those who are required to participate and is, therefore, more bearable."

"Direct physician involvement (which isn't needed and probably would not be requested) is not an issue here. The issue is the use of a therapeutic model for capital punishment."

In a Jan. 22, 1988 letter to Sen. Chichester, Amnesty International director William Menza wrote in part:

> ... I disagree with your comments: 'I can't imagine anyone thinking this wouldn't be easier than using the electric chair. There's less drama; it's less news. It's just easier.' I also find your comments most upsetting, because they seem to indicate that we are dealing with cattle and not with human beings. Your comments appear to reflect a kind of cold, indifferent dehumanization characteristic of political philosophies in the Soviet Union, or Iran, or even what was followed by some Axis countries during World War II.

The committee voted down LI by a vote of 27-12.

Newport News Republican Del. Phillip Hamilton re-introduced LI during the 1991 Assembly session, but again the proposal died in the House Courts of Justice Committee. The following August, the execution of Derick L. Peterson, who had to be administered two jolts of electricity almost 8 minutes apart before he was declared dead, forced legislators to reconsider. In 1994, the Assembly officially approved lethal injection as the default method of execution, with electrocution on standby.

Jon Sheldon insisted that the change to lethal injection was due to aesthetics. "We know that electrocution has a lot of problems, but it works fast. Smoking, all these problems, and that's why people don't like electrocution. It looks ugly."

There was always potential cruel and unusual risk in using LI as Virginia legislated. As the first drug in the three-drug execution protocol, midazolam, a sedative used in several botched executions in other states, was supposed to place the inmate in a coma, unable to feel the effects of subsequent drugs. However, if the midazolam did not work as intended, the subject was paralyzed by the rocuronium bromide, suffocating under fluid that quickly accumulated in the lungs. Then, as the third drug, potassium chloride, chemically burned the blood vessels, witnesses would have no clue that the inmate was being tortured, as they would see no outward reactions.

The cynical side of abolitionists may claim that the only reason a paralytic was administered after a sedative in the protocol was to spare witnesses from seeing the condemned person's distress.

In 2015, the General Assembly, the DOC, and Gov. McAuliffe acted to conceal LI procedures in heavier secrecy. This act was not to "inspire terror in the heart of the superstitious African" as in 1908 but to hide the processes from the media and the general public and to shield providers, such as pharmacies and drug manufacturers, from potential liability and political blowback.

In April 2016, McAuliffe, a Democrat, gutted a bill passed by the General Assembly that would have mandated the electric chair for executions if the state couldn't obtain the increasingly scarce drugs required for lethal injection. The three drugs had legitimate medical uses but had become challenging to obtain because of concern by the manufacturers that some states were using them to kill people.

"These manufacturers will not do business in Virginia if their identities are to be revealed," McAuliffe insisted in an attempt to justify the subterfuge and protect the suppliers. McAuliffe, a Catholic who claimed to be personally opposed to capital punishment, declared he was only trying to avoid using the electric chair, which he called a "reprehensible" method of execution.

McAuliffe instead introduced an amendment to allow unknown compounding pharmacies to manufacture the lethal drugs in secret. He also threatened to veto the General Assembly's electric chair alternative bill if it did not accept his amendment, creating a *de facto* moratorium on executions.

"All I'm doing today is providing a humane way to carry out capital punishment here in Virginia so we have options," he told the April 11, 2016 *Washington Post*. "If they do not take it up, I want to be clear, they will be ending capital punishment here in Virginia."

Like substance abusers jonesing for a fix, the use of unlicensed and unknown pharmacies was and still is common among death penalty states willing to break all public health rules to acquire their drugs. Compounding pharmacies, such as those used by Virginia, are not regulated by the U.S. Food and Drug Administration and have been linked to (non-execution) deaths due to unsanitary conditions.

According to the Death Penalty Information Center, a 2014 investigation by St. Louis Public Radio and the *St. Louis Beacon* found that the source of Missouri's lethal injection drug, pentobarbital, was an Oklahoma compounding pharmacy called The Apothecary Shoppe. This pharmacy was not licensed to sell drugs in Missouri, so to hide their dealings, a Missouri Department of Corrections official drove to Oklahoma with an envelope containing $11,000 in cash. That person gave the money to a contact at the Apothecary Shoppe, then returned to Missouri with the drugs in a suitcase.

An FDA and Oklahoma Board of Pharmacy investigation revealed 1,892 violations of state health codes at the pharmacy, including "questionable potency, disinfecting and sterilization practices." Employees, who were found to sometimes not even wash their hands after using the bathroom, extended expiration dates on drugs without proper testing. They also stored temperature-sensitive drugs in blue Igloo coolers instead of refrigeration units because it was too far to walk.

In April 2013, after a lethal meningitis outbreak was traced to a Massachusetts compounding pharmacy, the FDA inspected about 30 compounding pharmacies and reported unsanitary conditions in 29 of them.

Missouri should have been more wary of Oklahoma and their LI drugs. That same year, the Sooner State tried to execute Clayton Lockett. Witnesses watched Lockett struggle on the gurney in agony before officials rushed to close the curtain and stop the execution. Forty-three minutes later, Lockett died of a heart attack.

In Texas, corrections officials assured their compounding pharmacy that a drug sale would be "on the down-low." However, the pharmacy demanded its drugs back when its identity was made public.

In March 2011, the U.S. Drug Enforcement Administration confiscated Georgia's supply of one lethal injection drug, sodium thiopental, after that state illegally imported it from a shell company in Great Britain. In April, the DEA seized illegally imported sodium thiopental from corrections departments in Tennessee, Kentucky, South Carolina, and Alabama.

Fordham University law professor and death-penalty authority Deborah W. Denno stated in a 2007 Fordham Law Review that corrections officials nationwide "are just desperate."

"They're going to these pharmacies because that's the only place where they can get lethal injection drugs."

Some states even turned to each other in an "I'll scratch your back" arrangement to get the badly needed drugs. In 2013, Virginia provided Texas with a dose of pentobarbital. In 2015 Texas repaid the favor by giving Virginia enough drugs to execute Alfredo Prieto.

McAuliffe's hollow threat seemed to have the desired effect on jittery legislators, including the sponsor of the electric chair bill, Manassas Del. Jackson H. Miller.

"While this amendment is not ideal, it will ensure that Virginia continues to carry out the death penalty," Miller said in a written statement. "I will review the recommendation, but at this time, I intend to encourage the House to accept the amendments."

Rockingham County Republican Sen. Mark Obenshain and Richard Black from Loudoun also supported the change. "If it means the governor would kill the death penalty completely, then I would vote for the compounding pharmacy," Black said.

Republican Buckingham County Sen. Thomas Garrett Jr., a former prosecutor and ardent death penalty supporter, claimed McAuliffe ignored transparency with the amendment.

"I'd have favored an amendment that reinstated the firing squad over this ridiculous effort to have it both ways," he said.

The compounding pharmacies were not stupid – they saw piles of money to be made from Virginia and other states' dependence on secretive lethal injection drugs and wasted no time jacking up their prices. It took a Freedom of Information Act request by the Associated Press, reported on Dec. 12, 2016, to reveal that Virginia paid $66,000 for vials of midazolam and potassium chloride – drugs for which they once paid just over $500 before the enactment of the secrecy act. The compounding pharmacy's name was redacted.

The controlled substances were also possibly transported illegally into the state by bypassing the Board of Pharmacy. McAuliffe spokesman Brian Coy told the *Richmond Times-Dispatch* in September 2016 that "... with respect to lethal injections, this is the cost of enforcing the law."

In other words, break the law to enforce the law.

The request also showed that Virginia purchased $340 worth of rocuronium bromide from Cardinal Health, a pharmaceutical wholesaler in Ohio, without the knowledge of the drug's manufacturer, X-GEN Pharmaceuticals. X-GEN vice president of business strategies Jeff Granger told the Associated Press he was "surprised and concerned" by Cardinal's sale to Virginia.

Megan McCracken, of the University of California-Berkeley School of Law's Death Penalty Clinic, told NPR in January 2017 that Virginia's law made the poorly-regulated compounding pharmacies more desirable to do business with over large pharmaceutical companies, which the FDA more stringently regulated.

McAuliffe's proposal sparked harsh response from the opposition. Sen. Scott Surovell, a fellow Democrat from Fairfax, told the April 11, 2016 *Washington Post* that "Virginia gives more transparency to the purchase of furniture than it does to extinguishing human life."

The move also provoked sharp criticisms from Virginia's two Catholic bishops, Francis X. DiLorenzo of Richmond and Paul S. Loverde of Arlington.

The Man Behind the Curtain

> The selection process may include an assessment of the prospective team member's ability to work under stress, human relations skills, professional demeanor, and ability to perform the physical requirements of the assignment.
>
> -DOC Execution Manual; sec. H, "Execution Team," para. 1, *selection of execution team.* Feb. 07, 2017.

In the same 1994 Assembly session that approved LI, Virginia Beach Republican Del. Robert F. McConnell introduced his bill to allow murder victim family members to witness executions. Of the Bill, Newport News Democrat Sen. W. Henry Maxwell remarked, "We might as well start hanging out here on Main Street in Richmond and tell everybody to come and look at it."

The bill failed, but Gov. George Allen, as promised, issued an executive order allowing victim family members to witness executions from a separate room away from the media witnesses.

The new secrecy law concealed not just the contents of the drugs and their dubious transportation methods but the lethal injection procedures that administered them. Under the new protocols, witnesses no longer saw the prisoner enter the death chamber, so they had no idea when the execution process actually began. This procedure was a thumb in the eye to the American Bar Association's 2015 "Death Penalty Due Process Review Project 108B, Report to the House of Delegates," which called for execution processes to be disseminated in an "open and transparent manner." The ABA also required that those processes be viewable by media and witnesses "from the moment the condemned prisoner enters the execution chamber until the prisoner is declared dead," or the execution is postponed or canceled.

108B stated that:

> Because proper evaluations of the death penalty can only occur when execution processes are transparent, this resolution calls on jurisdictions to make detailed information available to the public about lethal injection drug protocols and execution procedures, to protect media and witness rights to view the entirety of the execution process, to conduct and make publicly available contemporaneous records of the minute-to-minute events of executions, and to provide for independent investigations of all flawed or troubled executions.

During the 2017 execution of Ricky Gray, witnesses watched as officials brought Gray into the chamber and strapped him to the gurney. Then, the curtains closed while the intravenous lines were inserted, which generally took mere moments. In this case, however, they remained closed for over 30 minutes. Corrections officials had no comment on why the curtain remained closed so long, but the next day they admitted they had trouble locating a vein – an unlikely scenario for a healthy, 39-year-old man.

Dr. Mark Edgar, an independent pathologist who reviewed Gray's autopsy report, stated that, in his opinion, Gray had experienced suffocation during his execution. "The anatomic changes described in Ricky Gray's lungs are more often seen in the aftermath of a sarin gas attack than in a routine hospital autopsy."

According to the 2018 DPIC report "Behind the Curtain: Secrecy and the Death Penalty in the United States," in 2017, "more than 60% of the executions carried out with midazolam produced eyewitness reports of an execution gone amiss, with problems ranging from labored breathing to gasping, heaving, writhing, and clenched fists."

The DOC stated that the execution was normal and had proceeded without issue other than the trouble finding the vein.

A Doctor in the House?

> We have secrets upon secrets upon secrets with Virginia's process of executing people in this state and it needs to stop.
> - Virginia ACLU Director of Public Policy and Communications, Bill Farrar, to WVIR-TV, March 2017.

After 1995, condemned inmates had the gruesome task of choosing between lethal injection and the electric chair, with LI the default if they refused to choose. In 2010, Paul Powell chose electrocution for the murder of a young girl. "There are the jolts, and it looked like it worked," recalled Powell's attorney Jon Sheldon, who witnessed. "And then there's a long time, eight or nine minutes, where nothing happens. They pulled the curtain closed, then the doctor came out, so you can't see who he is."

After the execution, Sheldon had an idea. "I thought this will not be hard to figure out who the doctor is," he recalled. "I went to the parking lot and looked at the cars, and there was one from out of state. It was the shittiest pickup truck you've ever seen. And I stood by that truck, and this old, decrepit dude comes out and goes to that pickup truck. I said, 'Hey, how'd it go?' [He replied] 'Yeah, all right.' I said, 'You're the doctor?' He said, 'Yeah.'"

According to the 2002 article "Health professionals and lethal injection execution in the United States," the use of physicians in lethal injection "medicalizes capital punishment by moving a process that has always been a function of the penal system into the domain of medicine." Hanging and electrocution had no medically related procedures other than verification that the prisoner had died and did not require direct physician participation.

With the insertion of intravenous lines, the injection of drugs, and the monitoring of vital signs, lethal injection, intentionally or not, fell under the practice of medicine. Perhaps the presence of a doctor, no matter how anonymous or secretive, was an intentional move to make lethal injections even more palatable, reassuring witnesses and others that the inmate would simply drift away, under the watchful eye of a trained professional, with no discernible suffering.

The article concluded that "Any form of participation in causing death by lethal injection is unethical because it violates the physician's role, thereby undermining trust ...The penal system, not the medical profession, is responsible for finding a way to perform executions."

These ethical concerns, therefore, forced the execution physicians underground. Post-secrecy Virginia protocol called for the doctor to remain hidden while determining the time of death via an attached heart monitor.

In Ricky Gray's case, the doctor used a stethoscope to confirm the death instead of a heart monitor, suggesting again that something had gone wrong.

"It seems like a violation of your Hippocratic oath," Sheldon explained. "People are going to start filing with the medical board trying to make you lose your license. So this doctor from North Carolina wanted to be anonymous."

Abolition Efforts Amidst Assembly-Line Executions

A New Abolition Coalition Faces the Fight of Their Lives

Death is an unusually severe and degrading punishment; there is a strong probability that it is inflicted arbitrarily; its rejection by contemporary society is virtually total, and there is no reason to believe it serves any penal purpose more effectively than the less severe punishment of imprisonment. The function of these principles is to enable a court to determine whether a punishment comports with human dignity. Death, quite simply, does not.

-Supreme Court Justice William Brennan concurring in *Furman v. Georgia*, 1972.

In 1988, Nelson County carpenter Henry Heller had just returned from a cross-country road trip when he realized he needed to get involved with something. "There was an Amnesty International group in Charlottesville, a human rights organization, so I decided to join it," he recalled. "I felt like I was doing something."

While there, Henry received a brochure about the death penalty. "Amnesty always had these nice brochures. And I just started reading it. And it was like, wow. I never realized this. There is so much more that's involved with the death penalty – innocent people executed, the cost of it, what it does to our society, the moral issues. And people who we're killing."

As Heller got more interested over the next few years, he found himself at a National Coalition to Abolish the Death Penalty conference. Then, he met Marie Deans.

"Marie came and spoke in Charlottesville at Lloyd Snook's church," he explained. "She was intense, very compelling. And the next thing you know, I'm going to her office in Richmond. Then, she summoned this group of people to talk about abolishing [Virginia's] death penalty."

By early 1991, the VAADP (Virginia Association Against the Death Penalty) had only recently folded due to its inability to secure funding, despite the group's great strides during the 1990 General Assembly session. They were a constant presence and provided testimony for what seemed to be a never-ending parade of death penalty expansion bills, such as HB 357, which expanded the death penalty for drug-related homicides, and SB 226, which prescribed the death penalty for deadly child abuse.

The group also, during the session, helped students at Eastern Mennonite College and the University of Virginia plan death penalty-related programs and secure speaking engagements at numerous faith groups and school assemblies.

VAADP co-founder BJ Brown Devlin recalled they also paid for a full-page advertisement in the *Richmond Times-Dispatch*. "That group organized a full-page ad with the signatory so that people could sign on against the death penalty. We bought the ad and collected the signatures. They were religious leaders who signed as well as regular citizens."

Despite all the hard work, abolition seemed too far out of reach for VAADP in that tough-on-crime, pro-death political climate. "As much as we would have liked to do that, gosh, I just don't know how," McConnell recalled.

But if Heller were to pursue abolition in post-VAADP Virginia, it would be a philosophical switch for him. Before joining Amnesty International, he was in favor of the ultimate punishment. "I felt like a lot of people, that if you've killed, then you deserve to be killed, and it was pretty simple. Eye for an eye, right?"

Live on Television

And at the beginning of the 1990s, only eight years after restarting executions, that "eye for an eye" retribution mentality and the notorious "brutalization effect" was gaining momentum. On June 20, 1990, Joseph Savino told the Associated Press that he hoped his scheduled execution the following week would persuade more people to oppose the death penalty. He conceded, however, that public reaction would probably be "ho-hum."

After dropping his appeals, Savino asked for a televised death by lethal injection rather than electrocution because a public execution would convince more people that the death penalty was wrong. "They do it in the middle of the night in the basement in some corner of the prison so selected people see it, and the next morning you want to read if the guy had last words," he explained.

He also wished to donate his organs and named the infamous Jack "Dr. Death" Kevorkian of Royal Oak, Michigan, as the doctor he would like to harvest them.

Gov. Douglas Wilder responded that state law, which had not yet approved lethal injection, forbade him from granting Savino's wishes.

"It's often death penalty supporters who blanch at the idea of public executions, dismissing such ideas as barbaric and crude," Roanoke College professor and VADP board member Dr. Todd Peppers wrote in the Nov. 5, 2019 *Richmond Times-Dispatch*:

> We can kill, but it must be discrete and behind closed doors. One wonders, however, whether proponents of capital punishment are less concerned about the tastelessness of a public broadcast and more worried that support for the death penalty might continue to drop if citizens saw the reality of state-sanctioned executions. Seeing human beings put down like old dogs isn't for the faint of heart. Nor is it good for politicians who support a policy grounded on the idea that the state should kill to show that killing is wrong.

On Oct. 17, 1990, Wilbert Lee Evans was executed despite interviews and statements that indicated (at the time) that he helped save the lives of 14 prison employees taken hostage in the 1984 death row breakout at Mecklenburg Correctional, making him worthy of clemency. Those pleas, however, fell on the very deaf ears of the U.S. Supreme Court and Gov. Wilder, who refused to grant them.

Evans had been sentenced to death for shooting Alexandria sheriff's deputy William Truesdale during an attempted jailbreak. In a phone interview with the *Washington Post*, Zita Truesdale, the slain deputy's widow, said, "We accepted his apology, and our sympathy goes out to his family. Things are never right in a situation like this. It's just closing a chapter on a life. From here, life goes on. We can now mentally bury my husband."

Several members of VAADP began a hunger strike the night before in sympathy for Evans.

Evans' eyes reportedly blew from his skull, and blood poured from under the mask during his execution. Jerry Givens claimed that Evans got a nosebleed from eating too much pork.

The Most Shameful Prison in America Finally Closes

Virginia scheduled to close the ancient, crumbling State Penitentiary on July 1, 1990, but construction delays at two new correctional facilities in Greensville and Buchanan Counties kept it open until December 14. A final inspection by the ACLU for the National Prison Project, Judge Robert Merhige Jr., and representatives of the attorney general's office revealed the buildings were filthy and vermin-infested; the heat was intolerable, and many of the toilets were stopped up. After this tour, the ACLU declared the penitentiary "the most shameful prison in America."

The night before the facility closed and the remaining four inmates transferred out, a southern drifter named Buddy Justus was executed in the electric chair for the 1978 rape and murder of a nurse, Ida Mae Moses.

Although the penitentiary was closed, the death chamber by law had to stay operational because the new chamber at Greensville Correctional was not ready. Then, in early February 1991, Joe Giarratano was brought into "A" Building to await an execution that never came.

The move of the death chamber from downtown Richmond 50 miles south to the rural community of Jarratt was described as cynical by death penalty opponents and a brazen effort to further keep executions hidden from the public.

The move notably changed the plans of abolitionists. "Even though it's out of sight, it's not out of mind," former VAADP assistant director Duane Hudson (*aka* King Salim Khalfani) told the July 23, 1991 *Richmond Times-Dispatch*. Hudson added that in preparation for the execution of Alfred Clozza, a prayer service was held at 8:00 p.m. on July 24 at St. Peters Catholic Church in Richmond. Participants would caravan to the prison to hold a candlelight vigil until the 11:00 p.m. execution. It was far different than the formerly short walk to the penitentiary.

The execution of Clozza was the 248th electrocution in the chair but the first at the brand-new Greensville death chamber. Clozza had been sentenced for the 1983 murder of a 13-year-old in Virginia Beach.

"The wooden piece of furniture itself is the same one that was in the penitentiary," DOC spokesman Wayne Farrar said. "Everything else, the wiring and so forth, is new."

The Aug. 21, 1991 execution of Derick Peterson called into question not just the morality of electrocution but pre-electrocution protocols. Chaplain Russ Ford was furious that corrections officers were allowed in the room where Peterson received last-minute pastoral counseling. "It was just a little peep show," he angrily told the *Richmond Times-Dispatch*. "They desecrated a sacrament with noisy laughing and gawking. They were on holy ground, and they had no business being there."

Peterson required a second jolt of electricity after a prison doctor named Barnes detected a heartbeat after the first 10-second jolt of 1,750 volts. "This man has not expired," Barnes reported, and after a 7-1/2-minute pause, a second cycle was administered. Peterson was finally pronounced dead at 11:13 p.m.

"It's like stabbing someone in the heart and, if they don't die, stabbing them again to make sure they're dead," Del. W. Henry Maxwell, a Democrat from Newport News, told the *Richmond Times-Dispatch*.

VASK Then VADP, Again

In the Fall of 1991, a group of about 13 people, including Heller and a few others from Amnesty International, assembled in a meeting room at a Richmond church at the request of Marie Deans to discuss organized opposition to Virginia's death penalty in light of the recent folding of VAADP.

Deans pointed out to the group that a then-recent Virginia Tech Center for Survey Research poll showed that while death penalty support among Virginians topped out at 80 percent, it decreased significantly to around 60 percent when given the option of life imprisonment, with no possibility of parole. Support fell to less than 57 percent when combined with some form of restitution to murder victims' families.

"This was important information," Heller recalled. "I said, let's do something with it. And that's where we came up with Virginians Against State Killing (VASK) because there was a Texans Against State Killing."

However, Heller discovered within a year that the organization's name was problematic in that it did not invite a conversation. "I remember calling a legislator's office saying, 'Hi, my name is Henry Heller. I'm the Director of Virginians Against State Killing." I'm like, I wouldn't talk to me. I just ended the conversation with the introduction."

The board decided to keep the acronym VASK but tweak the name to Virginians for Alternatives to State Killing to prompt the question of, "what is your alternative?" Yet still, Heller found "state killing" was killing the conversation.

"What are you trying to do here?" Heller recalled. "You're trying to get people to listen to you. Let's get out of the state killing thing, and let's just make it Virginians for Alternatives to the Death Penalty (VADP)." The organization's name officially changed in December 1995.

Heller recalled that the VADP name put off some of the Amnesty International members of the coalition. They considered themselves full-blown abolitionists, and the name should reflect an unmistakable goal.

"We put a t-shirt together. It said, 'An eye for an eye makes the whole world blind' on the front," he recollected. "And then on the back, we had, 'Why do we kill people who kill people to show that killing people is wrong?' And this Amnesty International contingent wanted to put 'I oppose the death penalty' under that. And I'm like, 'Well, you just cut off the conversation.'"

Heller explained that as soon as the Amnesty International people peeled away from the organization, he went to Blue Ridge Graphics in Charlottesville and removed the "I oppose the death penalty" line from the shirt template.

"That era's over," he pronounced.

Articles of incorporation as a 501(c)(4) non-profit were first drawn by board member Rebecca Edwards and attorney Steven Rosenfield in February 1993. VASK Headquarters (later VADP) were at E. Jefferson Street in Charlottesville. In addition to Heller, other board members included Victoria Almquist, David Burger, Rusty Dinkins-Curling, Judy Gaffney, Elizabeth Massie, Terry McCaffrey, and Margaret West

Heller recalled his experiences putting together quarterly newsletters for this new organization from his remote Nelson County home. "I'm not a great writer, but I learned how to write these things. Meg West did the newsletter's layout. The computer age was just beginning, and I'd send the stories to her."

For the first few years of VADP, that Virginia Tech Survey Research poll continued to be their "Bible." "We made a graph of every year that you can see that support for the death penalty was declining and support for the alternative was rising," Heller said. "Slightly, ever so slightly every year. It never went the other way."

Heller also recalled bumping heads with the faith communities in his stance to "start a conversation." "This was the whole thing of we want to abolish the death penalty. And I was more like, 'I'm trying to convey that there's an alternative to the death penalty.' And when you look at a brochure or bumper stickers – Yes, Virginia, there is an alternative to the death penalty. You're opening up a dialogue. People are saying, 'Well, what's your alternative?'"

Heller also feared legislators eager to lower violent crime rates were no longer listening to moral or religious arguments for abolition. "I was always trying to get different people to speak for alternatives to the death penalty, like an attorney or a murder victims' family member," he told *C-Ville Weekly* magazine. "Someone the legislators would listen to." However, he added that the faith community insisted on using the same speakers to argue for abolition based on religious teachings. He feared those mixed messages were counterproductive.

"Initially, it was rather tenuous," Kathleen Kenney said of the Catholic Office of Justice and Peace's relationship with Heller, Deans, and VADP. "I think they saw me as this ignoramus kind of walking in. And then Marie Deans was ... she wasn't my best friend, let's say. She was not easy, but she was committed to the core, and I gradually appreciated her work. Henry Heller was another extremely good person, committed again to the bones. We collaborated in whatever way we could, and my focus was very much the faith community and then trying to get them involved with VADP. It wasn't, for my part, adversarial. I focused primarily on the Catholic community and the interfaith community because I know how to talk to them."

Fear as a Political Commodity

Politicians jumping on the bandwagon to kill & murder, i.e., execute people because it's vogue now – in a hundred years, society will look back appalled (just like we look back appalled at the atrocities, 100 years ago ... and the beat goes on); those who forget the past ...

- Excerpt of an undated handwritten note from death row inmate Timothy Bunch. Courtesy Mary Ann McKee,

While there was not one execution in 1991, the year VASK organized, Roger Coleman was executed on May 20, 1992, kicking off a rapid-fire succession of killings that lasted well into Y2K. After Coleman came Eddie Fitzgerald on July 23, Willie Leroy Jones on Sept. 15, and Timothy Bunch on Dec. 10. These were followed by five executions in 1995, eight in 1996, nine in 1997, 13 in 1998, and 14 in 1999.

Despite genuine possibilities of innocence, reasonable doubt, and the reports of botched electrocutions, popular support never wavered during this appalling number of rushed sentences and executions.

As Frank Green wrote in the March 27, 1994 *Richmond Times-Dispatch*, "lawmakers were in no mood to be thought of as soft on crime."

1994 was a particularly tough year for abolitionists, death row inmates, and others simply trying to make penal conditions better for the ever-increasing number of prisoners sentenced to death. Many of these problems also were centered around the still-troubled Mecklenburg Correctional Center (MCC).

In June 1993, death row inmate Wayne Kenneth DeLong committed suicide a month before his scheduled execution by drinking a large amount of prison-made homebrew, injecting himself with cocaine, then hanging himself in his cell. The hanging resulted in a months-long security crackdown, culminating in April 1994 when officials found a two-shot Derringer pistol hidden in the rectum of a non-death row inmate in another section of MCC. Officials believed the gun got into the prison via a visitor.

Then on May 26 of that year, death row inmate Joseph Savino overdosed on heroin inside his cell and almost died. After recovering in a local hospital, officials sent him to Greensville Correctional. He was kept in a "strip cell" inside a storage building, with no clothes, no mattress, and no belongings. Savino insisted the heroin came into the facility via a corrections employee.

"Joe Savino was one of the funniest guys I've ever met," recalled Laura LaFay. "But he came from a small town in upstate New York where his entire generation of children was destroyed by a Catholic priest who raped them all. And by the time Joe was on the row, he said, 'Everybody I knew as a kid is dead, they all died of heroin addiction and suicide.'"

MCC officials could not determine how DeLong or Savino obtained the drugs. Six corrections officers were disciplined, but DOC said none were guilty of supplying cocaine to DeLong.

"Tough on Crime" Replaced "All White Jury"

"Tough on crime" sentiment swept Virginia in the 1990s and thrust Republican Gov. George Allen into office. Soon afterward, he announced his intention to change state policy to allow family members of capital murder victims to witness the killer's execution. Critics opposed the move, maintaining it would turn executions into public spectacles.

Before leaving office the previous January, Gov. Douglas Wilder encouraged Virginia legislators to extend its notorious 21-day rule. However, the Assembly would have none of it and let the restrictive rule stand.

Meanwhile, skyrocketing public support for harsher penalties drove Virginia to sentence five to 10 people to death and execute up to 14 people in a year. In the 1990s, the phrase "tough on crime" replaced "all-white jury" as the most fearsome and dangerous three-word phrase in Virginia criminal justice.

Government enthusiasm for judicial killing spread like a plague from Virginia throughout the Deep South. Arkansas Gov. Bill Clinton theatrically returned to Arkansas before the New Hampshire primary in 1992 to "preside" over the execution of Ricky Rector, a profoundly brain-damaged Black man who was executed for the 1981 murder of police officer Robert Martin.

In 1995, South Carolina Attorney General Charles Condon was so impressed with Arkansas' successive executions of three inmates that in an Aug. 7, 1995 *Newsweek* article titled "Anger and Ambivalence," he seriously proposed an "electric sofa" to "juice several inmates at a time."

In 1997, Florida Attorney General Bob Butterworth boasted of the state's malfunctioning electric chair, which caused at least two inmates, Jesse Joseph Taliaferro and Pedro Medina, to explode into flames during their executions. He laughingly said in a March 25 Associated Press story that people who commit murder "better not do it in the state of Florida because we may have a problem with our electric chair."

A federal judge with the unlikely name Alleyways Kozinski stated in a 1995 *New York Times* editorial that "We have constructed a machine that is extremely expensive, chokes our legal institutions, visits repeated trauma on victims' families and ultimately produces nothing like the benefits we would expect from an effective system of capital punishment. This is surely the worst of all worlds."

The Virginia Capital Representation Resource Center (VCRRC)

Indeed, the enthusiasm for death in 1994 was at its strongest since the death penalty was reimposed by Gov. Mills Godwin 20 years earlier, but there were also two bright spots for abolitionists in the first half of the 1990s. Earl Washington Jr. had his death sentence commuted to life in prison (leading to his eventual exoneration) thanks mainly to the work of Deans and Giarratano. Then, in April 1992, the VCRRC, one of 19 capital resource centers around the country, opened its doors. The Virginia Bar Association started the centers in direct response to the lack of legal counsel to capital inmates in state and federal habeas petitions. The multi-pronged goals of the center – which according to the first director, Barry Weinstein, took no position on the death penalty – included providing legal services to indigent persons facing death sentences; promoting and providing improvements to the administration of justice; and helping facilitate the efforts of attorneys working pro bono on behalf of death-sentenced inmates.

The center's origins date back to 1986, when a class-action lawsuit filed by Joe Giarratano (*Giarratano v. Murray*) under U.S. District Court Judge Robert Merhige Jr. found the capital representation system in place in Virginia at the time was grossly inadequate. However, it wasn't until 1989 that a joint congressional subcommittee recommended that the Virginia Bar Association (VBA) explore the feasibility of creating a capital resource center. VBA executive committee chairman F. Claiborne Johnstone Jr. stressed the necessity of the center to ensure competent representation for capital litigation as a due process issue, not pro- or anti-death penalty issues. Attorney Gerald Zerkin and Petersburg commonwealth's attorney Ray Lupold joined Johnston to manage the project.

A board of directors secured $90,000 in seed money from the VBA in 1990 and 1991. Then in April 1992, they secured federal funding totaling 70 percent of their budget.

Executive director Rob Lee explained how the office worked. "If the Supreme Court of Virginia affirmed their death sentence, that was when we most typically got involved," he said. "There's the trial and the appeal, there's the state post-conviction review, and then there's federal post-conviction review. When people got out of direct appeal, their right to trial counsel ended. And so, we would become involved by recruiting counsel to work on the certiorari petition." Lee said either his office would take the case or they would contact law firms with expertise in that area to do so.

In the first two years, in addition to obtaining clemency for Earl Washington Jr., the VCRRC obtained executive clemency for Giarratano, Herbert Bassette, Joe Payne, William Saunders, and nine others.

The Effective Death Penalty Act

As part of their 1994 'Contract with America" platform, Republican congressional members passed the "American Effective Death Penalty Act (AEDPA)." It garnered little notice until April 18, 1995, when Timothy McVeigh detonated a fertilizer bomb in front of the Murrah Federal Building in Oklahoma City. With both political parties clamoring for a death sentence for McVeigh, augmenting a sudden interest in swift executions by the American populace, Republicans seized the opportunity and attached this act to an anti-terrorism bill endorsed by President Bill Clinton. With Clinton's approval, the bill avoided amendments and was passed into law.

The new AEDPA law imposed an unprecedented one-year statute of limitations on filing a habeas petition in federal court. The law also allowed states to establish procedures that caught capital inmates in "Catch-22" scenarios by denying them legal assistance that prevented them from meeting these one-year deadlines.

Lee pointed out in a 2022 interview that the AEDPA had a chilling effect on Virginia's death row. Before its passing, if federal district court judges found there had been a constitutional violation at trial, they could allow facts to be developed, hold a hearing, grant relief, or even order a retrial or re-sentencing, if necessary.

"After the AEDPA, they could only do that if they found the state court decision was unreasonably wrong," he explained. "They could find it wrong, but unless they could establish it as *unreasonably* wrong, they had to stand by and let this arguably wrong decision stand." According to Lee, with no guiding standard of what was considered "unreasonably wrong," this further streamlining of the process "ramped up the executions because nobody was getting much review."

Despite the urgent need for the centers, especially in the face of AEDPA, in 1996, the federal Judicial Conference Committee on Defender Services made the situation even more dire by eliminating the federal grant for every capital resource center across the nation, including Virginia's. This broad brushstroke left them wholly dependent on state funding.

With the federal dollars gone, Virginia's legislature and Attorney General Jim Gilmore had little interest in spending more money to defend "convicted killers" and refused to replace the lost funding. In response, VCRRC attorneys began to submit vouchers for appointed work in federal cases and contributed all funds received to VCRRC. Until 2021, VCRRC was the only resource center in the U.S. that could continue operating.

In 2022 the VCRRC still operates, defending post-conviction capital defendants in several states and the federal level.

All About the Money

Henry Heller recalled that during the mid-1990s, VADP accumulated about 1,000 members and raised small amounts of money by appeals through the newsletter. "Then, we started sending out fundraising letters," he noted. "That was another thing I'd have to put together [as a volunteer], a yearly fundraising letter."

Those first few years, a substantial fundraiser for VADP was the Virginia Peace Pilgrimage, a 165-mile walk over five days from Appomattox to Yorktown. The departure and end locations were deliberately picked because they marked the endings of two wars fought on American soil. Heller, who walked 140+ miles, reported in the newsletter that the five days "give me plenty of time to think about my friends on death row, friends that have died and been executed, and others that I have encountered in the movement to abolish state-sanctioned killing."

"The pilgrimage has left me exhausted and empowered, knowing that we can make a difference; all we have to do is speak out and let ourselves be heard. By not getting involved with all that's wrong with our society, we're accepting these injustices."

Donations were made either per mile or in a lump sum. Since abolition in Virginia was not a possibility, national grants were non-existent and reserved for states that at least had abolition on the horizon.

Smokey and the Beaver

While Gov. Allen remained busy being tough on crime and installing a new witness room at Greensville Correctional Center's death chamber, he did show mercy to a Fairfax beaver by saving him from lethal injection.

"We can save the life of Mr. Beaver," Melissa Dickie, a spokeswoman for the governor told the Aug. 13, 1995 *Roanoke Times*. "The logistics are still being worked out, but we can save him."

The unnamed beaver dropped so many trees in Fairfax County's Burke Lake neighborhood that fed-up county officials ordered him euthanized.

Instead of lethal injection, Fairfax Supervisor Elaine N. McConnell volunteered to take the beaver to her Page County farm if he could be captured.

Similarly, in December of 1994, Danville commonwealth's attorney William H. Fuller III said he would ask that Smokey, a retriever whose death sentence garnered international sympathy, be spared execution.

Danville General District Court Judge T. Ryland Dodson sentenced Smokey to die by lethal injection after convicting the dog's owner of harboring a vicious animal. Jackson appealed the sentence to Circuit Court. Even former Secretary of State Henry Kissinger said he was worried about Smokey and might try to negotiate a pardon.

Once Smokey was pardoned, his owner, Craig Jackson, said, "He'll have a good ol' plate of (deer) hindquarters waiting for him."

From 1978 to 1997, the city of Danville tried 23 potential capital crimes, with nine death sentences handed down. Smokey was Henry Kissinger's only intervention.

1995: Truth in Sentencing

A Dec. 13 stay issued by the Supreme Court in the case of Coleman Gray and a one-week stay issued for Walter Correll, who was scheduled to be executed on Dec. 28, kept 1995 from being a record year for Virginia in the number of executions, with five. Dana Edmunds was executed on Jan. 25, Willie Lloyd Turner on May 25, Dennis Stockman on Sept. 27, Mickey Davidson on Oct. 19, and Herman Barnes on Nov. 13.

Texas led the nation in 1995 with 19 executions. Missouri executed six, and Virginia tied Illinois, with five each.

But the number of death sentences imposed in Virginia for crimes committed after Jan. 1, 1995, began dropping when the alternative of life without parole, or LWOP, was instituted as an exact sentence as part of a "truth-in-sentencing" initiative. Previously, capital murderers sentenced to life could be eligible for parole after serving 25 years.

The LWOP law coincided with Virginia abolishing parole for all crimes.

However, there was a loophole in LWOP. Virginia was one of only three states that offered juries a choice of sentencing a capital defendant to life or death but refused or neglected to inform the jury that a life sentence meant no possibility of parole.

It wasn't until juries started receiving complete and truthful sentencing options that new death sentences dropped more dramatically. David Bruck, Clinical Professor of Law and director of the Virginia Capital Case Clearinghouse at Washington & Lee University, told the *Richmond Times-Dispatch* that "Virginia excludes evidence that every other death penalty state allows juries to have, so it's not surprising that sooner or later the

Virginia rule was going to be struck down by the federal courts."

By November 1996, only one jury and one judge had issued a new death sentence for a capital murder committed after Jan. 1.

William Geimer, a professor of law also at Washington & Lee University, did not think this development was a fluke, telling the Nov. 24, 1996 *Richmond Times-Dispatch* that "I do think that not only is the knowledge of life without parole affecting juries, it's affecting negotiations" for plea agreements.

During that 1995-96 period, all six defendants convicted of capital murder by juries and sentenced under the new law were given life without parole, with only two death sentences. Compare these figures to 1994, when juries sent ten defendants to death row.

Richard Dieter, executive director of the Death Penalty Information Center (DPIC) in Washington, said Oklahoma, Indiana, and other states that implemented LWOP experienced similar outcomes. "When three options are there: death; life without parole; or life with parole, then the jury, if they have those three choices, will often pick the middle ground."

VADP director Heller continued to point out a national poll that showed that while 83 percent of Virginians favored the death penalty in 1995, that number dropped to 40 percent if there was no possibility of parole for a minimum of 25 years and restitution paid to victims' families. Obviously, he maintained, public opinion on capital punishment had shifted since the 1980s.

But maybe not – in 1998, admissions to death row at Sussex I Prison jumped significantly, with nine new inmates sentenced to death.

"While higher than average, is not statistically significant," claimed Attorney General Mark Earley spokesman David Botkins. "It indicates that those who thought the relatively low figures in 1996-1997 were attributable to [capital sentencing] juries being told defendants were ineligible for parole on a life sentence - were wrong."

The uptick caught Heller and VADP off guard. "It doesn't make any sense with everything they've done, [including] the abolition of parole," he told the *Times-Dispatch*. "Juries aren't supposed to be giving death when there's the alternative of life without parole."

Dieter suggested in the same article that the reasons for the increased number of new death row admissions were more nuanced. "It can also be that the public seems to have a lag in terms of when a life without parole sentence comes in and when they begin to trust that it really exists and means what it says," he said. "That takes time as well. I am still confident the public around the country will choose life without parole more often as they know about it and feel confident in it."

The Case of the Gun in the Typewriter

Long-time death row inmate Willie Lloyd Turner once claimed to journalist Laura Lafay that he resented corrections officials' attempts to make him "sound like an amateur, like a fool."

Turner turned the tables on them.

A firestorm of controversy surrounded the execution of Turner for the 1978 murder of W. Jack Smith, Jr. Turner's death by lethal injection on May 25, 1995 ended what was at the time the most extended death row term in Virginia history. The 49-year-old had refused to seek clemency from Gov. George Allen after being turned down by the U.S. Supreme Court.

The controversy surrounded not the execution but what happened one hour afterward.

On death row, Turner wrote an 800-page account of his 15 years of incarceration titled "The Real Deal" on a Smith-Corona typewriter. Weeks before his execution, he told his attorney, Walter J. Walvick, that he should take a good look at the typewriter after his execution. Walvick thought little of the comment at the time.

After Turner was pronounced dead at 9:08 p.m., corrections officers helped Walvick load that typewriter, case and Turner's personal belongings into his car. After speaking to two journalists, Laura LaFay and June Arney, he asked them to join him and his wife in an Emporia Hotel room, where they would look at the typewriter per Turner's request.

LaFay told Walvick that Turner wrote the word "Gun" two days before his execution and showed it to her.

Once in the room, Walvick opened the typewriter case with the two reporters as witnesses. Inside they found a compartment sealed with chewing gum and a paste made from water and dried coffee creamer. Popping the seal, they were stunned to find inside a custom-made cavity wrapped in tissue paper a loaded Smith & Wesson .32-caliber revolver, a plastic bag containing 14 extra bullets, and a scrap from a package of anti-fungal cream that said "SMILE."

Walvick exhaled. "Son of a bitch."

"[Walvick] had no idea ... he thought he was just giving him a typewriter," recalled Julie McConnell of the incident. "And essentially, I think that was very Willie Lloyd Turner. He was saying, 'I could have done something with this, but I chose not to.'"

"You could hardly believe it," Walvick admitted to the May 27, 1995 *Richmond Times-Dispatch*, adding that with the shock came "a tremendous sense of personal pride because he did have a gun but didn't use it."

Walvick surrendered the gun to Emporia police, who turned it over to the DOC to Walvick's disappointment.

"I only wish that I had called the Virginia State Police, instead," he told the May 30 *Times-Dispatch*. "They wouldn't have given it up."

Less than 48 hours after Walvick found the gun, director Ron Angelone issued a three-page statement declaring a prison investigation had found no evidence "that the gun was ever inside the facility." The statement concluded that since Turner's fingerprints were not found on the weapon or the bullets, they could not possibly have been in his possession.

"Much has been said about the fact that this was Willie Lloyd Turner's last attempt to embarrass the Department of Corrections," Angelone told the May 28, 1995, *Baltimore Sun*. "People that knew Turner have indicated that they believe that he would have wanted to leave his signature on that gun in the form of fingerprints."

Angelone also speculated that if Turner "really had wanted to embarrass the department," he would have mentioned the typewriter in his last words before execution.

Lloyd Snook, who represented Turner from 1980 until 1988 before Walvick took over, called Angelone's comments "a rather obvious attempt to cover up a political embarrassment."

Jan Elvin, of the ACLU's National Prison Project, agreed, telling the *Richmond Times-Dispatch* that "I think, knowing his sense of humor, it was also a message to the Department of Corrections that you all think you have your act together and look at this."

"This is truly astounding that a gun could have been smuggled in there."

The incident did indeed embarrass the DOC, who quickly insisted the discovery was a ruse orchestrated by Walvick. Walvick angrily denied the accusation, claiming he was "falsely accused of perpetrating an elaborate hoax."

Gov. George Allen, whose "no parole" policy was filling Virginia's prisons, was also humiliated by the incident. In addition to blaming Walvick, he claimed in fumbling, poorly-worded statements that "It's an allegation . . . and (we) shouldn't assume a statement by his attorney is true or false ... We'll investigate, and if true, we'll see who is culpable ... we certainly don't want inmates to have contraband or guns. At this point, I don't think you should accept as fact that Turner had a gun in his typewriter ... If it is true, then we certainly have a lot of questions as to how it did get in there and why it wasn't detected."

This incident was the worst of several that plagued Virginia's booming prison system just after Allen brought in Angleone as director. During a disturbance in 1995 at Buckingham Correctional Center, four inmates were shot, and the warden was stabbed in the face. A few months later, the prison law library burned. At Nottoway Correctional, several guards were wounded when a shotgun was accidentally fired during a riot and escape attempt.

Critics of Virginia prisons claimed that inmates responded to a series of "provocative indignities, restrictions, and curbs on personal property" under Angelone and Allen's administrations.

These disturbances were absent before Angelone's harsh presence and policies, which took away or restricted prison jobs, personal property, and visitation. The DOC had become less about corrections and more about basic warehousing.

Marie Deans was especially unforgiving to Angelone, telling the *Times-Dispatch* that "What he's doing is creating people who are even more dangerous when they come out of prison than when they went in, and that is not good for any of us."

"We do not run a boy's camp. We run prisons, and we're trying to make the system safer." Angelone responded. "I'm getting tired of every time people act like juveniles and are irresponsible that somebody's going to stand up for them and say it's the system." Angelone also ominously warned critics and the news media they are "playing with fire" and risking inmate problems when making or reporting allegations of mistreatment.

During these years, the Virginia news media was equally frustrated in their dealings with the DOC. Under Gov. Allen, Virginia's prison system bloated into the state's largest agency, with 40 buildings holding 25,000 inmates. However, it had become impossible to know what was going on inside these buildings, as Allen and Angelone initiated a media blackout that banned reporters and photographers from talking to either inmates or employees. Any news from inside the system came scrubbed through Angelone or his spokesman David Botkins.

Prison Chaplain Henry Gerrard told the *Times-Dispatch* that Turner did not use the gun because he wanted to spare his family further pain. He also believed that Turner was trying to show he had changed.

Walvick told the *Washington Post* that Turner told him shortly before the execution to look in the typewriter after he was dead. Walvick claimed that Turner added, "I didn't use it because of you," a statement he then believed referred to the gun.

Smile

After deciding he wasn't satisfied with the two-day internal whitewash of the gun situation, Gov. Allen ordered a full state police inquiry. Public Safety Secretary Jerry Kilgore, who oversaw the DOC and the state police, insisted the abbreviated internal investigation was done correctly. He told the *Washington Post* in a nonsensical explanation that "Corrections has hit what they consider a brick wall and feel they can't go any further."

A half-dozen police investigators worked on the case full time for seven weeks. They tracked dozens of leads and interviewed and conducted lie-detector tests on inmates, visitors, death row family members, and corrections officials.

Then, almost two months after Turner's execution and the discovery of the gun, investigators looked again into that infamous typewriter and found two hacksaw blades.

Shocked legislators claimed the discovery raised many questions about the competence of the original two-day DOC investigation, given that investigators completely overlooked the blades during their initial search of the typewriter.

The heavily redacted July 31, 1995 State Police report, titled "Delivery of Firearms to Prisoners (Death Row Inmate Willie Lloyd Turner)", and obtained through FOIA, stated that a paralegal, Caroline Schloss, was told by Turner that he "possessed handguns while he was incarcerated at both Mecklenburg and Powhatan Correctional centers prior to his transfer to GCC (Greensville Correctional Center)."

Schloss also told investigators that she questioned Turner about an ending to his book during one of her last contacts with him. "Turner told her not to worry, there would be a lot to write about after he was gone."

An inmate named Allen told investigators that he believed Schloss brought the gun in to Turner. When asked why she would do that, he replied "I don't know why Caroline did it. She loved him enough that she quit her job for him."

Interviews with fellow D-Unit inmates produced a myriad of results and explanations. One claimed that the gun had been passed to Turner inside an empty box of Ritz crackers. Another inmate, Terry Anderson, insisted that a female corrections officer brought in the gun. Aldwayne Blackwell claimed that a nurse brought it in.

Turner told Schloss he never intended to use the weapon but to embarrass a night shift supervisor and get him fired.

According to the report, a firearms examiner determined that the gun had not been taken apart. Joe Giarratano explained, however, that was exactly how it got on death row. "The gun came in piece by piece," he disclosed. "A piece of it came in inside a television set. We were able to send TVs out to get them repaired. And during the repair process, somebody put the gun piece in there, covered it up. I think they used a lead box, so it wouldn't [show] through the x-ray."

"Another piece came in by a guard, who didn't know what he was bringing," Giarratano continued. "I can't remember if it was a piece of the gun or the bullets themselves. He probably thought he was bringing dope in or something. He didn't ask any questions. Another piece came in inside a radio."

Ultimately, the report concluded that investigators could not identify a person or persons who brought the gun into the prison, nor could they conclude that the weapon was ever on death row. Instead, the report weakly stated there was ample evidence that the typewriter case had been modified in such a way as to "elaborately conceal" the 32 caliber, four-inch barrel revolver found inside. "Furthermore," the report closed, "the evidence suggests the gun was likely concealed in the typewriter prior to it being removed from Greensville Correctional Center."

That last statement seemed to be the investigation intentionally leaving open the possibility that Walvick put the gun there.

Survey Calls the Death Penalty "a Hollow Deterrent"

As the Turner incident settled, and as the death penalty's height of popularity was about to peak in Virginia and across the entire Deep South, a national survey of law enforcement professionals appeared that should have thrown a wrench into the capital sentencing juggernaut. The Peter D. Hart Research Associates survey, conducted in January 1995, of 386 randomly-selected police chiefs and sheriffs across the United States listed the death penalty dead last in reducing violent crime, with only one percent citing it as their primary focus. Law enforcement also rated the death penalty as the least cost-effective method for controlling crime. More efficient and cost-effective methods included reducing drug abuse, improving the economy, providing fewer barriers to prosecution, longer prison terms, more police officers, and fewer guns on the streets.

Of the survey, former New York police chief Patrick Murphy wrote in the Feb. 13, 1995 *USA Today* that "There are better ways to spend our crime-fighting dollars. Society can be protected, criminals made to pay for their crimes and grieving families given some closure by a sentence of life imprisonment with no possibility of parole."

"It is time for politicians to put away the rhetoric and listen to the experts."

The report landed with a thud in Virginia. University of Iowa law professor David Baldus, who wrote extensively on the role of race in the death penalty, said, "Because of the new wave of conservatism, the death penalty will be more difficult to resist. The pressure is on for governors and judges ... to speed things up."

Support of abolition was unlikely, especially in the wake of several horrific, high-profile crimes in the mid-and late-1990s. Few people shed tears when an unapologetic

Timothy McVeigh was executed (although VADP held a prayer vigil in Richmond). Many Americans were also angered in 1994 when Susan Smith was sentenced in South Carolina to life in prison rather than death after drowning her two young children, then claiming a mysterious Black man had committed the crime. *Newsweek* writer David Kaplan wrote, "At the water cooler and in the streets of Union, S.C., people argue about what fate the Susan Smiths of the world deserve."

Many Americans also believed "Unabomber" Theodore Kaczynski deserved execution for mailing letter bombs that left three people dead and 22 others injured.

"There is a zeal for prosecutors, judges, and state governments to empty their death rows," Henry Heller wrote in an end-of-1995 recap mailed to VADP members. "Death rows are filling up all over the country, and there is a need for space. It's what politicians have promised constituents to get votes. We've been promised that more executions will make us safer and keep others from committing similar crimes."

"Virginia's death row population is 57. This is about ten more than two years ago." He closed by noting that many of the newest inmates on death row were between 18 and 25 years of age.

Atkins v. Virginia Prompts Nationwide Change

At midnight on Aug. 16, 1996, Daryl Reynard Atkins and his companion William Jones abducted and robbed an air force mechanic named Eric Nesbitt. After forcing him to withdraw money from an ATM, they took him to a rural location near Hampton and shot him eight times. Both men testified during Atkins' trial, but both blamed each other for the killing.

Since a defense psychologist testified that Atkins was "mildly mentally retarded" and had a functioning I.Q. of only 59, the jury found Jones's version of events more credible. The court accordingly found Atkins guilty and sentenced him to death. On appeal, the Supreme Court of Virginia affirmed the conviction but called for a new sentencing hearing after finding that the court used an improper sentencing verdict form. At the retrial, Atkins was again sentenced to death.

The U.S. Supreme Court reviewed the death sentence and, in a 6-3 decision, maintained that the Eighth Amendment's ban on cruel and unusual punishments prohibited the execution of someone with an intellectual disability, such as Atkins. "The Constitution places a 'substantive restriction on the State's power to take the life of a mentally retarded offender.'" The decision also left it to the states to define who is intellectually disabled.

The Court used three lines of reasoning in their decision: that prevailing standards of decency forbid the execution of intellectually disabled offenders; that intellectually disabled defendants do not act "with the level of moral culpability that characterizes the most serious adult criminal conduct that do not warrant a death sentence;" and that those defendants are far less capable of securing the upper-level defense needed in capital cases, creating a dangerous opportunity of a death sentence being imposed on someone who did not commit a capital crime.

Atkins was remanded to prison but Virginia was not about to let the U.S. Supreme Court push them around. Since no opinion had been explicitly rendered to his disability, the commonwealth's attorney pursued yet another lengthy jury trial in a Yorktown courthouse in 2005 to ensure that this time the Black man Atkins would be executed.

After testimony from about 100 witnesses, the jury reasoned that being around lawyers for seven years provided enough intellectual stimulation to bump Atkins' I.Q. to 70, putting him precisely one point over the state minimum of 69. He was thus declared competent to be put to death under Virginia law. His execution was set for Dec. 2, 2005.

In a surprise and extremely rare move, The Supreme Court of Virginia unanimously overturned the lower court's ruling, but not directly because of Atkins' disability. The court agreed with Atkins' attorneys that the 2005 jury should not have been told that in 2002 he had already been convicted of capital murder and sentenced to death. That statement, they agreed, prejudiced his sentencing.

On Jan. 17, 2008, at yet another hearing, Atkins received multiple life sentences when it was discovered that the prosecution in the 1998 trial coached co-defendant Jones to revise his statement when it did not sync with forensic evidence in the case. In addition, an audio analysis expert testified that 16 minutes of the two-hour recording of the interrogation could not be found. Leslie P. Smith, who was Jones's original attorney, testified that during the interview, prosecutor Cathy Krinick turned off the tape recorder when Jones' statements "were inconsistent with forensic evidence."

According to the *Washington Post*, Smith testified that prosecutors coached Jones for 15 minutes to produce false testimony against Atkins that better matched the evidence.

The *New York Times* reported that Smith claimed he was advised by legal ethics authorities with the Virginia State Bar not to divulge that he had witnessed "brazen misconduct" by a prosecutor coaching a witness then hiding it from Atkins' attorney.

Judge Prentis Smiley Jr. said, "The court finds there was favorable, potential impeachable evidence possessed by the commonwealth" and "had he [Atkins's attorney] been given the evidence, the outcome might have been different."

The Atkins case directly impacted another Virginia death row inmate, Percy Levar Walton. "He was extremely mentally ill, schizophrenic, and not being treated," recalled attorney Rob Lee. "He lived in a cell with nothing. He had maybe a radio at one point and broke it. No TV. His belongings were this pile of salt and pepper packets. And he just walked [back and forth], mumbling and screaming, and the guys on the row called him 'crazy horse.'"

While VCU health officials testified to the severity of Walton's illness, a DOC official testified that Walton was merely disappointed that his life had not gone where he thought it would. And the jury bought it.

"I think the death sentence interfered with the willingness of the DOC to treat them," Lee explained of inmates like Walton. "Levar had a scheduled execution, was very near to being executed. And a contract doctor who was doing rounds there saw how [disabled] he was and wanted to do a workup on him." When Walton scored a 66 on an I.Q. test, Lee moved forward on getting another hearing for him.

After the Atkins decision, the I.Q. test, and the hearing, Gov. Tim Kaine commuted

Walton's death sentence. He was sent to the Marion Correctional Treatment Center, where he still receives much-needed treatment and is even seeking his GED.

Lee described how mentally ill inmates like Walton improved when essentially freed from their death sentence. "The pressure to kill them is removed, and they're treated like any other mentally ill person in the prison system, and they're better."

Today Daryl Atkins remains incarcerated at Nottoway Correctional Center, and it remains unconstitutional nationwide to execute anyone with an intellectual disability.

Journey of Hope Comes to Virginia

> When [murder victim] families are at the lowest point in their lives, when they're grieving and hurting and trying to make sense of something that doesn't make any sense, the first thing they're offered is another death. [Deaths that are] used by politicians and [by] prosecutors to build careers, to get convictions and to make headlines.
> -Pat Bane, director of Murder Victims Families for Reconciliation, in the
> *Richmond Times-Dispatch*, Jan. 30, 1996.

In 1993, while Bill Pelke served on Marie Deans' Murder Victim Families for Reconciliation (MVFR) board, he had an idea to take a group of their members on a speaking tour through Indiana. The tour would allow them to share their stories of heartbreak and their attitudes regarding the death penalty. So with the blessings of the MVFR, he, along with Sam Sheppard, Marietta Jaeger-Lane, and Suzanne Bosler set up Journey of Hope as a separate organization.

"I was also invited to come," recalled Northern Virginia resident George White, whose wife was murdered right in front of him in an Alabama robbery. He was then arrested, convicted, and sentenced to life in prison for the killing and served seven years before evidence hidden by the prosecution exonerated him. "That's where I first met Bill and the other Journeyers. The idea was to hold a 17-day public education tour in Indiana. It was to bring together other murder victim family members who opposed the death penalty, death row family members, and others with stories to tell."

The group traveled and spoke in colleges and universities, high schools, churches, anywhere they could get in, with their arresting stories that established credibility surrounding the problems with the death penalty. The Indiana tour was so successful that they held Journeys in Georgia, California, and New Mexico over the ensuing years. Then, from Sept. 21 through Oct. 6, 1996, they toured Virginia.

A flyer for the Journey stated that "MVFR members describe their experience of losing a loved one through murder and their eventual recognition, unique to each one, of how the hatred and desire for revenge is destructive to themselves and our society as a whole."

The Journey's stated goals in Virginia were to reduce the number of death sentences, abolish the 21-day rule, encourage legislators to find alternatives to the death penalty, and identify murder victim family members who also sought alternatives to the death penalty. Finally, they wished to build VADP membership and visibility.

The Journey arrived at a crucial time – twelve Virginia death row inmates were scheduled to die in 1996, more than doubling the number of executions the previous year. While appeals were running out for many of them, a new law designed to speed up the execution process was signed in 1995. The law stipulated that once the Supreme Court of Virginia and the Fourth U.S. Circuit Court of Appeals denied the inmate's appeals, either the attorney general or the commonwealth's attorney could seek an execution date from the trial court. That court then was bound to hold a hearing within ten days of receiving the request, and the execution date then had to be set within 60 days of the hearing.

The law also handed the Supreme Court of Virginia original jurisdiction over state habeas petitions, eliminating two processes, the trial court and the Virginia Court of Appeals. Capital defendants seeking habeas relief instead returned to the same court that had just denied their direct appeal. Accordingly, an ABA report found that between 1995 and 2013, the Supreme Court of Virginia granted relief in only one habeas petition out of dozens and dozens submitted.

Attorney General Jim Gilmore's spokesman, Mark Minor, hailed the development, telling the Associated Press that "The bottom line here is that state and federal law has changed. No longer are we going to have death row appeals carrying on for 10 or 15 years."

VADP Director Henry Heller responded that they were "outraged at the rate at which the state is proceeding to empty its death row."

Once in Virginia, Sister Helen Prejean – whose book "Dead Man Walking" had just been made into a movie – kicked off the Journey of Hope's 17-day itinerary to a packed house at the Cathedral of the Sacred Heart in Richmond. This event was followed by similarly well-attended gigs around Hampton Roads and Williamsburg.

On Sept. 23, the Journey gathered at the state Capitol, where Rep. Robert C. Scott and future Virginia Gov. Tim Kaine joined them.

"Violent crime is probably one of the biggest problems we have here in Richmond, but the death penalty is not the answer," Kaine told the crowd. "We have to find a way to end violence of all kinds." A trial lawyer, Kaine had defended several death row inmates, including Lem Tuggle Jr. and Richard Whitley.

"The Journey was a major undertaking," Heller recalled of the "mixed blessing" of the Journey, its 30 people, and its $50,000 budget. "Logistics, housing, meals, transportation, getting the press there ... And, you know, we got through it, but ... I was just trying to double-check everything."

Despite the logistical and personnel issues, Heller maintained that the Journey was a financial turning point for VADP. "Finally, it brought us a little money, which allowed us to bring in more money. And all of a sudden, there was a little cushion."

After the Journey, VADP board chair Steven Rosenfield wanted to hire Heller full-time as director, but Heller turned him down. "I'm like, 'I'm a laborer, man. I work for a living, you know!'" But they reached a compromise where Heller would take off

Wednesdays to do his VADP work and get paid for that one day.

After the Hampton Roads presentations, the Journey rallied at Greensville and Mecklenburg Correctional Centers before touring the Shenandoah Valley, with additional stops in Farmville, Charlottesville, and Danville. The group spent the first week of October in Northern Virginia.

George White recalled that the Journey was welcome wherever they went. "That's one of the blessings from our personal losses that we bring. People can continue to disagree with us, but it's hard to dismiss our experience. I've had occasions where I've gone to speak, and people haven't known where I was coming from initially. I would say, 'I'm against the death penalty.' And somebody would respond, 'Well, you'd feel differently if it happened to someone you loved.' And I have a response to that. 'You're right, I did feel differently when my wife was murdered. Let's talk about it.' And that's generally the approach that we take."

"I don't want to debate the death penalty. Debating is about winning and losing. I want, and we as an organization, just want to tell you about our experiences. We'll listen to you if you listen to us. And that's been our philosophy."

Another benefit of the exposure and money the Journey brought was the erection of a billboard along eastbound I-95 in downtown Richmond. The banner read, "Yes, Virginia, there is an alternative to the death penalty!" the VADP logo, website, and phone number were prominently displayed underneath.

Not Abolition – Alternatives

Heller maintained that by the close of the 1990s, as the number of executions reached its zenith, he again focused on advocating for alternatives to the death penalty, not full-blown abolition. "I had these brochures made up, and I'd always keep them in my pocket or my bag," he recalled taking advantage of the visibility of the Journey of Hope and the billboard. "I was constantly putting brochures everywhere. It was just all about education."

"But I wasn't advocating abolishing the death penalty," he clarified. "To me, abolishing the death penalty was something in the future that was going to happen hopefully at some point."

Lem Tuggle Jr. Executed

The future abolition of which Heller spoke would come too late for death row inmate Lem Tuggle Jr. On Dec. 12, 1996, Tuggle, the last surviving 1984 death row escapee, was executed at Greensville Correctional Center after 13 years on the row. Tuggle was described as the poster boy for Gov. George Allen and Attorney General Jim Gilmore's 1995 abolition of parole and truth-in-sentencing initiatives. At the time of the Havens murder, he had been on parole for the 1971 murder of Shirley Brickey. Gilmore reasoned that "if these new sentences had been in place when Lem Tuggle was convicted of killing Shirley Mullins Brickey, he would not have been on parole the day Havens was shot."

The parole board had, in fact, turned Tuggle down three times for parole before granting it on the fourth try.

BJ Brown Devlin recalled seeing Tuggle one last time before his execution. "My last visit to death row, I was pregnant with my first child," she explained. "And Lem asked me if I was tough enough to be a parent. Not in a mean way. In a friendly way. I was certainly not starry-eyed and thinking these people had all been railroaded or anything like that. I knew what they had done. But I also knew that they were broken human beings and still children of God."

Another Moratorium Request

> I see no reason to have a [death penalty] moratorium because all one would be doing would be delaying justice."
> -Former Governor and U.S. Senate candidate George Allen, responding to
> a reporter's question, Sept. 17, 2000.

Heller's goal of advocating for alternatives to death received companionship from the American Bar Association (ABA). In 1997 they passed a moratorium resolution calling on every death penalty state to suspend executions until cases could be administered "fairly and impartially" and that they could be managed constitutionally, with minimal risk of executing innocent persons.

This moratorium also established guidelines for indigent counsel, including the appointment of two experienced attorneys at each stage of a capital case. That counsel, in turn, should be provided the necessary time and funding for proper investigations to level the playing field, including the procurement of expert witnesses and other services.

This national call for a moratorium preceded a similar resolution passed by the Charlottesville-Albemarle County Bar Association. The main point of this resolution was to minimize the risk of executing an innocent person by building more safeguards and fairness into a system that seemed hellbent on just speeding up the process.

"I got the Charlottesville-Albemarle Bar Association to take up a resolution calling for an end to the death penalty," recalled Steven Rosenfield, who spearheaded the initiative. "I invited the ACLU's death penalty person in Washington, D.C. to come down. So, there was going to be a debate at our bar luncheon. But I could not find a prosecutor. So they asked me to talk. And I gave my stump speech, knowing the statistics pretty well. By a two-to-one vote, we passed a resolution calling for the end of the death penalty."

Rosenfield added that a similar resolution also passed the Harrisonburg Bar Association by a single vote but failed in the Henrico Bar Association, highlighting the split opinions on the death penalty. "I sent out countless requests, and those were the only ones that allowed me to come and talk about opposing the death penalty. So, there was a small effort getting lawyers to oppose it."

More Calls for a Moratorium – One from an Unlikely Source

In Virginia, we've fixed it! It's moving faster than ever!
-Gov. Jim Gilmore, responding to a member of the clergy who told him,
"We really need to do something to fix the death penalty," July 13, 2000.

Following on the heels of the ABA and the Charlottesville Bar calls for abolition at the tail end of this murderous decade were two more calls for slowing down or temporarily stopping the implementation of death from two seemingly polar opposites – the Virginia ACLU and "700 Club" host Rev. Pat Robertson.

On April 8, 2000, in a keynote speech, Robertson told an audience at the College of William and Mary School of Law that he believed the death penalty was morally justified; however, it was applied unfairly to African-Americans and the poor and did not provide opportunities for mercy. Robertson unbelievably called for a temporary moratorium on executions to fix these issues yet noted he was not ready to "crusade for it."

The admission stunned and gratified then-University of Florida Professor Michael Radelet, the director of an organization called "Moratorium 2000." "Pat Robertson coming out in favor of the moratorium is like the Pope coming out in favor of condoms," he told the April 11 *Gainesville Sun*.

In a 2022 email, Radelet clarified his message. "My first thought was that it showed that yet again, the more people know about the death penalty, the more likely they are to oppose it."

Over in Lynchburg, Rev. Jerry Falwell split with his fellow TV pastor on the issue, stating that he did not support a moratorium and that the time between conviction and execution be cut even more. "As far as human beings can devise a judicial system, Americans have done it the best," he told the April 12 *Richmond Times-Dispatch*. "I'm not willing to abrogate our judicial system on the premise that we may possibly have set free a guilty person or convicted and executed an innocent person."

On the same day Robertson spoke out for a moratorium, the Virginia ACLU released a bombshell report titled "Unequal, Unfair and Irreversible: The Death Penalty in Virginia."

The study came when concerns about wrongful convictions nationwide were at an all-time high. Polling showed support for the death penalty in Virginia had declined from a high of 80 percent in 1994 to 66 percent in 2000.

Abolitionists embraced the study, claiming it proved the death penalty's corruption, arbitrariness, and biases. Kent Willis, who was executive director of the Virginia ACLU chapter, claimed that the report "casts a dark shadow over the death penalty in Virginia."

Willis had long been involved in the fight to end capital punishment in Virginia through the lens of the ACLU. In a 2021 interview, he recalled how difficult it was in the late 1990s and early 2000s to push abolition or moratorium legislation. "I was already opposed to the death penalty when I became executive director. The first job I created after getting some more money was someone else to do [abolition] lobbying in the General Assembly because it was a frustrating place to be, and it continues [to be an] incredibly frustrating place."

Most frustrating to Willis in the Assembly was what he called "the language of benign deception" or "talking between the lines." "We lobby from day one for the abolition of the death penalty, but you have to be practical [in] that there were bills introduced, but largely symbolic. And then the other strategy was to work around the edges, and try to do basic criminal justice reform that would decrease the opportunities for capital punishment cases, and possibly grab hold of this notion of life without parole."

Willis recalled that the report was primarily *Virginian-Pilot* reporter and Northeastern Law School student Laura LaFay's idea. "She called me and said, 'I'd like to come be with you for six months and do a study of what's going on with the death penalty in Virginia.'" Assisting in the study was defense attorney Gerald Zerkin, capital defender Rob Lee, Marie Deans, Henry Heller, Professor Richard Bonnie, and numerous others.

LaFay credited David Oshinsky's 1997 book "Worse than Slavery: Parchman Farm and the Ordeal of Jim Crow Justice" with putting her writing on the death penalty in context, leading to her proposal to create the study.

"People were, at that time and probably still are, very visceral about the death penalty," she noted. "[They think] 'Murderers should die. They're evil.' And you would always hear the state say, 'This thing has been through the state court, the federal court, reviewed a million times. This guy is guilty and needs to die.' And there's no easy way to explain to anybody ... they think, you kill someone, you should be killed as soon as possible because the death penalty was about vengeance."

The report's principal findings noted deep-rooted, pervasive problems in Virginia's capital punishment system, from charging to conviction to legal counsel to courtroom proceedings to executive clemency. Among them:

- Geography played a significant role in who received a death sentence in Virginia. Between 1978 and 1997, eight (out of 133) jurisdictions imposed one-third of Virginia's death sentences. However, those eight jurisdictions suffered only ten percent of the state's capital murders. Prosecutors in those jurisdictions routinely sought the death penalty, while prosecutors in other jurisdictions never or rarely sought it. Also, of these 133 jurisdictions, 113 had white commonwealth's attorneys, with only eight Black.

- Race remained a controlling factor in the administration of Virginia's death penalty. According to the FBI's *Supplemental Homicide Reports* for 1978-1997, 41 percent of victims of capital crimes in Virginia were Black. Yet of the 131 crimes for which a death sentence was imposed during the same period, only 20 percent involved Black victims. Also, a Black offender who robbed and murdered a white person was four times more likely to be sentenced to death than a Black offender who robbed and murdered a Black person.

- Virginia had no enforceable structure for ensuring that competent lawyers represented indigent capital defendants. Ninety-seven percent of those sentenced to death since 1977 were too poor to afford a lawyer. Published statistics also showed that trial attorneys appointed to represent Virginia's death row inmates were six times more likely to be the subject of disciplinary proceedings than other lawyers.

- Virginia's appellate courts rarely corrected errors that occurred in capital trials. Between 1978 and 1997, the Supreme Court of Virginia reversed a meager eight percent of the death sentences it considered. In contrast, the national average reversal rate by state supreme courts was 40 percent. During the same period, the Fourth U.S. Circuit Court of Appeals, the court of last resort for the condemned, granted relief in only one of 131 cases.

- As a result of these judicial rushes to execute, the study found that Virginia governors stopped more executions than the governors of any other state. In almost all cases, the governor's action resulted from reasonable doubts about guilt. These included concerns raised by evidence that juries never heard and that higher courts would not consider.

- Finally, the study found that Virginia's record-keeping systems for capital cases "are so rudimentary, incomplete, and inaccessible that there is no efficient way to compile objective data about the death penalty here." It further pointed out that crime statistics had to be gleaned from the FBI because Virginia had "no central repository for information about the way it administers the death penalty and no reliable method of compiling data about capital prosecutions." Even the number of capital indictments since 1976 was not known.

Predictably, death penalty supporters disparaged the study. Attorney General Mark Earley called it "biased and erroneous" in the April 16, 2000 *Virginian-Pilot*, but presented no data to support his assertion, other than pointing to the layers of judicial review through which death sentences pass as evidence that truth always prevailed.

Danville commonwealth's attorney William Fuller was particularly irked about the spotlight on death sentencing and executions in his jurisdiction. Thanks to him, Danville had the highest per capita death sentence rate in the state at 68.88 per 1,000 residents. As mentioned previously, of the 108 murders in Danville between 1978 and 1997, Fuller charged 18 defendants with capital murder and sought the death penalty for 16 of them, winning nine executions.

One that got away from Fuller was Calvin Swann. Jurors sentenced him to death in 1993 without being informed that Swann had been clinically diagnosed as schizophrenic and psychotic and spent the previous 25 years in prisons and state psychiatric institutions. Even Gov. Gilmore could not stomach that travesty and promptly commuted Swanns' death sentence to life without parole in May 1999.

Fuller's eagerness to seek death was possibly surpassed only by Prince William County commonwealth's attorney Paul Ebert, who during his 51 years in office pursued 14 capital crimes, and won nine executions.

States With No Death Penalty Share Lower Homicide Rates

-Page 1 headline, *The New York Times*, Sept. 22, 2000.

VADP held its first statewide conference in the new millennium on Oct. 14, 2000, at

Westminster Presbyterian Church in Charlottesville. Guest speakers included Joe Jackson and Bill Burke, authors of the book "Dead Run – the Shocking Story of Dennis Stockton and Death Row in America."

It was a somewhat bittersweet occasion – Virginia was coming off two extremely high execution years, with 14 killed in 1999 and eight in 2000. But there were bright spots, including a record-high fundraising campaign in the summer and the opening of a new office at the Virginia Organizing Project. Efforts to raise awareness of moratoriums gained substantial momentum when numerous organizations signed resolutions to temporarily halt executions. These organizations included the Virginia College of Criminal Defense Attorneys, the Charlottesville City Council, and the State Black Caucus. Numerous faith groups also spoke up in support, including the Catholic Diocese of Richmond, the Episcopal Diocese of Virginia, the Virginia Council of Churches, the United Methodist Church of Virginia, and the Charlottesville Friends Meeting, in addition to many individual churches across the state. Editorials supporting either a moratorium or an end to the death penalty appeared in the *Virginian-Pilot*, the *Staunton News-Leader*, the *Potomac News*, and the *Richmond Free Press*.

The conference also introduced VADP members to the Virginia Mitigation Project. "The project will monitor all capital cases, including those murders which fit the statute but are not charged capital ... Without such monitoring, no one in Virginia, including the governor and the courts, actually knows how the death penalty is applied and works in Virginia."

The VMP also included Charlottesville attorney Bruce Williamson as President. Vice President was Alexandria researcher Gayle Harris, and Chip Wright, a Richmond Attorney, was secretary/treasurer.

Lynchburg's Death Penalty Awareness Week & New Chapters Considered

In 2001, Feb. 18 through 25 was Death Penalty Awareness Week in Lynchburg. Over 5,000 central Virginians attended one or more presentations co-sponsored by VADP and five area colleges and universities, including Liberty University, Lynchburg College, Randolph-Macon Women's College, and the Virginia University of Lynchburg.

Sister Helen Prejean spoke as usual to a packed house of 800 at Randolph-Macon, and formerly wrongfully-convicted death row inmates Michael Graham and John Fortis also spoke to overflow crowds.

Also, in April of 2001, VADP looked again to expand with chapters in various parts of Virginia where support was high. A guideline stated that VADP chapters' goals included "promoting the alternative to the death penalty that Virginians have preferred through successive years of polling: life with no possibility of parole for a minimum of 25 years, combined with restitution to the victim's family." A Northern Virginia chapter was organized in 1995, followed by Charlottesville, with Anne Meador selected chair.

VADP members also provided contacts and vigil information in Waynesboro, Richmond, Lynchburg, Farmville, Norfolk, and Moneta, home of Smith Mountain Lake.

Looking Back ... and Looking Forward

In summing up the first 20 years of Virginia's death penalty "modern era," Kent Willis observed that "There's a notion that justice was the end. Justice was the goal, let's do it, and let's do it quickly, and justice will take care of itself. There's an argument to be made for that."

"The truth is, when you start looking at all the little pieces that make up death penalty adjudication, you see thousands of little ways to undermine it. The Virginia court system looked for every way to undermine even the notion of procedural due process. Much of our [ACLU] effort went into reforming the death penalty rules to create a more progressive landscape."

"And then even when there were some breakthrough reforms, they weren't really breakthrough reforms. Every time they added something that seemed to make it work better, there would be just enough loopholes so that it didn't work much better. And the 21-day rule was just nuts. It didn't make sense. And the history of the 21-day rule is an exact parallel to the history of the death penalty law in Virginia. Look at how it started out so unfair and how the reforms have never really reached the intended goal."

Almost Executed: Michael Graham and Albert Burrell

> I would have been dead due to the 21-Day Rule.
> -Wrongfully convicted Roanoke man, Michael Graham, speaking to the
> 2001 Virginia General Assembly.

In 1987, two Roanoke men, Michael Graham and Albert Burrell, traveled to Louisiana for a two-week search for construction work that turned into a 14-year living hell on Angola Prison's death row.

While in Louisiana, law enforcement arrested Graham and Burrell for the murder of an elderly Downsville couple, William and Callie Frost. No physical evidence linked Graham or Burrell to the crime scene, and prosecutors intentionally withheld exculpatory evidence during the trial while calling three witnesses who later recanted their testimony.

The chief witness, an inmate named Olan Wayne Brantley, had a record of mental instability and was known in prison as "Lyin' Wayne." In a plea deal with the prosecution, he claimed Graham had confessed to the murders while they shared a cell. Another female witness, Burrell's ex-wife, Janet, was told by police to either implicate Graham and Burrell or they would take her children away. A third witness, a 14-year-old female, simply lied.

Graham and Burrell were both found guilty and sentenced to death.

Five months after Burrell was convicted, Janet Burrell, who was already remarried to Burrell's brother, James, retracted her testimony. She claimed she lied because she wanted to get custody of their child, awarded to Albert before the murders.

In December 2000, Judge Cynthia Woodard granted a request by Graham for a new trial based upon claims that the district attorney, Tommy Adkins, had wrongfully withheld evidence from the defense. Burrell was also granted a new trial after the Graham ruling.

After 14 horrendous years, the court finally dismissed the charges against them. Judge Woodard noted that "the case against Mr. Graham and Mr. Burrell is so weak that it should never have been brought to the grand jury." Graham had come within a heart-stopping 17 days of execution.

When released from Angola, officials gave the men a $10 check for transportation (even though the bus fare to Roanoke was $127) and a state-issued denim jacket several sizes too large. "Talk about a crime? That's a crime," John Holdridge, the lawyer who proved Graham's innocence, told the press.

Burrell instead got into his stepsister Estelle's pickup truck to her ranch in East Texas, where he lives today. Of the crime, he always said, "I didn't have nothing to do with that."

To add even further insult, the Second U.S. Circuit Court of Appeals in Shreveport, on Jan. 13, 2016, upheld a 2008 lower court ruling that denied any wrongful conviction compensation claimed by the two men. Ten dollars and an ill-fitting jacket were all they would receive from the Great State of Louisiana for 14 years wrongfully convicted.

Graham appeared in front of the 2001 Virginia General Assembly to tell his story and send a strong message: "If this would have happened to me in Virginia, I would have been dead due to the 21-day rule."

Despite Graham's plea for Virginia to end this medieval law, the 21-day rule, although tweaked, is still in effect.

Abolition as a Matter of Faith

"Healing the Memories, Redeeming the Present, Reshaping the Future"

In the center of Richmond, there is a small plot of ground near the intersection of Belvidere and Spring Streets, where 245 people violently died. Not even Virginia's civil war battlefields experienced as much concentrated killing as this small plot.

This spot is where the Virginia State Penitentiary's death chamber was located. One chilly day in February 1992, as the penitentiary was being demolished, the faith community stepped in to commemorate those inmates and the dark history of the institution, which sat at that location for 191 years. "We decided that this was sacred ground because so many people had been killed," recalled Kathleen Kenney, associate director of the Office of Justice and Peace for the Richmond Catholic Diocese from 1991 to 2004. "And this was an opportunity to raise consciousness about the death penalty and make a faith-based, spiritual blessing of the ground while acknowledging the executions that had taken place there."

On that day, with the penitentiary being reduced to rubble, 50 religious leaders representing Christians, Jews, and Native Americans gathered outside the 20-ft wall for an ecumenical consecration of this location where the state killed so many men and one woman. "Judy Bennett (Coordinator for Interfaith Action for Humane Corrections) was primarily in charge. There was a very large contingency of clergy and rabbis and so on," Kenney recalled. "We gathered there and had a ceremony, and it heightened the consciousness about what it means to kill somebody."

The attendees formed a circle around a small box filled with dirt from the penitentiary site. John Black Elk of the Mattaponi Reservation in King William County burned leaves of grass, then beat a drum as other participants read prayers. At the conclusion, each person filled a small container with dirt from the box and then took it home to mix with earth in their back yards.

Participants in the consecration included Bishop Walter Sullivan; the Rev. Carroll Jenkins, Executive for the Presbyterian Synod of the Mid-Atlantic; Rabbi Myron Berman of Temple Beth-El; the Rev. James McDonald, general minister of the Virginia Council of Churches; and the Rev. George Ricketts and Pastor Russ Ford, of the Chaplain Services of the Churches of Virginia, among others.

"This land had blood on it," Kenney recollected, "and it was like a blessing and a purifying."

A Small Band of Volunteers

> We think society is entitled to retribution.
> -Urchie Ellis, spokesman for Americans for Effective Law Enforcement,

> on expanding eligible death penalty crimes, quoted in the *Staunton News-Leader*, Feb. 24, 1977.

The most substantial and visible opposition to the re-introduction of the death penalty in Virginia after the 1976 *Gregg* decision came from Virginia's faith communities. Within hours of newly-elected Gov. Mills Godwin's announcement that he planned to reimpose capital punishment, leaders from the Catholic, Episcopal, Presbyterian, Greek Orthodox, and Jewish communities scheduled a news conference on Jan. 13, 1977, vowing to vigorously oppose it.

Those leaders, led by Bishop Sullivan, included Bishop Robert Nall and the Rev. Canon Fletcher Lowe of the Episcopal Diocese, Presbyterian Minister Rev. James Payne, Rev. Constantine Dombalis of the Greek Orthodox Church, Rev. George Ricketts, and Rabbi Myron Berman. In a comforting display of unity, these leaders announced an ecumenical prayer vigil on Sunday, Jan. 16, at the Virginia State Penitentiary in Richmond for Utah prisoner Gary Gilmore, who had been executed by firing squad the previous week.

"Bishop Sullivan had a track record of working with the major denominations and the Islamic community members," Kathleen Kenney recalled in a 2021 interview. Kenney worked closely with Sullivan and witnessed his leadership abilities up close. "He had taken a leadership position in the ecumenical community on many issues, and my understanding is it really started with the whole racism issue and civil rights."

"Bishop Sullivan was a rallying point," recalled retired penitentiary chaplain Russ Ford. "When he was there, the other bishops would be there. The other bishops were great guys. Bishop Vache was a personal friend, and he would be somebody that worked and pushed... then Bishop Lee and the Episcopals. George Ricketts was instrumental in pulling those guys together."

Sullivan also had as many detractors as supporters. He was always in the crosshairs of the far right-wing *Richmond News Leader* and *Times-Dispatch* editors. One editorial was so withering that 800 allies bought full-page advertisements in both papers supporting him. Many old-school Virginia Catholics urged the Vatican to remove him as bishop. But because of Sullivan's activism, young priests leaving seminary training frequently came to Richmond.

The Penny Resistance: Gorman versus Virginia Electric & Power

> There is certainly no joy when someone is killed, even by a legal process. But it makes clear that the public can express its anger in an appropriate and legal way against those who violate our laws in a violent and capricious manner.
> -Attorney General J. Marshall Coleman in the *Newport News Daily Press*.
> May 26, 1984.

While Virginia's anti-death penalty modern-era sentiment was rooted in faith communities, other pockets of opposition arose based on social, cultural, moral, and even economic principles.

In the early 1980s, North Richmond residents and abolition leaders Dr. Jerome Gorman and his wife Donna were appalled that their tax dollars would help electrocute prisoners. They came up with an ingenious form of protest that a utility provider found neither appropriate nor legal, as defined by Coleman.

On March 15, 1984, they mailed the following letter to Virginia Electric and Power Company, known as VEPCO, Virginia's largest electrical utility:

> Dear Folks,
> One cent (1¢) is withheld from our electric bill. This is done to oppose the electrocution of prisoners in Virginia. Euthanasia of prisoners is morally wrong. How many kilowatt-hours are required to kill a human? How much does VEPCO charge for the electricity required to kill a prisoner?
> Thank you.
Yours Truly,
Donna B. Gorman
Jerome D. Gorman

In the Gormans' opinion, more creative responses than just judicial efforts and legal protest were needed to broaden support for abolition. They called their method of hitting in the wallet by withholding a penny from their electric bill the "penny resistance."

"In a very real way, the electrical network links our home to the electric chair," they stated in an undated written statement. "We have ended our silent complicity in the premeditated killing of prisoners. While holding back one cent from our Virginia Electric and Power Company bill, we informed VEPCO of our objection to electrocution."

Counterpoint

VEPCO was not sympathetic to their protest. On March 27, Customer Relations Supervisor J. S. Lewis, after a somewhat facile introduction, responded to their letter:

> We recognize and support the right of individuals to hold various opinions on various issues. However, these are individual value judgments and not conditions which determine nor control the provision of electric service by VEPCO. There are other legitimate avenues for you to address this issue. We are not permitted nor will we allow exceptions in billing due to personal opinions. Your failure to pay any part of your electric bill is a delinquency on your part and for us to excuse it would be discriminatory and therefore improper.
> Sincerely, J. S. Lewis, Supervisor – Customer Relations.

Point

On March 30, the Gormans replied:

Thank you for your letter of March 27, however you did not answer the two questions in the letter of March 15th. How many kilowatt-hours are required to kill a human? How much does VEPCO charge for the electricity required to kill a prisoner?

Yours truly, etc., etc.

Counterpoint

On April 6, VEPCO responded:

In specific response to the questions posed, we wish to respond that we do not know the answers, nor do we ever intend to make the determination. We further feel the questions are in poor taste. Our position in this matter is as stated in my March 27 letter.

Sincerely, J. S. Lewis, Supervisor – Customer Relations.

Point

On April 7, the Gormans repeated their two questions, then added that:

It is unjust that we are compelled to purchase electricity from a sole-supplier firm which appears indifferent to the use of its product for premeditated killing of humans. Tragically, your two letters inform us that VEPCO has little concern whether its product is used for stir-fry cooking or fry those in stir. Could you please refer our questions to someone in VEPCO who will answer them?

Yours truly, etc., etc.

Counterpoint

In an April 11 response, Supervisor Lewis took a more passive-aggressive approach in explaining the benefits of the constitutional republic under which we all live:

The conviction you hold relative to capital punishment is laudable within the context of your right to hold such an opinion ... However, we thankfully live in a society where the rule of law is supreme, and under the law, the act to which you object is authorized under prescribed conditions.

... Reasonable citizens may disagree over capital punishment, and while I make no personal or corporate statement here, I wish to reiterate that capital punishment is the law of the land. We will obey the law, which by the way, is the exact duty of each and every citizen.

... Specifically addressing your specific questions, it is our position that it is not our responsibility to make the requested determination, the request is in the poorest of taste, and we will not now nor in the future dignify the same with a reply. We are firm in this position.

Sincerely, J. S. Lewis, Supervisor – Customer Relations.

Point

On April 13, the Gormans upped the ante:

> Dear Mr. Lewis, In a very real way, the electrical network links our home
> to the electric chair and death chamber. We have ended our silent complic-
> ity in the killing of humans by electrical euthanasia. Our letter of April 7
> asked you to refer our questions to someone in VEPCO who will answer
> them. Please respect that request.
>
> The questions are the same: How many kilowatt-hours are required to kill
> a human? How much does VEPCO charge for the electricity required to kill
> a prisoner?"
>
> > Yours truly, etc., etc.

Not receiving an answer, on May 5, the Gormans wrote to VEPCO Vice President
Paul Edwards:

> Dear Mr. Edwards. ...We have been corresponding with Mr. J. S. Lewis ...
> Though we have repeatedly asked for answers to plainly worded questions,
> Mr. Lewis has not provided the information requested. Would you please
> look into this matter and inform us of your findings? Thank you.
>
> > Yours truly, etc., etc.

Counterpoint

On May 11, 1984, VEPCO VP Paul Edwards succinctly responded to Gorman's letter
but did not answer it:

> After reviewing the previous correspondence on this matter, I find our
> prior reply to be appropriate.
>
> > Sincerely, Paul G. Edwards.

Clearly, during several more back and forth arguments, the Gormans had become the
sand in VEPCO's swimsuit. After their repeated withholding of one cent from their bill,
Customer Relations Supervisor Lewis began making thinly-veiled threats, saying in part:

> Your failure to pay in full for services rendered is unacceptable, not only
> because it deprives the company of funds justly earned, but it violates the
> Company's terms and conditions for supplying electricity on file with and
> authorized by the Virginia State Corporation Commission ... Your failure to
> adhere to the aforementioned terms and conditions subjects your service
> to whatever action is appropriate under the law. You have other legitimate

avenues to address this issue. Deducting a portion of your electric bill is not one of them."

Sincerely, J. S. Lewis, Supervisor – Customer relations.

In June, and the middle of their *contretemps* with VEPCO, the Gormans became aware of a June 29, 1978 article in the *Richmond News-Leader* titled "State Preparing Chair if Needed." The story stated, in part, "Already Virginia Electric and Power has installed a new transformer to channel killing amounts of current to the [electric chair]. VEPCO said the transformer replaces one the utility removed during a flood emergency when capital punishment was effectively outlawed."

This development triggered a request from the Gormans for an explanation from Mr. Lewis:

Since receiving your letter of June 7th, the enclosed article from the Richmond News-Leader (June 29, 1978) has come to our attention. We note an apparent conflict between your letter of June 7th and the mention of VEPCO in that news article. Is the newspaper report in error? We would appreciate your comments.

Yours truly, etc., etc.

Getting no response from VEPCO, the very next day, the Gormans expanded their "penny resistance" by also withholding one cent from their C&P Telephone bill:

For religious, moral, cultural, and social reasons, we cannot support the death penalty. This deeply-held belief leads us to resist the involuntary obligation which the state of Virginia imposes on us to help pay for this cruel and inhuman atrocity. To end our silent complicity in the premeditated killing of Virginia prisoners by electric euthanasia, we again hold back one penny from the Virginia state tax on the A.T.&T. Information Systems portion of our telephone bill.

In fidelity to a merciful and just God and in solidarity with those children of God who are on death row, we are

Yours truly,
Donna Gorman
Jerome Gorman

"VEPCO was going to turn our power off," Donna Gorman said in a brief 2021 conversation. It was a move that could have had disastrous repercussions for her, her husband Jerome (who died Feb. 7, 2015), and their 12 children at their rambling North Richmond home. "So we eventually paid it off. It was a dollar and some change. And then we started all over again!"

The penny resistance continued into 1987, with the cycle of VEPCO threatening to cut their electricity, the Gormans paying the arrears, then starting all over again.

Texas inmate and author of the 1983 book "Deathman Pass Me By," Philip Brasfield, wrote to the Gormans to congratulate them on their penny resistance initiative. He added, "if you want to do more than withhold taxes, I suggest that you contact a good friend of mine who is actively engaged in death penalty opposition work and frankly needs all the support she can get at this time. Her name is Marie Deans, Director of the Virginia Coalition on Jails and Prisons."

By April 1986, another protestor joined the Gorman's penny resistance effort. Thirty-year-old Jon Klein, a drifter, construction worker, and volunteer for the VCJL, explained in a press release that he would not pay taxes to the Commonwealth of Virginia "because of its use of the death penalty and its collection of barbaric jails and prisons."

"I came to the conclusion that if I wouldn't allow my money to be used to help finance the killing and torture in Central America, then I couldn't finance the killing and torture going on right here in Virginia," he wrote. "Murder and crime are serious problems, but they are not solved by strapping people into the electric chair or by warehousing them in dehumanizing institutions."

The Gormans even published a mailed newsletter, *Penny Resistance*, filled with legislative updates, quotes, and reprints of death penalty-related articles from around the country.

"A Ritual of Final Revenge:" The Faith Community Steps Up

The first chaplain service was organized for the penitentiary in 1919 to serve all inmates, not just those on death row. In 1951 a group of Black Virginia Union students led by Odie Brown was with the Martinsville Seven when they were all executed for raping a white woman.

But the service took on a new urgency in 1976 when Gov. Mills Godwin signed the death penalty back into law after a 14-year hiatus. Russ Ford was already with the service, and he and a few others volunteered to minister to inmates as they entered the newly-formed row.

"It sort of put a lump in my stomach," Ford, a Baptist, recalled of those early planning meetings in 1977. "I mean, we would have to work with it, and it bothered me. I was against capital punishment ...We all opposed capital punishment. The chaplain service had a policy, and its board voted to be against it."

Ford forged strong relationships with the men on the row. "What happened was I got in and did really well with the men. And some of the other chaplains didn't relate to them well. They were in youth services or other places, and they weren't clicking with the men. So, [director George Ricketts] asked me just to go in and take it, and I went on from there."

Ford described how the crumbling State Penitentiary infrastructure contributed heavily to the behaviors of inmates, the guards, and anyone else who all functioned in seemingly impossible circumstances.

"The penitentiary was out of control," he recalled. "The staff did not have a handle on the prison. The inmates, they had a handle. It was so antiquated – the locking mechanisms didn't work. In the summer, it was not unusual on top of that tier C [maximum security] ceiling to be 115, 120 degrees. It was just incredible heat, and you sweat all through the summer. The windows would be broken out in the summer to get air in. Then the state would not fix them for a long time. Then after some grievances and some lawyers involved, they would replace the broken windows. Then you frigidly made it through the winter. I'm serious on the top tier it was so frigidly cold, I hated going up and doing rounds. And there were pigeon droppings everywhere."

"I was only in there once," recalled civil rights attorney Philip Hirschkop of a visit around 1969. "They fought like hell to keep me from going in there. I had several court orders to go there, and they would appeal them. But it was totally bare-bones. There was very little air moving. During the winter, it was cold as hell. And, you know, when I was there, there were no mattresses from the section I saw, but it was stark. It was what you see in the movies when you're trying to see an old-fashioned horrible penitentiary."

Attorney Michael Millemann in 1969 co-authored with Hirschkop a devastating portrait of the penitentiary in the *Virginia Law Review* titled "The Unconstitutionality of Prison Life." He recalled in 2021 how the environment around the "A" Building basement death chamber was swarming with rats and cockroaches.

Ford also recollected that an early religious leaders forum did many good things on the row and brought together the most they could muster of influence from the mainline denominations, including the impact of Bishop Sullivan. In fact, in 1976, these faith leaders proposed legislation to establish a fund to compensate victims and their families of capital crime. It became law in July 1977 and continues in 2022 as the Virginia Victims Fund.

"Violence Breeds Violence."

Bishop Sullivan was known for his social justice work and being unequivocally pro-life. As early as 1976, as Virginia re-started the death penalty after the *Gregg* decision, Sullivan was right in there, addressing the General Assembly, telling them that "Violence breeds violence, and capital punishment is violence."

Fr. Griffin insists that Bishop Sullivan – who died in 2012 – remains a hero because his pro-life stance was so tenacious. "It was unmistakable. It was a right-to-life thing. I've always said that it's hard to be pro-life consistently because you know that you hate abortion, you know you hate murder, and you know you hate murderers, but their lives are created in goodness by God. So, it's hard to be across the board pro-life."

As for Sullivan, "He never wavered. [It] got him in trouble … but he was one person who consistently upheld human life, whether it's an inmate, gay person, woman, poor person, whatever."

In a 2021 interview, BJ Brown Devlin recalled similar experiences with Sullivan when she came to Richmond in 1985. "I came to Richmond as an associate director in the Office of Justice and Peace, and it was possibly August when I made my first visit with Bishop Sullivan to death row. My job responsibilities included supporting prison ministry in the diocese, the bishop's commitment to that, and supporting work towards abolition. Although, we didn't use the word abolition quite so much at that time."

Devlin stressed during this time that Bishop Sullivan was adamantly opposed to a proposed switch to lethal injection, which was suggested among some legislators starting in 1988. "He opposed the change to lethal injection because what we're doing is wrong. And we shouldn't whitewash it. We shouldn't pretend it's not wrong," she recalled. "He went down to the General Assembly himself to a committee to testify. Now, for him to go down himself meant it was a priority for him. He did not lightly travel down there. He would send staff like me, or he would send the Chancellor."

A Requirement of Faith

As Devlin noted, in the mid-to-late-1980s, as more faith leaders joined Bishop Sullivan in taking up the cause, death penalty abolition was only a long-range goal. Advocates instead petitioned lawmakers to slow the pace of executions and stop death penalty expansion laws. "We had a strong coalition of religious leaders with Bishop Sullivan sort of seated at the head of the table," recalled Julie McConnell. "Rabbi Jack Spiro and a whole group of interfaith leaders would help us by coming and testifying at committees when they were trying to expand the death penalty. And just anything we could try to do to make the system a little more fair."

Devlin claims that at the beginning, there was less grassroots organizing and more of what she called "a great deal of witness." "The leaders of the faith organizations [would say] that opposition to the death penalty has roots in your faith commitment," she explained, adding that opposing the death penalty was not supposed to be foreign to anyone's religious commitment. "I was there to give any kind of legitimacy from respected religious leaders to opposition to the death penalty. It was just a matter of getting that out there and getting the first steps, saying, 'this is not the lunatic fringe here, people; this is a requirement of your faith.' The grassroots organizing piece would come much, much later."

The Roles of Faith Volunteers, Vigil Organizers, and Donors

As a Christian, it seems obvious that we should not be killing people. It's just wrong. There's a lot of scripture against killing and, "Oh, and do not repay evil with evil," and Jesus forgiving the adulterous, stopping an execution ... there's so much in the Bible about forgiveness for wrongdoers.
    -Vigil organizer and death penalty abolition volunteer Virginia Rovnyak,
                                          in a June 29, 2021 interview.

For decades, laypeople stepped up to organize execution vigils, schedule death penalty discussions in churches, lobby legislators, donate money, and keep the focus on the inequities of the death penalty. They worked both within and outside their faith communities for no money or recognition and may be considered among the true silent heroes of the abolition movement.

Debbie Simpson: From Follower to Leader

Fredericksburg resident Debbie Simpson claimed her mother always considered her a follower. "And I was fine with that," she said in a 2021 interview. "I was a childhood stutterer. I was quiet. And I wasn't jumping on board with this thing called leading. It's my story of how that turned around for me."

Simpson traced her work in the abolition movement to the mid-1990s, when she attended a Cursillo program and later a two-year spiritual direction course through the Spiritual Direction Institute (SDI), organized by Monsignor Chester Michael in Charleston, S.C. Later, following an illness diagnosis, she professed to be a little lost in what God had in mind for her.

"It must've been about 1998, every time I turned around, there was another execution," she recalled. After reading church teachings on capital punishment and reviewing Virginia's position on the matter, she decided to attend an execution vigil at Greensville Correctional Center for Thomas Royal, who was executed for the 1994 shooting death of Hampton Police Officer Kenny Wallace.

"When I left the vigil that evening, I got in my car, and it was just this flood of what have I just witnessed, what have I just experienced," she professed. "I can't believe we're doing this. After months of trying to discern the right thing to do, I jumped off the fence, and I firmly landed on the side of abolition. And so that's when there was a shift for me. I knew that taking people's lives was wrong."

Later, at an alumnus gathering of SDI graduates, Monsignor Michael asked her to speak to a class about death penalty abolition – something she had never done before. "I was jittery and shaky," she laughed, but Michael encouraged her to talk about the topic from a faith perspective. "And that's where I had the most comfort, from the wisdom of the Christian faith tradition. It was a springboard."

The talk went so well that Simpson joined VADP and started gathering signatures of others interested in abolition. Whenever the state scheduled an execution, she mailed a letter to them in those pre-computer days, asking them to participate by contacting their legislator or attending a vigil. "Bishop Sullivan helped found the Pax Christi Movement, and he was a very justice-oriented man. And he came out with things that the Richmond Diocese could do for creating awareness," she recalled. "Toll the church bells on the night of an execution, wear black armbands on days of executions, put it in your church bulletins. And so, I would encourage other people to do the same. I was with a small church in the Richmond diocese, and they were very amenable to having announcements placed in the bulletins."

"I wrote letters to the editor," she added. "And I wore my abolition gear. And I just went wherever my feet could take me."

Simpson attended several execution vigils at Greensville Correctional between 1999 and 2003. "I remember one of the first ones that I had attended. It was a pretty large group of people, and we had passed the time of 9:15 p.m., and then we all lined up along the roadway with candles lit until the truck carrying the body went by. We were lined up, and this man [came] out of the facility, began at the front of the line, shook everybody's hand, and said, 'Thank you for coming. Thank you for being here.' And I realized he was the prison spiritual director. He had just journeyed with this condemned man. It was very touching that our presence mattered so much to this individual after all he'd just gone through."

For three years, starting in 2009, Simpson felt called to speak about death penalty abolition at the General Assembly's Republican-controlled Courts of Justice Committee, but she could not summon the nerve. "It was bugging me," she recalled of her hesitancy, "I'm supposed to go do this. [But] I don't want to do this."

She decided that 2012, with two death penalty expansion bills on the docket, would be the year, so she wrote her three-minute speech. "Be precise, be succinct. I've got three minutes. That's it. Make the best of the three minutes," she repeated.

After several delays, she finally got her chance. She stood and said, "Chairman [Rob] Bell, members of the committee, my name is Debbie Simpson. I'm a spiritual director. For the past ten years, I've been sitting in the meeting rooms of the justice committees when bills related to capital punishment have been proposed, but I've not elected to speak before until today ...."

After her nerve-wracking speech, Northern Virginia Delegate Charniele Herring approached her in the hallway and put her arms around her. "I didn't know her. She didn't know me. And she hugs me and says, 'Thank you.' And I said, 'Well, thank you for the one vote.'"

Sure enough, Del. Herring was the lone vote against expansion on that committee that year.

Simpson's story is not unique in faith-based abolition circles in that she did all these activities on her own, guided only by her convictions while transforming from a follower to a leader. "All my life, I never paid attention," she admitted. "And I'm thinking, 'Well, I'm just a normal person.' But once you start paying attention, you'll see it too."

Elise Cleva: The Power of an Individual

Arlington resident Elise Cleva traces her anti-death penalty work back 20 years to Bishop O'Connell High School. "The topic of capital punishment came up in some of the theology classes that we were required to take," she recalled. "It was one of several issues under the respect for human life umbrella. And I remember feeling particularly compelled by it because it seemed so barbaric to me that my state and others would continue to execute people when we have supermax prisons to keep dangerous people away from others."

After graduating from the University of Virginia, she moved back to Arlington and got involved in more social justice work through St. Charles Borromeo Catholic Church. One of the committees that she joined included encouragements to parishioners to write letters supporting clemency when there was an execution. Through this work, she learned about the VADP vigils.

"During that time, I think there was only one execution, but I remember publicizing the VADP vigil for that execution in the church's bulletin." That 2010 vigil was for Teresa Lewis, the first woman executed in Virginia since 1912. It was held at the Clarendon Metro Station, a brief two-minute walk from the parish.

In 2015, after taking a position working for Falls Church Del. Kaye Korey, Cleva decided to become more involved in VADP when the organizer of the Arlington vigils stepped down. She contacted executive director Michael Stone, offered to be the vigil coordinator for the area, then organized vigils at Unitarian Universalist Churches in Arlington and Fairfax. She also assisted Del. Korey with drafting letters supporting clemency for Alfredo Prieto.

"After about 16 years of being active on death penalty issues, I didn't believe that we would see it abolished in my lifetime," Cleva said. "That's how intractable it seemed to me in the State of Virginia." Unlike a few skeptics, Cleva also believes the abolition will be permanent.

"A commonwealth that I'm part of affirmed human dignity," she declared, "And I guess it's a lesson not to give up. With advocacy, it feels like you're screaming, and nobody is paying attention. And the power of an individual or even a small group of individuals is negligible. But there can be a convergence of several different factors that completely change the game and create an environment where the small efforts of many individuals over many years suddenly have more of an impact."

Robert More: "I Have a Brother on Death Row. So Do You."

"The idea of state officials taking a person out of his cell, walking him to this little room, strapping him to a gurney, putting an IV in his arm, asking him if he has anything he wants to say, and then deliberately injecting lethal drugs into him and killing him ..." More's voice trailed off as he gathered his thoughts. "It's just appalling to me that our government is in the business of killing people to teach the lesson that killing people is wrong. It's just such a contradiction to what I think our values should be."

Fairfax resident Robert More, a retired federal environmental lawyer and devout Catholic, maintained that his opposition to the death penalty stretched back decades. However, it wasn't until more recently, when he conflated the violence of the death penalty with the supposed need for war, that he became an active advocate both against war and America's use of the death penalty.

"I probably started with the church's traditional teaching about a just war approach," he remembered, "where war is a regrettable evil but sometimes necessary and justified. I would say that around 2008, I became convinced that [war] was always contrary to God's will. There's no excuse for the barbarity of war anymore because there are so many alternatives to war."

"But I'd say when I joined Pax Christi and became committed to ending all kinds of violence, I became more interested in working on the death penalty, along with other issues."

In 2009, he attended a death penalty conference held at Our Lady Queen of Peace Parish in Arlington. Then, in 2010, he went to Columbus, Georgia, for the annual School of the Americas Watch protest. There is where he found a T-shirt that read, "I have a brother on death row. So do you."

"It brought tears to my eyes. It still does," he confessed. "I bought it, and it touched me and made me think that I needed to do more in this area."

He attended a Diocesan Peace and Justice Commission conference on the death penalty a year or two later. Speakers included Michael Stone, who was at the time the Virginia coordinator for the National Coalition to Abolish the Death Penalty. Other speakers included VADP executive director Steve Northrup, former executioner-turned-abolitionist Jerry Givens, and Terri Steinberg, whose son Justin Wolfe was on death row for a crime he did not commit. "That was a great conference," More added, "and as a result, I became more convinced that I needed to be involved politically and not just thinking about the death penalty as a moral issue."

He accelerated his involvement. In 2012 he started a Pax Christi group at St. John Neumann Parish in Reston. Then in 2013, that group started monthly prayer vigils for peace. He also, in 2015, helped organize a prayer vigil during the execution of Alfredo Prieto.

"It was quite moving," he recalled of the vigil. "We started at 8:30, with the execution scheduled for 9:00. And we spent that half-hour with an introductory prayer, then the group just shared why they were concerned about the death penalty, and I got a lot of good perspectives. One guy, for example, was very conservative. And he said he used to be a supporter of the death penalty, but then he got involved with prison ministry and saw who these people were. And that changed his mind."

More freely admitted there is still a level of acceptance for the death penalty in the American Catholic communities, which place a heavier emphasis on abortion. "And this fellow, the head of the Respect Life Committee for the parish, focuses mainly on abortion. But he supported us in death penalty abolition because of his experience in prison ministry. So he's bought into this consistent ethic of life. And his group, which tends to be conservative and mainly concerned about abortion, he brought them along as an ally. We gained probably a wider acceptance than we might have otherwise."

Like most Virginians, death penalty abolition in 2021 caught More somewhat flatfooted. "I didn't have any big hopes that the death penalty would be abolished soon. I hoped it would fade away over a long time, but I wouldn't have expected abolition in 2021."

"Then, when I saw the governor sign the bill, I got all choked up. And I cried."

Carissa Phillips: Finding Herself on a Journey

While growing up in Evangelical churches in Dallas, Texas, Charlottesville resident and VADP board member Carissa Phillips admitted she gave the death penalty little thought, despite the lightning pace of executions occurring in her home state. "I had never dealt with how I felt about the death penalty." She admitted in a 2021 interview. "I hadn't dealt with that kind of cry for vengeance that our society has ... And that makes me so sad. But, you know, it's not an issue that many evangelical churches wrestle with. It's just kind of expected. It's not challenged. Sadly, the preciousness of all of human life doesn't seem to be consistently applied in many evangelical churches."

After moving to the Charlottesville area, Phillips, around 2015, became a part of Vineyard Church and started following Philadelphia-based Christian activist and author Shane Claiborne. Reading Claiborne started her – like Joseph Campbell's reluctant warrior in "The Hero's Journey" – on a winding voyage deep into the abolition movement. "I followed a lot of the social justice issues that he had taken up throughout his life, but the one that surprised me the most was the death penalty."

"Seeing his work in his book 'Executing Grace' was impactful for me," she added. "And then that kind of led me to Bryan Stevenson and his book 'Just Mercy.'"

After experiencing "Just Mercy," Phillips suddenly found herself in front of the U.S. Supreme Court at the 2017 40th-anniversary rally to abolish the death penalty. "It was very random. I went all by myself," she laughed at her sudden calling. "I knew not one soul. I recognized Shane Claiborne's face, but that was about it. I just knew I had to be there."

She then recalled a chance meeting on an airplane a week after that as she returned from a work trip. "I was coming back to Charlottesville, and the man sitting next to me on the plane was very chatty. I told him about this experience in front of the Supreme Court, seeing a man named Derrick who had been on death row in Ohio for more than 20 years and purposely getting arrested again to protest the death penalty. And he immediately connected me to Michael Stone."

Shortly after that, she attended a VADP supporters meeting in Charlottesville to get more involved. "That's where I finally met Michael. And I had no idea anybody in my town was doing anything about the death penalty, so I was eager and ready. I think I got the application to be on the Board within 24 hours."

After joining VADP as a board member in 2019, Phillips began engaging her fellow evangelicals in discussions, finding, as she suspected, there was very little knowledge among them of the death penalty's corrupted processes. "When I started talking about [Claiborne's] book, and how the death penalty was vengeance for the sake of vengeance, and so horribly applied, and so connected to white supremacy and lynching, nobody knew how to process that information. Nobody had heard that before. Even my Black friends in the church hadn't heard that before."

To help with that educational effort, Phillips and VADP invited Shane Claiborne, along with former death row inmate Joe Giarratano and murder victim family member Linell Patterson, to speak at her church. "I think [Claiborne] had name recognition in the evangelical world," she explained. "But we got about 100 evangelicals to show up for that talk, which, to me, was sad. I felt like if it had been another social justice issue, there would have been a lot more. But my pastor was super supportive."

At the beginning of her journey, Phillips claimed to see the murder victim's family members tell their stories was most moving to her, that they weren't seeking vengeance on the person who killed their loved one. "That was kind of the first most impactful thing to me. Then, seeing people like Jerry [Zerkin] on the board, who have worked to free these people for decades ...."

Phillips celebrated abolition with a dance party at her house. "it's interesting. I am a pacifist when it comes to war. And it felt like [abolition was] the end of a war. Almost like our leaving Afghanistan as a nation, it felt very similar. Like, 'It's about time.'"

Virginia Rovnyak: Saber Rattling

When elected President, Ronald Reagan frequently engaged in what Lynchburg Pastor and Liberty University President Jerry Falwell called "saber-rattling" in responding to the Soviet Union's aggressiveness. In response, Charlottesville resident Virginia Rovnyak recalled that people spontaneously rose out of some local churches and formed peace groups. "What got me in was adult Sunday school class at my church, Westminster Presbyterian. And I joined this peace group, so it was probably the winter of 1980 or 1981. And I'm still there. And, it was through that peace group that I became aware of the death penalty and the moral and religious issues [surrounding it]."

"Because I'm a Christian, I follow Jesus' model. And he did not act violently toward his captors, and he forgave them. So I would say, look at Jesus' model for that."

Rovnyak recalled some of her first actions in abolition. "The earliest piece of paper I have with my name on it is around winter of 1989, 1990 when I wrote something in the peace center newsletter urging people to write in support of Joe Giarratano. So, I was a death penalty opponent by that time, if not before."

In the 1990s, as Rovnyak wrote to legislators and lobbied them in Richmond, she also worked with fellow Westminster parishioner Betty Gallagher to sponsor a vigil in Charlottesville on the day of executions. "On the Sunday before an execution, we would announce the vigil in the church and ask people to ask the governor for clemency."

Her efforts began bearing fruit. A few years later, one member told her, "You know, I never really thought much about the death penalty until you and Betty started talking about it."

The comment was encouraging and made her comprehend the reality of the death penalty's brutalization effect. "We've had the death penalty so long that it's just something out there. And you don't think about it."

One execution that affected her was that of Wilbert Lee Evans. After his execution, he was buried with a copy of Supreme Court Justice Thurgood Marshall's opinion on capital punishment in his hand. "It enabled him to stand up when he walked to the death chamber," she explained, adding that the politics played in the life-or-death case by Gov. Douglas Wilder was infuriating. "What makes you want to tear your hair about that is that Wilder at the time was thinking of running for president, and he wanted to be tough on crime."

Del. Kenneth Plum, a staunch abolitionist, recalled in a phone call to *The Intercept* journalist Liliana Segura in April 2021, "So much of the discussion about [the death penalty] was whether or not you could get reelected if you voted to get rid of it ... And when I look back on this, it's disappointing to realize that that was the driving force for keeping it in place for a lot of people."

Despite the aggressiveness of executions throughout the 1990s, Rovnyak never considered giving up the fight because of the persistent efforts of Marie Deans and VADP Director Henry Heller, among others. "Henry was just so energetic, certainly an inspiration. Henry was always a speaker [at the peace center], and he was supposed to talk for five minutes then go on for 20 ...."

Rovnyak recalled a light-hearted anecdote regarding Heller of those shoe-string budget days. "I think it was the Church of the Brethren. We had these large coffee urns, and we plugged two of them into one outlet and blew a fuse. 'Pastor, where's the fuse box?' He had no idea. So we had to get a bunch of extension cords to run from different places."

Rovnyak also recalled the vigil they held for the execution of Mir Aimal Kasi in November 2002. "Kasi was a Pakistani man who killed two people outside the CIA headquarters," she explained, "so there was much international attention. They didn't allow counsel from Pakistan. Betty and I stood on the corner with signs [not in] protest [but] a prayerful vigil. It's at night, November 2002, and my sign was big and legible, and everybody took my picture."

That picture got picked up by the Associated Press and went international. "My face went all around the world," she laughed, explaining that her husband had a brother in New Jersey, and a co-worker asked him, "Don't you have a relative named Virginia Rovnyak?" He answered, yes! That's my sister-in-law. "So I've had my 15 minutes of fame."

Rovnyak remained focused but realistic with her work until abolition passed. "You have failures and successes ... I mean, frustrations, such as in 1990 when Attorney General Mary Sue Terry, again, for political reasons, refused a new trial for Joe Giarratano. And also, in 1990 when Wilder let the execution of Willie Evans go forward."

"And then in the 2000s, we were in Richmond every General Assembly fighting additions to the list of capital crimes." She recalled that the list of death penalty-eligible crimes was becoming so long that a Republican legislator on the Courts of Justice Committee actually remarked, "You add these on, pretty soon we'll be adding the gardener."

Rev. Canon Fletcher Lowe: Halleluiah!

Rev. Lowe, who founded the Virginia Interfaith Center for Public Policy in 1982 and worked tirelessly for abolition for decades, got to see it made real before passing away on Aug. 25, 2021. In a March 25, 2021 *Richmond Times-Dispatch* editorial, he pointed out several legislators who he considered allies in the abolition fight over the years. These included Hanover County Del. Frank Hargrove, Fairfax Del. Kenneth Plum, Suffolk Del. Sam Glasscock, Newport News Del. Ted Morrison, Fairfax Sen. Joe Gartlan, and Richmond Sen. Henry Marsh.

"Finally!" Lowe joyfully exclaimed, "With the stroke of his pen Wednesday, Gov. Ralph Northam ended the death penalty in Virginia – Halleluiah!"

Impressions of Death Row

Mass was not a death watch but an expression of thanks to one who had become a part of our lives. Eddie [Fitzgerald] expressed no bitterness or excuses for his past. He knew he had to pay his debt to society and was spiritually ready. He recognized that he came to Mecklenburg 12 years ago as "a sick person from years of drugs." He thanked those present because for the past 12 years he had experienced the unconditional love of people in the diocese. The month before, he wrote in a letter, "although my time has come to an end on earth, I fear not. I know that Christ is holding me tightly in his loving arms and will protect me from evil. He will walk with me into heaven in a few short weeks."

-Statement by Bishop Walter F. Sullivan before the execution of Eddie Fitzgerald, July 1992.

In his 2003 book "Kiss of Death" John Bessler wrote that the ban on television cameras from America's execution chambers took away two of death penalty abolitionists' most potent arguments. First, it obscured the faces of execution participants, such as the condemned inmates and the execution teams. Second, it robbed the viewing public of their ability to witness a violent act of killing performed by the state on their behalf.

The state constantly conned the populace in presenting death row to them. The absence of objective, factual coverage forced average citizens to perceive death row inmates as the "worst of the worst," subjectively painted as dehumanized monsters by the state and DOC PR machines. Death row inmates' lives were reduced in the public eye to a single act and an unflattering mug shot taken at the worst moment of their lives.

Worse, the general public could, as a result of the dogged secrecy surrounding death row and executions, wrongfully envision the condemned as ruthless, scheming white male James Bond villains like Blofeld or evil geniuses like Hannibal Lecter, worthy of being killed quickly before they inventively slithered away unnoticed at the first escape opportunity, abetted by supportive minions, to continue their brutal and cunning crime waves.

As a result of this unfamiliarity, the public may also have regarded the concealed inmates' expressions of regret or sorrow for their crimes or their jailhouse religious transformations as crude, insincere ploys to gain sympathy or even executive clemency.

And in the end, no matter how botched, bloody, smoke-filled, fiery, or gruesome the execution, those in charge blandly told a nodding populace that "the execution proceeded without incident."

Death row chaplains, ministers, and advocates such as Marie Deans and many others met these invisible inmates and saw them not as monsters but as fellow human beings. They may have committed horrific crimes, but they were parents, siblings, and children, like anyone else.

When asked if they saw any monsters or evil geniuses, many faith leaders and chaplains, who spent years meeting and ministering to dozens of death row inmates, describe something far different than the manufactured stereotype.

Kathleen Kenney: "My first introduction [to Bishop Sullivan] was taking him down to Mecklenburg to do a Mass with the guys on death row. And it took a lot of negotiating. They had a library there, and they had to figure out how to keep the guys from the different pods separated, so there were cages from floor to ceiling. And then a fenced-in place where Bishop Sullivan and I could go."

"Sullivan was just great with them. He just treated them with respect, kindness, and care. And these were human beings. These were people."

"Jim [Griffin] was great. Some of the guys who had these small churches down around Mecklenburg had difficulty getting close to some of these guys on death row and then asked to accompany them [to the death chamber]. It was traumatic. But Jim loved doing this ministry. And then he was able to befriend somebody, walk with them, and be there when they're put to death. And I'm sure it took a lot out of him, but ... I always knew I could call Jim and say, 'I need somebody for the prison ... to go to this prisoner or just to death row or whatever.' Even now, I know I could call him."

"And what struck me was how these men ... I know some of them had done pretty awful things, but they were so simple and ... a lot of them, you could tell, had a very low I.Q., and very little education. And these guys' simplicity would show my prejudice, my preconceived notions."

"And they just responded to the bishop. I think I would've felt safe being in an open room with them. Of course, the prison would never allow it, but these are guys who would meet one on one with Marcelline [Niemann]."

Marcelline Niemann had been a Sister of Charity until the Second Vatican Council of 1964 when she left the order but continued to commit her life to education and ministering to death row inmates. She was known for her flowing, colorful dresses, her love of poetry "and a little amber in a glass." The death row inmates also loved her, and she was a fixture both at the State Penitentiary, Mecklenburg, and Greensville Correctional Centers.

Death row inmate Eddie Fitzgerald wrote to Marcelline around 1990 and told her in part, "If you promise not to be sad I will be honored to have you visit me in Greensville. Seeing you now and then back when we could all get together in the pod area was always a fun and loving time. I don't want that to change."

"Keep the faith,

Eddie."

In another undated letter that is a two-page single sentence, Syvasky Poyner wrote to Niemann, asking her if she could help him raise $12 to buy a dust cover for his typewriter. He closed by saying, "... I am so thankful to you well as for me today I am in the best of heather today and I believe everything is goning (*sic*) to be alright and the reason that I say that is that I know that the Lord is with me always and that I have nothing to worrie (*sic*) about ...."

"Your friend always,

Syvasky Laffayettee Poyner."

Marcelline Niemann died Aug. 2, 2021, on her 97th birthday, just before she could be interviewed for this book. Her friend Mary Ann McKee provided the letters.

Russ Ford: "My experience with the men is ... I see them for who they are, not for what they did. I was there to be with them and help them. I wasn't there to condemn them. I was a counselor, a pastor. And Marie [Deans] and I worked together. So, we had that one-two punch that made this thing work. There weren't reports of anything positive about the executions in pastoral care when I started. The men died struggling."

Ford worked for ten years as the death row chaplain with the Virginia chaplain service. After that, he worked for three years with Gateway Parish, a nonprofit ministry he formed, to work with people who had been affected by violent crime.

"The men on [death] row were a different situation entirely. Before the [1984] escape, the Briley brothers were the head jokers. They were physical, and they ran the row. They did what they wanted to do, and the state didn't pay attention. They just looked away from it. Marie Deans had a big impact when she organized the row with Joe Giarratano, and they set up in each tier a man to help out other inmates [stop the] inner strife. I found them to get along pretty well throughout my time. I would say that they got along better than people in the general population."

Former VAADP director and attorney Julie McConnell: "I'm not naïve enough to think that they're not capable of what they're convicted. I mean, I know that Willie Lloyd Turner did kill the store owner. I think it's a classic case of panicking and not something he necessarily went in there planning to do. I will say this about Turner, he never made excuses. He didn't say, 'Somebody made me do this.' He accepted full responsibility for it."

"I would spend hours with them, and they never tried to do anything to hurt me. No guards were making sure that I was protected either. So no, I didn't sense that. They never threatened me or made me feel uncomfortable. They were human beings, you know."

McConnell also visited Turner, Dennis Stockton, and Joe Wise after DOC moved them to Powhatan Correctional, a facility judged by prison rights advocates as one of the worst prisons in America, where "feces throwing" was a pastime.

"Marie Deans dealt with Mecklenburg, and I dealt with Powhatan," McConnell continued. "So we kind of divided and conquered that way. Stockton was a closed book, but Turner and Joe Wise were much more – I don't know what the right word is – personable, open, and appreciative of the interaction. So I got much closer to the two of them. And I was there at Greensville when they executed Turner. Ten minutes before the execution, I was inside with him, and then I went outside, which was really hard. You know, I was like 23 years old."

Father James Griffin: "I was Bishop Sullivan's secretary, which meant driving him around to master of ceremonies and confirmations. And he and I went down to death row the first time that first year I was his secretary. I was ordained in 1982, so that fall, we went down. And Sullivan said, 'You go talk to Joe [Giarratano], I'm going to talk to ...' whoever he was talking to. I talked to Joe, and he asked me to do Christmas Mass a couple of months later, and that was my start on death row."

"[I remember] Doug Buchanan. I believe his mother had cancer, and his father was playing around with another woman while his mother was still alive, which set him off. And he murdered his father and murdered his little brother and sister as they got off the school bus ... I don't know that he was in trouble before that, but I know that's his purported crime. And I remember being with him the day he got executed by lethal injection, and it was a rainstorm outside of Greensville. We had to put our feet on the bars because the water was rising in his cell. It was the last day of his life. And he's sitting there eating his last meal, and the cell is flooded."

BJ Brown Devlin: "I remember very clearly my first visit [in 1985], and every visit was a little different. The first time I went, they brought us right up to the row. And we spent some time just chatting through the bars. Eventually, the guys were shackled and led to the law library for Mass, and then they were unshackled once they were in the library. And we celebrated Mass together. Other times, they would bring the guys down to a common area room, shackled for the trip, unshackled while they were with us."

"What struck me, particularly on that first visit, was they were so young. These guys were not old hardened criminals. The substance abuse that was a factor in their crimes was so obvious. Also, mental illness was probably a little less up in your face. But they were so young and under the influence, people who had a history of substance abuse."

"It wasn't that they were the worst criminals per se. This one guy who was gay happened to have committed his crime in the wrong county. Anywhere else, it wouldn't have been a capital case."

"Circumstances catch them. They're caught by addictions. They're just wounded people who did stuff they shouldn't have done. But killing them did not undo anything, and it didn't address anything."

"I was young ... but certainly not starry-eyed and thinking these people have all been railroaded or anything like that. I knew what they had done. But I also knew that they were broken human beings and still children of God."

Devlin recalled toward the end of her time in Richmond a tour of the penitentiary and the death chamber. "We went on a 'surprise tour' of the Virginia State Penitentiary. Our visit was to publicize the inhumane conditions, the maggots in the showers, the food, the broken windows, the birds flying around, and all that crap. We showed up one morning around 8:00 and asked for a tour, which the warden [allowed]. This young guard takes us through the cell blocks and the yard, then he says to us, 'Do you want to go to death row?' And you know, you're in a prison with a guard who is your only way out, so there's only one answer, right?"

"But this guard wanted to make sure we saw everything, so he took us to the electric chair. And he's showing it off, the leather straps, the iron restraints, taking them off, where they hang on the wall, and he drops one at my feet. And I just remember looking down and saying, 'I will not touch that because that is evil.' That gave me the privilege of clearly seeing the evil done in our name."

Cari Rush Willis: "For six years, I served as the volunteer chaplain to four guys on death row in Virginia. I walked with one of them to his execution. I would show up on the first and third Thursday of the month and spend one hour with each of them. We spent our time together thinking about the deep things of God, sharing life stories, and laughing uproariously about something silly. Their friendships would change my life and my ministry. They showed me unconditional love and what the irrational love of God can do to transform a life. I still stay in touch with three of the men who were on the row. I will forever be grateful to God for opening this door for me as I have met the most amazing people who have become very close brothers and friends."

Lynn Litchfield Divers: "I was brought up in the church to love people, even people who make mistakes. I even follow someone who was crucified for a crime. And yet, when I went to love Teresa [Lewis] to say, 'Okay. What's happening to her is unfair,' people turn their backs. They close their ears and hearts because they didn't want to be seen as a bleeding-heart liberal or ... you know, you do the crime, you do the time. It was such a culture. They wanted me to love her but not cause any trouble, not love her enough actually to care about what's happening to her."

"So, I could abide by all the rules that the prison had ... but when I am present as your chaplain, I am present as your chaplain. And you're not an inmate. You are a person sitting before me that is a child of God, first and foremost. And I think that's one reason I was so effective in prison ministry that I met people where they were and tried to help them go where they wanted to go. If they wanted to get better, I could help them. If they didn't, then that's on them. But most of the women I worked with [at Fluvanna Correctional Center for Women] were so eager and hungry for a different way of life."

Former *Virginian-Pilot* journalist Laura LaFay: "Several people that I met, the best time in their life was their time on death row. And one guy, in particular, Larry Stout, told me that. There was a tradition on the row that whenever a new condemned person came in, everybody would pool their money and go to the commissary and bring that person kind of a 'welcome to the row' gift."

"This just stunned Stout. Nobody had ever given him a present in his life. People cared enough about him to teach him how to read. I wrote a story about him, in which I just included his horrible, nasty background that should have been presented as mitigation in sentencing and never was. The *Virginian-Pilot* refused to consider publishing it. That's kind of why I left The *Pilot*."

Sister Mary Eileen Heap, a Benedictine nun and St. Gertrude's School faculty member since 1976, joined George Ricketts, executive director of the Chaplain Services, in 1983 and began ministering as a chaplain in the Virginia State Correctional System. She, Ricketts, and Russ Ford were some of the first ministers on death row after the resumption of the death penalty in 1982.

In early August 1984, Heap met with Gov. Charles Robb to urge him to meet the men on death row personally, and to commute the death sentence of Linwood Briley, a move extremely unpopular at the time, as almost everyone wanted Briley executed.

"I am going to ask him to talk to the men and make his own decision," she told a UPI reporter of the conversation. "He could make his decision more on a human basis, not a political basis."

Sister Heap was with Briley when he was baptized on Aug. 2 and met with him a few days before his execution, describing him as "very peaceful."

She died on June 4, 2006.

Lurching Toward Abolition

VADP Pushes Forward on a 20-Year Journey

> The day when Americans stop condemning people to death on the bases of race and inequality will be the day when we stop condemning anyone to death at all.
>
> -David Bruck, "Decisions of Death." Undated article.

In June 2002, VADP executive director Henry Heller had enough. "I'm just burned out. I'm tired of fighting," he told the June 18-24 edition of *C-Ville Weekly* after 11 years as the largely unpaid director of VADP.

"It's like I got to quit. I have to stop working. So, I did," Heller explained in a 2021 interview. The switch had turned off; Heller walked away and never looked back. "I wasn't anywhere to be found. I was of no help. But I'd hear some stuff here and there, and they're talking about vigils and abolishing the death penalty and whatever ...."

VADP Board Chairman Steven Rosenfield told *C-Ville Weekly* that "Henry committed so many hours of free time to the movement. I think he resigned from emotional burnout from having too many responsibilities."

Another reason Heller walked away was due to a philosophical split with other VADP members who wanted to stop advocating for a moratorium – which he believed was the place to start – and go straight for the throat of full-blown abolition. "The vision became 'I oppose the death penalty' and the abolition of the death penalty," he explained. "We're going to do vigils, we're going to tell people why the death penalty is wrong, but we're not asking that question [what's your alternative?]. We're not opening dialogue."

A New Director

Upon Heller's resignation, Board Chair Steven Rosenfield hired an activist and former Lynchburg Professor named Jack Payden-Travers, who with his wife Christine had moved to Richmond in 1984 when she became the assistant minister at St. James Church on Monument Avenue. Coincidentally, Payden-Travers had earlier met Marie Deans through the Friends Meeting House by bringing her meals after she became bedridden with a severely broken ankle.

"[Marie and I] got to be fairly good friends," he said in a 2021 interview. "And that sort of clinched it. And, of course, my doctor in Richmond ended up being Jerome Gorman."

A Yonkers, New York native, Payden-Travers had a long history of social and judicial activism and had been exposed to Virginia's death penalty at the 1984 Linwood Briley execution. "I'd only been in Richmond maybe two or three weeks when Wendy Northup, who was directing the Richmond Peace Education Center, invited me to come over to join the vigil. And I just thought I was going to a candlelight vigil, and the bishop would be there, and whatever. I was shocked at the vitriol, the anger, and vengeance coming from the west side of Spring Street. They had signs; I remember one 'Chicken Fried Briley' and 'Fry Briley Fry.' Wow, I was just amazed."

Payden-Travers also recalled meeting attorney and future Virginia governor Tim Kaine and his wife through the Friends Meeting House. At one meeting, he mentioned a recent incident where some young boys threw a brick through their West Avenue home's front window and how he was hesitant to prosecute them.

After the meeting, Kaine approached him. "Jack, if you don't prosecute those people, there's a good chance I will end up defending one of them on death row someday," he warned. "You'd be surprised at the people on death row who don't know why they're there. And it's all because there was no accountability from the very start."

Payden-Travers elected to prosecute and stood before the same judge when he was arrested years earlier for sitting in at U.S. Senator Paul Trible's office over the issue of U.S. aid for Central America.

The Payden-Travers then moved from Richmond to Calloway, Virginia, where he became the Plowshare Peace Center director. They then landed in Lynchburg, where he became a professor at Lynchburg College (now Lynchburg University) and the Lynchburg Peace Education Center director.

He later lost his job at the college over a city ordinance that prohibited five or more people from meeting on a city street without a permit. "We had these vigils against the bombings in Afghanistan, and I didn't believe in permits," he recalled. "And I guess after the second or third vigil, we ended up with five people on the picket line, and all of a sudden, four police cars came out of nowhere, and I got arrested and ended up in court. And so, at the end of that first term, I lost my honors course that I was teaching."

Refusing to accept what he called the "slave labor" of adjunct teaching, he applied for the director position at VADP. "VADP was looking for a director because Henry didn't want to go full time. And the board had gotten a $40,000 grant from the Public Welfare Foundation. And they had another grant from a local donor, so they decided to go with a full-time director. Well, I applied."

Payden-Travers spoke highly of Heller's dogged commitment during his eleven long years as director. "VADP wouldn't have lasted all those years between the 1990s and 2002 if it wasn't for Henry, the Jewish carpenter, as he likes to call himself. He worked part-time as a carpenter, but I think he put full time into VADP, and he just didn't want to get paid for it. He was just amazing."

After getting the job, Payden-Travers descended straight into the abyss when John Allen Muhammad and Lee Boyd Malvo were caught and brought to trial.

Beltway Snipers

Muhammad and the 17-year-old Malvo became infamous figures as a sniper team that terrorized Maryland, Washington D.C., and the I-95 corridor of Virginia for 20 days in October 2002. A talented mechanic, Muhammad made a sniper nest out of the trunk of his car, where Malvo hid and shot people Muhammad targeted as they did everyday things, such as pump gas or leave a restaurant. Altogether the two killed ten people and injured three more.

Like the Penn Brothers in the 1960s, the Brileys in the 1970s, and the Southside strangler in the 1980s, Richmond, D.C., and Maryland became gripped in fear and paranoia due to the seemingly random killings. Law enforcement received a tip to look out for a white commercial van and, with guns drawn, stopped each one they saw. Everyone was vigilant; Richmond schools near I-95 pulled shades and kept children in the classrooms all day. Teachers and cafeteria workers delivered student lunches to their desks. People knelt low behind their cars while gassing up. Everyone looked over their shoulder.

After a shooting at a Ponderosa Steak House in Ashland, this author's wife, Susan – out of utter frustration of more gun violence only ten minutes from the house – penned an unpublished response which read in part:

> Ashland, where this shooting occurred, is an idyllic place, long self-proclaimed and promoted as "the center of the universe." And now, thanks to satellites, it is. The media frenzy has already descended. A single bullet has ravaged this slow-paced historic railroad & college town. We pray for the victims, and though consciously fighting the impulse, we unwillingly wait for the other shoe to drop. We will not hide, but we will use caution. The Exxon & Texaco that sit right on the vastly underused beltway near our house are off-limits. We'll use a small neighborhood station that's a little more out of the way. The first call I make in the morning will be to our three children's principal to see how they propose to protect the students in this "campus style" elementary school. I'll dig up the license plate number I scribbled a few days ago on a white Chevy Astro commercial van with the pristine ladder on top (no paint spots, I had noticed at the time) and pass it along for what it is worth ....

Payden-Travers also recalled an incident at a gas station during this tense time. "The month I took over, the sniper shootings started in D.C. I remember trying to fill my gas tank on Route 29 as I was coming south from a meeting in Washington for VADP. I heard these gunshots, and I hit the ground. It turned out where [Route] 17 comes into 29, there's a shooting range across the street."

After several shootings, Muhammad and Malvo upped the ante by arrogantly taunting the police. After one shooting, they left a note: "Mister policeman, I am God." Another time the pair demanded $10 million to stop the shootings. Ultimately, someone called a tip line and pointed them to a Montgomery, Alabama, liquor store shooting weeks earlier, where Malvo had dropped a brochure. A fingerprint recovered from the brochure matched a print on file with the Dept. of Immigration. This evidence provided law enforcement with their first suspect.

Muhammad had nurtured a bizarre mentor-protege relationship with Malvo after losing his own three children in a custody dispute. Muhammad allegedly controlled every aspect of Malvo's life, imposing a rigorous exercise program and a curious diet that reportedly consisted at one point of only honey and crackers. He also taught Malvo how to use a gun, and they practiced on a tree stump in a neighbor's yard before switching to human beings.

After a reported sighting at Broad Street and Parham Road in Richmond, dozens of police closed the intersection. They converged on a painter's van, with rifles and handguns drawn, only to find very real and very terrified painters inside.

On Oct. 24, 2002, police surrounded Muhammad and Malvo at a rest area near Myersville, Maryland, and took them into custody.

Since they committed crimes in several states, authorities had to decide where the pair should be tried first. Maryland, Virginia, and Alabama all wanted a crack at them – especially Maryland, as six killings occurred there. That state, however, had a death penalty moratorium in place; therefore, in a unashamed decision, U.S. Attorney General John Ashcroft assigned the case to Paul Ebert, commonwealth's attorney of Prince William County, Virginia.

Virginia (especially Prince William County) was considered far more likely to impose death sentences, even for the 17-year-old Malvo. Virginia also had a unique law that allowed it to seek the death penalty against terrorists, which did not require the state to establish who actually fired the shots. This statute removed a major prosecutorial hurdle, as the identity of the triggerman in some of the shootings was questionable.

Capital defense attorney Matthew Engle noted that since the case spanned multiple states, the federal government should have tried it. "But, no, the whole point was that Virginia would quickly give [Muhammad] a death sentence, then ram him through the appellate and post-conviction process, and kill him in a way that the feds couldn't or wouldn't at that time."

Virginia indeed seemed more interested in procuring death sentences than fair trials for the two, which the U.S. Constitution guarantees even the most atrocious murderers. Attorney General Jerry Kilgore went on Fox News and bragged, "We can try this juvenile [Malvo] as an adult and subject him to the death penalty, and we can move quickly."

"You know, that does not speak well of where we were as a state back then," lamented Engle.

Jack Payden-Travers was equally troubled by the rush to seek a death sentence. "We're very concerned about prosecutorial vigilanteeism[sic]," he told the Virginian-Pilot on Oct. 30, 2002. "The debate is who can hang the highest and fastest, rather than how we can bring a healing process."

While the trial venue was later changed to Virginia Beach, on Nov. 17, 2003, Muhammad was convicted of all four counts against him: capital murder for the shooting of Prince William resident Dean Harold Meyers; capital murder under Virginia's antiterrorism statute for homicide committed with an intent to terrorize the government or the public; conspiracy to commit murder; and illegal use of a firearm.

As predicted, Muhammad received a death sentence.

Malvo was found guilty of one killing in Fairfax County and guilty of a firearms charge in a separate trial. He also pleaded guilty to a second killing in Spotsylvania County. He received a life sentence. He later pleaded guilty to six murders in Maryland.

Payden-Travers recalled that he couch-surfed for three months monitoring the trials, coordinating vigils outside the courthouse, and promoting the abolition of the death penalty. "Muhammad's trial started in late September, early October. And then Malvo's didn't wrap up until Dec. 23 or 24. And I lived in Norfolk Monday through Friday at the Catholic Worker and then came home to Lynchburg on weekends."

Payden-Travers also recalled how VADP stumbled into some money to keep operating. Before the Muhammad jury began deliberations, the organization received a $10,000 grant from an anonymous source to erect a billboard in Virginia Beach decrying Virginia's juvenile death penalty. He was on his way to meet with a billboard executive to sign a contract when he got a call from the donor, who said, "We've just received word from the defense counsel that they don't want the billboard. So please don't sign the contract. That money is yours to use for VADP."

"We were just about broke," laughed Payden-Travers, who had cut his own pay to remain solvent. "It always seemed that we were always borrowing from Peter to pay Paul. We were lucky we could publish the next newsletter."

Lost in D.C.

After being sentenced in Virginia, Muhammad went to trial for six slayings in Montgomery County, Maryland. Virginia claimed that since he was a death row inmate, they would transport and provide security to Maryland for trial.

Jon Sheldon, who later was Muhammad's attorney, told an unreported story of what happened as three corrections officials escorted Muhammad from Sussex I prison in Waverly through Washington D.C. "They put [Muhammad] in a van with a driver and two security escorts, driving him to court in Maryland," he explained. "But they've never been to D.C. before, and they get lost. This is before GPS and phone maps. They're bickering among themselves, and the driver decides to pull over by a park. The three of them get out, and they start talking about how are we going to find the courthouse? What are we going to do?"

As the men stood outside the van, they realized one did not have his rifle. "They go, where's your gun? And he's like, oh, I left it in the van." The men looked toward the van, and even though Muhammad was shackled, he squirmed into the backseat and, with his mouth, picked up the gun, put it on his lap, and disassembled it with his cuffed hands. "Now they're afraid to get back in the van," Sheldon continued. "The guys are standing there, wondering what are we going to do? And John just starts laughing, and he goes, 'It's just in pieces. Come and get it.'"

The inept team finally got Muhammad to Maryland, where he was tried, found guilty, and sentenced to multiple life terms. Back in Virginia, Spotsylvania County decided not to charge him in the death of a Philadelphia man at a gas station in Spotsylvania since the Supreme Court affirmed his death sentence. Hanover County also chose not to charge Muhammad for wounding a man outside the Ashland Steakhouse.

The notoriety of the beltway sniper case had an oddly negligible impact on attitudes toward the death penalty. Del. Robert McDonnell, who later became Virginia's governor, told the *Virginian-Pilot*, "Those who have strong moral beliefs for or against the death penalty won't change their minds because of this case. Having said that, I'm still convinced there's strong public support for Virginia's law."

Playing Politics

As VADP executive director, Jack Payden-Travers was a hands-on participant in the mechanisms of the General Assembly during sessions. He recalled meeting Virginia Beach Sen. Ken Stolle, who sat on the Courts of Justice Committee. "He wasn't about to let [an abolition] bill ever get out of the Justice Committee," he recalled. "But Stolle was a person you could have lunch with. So I would be in the cafeteria, and if I saw him, we'd sit and have lunch, and we would talk about it."

"Working at the General Assembly put me in touch with people that if I'd just stayed in the office in Charlottesville and had just gone in for the hearing, I would have never known."

He recalled another conversation with Norfolk Del. Ken Alexander, who worked as a funeral director and mortician. "I asked him one day, 'Why were you opposed to the death penalty?' And he said, 'Well, I see the bodies after they're electrocuted. Once you've seen an electrocuted body, you can't be in favor of the death penalty.'"

Before the Muhammad and Malvo shootings, the 2001 General Assembly considered 16 death penalty bills and even modified the much-maligned 21-day rule by passing post-conviction DNA testing for capital cases. These included HB 1656, which expanded the statute to include the murder of someone going to testify as a witness (defeated in House Courts of Justice 9-13); HB 2345, which abolished the 21-day rule in capital cases (defeated in House Courts of Justice 10-11); and several bills which called for a moratorium on death sentences until the completion of the Joint Legislative Audit Review Committee (JLARC) study. All of these were also defeated. Frank Hargrove's perennial bill, HB 1827, which called for death penalty abolition, was also defeated in the House Courts of Justice 0-23.

By 2002, death penalty abolition, or even a moratorium, had little support because of the one-two punch of the beltway snipers and the Sept. 11, 2001, terrorist attacks.

Republican Del. Vincent Callahan, previously a death penalty supporter, advocated for a two- to a three-year moratorium in light of the JLARC study. Sen. Stolle, however, told the *Virginian-Pilot* that several of his fellow legislators who had been considering a moratorium decided to abandon the effort "in light of Osama bin Laden and people who fly planes into buildings."

Anne Hamilton, spokesperson for a Northern Virginia abolition group called Citizens United Against the Death Penalty, told the Oct. 1, 2001 *Richmond Times-Dispatch* that "We are still – like everyone else – sorting through the aftermath and deciding if this helps us or hurts us. Not everyone in this country is gung ho, kill, kill, kill. Many people in this country are using this opportunity to reflect."

One bill introduced in the 2002 GA session highlighted legislative disdain for abolition and moratoriums. The bill would force people who opposed capital punishment to specify that if they were murdered in a capital offense, their estate would foot the bill for the killer's lifetime incarceration.

The bill went nowhere.

VADP Support Projects

By 2004, as the capital defense offices got up and running, one of the many projects VADP initiated for death row inmates was the Death Row Support Project, which offered assistance and support for those on the row and their families. The DRSP was the brainchild of a former death row inmate, Michael Williams, whose sentence had been commuted to life in prison. He had reached out directly to VADP with ideas on how the organization could better assist those families facing the death penalty.

In addition, VADP maintained its death row pen-pal program, which matched inmates with compatible members for correspondence. VADP members also actively visited death row families, especially as executions neared, and continued to organize vigils around the state on the day of executions. An 8-12-page newsletter, *VADP Action*, published three times per year, kept members updated with news about the men (and woman) on death row, an overview of national death penalty news, reviews of death penalty literature, and announcements of upcoming activities. In 2004, the VADP.org website generated over 2,000 hits per month.

VADP held its 2004 annual conference on Oct. 2 at St. Mark Lutheran Church in Charlottesville. Keynote speakers included Alan Gell, Ida Reid, whose brother was executed two months later in December, and Ed Morrison, a murder victim family member. Workshop sessions helped members work the media and how to lobby the General Assembly. Payden-Travers announced at this conference that VADP would be represented at the Second World Conference Against the Death Penalty. He would also table at the National Coalition to Abolish the Death Penalty national conference at Gallaudet University in Washington D.C. later in October.

It was an impressive workload for such a shoestring operation.

The Journey of Hope Returns

In 2005, Payden-Travers, seemingly always traveling, went to Texas to participate in the Texas Journey of Hope. While there, he spoke to founder Bill Pelke about bringing the Journey back to Virginia. "[VADP board member] Arie Cohen had just gotten his Ph.D. and was at James Madison University," he recalled. "So I did programs with Bill at [JMU]. After that program, Henry, Bill, and I planned out the Virginia Journey."

Like the 1996 Journey, murder victim family members, parents of death row inmates, and those executed, exonerees and activists planned an extraordinary 122 death penalty presentations over 17 days from southwest Virginia to Northern Virginia to the Eastern Shore.

Payden-Travers recalled the financial strain of such an operation. "We flew people to Lee County to do a presentation. And we stayed in hotels. And I can remember writing checks for $40,000 to drive people all over the state and do all those presentations and just hoping that they wouldn't bounce," he laughed. "And when we finished the Journey, I figured out that we were $17 in the black."

Payden-Travers added that the Journey could have made more money, but a Texas woman working as the Journey accountant embezzled an unknown amount from the organization and wasn't caught until the following year.

Despite the unfortunate financial situation, the 2006 Journey was a success. VADP doubled its mailing list and picked up 1,500 more names for a moratorium campaign petition later sent to Gov. Tim Kaine.

As lieutenant governor, Kaine was friendly to abolitionists. In 2006 he ran for governor against Attorney General Jerry Kilgore, who made Kaine's opposition to capital punishment an election issue. The tactic backfired, and Kaine won decisively.

"The fact that I was elected told me something about changing popular views of the death penalty," Kaine told the March 25, 2021 *Richmond Times-Dispatch*, "and that gave me complete freedom to veto all the death penalty expansion bills that came up when I was governor."

VADP also was sure to trumpet the results of a two-year study titled "Equal Justice and Fair Play." In assessing Virginia's capital statutes against 85 recommendations made by the Illinois Capital Punishment Study Commission, the study found that Virginia was in partial compliance with only 12 of the recommendations to guard against the wrongful execution of the innocent and failed to meet 47 of the recommendations.

2008: A Change of Leadership and Direction

At the end of January 2008, Jack Payden-Travers stepped down as executive director of VADP to start a new position as the education associate for the ACLU's Capital Punishment Project in Durham, N.C. At his leaving, VADP had amassed over 4,500 names on their mailing list and had a working budget that varied from $80,000 to $100,000 per year, with a large percentage coming from individual donations.

VADP board chair Jon Sheldon hired Beth Panilaitis as the next executive director. In a 2021 interview, she recalled getting a phone call from Doug Smith, executive director of the Virginia Interfaith Center, where she briefly worked an internship in 2004. "He didn't even say hello," she recalled. "I picked up and said, 'Hello?' And he said, 'Death penalty – for or against?' And I said, 'Against. Is this Doug?' And he said, 'Excellent. I have a job that you should apply for.' And that's actually how I got involved with VADP."

Panilaitis worked an internship at Powhatan Correctional Center as a VCU undergraduate, so she was exposed to the Virginia correctional system first-hand. "I think professionally, I realized that I needed to challenge myself to live into the values of being a social worker and respecting the dignity and worth of all human beings. And there was this awakening that I had about the criminal justice system and the death penalty. I hadn't thought about it that much up until that point."

Under Sheldon and Panilaitis, VADP gravitated away from being an activist organization into being more policy-driven. "I think trying to convince lawmakers to abolish the death penalty while also having this foot in the camp of advocating for folks on death row was a difficult balance," Panilaitis explained. "And I think Jon had this idea of letting the defense community take care of folks on death row."

There was a difference between Jack [Payden-Travers] and Beth," explained Sheldon. "Jack was the right man for his time. We wouldn't have got to abolition without Jack, and I don't know who else would've done it. But he did great work."

Sheldon also noted that there was an uptick in funding during this time. "I worked hard to get funding. We applied for grants, and we got them. I went to [author] John Grisham, and he gave me a check for $25,000. He just said, 'Here you go, make good use of it.'"

Sheldon also introduced more structure to the organization, including training fellow board members on how to raise money and recruit other board members to increase turnover, keeping minds and voices fresh. "This is what you do [for funding]," he explained of his messaging, "You ask for a specific amount. And we started a structure where every board member had to call a certain number of people and ask them for money. And every board member had to recruit another board member."

Sheldon's strategy was for VADP not to be identified solely with an individual or a character. Energy, revitalization, fundraising, and turnover was his strategy. "As long as you recruited several board members, you can get out. And we recruited a lot."

Sheldon even dramatically reformed the seemingly mundane task of taking minutes at board meetings. "People had taken minutes like a court reporter. Beth says this. Steve says that. Who gives a shit? What was decided? So our minutes became several sentences, less than a page, and it had to be decisions made and actions to be done. That's it."

Sheldon and Panilaitis also hired Matt Selman as an administrator, leaving Panilaitis to travel and visit with everyone she could to survey the criminal justice landscape and laser-focus on the organization's priorities. "Matt was important," Sheldon noted. "He worked for pay at first. Then he worked for nothing. Then he worked 20 hours. Then he worked full-time. Matt filled so many gaps in what that organization needed. It wouldn't have happened without him."

Before Virginia executioner Jerry Givens came out as an abolitionist, Sheldon introduced him to the VADP board. "[*Richmond Times-Dispatch* reporter] Frank Green connected Jerry and me," Sheldon recalled. "I talked to the board, and I said, 'Listen, this is the executioner. He believes in the death penalty. He believes what he did was good. But he's a good man, and this is somebody whose perspective we could use.'"

"I did not minimize Jerry's view at all. But it did seem clear to me that he'd be of great value for what he was, not for something he might become. But he did become an advocate against the death penalty. And then the more attention he got, the more outspoken he became."

Panilaitis recalled that VADP's partnering with Witness to Innocence helped tremendously with their educational initiatives. Witness to Innocence is a collection of former death row inmates who had been wrongfully convicted and sentenced to death but were later exonerated, sometimes decades after their convictions.

Most death penalty abolitionists usually have to speak "from the head" when presenting reasons to abolish, citing objective details such as cost, racial and class bias, and the possibilities of innocence. However, the exonerees from Witness to Innocence speak "from the heart," as their personal stories present far more compelling examples of the problems with wrongful convictions and racial bias in America's death penalty. Their website states, "The cornerstone of Witness to Innocence's work is our legislative and advocacy efforts fighting for death penalty abolition state-by-state and nationwide. Death row exonerees, and the issue of innocence, have been pivotal in every state that has abolished the death penalty in the last 15 years."

"Having the voice of somebody who could say 'I came within days of being executed and here's my personal story' was very strong," Panilaitis admitted. "We did a week-long tour where we drove everywhere around the state, and we talked to universities, faith communities, and pretty much whoever would listen."

Panilaitis recalled a startling experience driving around with one of the exonerees, an older Black gentleman, Shabaka WaQlimi. WaQlimi had come within 15 hours of being executed by the state of Florida in 1983 for a 1974 murder he never committed. As they drove through Lynchburg, he suddenly told her, "I got to call my wife and make sure that my life insurance policy is up to date."

She asked him what he meant, and he replied, "I'm driving around with a young white lady in a place called Lynchburg, like, with my track record, are you kidding?"

"For me, from a racial justice standpoint, this was an eye-opening experience," Panilaitis explained. "And in those couple of days, I had a guy at a gas station ask, 'Ma'am, are you okay?' I said, 'Yes, yes, sir, I'm fine.'"

The Triggerman Bill

Panilaitis recalled she and Selman working in that tiny office with no windows in downtown Richmond while she lobbied the legislature during the 2008, 2009, and 2010 General Assembly sessions. Even though executions were tapering off in those years (four in 2008, three in 2009, and three in 2010), she still met fierce resistance. "People didn't even want to be seen with me," she admitted. "Once they realized that I was the death penalty lady, it was like, 'I don't want to be associated with you.' So it was very much the climate – nobody was going to say that they were in favor of abolition [except] Frank Hargrove and Joe Morrissey." She soon found that partnering with lobbyists from the ACLU and the Catholic Conference was far more productive, and that legislators were more willing to talk to them than just "the death penalty lady" by herself.

In 2009 the General Assembly introduced numerous expansion bills, including increasing death penalty eligibility to those who kill game wardens, off-duty police officers, and firefighters. However, the most critical expansion bill came in 2010 and was called the "triggerman" bill. This expansion bill would have extended murder charges and made eligible for the death penalty anyone complicit in capital murder, in any way. This law could have ensnared cab drivers, passengers, doctors, literally anyone who assisted, unwittingly or not, in a murder.

The heavily favored bill passed in both chambers.

Gov. Tim Kaine, however, vetoed all these expansions, including the triggerman bill. Still, the fear lingered among abolitionists that the bill had more than enough support to override the veto. To prevent that from happening, Panilaitis knew that several legislators who had voted for the bill would need to vote against it to maintain the veto. So, she and Chris Ramos of the Catholic Conference embarked on an "epic" 500-mile road trip around the state to convince certain legislators to switch their votes and keep the veto intact. And one of those legislators they convinced to change his vote was Ralph Northam, who 11 years later was the governor who signed the abolition bill.

"We went to his office on the Eastern Shore and met with him," Panilaitis recalled. "I said, 'You are a healer; this is what you do. Let's not expand a broken system.' And he was one of seven legislators, including Creigh Deeds and John Edwards, who changed their vote."

VADP, the Catholic Conference, and the ACLU heavily prepared for the final hearings. "We had a good amount of notice, and we pulled out all the stops in a very organized way," Panilaitis said, adding that she helped introduce Jerry Givens to the legislators. "That was one of the first times that he had spoken publicly. He opened up and said, 'I killed 62 people.' The look on legislators' faces was like, 'What? Do we need to call capital police?'"

In addition to Givens, Linell Patterson talked of being a murder victim family member. Mark Herring was possibly the first sitting commonwealth's attorney to speak out against the death penalty. "That was where we leveraged the legal community to get him on board," Panilaitis said, "And that was huge."

Jon Sheldon also spoke of how much money the triggerman law would cost the state. He explained that his argument, called the Attorney Full Employment Act, "Was going to give the death penalty [to] the trigger man, and the death penalty [to] the non-trigger man. They're going to have to have separate counsel. One of them is going to snitch against the other. One of them will get death; one of them won't. You're going to end up in the same place but paying all of us lawyers so much money. That's all it is."

Sheldon also revealed a crucial player in the eventual defeat of the triggerman bill – the hard right-wing attorney general, Ken Cuccinelli. He forbade his capital litigation unit (the "death squad") from advocating for any legislation that expanded the death penalty.

Thanks to their lobbying and presentation, the triggerman bill remained vetoed, to the shock of hardcore advocates convinced they had the votes to override. It was a close call – VADP estimated that passage of the bill could have doubled the number of executions.

Amid this victory was a lot of vitriol directed at Panilaitis and VADP. She recalled being invited to a radio show, and when she was on the air, they told her it was a call-in show. "It was an hour of people calling in with the most horrific, ugly questions you could imagine. Saddam Hussein had recently been killed, so there were questions about, 'Well, what about Saddam Hussein? Do you think ...' I mean, it was like, let's pull out everything."

"On occasion, especially around executions, we would receive threats. Those moments were disheartening."

All About the Money

After the significant 2010 triggerman victory, VADP received the bad news that Tides Foundation funding, which totaled between $30,000 - $40,000 per year, was not getting renewed. They were instead investing in states where abolition looked more promising, and unfortunately, Virginia was not one of those states. With no money to pay her, Panilaitis regretfully stepped down as executive director.

"I stepped down and handed things over to Matt Selman to keep the lights on," she lamented, recalling the conflicting emotions of her decision. "We had this amazing victory; we did something that folks did not think we could do. And we didn't have enough money to stay as an organization."

After Panilaitis stepped down, board member Steve Northup raised his hand and volunteered to keep the organization afloat until a new director could be hired – a task that took a little over four years. "When I left, they realized that if Steve was willing to do this and be the lobbyist, and if Matt stayed on to do the administrative stuff ... that's how they navigated it."

But Beth Panilaitis was not finished with the death penalty fight – she became a VADP board member from 2011 until 2016, with Northup filling in as director from 2010 until 2015. Like clockwork, Northup had to contend with that stubborn triggerman bill appearing in the General Assembly every year, with the last effort in 2015.

"I worked as a volunteer executive director of VADP because we were flat out of money," Northup said in a 2021 interview. 'We had lost grants. We were not among the states viewed by the national organizations and the national funders as being close enough to abolition toward the kind of funding you need to do things, like hire people. But we had no money to pay an executive director."

Northup recalled that while he had resigned from the board of directors to serve as volunteer executive director, that board's strength and determination kept VADP in business during those lean years from 2011 to 2014. "We had a good board then. I [eventually] got a grant that enabled us to hire a real executive director and pay him a salary. And that's how we hired Michael Stone."

"I could not give more kudos to Steve," Panilaitis explained. "He did an amazing job and gave a gift to VADP of willing to do that as a volunteer."

Those were lean execution years as well. Jerry Jackson was the only one in 2011. There were none in 2012 and 2014, and Robert Gleason was the only one in 2013. Alfred Prieto was the lone execution in 2015. Clearly, the death penalty was falling off Virginia's radar.

With executions swiftly dropping, the legislature still stubbornly sought to expand the death penalty. One proposed bill, re-introduced after a couple of policemen were ambushed on their way home, was dubbed the "blue lives matter" bill. Under Virginia code, since the police officers were off-duty and in street clothes, those weren't automatic capital cases. Legislators, in turn, wanted to make those cases eligible for death sentences.

The bill may have been well-intentioned but was fraught with potential abuse. For example, if a policeman or firefighter had a dispute with a neighbor, and it escalated to where the neighbor killed the officer, it could be prosecuted as a capital offense, even though the murder had nothing to do with his status as a policeman.

With executions becoming so rare, coupled with jury reluctance to impose death sentences, far better defense methods, the leanest death row in decades, and the willingness of the General assembly to slow and even stop the constant expansion attempts, Michael Stone took over as the new executive director in early 2015 with a five-year plan.

It was time for VADP to set that "big fat hairy goal."

Capital Defense Offices Open

Starting the Abolition Snowball

> The playing field was leveled, and with a level playing field, the death penalty was going away. It just changed everything.
> -David Johnson, executive director of the Virginia Indigent Defense Commission, on the capital defense offices' critical roles in abolition.

Before 2002, indigent defendants facing a capital murder charge were frequently represented by a public defender's office, if one was even available in their jurisdiction and who may have lacked experience in the intricacies of death penalty cases. The other option was a similarly inexperienced court-appointed lawyer.

Capital defender Douglas Ramseur pointed out that a considerable downside to court-appointed lawyers was getting the trial judge's approval for any expenditures, such as psychologists or other mitigation experts. This process was done in open court and tipped the defendant's strategy to the prosecution.

This imbalance resulted in prosecutors obtaining capital murder indictments in eight out of every ten murders charged as capital, with over 30 percent going to trial. The overwhelming majority of those cases ended in a death sentence. Between 1976 and 2004, Virginia tried 166 capital defendants, with 140 of them sentenced to death – a breathtaking 84 percent.

Corinna Barrett Lain and Ramseur wrote in their 2021 report "Disrupting Death: How Dedicated Capital Defenders Broke Virginia's Machinery of Death" that the overall reversal rate of death sentences in Virginia, combining all levels of review, was an anemic 18 percent – half the rate of runner-up Missouri and a mere one-fourth of the national average, with 68 percent of death sentences reversed. These factors made Virginia by far the most successful state in the Union at converting death sentences into executions.

Many pre-2002 capital defense attorneys, such as Gerald Zerkin, Steve Rosenfield, Steve Northup, Craig Cooley, Richard Bonnie, and Lloyd Snook, among many others, were dedicated, hard-working, and excellent at what they did against almost impossible odds. However, others were not only overwhelmed but just flat-out terrible lawyers. A federal judge called one attorney's direct appeal on a habeas review "a shameful disgrace." Another federal judge in a capital case called the attorney's work "virtually a complete absence of representation."

Consequently, because the prosecution and their unlimited resources were so crushing in the first guilt-or-innocence trial, the second sentencing trial became almost perfunctory, with some lasting less than one day. At his client's 1997 trial, one attorney claimed that he did not prepare at all for sentencing because he had the impression "the case was going to plead out." Despite concerns about that attorney's competency, the client lost his appeals and was executed in 2006.

In a 2015 article titled "Virginia's Vanishing Death Penalty" at Slate.com, Duke University Law professor Brandon Garrett recounted how Edward Bell's lawyers in 2001 presented almost no case at all during sentencing. "The judge overseeing a request for an appeal asked the lawyer how could one present 'literally no mitigating evidence,' because after all, 'it couldn't get any worse' than presenting nothing," Garrett wrote. "The judge found the lawyer inadequate but decided that correcting those failures would not have made enough difference in Bell's case. Bell was executed in 2009."

When warned by the Supreme Court of Virginia to fix these problems, The Virginia State Crime Commission issued a report in 2002 recommending the creation of several regional capital defender offices. The report claimed that creating these offices would fix the capital defense problem while saving money. "There are some cost savings, but it's an expertise issue," a spokesperson for the State Crime Commission told the *Newport News Daily Press*, adding, "It's such a complex area."

The General Assembly responded to the report by voting into law a bill sponsored by Republican Ken Stolle to create capital defense offices in Richmond, Norfolk, Roanoke, and Manassas (later Arlington). "I think it went a little further than I thought it would," Stolle told the March 26, 2021 *Virginia Mercury*. "But I think a lot of people didn't realize the problems (with the old system)."

"A Rich Person's Defense"

True to David Johnson's word, the creation of the four regional offices in October 2002 did indeed level the playing field (or, in the words of Lain and Ramseur, "neutralized systemic unfairness"). The offices provided low-income defendants facing a death sentence access to a highly-educated, well-funded expert team of independent lawyers specializing only in capital cases. Some of these lawyers said they gave poor people "a rich person's defense."

Douglas Ramseur worked on and off at the capital defense offices for 18 years. He pointed out the hazards of being a court-appointed lawyer in a capital case, particularly in a rural area. "It affects you when you know that judge controls the purse strings," he told *Mercury* journalist Ned Oliver, adding that if the lawyer was fighting the wrong fight or was needlessly dragging out the case, they ran a risk of not getting appointed the next case.

Ramseur pointed to his case in Louisa County, where his Black client, Darcel Murphy, was to be tried in a courtroom under a life-size portrait of Confederate leader Robert E. Lee. Before the trial began, Ramseur filed a motion to have the portrait removed. "I came in defending my African-American client who said, 'I don't think that's appropriate in this courtroom,'" he explained. "That's something that would have been much harder for a local lawyer serving at the pleasure of the judge to do."

VADP board chair Kristina Leslie, as a capital defender in Northern Virginia and a woman of color, had a unique perspective on these predominantly white, male-dominated, and sometimes Confederate-saturated capital defense environments. She recalled many times she and her client were the only Black people in the entire courtroom –

including those portrayed on the walls. "The portraits in the courtroom are all grand people from the Confederacy, all white men, and looking down on you," she explained.

She recalled additional imagery in a county courthouse just a few miles north of Richmond. "I don't know if it's still there, but as soon as you walked in, the first thing you saw was this big painting, and it says what punishments people used to get for certain crimes, like, lashes and whippings," she recalled in a 2021 interview. "It literally is the first thing that you saw. And it's just this air of supremacy and intimidation when you're walking in."

She contrasted this pompous white Confederate and supremacist imagery with the dress and treatment of her Black defendants. "Our clients were dressed like [they are] in other countries, in shackles and chains and jumpsuits connected together. It brings up the images of slavery and dehumanization."

Leslie was also reflective on the emotional struggles of defending a client convicted of a gruesome crime. "Bryan Stevenson said it best; no one should be judged by their worst moment," she said. "And you just really have to take a step back and look at the whole picture. Given the right circumstances, I think anyone could end up where some of our clients are. If you were treated that way brutally, day in and day out, who's to say that, at our breaking point, we all couldn't potentially do something like that? We have the switch that we can turn off or stop, but not if you were never given that [switch], or it was beaten out of you."

Ricky Gray was convicted of brutally killing the beloved Harvey family in Richmond's south side in 2006 and remains possibly one of the most reviled men in Richmond. Leslie spoke of how his personality not at all matched the savagery of that killing. "I'd never met Ricky in person, but he was a talented artist. He would send us birthday cards or Happy Mother's Day cards. We just see these aspects of these people, and that's really who they are, at their core, and it's just trying to convey that to other people."

Leslie echoed many other defense attorneys on what their investigations revealed about their clients' and relatives' upbringing and what they seemed to have in common. "What we do in these investigations, we look into [not just our] our client's life, but we also investigate their parents, their grandparents, and usually go out two to three generations laterally – cousins, aunts, uncles. And you start seeing these patterns: physical trauma, sexual trauma, poverty, systemic racism."

"And so, once we identify all those documents and interview different people that knew them along the way, we try to tell their story in a way that's compelling to show some humanity."

In addition to highly-trained attorneys, the four offices employed mitigation specialists and investigators who delved deep into their clients' backgrounds. They looked for information that could blunt a guilty verdict by helping explain circumstances, such as childhood trauma or intellectual disabilities, that contributed to the crime. In some cases, mitigation specialists flew to Central America and Eastern Europe to investigate the horrendous conditions where a client grew up.

In most cases, once prosecutors and commonwealth's attorneys saw the defense team's overwhelming mitigating evidence, they simply took death off the table and offered a plea deal. Juries were often unwilling to sentence to death (for those who chose to go to trial and pursue death) after seeing the capital defenders' findings.

"You can count on your fingers the number of cases that went to trial with the death penalty as a sentencing option since the creation of the capital defender offices," explained Matthew Engle. "I don't know the exact number, but not many."

And, at Washington & Lee School of Law ...

Engle pointed out that before the capital defense offices, it was the stellar work of a capital representation center at Washington & Lee Law School under Bill Geimer and Roger Groot (and later David Bruck) that began changing the complexion of capital trials. "When I was a student from 1998 to 2001, it was routine for death penalty cases to always go to trial. It would be a two or three-day trial. A one-day trial got rarer as time went on, but it was not unheard of."

"The standard of representation in death penalty cases in Virginia was abysmal," he continued. "People weren't filing motions, and they weren't doing pre-trial litigation. They weren't investigating these cases. They were doing rush job trials, and everybody was winding up on death row. Then the appellate courts just weren't giving it the level of scrutiny that they should have."

Engle said it was the pioneering efforts of this program that helped attract top-notch talent to staff the capital defense offices when they opened shortly afterward. "I don't want to overstate it and act like it was just W&L creating this. But there's a direct line, in my opinion, from professors Geimer and Groot in Lexington to the creation of the capital offender offices."

All About Results

> First, we execute the severely mentally ill. Second, we execute offenders who have themselves been terrorized, offenders who are just as much a product of profound violence as they are its perpetrators. And third, we execute not for exceptionally bad crimes, but rather for the exceptionally bad luck of having poor representation, or being in a county where the prosecutor has a proclivity for capital charges, or committing Black-on-White crime. Take these categories away, and the death penalty is an empty shell.
>
> - Corinna Barrett Lain, "Three Observations about the Worst of the Worst, Virginia-Style," *Washington & Lee Law Review Online*, May 4, 2021.

In his 2019 article "The State of the Death Penalty," Brandon Garrett pointed out that Virginia's results after establishing the capital defense offices were not irregular. For example, when New York re-introduced their death penalty in 1995, the legislature also created a statewide capital defender office. As a result, few death sentences were imposed, and each was reversed on appeal.

The creation of regional capital defense offices in Pennsylvania, Georgia, North Carolina, and Texas also resulted in steep declines in new death sentences.

In Virginia, the decline was nothing short of miraculous. Of 250 capital cases tried between 2004 and 2017, only ten went to trial with death a possible outcome. Of those 10 cases, four resulted in a death sentence. One was commuted on appeal to a life sentence. Another of those four received a gubernatorial pardon when it was discovered that prosecutors used false evidence to convince the jury to sentence to death. Of the remaining two, one was commuted when Virginia abolished the death penalty. That left only one of 250 put to death.

"Capital defenders ground Virginia's machinery of death to a halt by beating death sentences one capital case at a time," concluded Lain and Ramseur. "And if that can happen in Virginia, where the deck was stacked against capital defendants in almost every conceivable way, it can happen anywhere."

The Tragic Story of Teresa Lewis

The Only White Woman Executed by Virginia since 1896

> To: Mr. Porter
> I'm the one on death row. I would like to know if there is any way possible that I could take up some classes in school. I already have my high school diploma. Can you please check into this and let me know. I'm really interested in doing a lot. Thanks so much.
> -Death row inmate Teresa Lewis, inmate request form, Fluvanna Correctional Center for Women, dated 7-9-2004 – six years before her execution.

Mary Snodgrass, a 28-year-old woman labeled "disreputable" by the press, became the first white female Virginian to be executed in over 120 years when she was hanged near Coeburn in 1896 for killing her illegitimate, biracial child in a wood stove. "The infuriated people wanted to lynch her," reported the Jul. 24 *Chattanooga Press*, "but the promise of speedy justice caused them to allow the law to take its course." The story, which was picked up by many national papers, including the *Los Angeles Times*, also reported she had been married at age 16 to a "worthless man, but they soon separated."

It would be 114 years before Virginia executed the next white woman. Her name is Teresa Lewis.

Attractive People Don't Get Executed

It is well-documented that the criminal justice system, especially the death penalty, has not just a racial but a gender bias – more specifically, a "beauty bias."

For 400 years, white Virginia women who killed but exhibited contemporary ideals of grace and beauty were never executed. Jurors and judges who saw white and heterosexual female defendants demonstrating feminine, submissive, nurturing, or chaste traits treated them more as victims worthy of mercy.

In her 2002 paper "Executing White Masculinities: Learning From Karla Faye Tucker," Joan Howarth found that commutations of death sentences across the U.S. support this phenomenon. Nationwide, women overall have had a more significant number of life-sparing clemency petitions granted than their male counterparts. A smaller subset of white, wealthier women was "practically immune to being capitally charged, and such women are rarely sentenced to die."

On the flip side, Howarth's paper found that judges and jurors perceived coarse, aggressive, lesbian, or sexually promiscuous women as a societal threat and thus deserving of severe punishments, including death. Simply, these women are considered "unladylike." They are dehumanized by being defeminized.

In 2010 Teresa Lewis faced this harsh bias. She grew up the child of an alcoholic. She had a pill addiction, was overweight, and lived in a mobile home in a rural part of Virginia. Worse, she had a broken tooth.

"We don't tend to execute attractive women," explained Lynn Litchfield Divers in a 2021 interview. From 1997 to 2009, Divers was a chaplain at the Fluvanna Correctional Center for Women under the umbrella of the Chaplain Service, which later became a nonprofit called GraceInside.

Divers ministered to Lewis for six of her seven years on death row. "We don't execute cute people. There is bias when there are attractive people in our system. And bless Teresa Lewis, you know, I hope if you're listening, Teresa, you're not offended by this. But physically, she wasn't the most attractive lady. If you looked at pictures of her, I think that did not do her any favors."

Teresa Wilson Bean Lewis grew up poor in an emotionally strict household in Danville. At 16, she dropped out of school to marry and leave home. She had a daughter and a son from this first marriage, which lasted just a few years.

Lewis suffered from depression and various physical ailments throughout her adult life that caused her severe pain and prevented her from holding a steady job. Between 1987 and 2000, she had 49 different jobs. Her depression and pain also led to a prescription drug addiction that wreaked havoc with her judgment and contributed to her dependence on the opinions of others.

Lewis met her future husband, Julian Clifton Lewis Jr., in 2000 at their employer, Dan River Mills in Danville. They soon moved in together and later married.

In December 2001, Julian's older son, Jason Clifton Lewis, died in a car accident. Julian was the beneficiary of his son's life insurance policy worth $200,000. He received the money and placed it in an account with Prudential Securities. The money was only accessible by drafts with Julian's approved signature.

In February 2002, Julian bought a mobile home and five acres of land for himself and Teresa in Pittsylvania County. Then, in August of that year, Julian Lewis' younger son, Charles (C.J.) Lewis, a United States Army Reserve member, was summoned for active duty. In making final arrangements in the event of his death while on active duty, C.J. purchased a $250,000 life insurance policy and wrote a will, with both identifying his father as his primary beneficiary and his stepmother, Lewis, as the secondary.

A Chance Meeting

Lewis's mother's death in 2002 pushed her further into a depressed state. Then, in September of that year, at the Danville Walmart, she met two men, Rodney Fuller and Matthew Shallenberger. After speaking, Shallenberger and Lewis exchanged phone numbers. The following week she and her 16-year-old daughter began sexual relationships with both men, during which Lewis told Shallenberger of the insurance policies. They then decided that Shallenberger, with Fuller's help, would kill Julian and split his Prudential account proceeds, which was a little over $100,000.

Shallenberger saw an easy mark with Lewis, noting bruises that made him believe her husband beat her. He figured that she would help him achieve his atrocious dream of moving to New York to become a drug runner and a hitman. In an Aug. 22, 2003 letter written from prison to an unknown girlfriend, he noted that:

> The only reason I had sex with the woman [Lewis] was for the money to get her to "fall in love" with me so she would give me the insurance money. One of my brothers made me an offer I couldn't refuse, he was going to start selling me kilos of pure Columbian [unreadable] for 12 grand a pound and pounds of weed for 200$. I'm sure you realize how cheap that is. I just couldn't overlook it and I needed the money to get started.

Divers believed from the beginning that it was Shallenberger, not Lewis, who proposed the murders, and those later letters and affidavits supported her opinion. "Teresa had an I.Q. of 70 on one test and 72 on another, and Shallenberger [tested at 113]. I do not think she understood the consequences of her choices ahead of time," she recalled. "I think she was eager to please Matthew Shallenberger. And I think she went along with those ideas because she was so eager to please him."

Lewis also had no record of violence. She had only one prior offense for forging a prescription and had never violated her probation.

"If you just met Teresa, I don't think that you'd notice that she was slow. But if you spent any significant amount of time with her, that revealed itself," Divers continued. "The way she tried to please, the way she'd ask questions, she was an adult child of an alcoholic. So, she had these people-pleasing mannerisms down. She'd ask you what you think. She'd want to know what you thought before she made any kind of thinking or decision on her own."

"I certainly would hold her accountable, but I don't know that I could hold her responsible."

Two Murders

In late September, Lewis told a friend that she was just using her husband Julian "for money and that he would buy her things." Another acquaintance who had known Julian and Lewis for several years heard her say that if Julian died, "she would get the money, and if [C.J.] was killed and Julian was dead, she would get that money, too."

These conversations would later help the prosecution prove the case against her.

On Oct. 23, 2002, Lewis met Shallenberger and Fuller at a shopping center in Danville and gave the men $1,200 in cash to purchase guns and ammunition to kill Julian. A friend of Shallenberger, Antwain Bennett, bought two shotguns, a pistol, and ammo for all three.

After a failed attempt to kill Julian as he traveled from work in early October, the three learned that C.J. would be with his father at home on Oct. 30, 2002. They then decided to kill both simultaneously, which would increase the payout to around $350,000.

During the early morning hours of Oct. 30, Shallenberger and Fuller entered the mobile home through a back door that Lewis had left unlocked. Each man carried a shotgun.

The two men first awakened Lewis, who was in bed with Julian, telling her to get up. After she left the bed and walked into the kitchen, she heard Shallenberger shoot her husband multiple times.

Fuller had gone into C.J.'s room and shot him three times, but he did not die. He had to go back in and shoot him twice more.

After dividing $300 recovered from Julian's wallet, Shallenberger hugged and kissed Lewis, telling her he was sorry she "had to go through something like this."

After the two men left, Lewis waited about 45 minutes and then made two phone calls to her former mother-in-law and a close friend before calling 911 at 3:55 a.m. She told them that a burglar had entered their home and had shot her husband and adult son. She also said to them that both Julian and C.J. were dead.

At 4:20 a.m., Sheriff's deputies Harris Silverman and Corey Webb arrived and found Julian still alive. He reportedly made "slow moans" and uttered, "Baby, baby, baby, baby." Deputy Webb asked the victim his name, and he responded, "Julian." Then, when Webb asked Julian if he knew who had shot him, Julian answered in a faltering voice, "My wife knows who done this to me."

Webb then reported that Lewis did not appear upset after Julian died, but that could have been attributed to many anti-anxiety medications she took both before and after the shootings.

Less than one week after the murders, Lewis showed up at Prudential with a $50,000 check purportedly signed by Julian and payable to her. A bank employee refused to cash the check because the signature did not match Julian's signature in the records.

A few days later, after questioning, Lewis fully confessed that she had offered Shallenberger and Fuller money to kill her husband.

At her trial, Barbara Haskins, a court-appointed forensic psychiatrist, verified that Lewis' cognitive testing showed a Full-Scale I.Q. of 72, with a verbal I.Q. of 70, and a performance I.Q. of 79. Dr. Haskins believed that Lewis was competent to make plea agreements. In addition to a low I.Q., Lewis's attorney Jim Rocap said she had an addiction to pain pills and was diagnosed with a dependent personality disorder by three different forensic psychologists.

Her defense attorneys advised her to plead guilty to avoid a jury sentencing while appealing to the judge to show some leniency since she cooperated with investigators. Eager to do what she was told, she pleaded guilty to seven felonies: two counts of capital murder for hire, one count of conspiracy to commit capital murder, one count of robbery, and three firearms charges.

A Criminal Mastermind

The plea didn't work as intended. The Pittsylvania Circuit Court found Lewis' crimes to be "wantonly vile, horrible, or inhuman" and sentenced her to death for each conviction of capital murder for hire, as well as prison terms on the firearm charges. Judge

Charles Strauss called her the "mastermind" of the crime (despite her I.Q. of 72) and "clearly the head of this serpent."

Even though Lewis confessed her role in the killings and identified Shallenberger and Fuller as the gunmen, the prosecutor did not consider her cooperation and instead struck a quick deal with Fuller to recommend a life sentence for him in exchange for his cooperation against Shallenberger. This deal led Judge Strauss to sentence Shallenberger to life in prison also because he considered it unfair that one triggerman should get the death penalty when the other received a life sentence.

Strauss admitted in a short 2018 discussion with this author in a Chatham coffee shop to having little latitude in Lewis' sentencing since she pleaded guilty. When asked if he had to do it all over again would he sentence her to death, he deflected, answering that if he had to do it all over again, he would not become a circuit court judge.

He did admit that he was then against the death penalty because he disagreed with the process behind it.

Triggermen Shallenberger and Fuller went to serve their multiple life sentences at Wallens Ridge Maximum Security Prison.

"Law-and-order" Attorney General and staunch pro-life Catholic Ken Cuccinelli was quick to exploit the gender stereotypes in the case. He argued in carefully chosen language that the death sentence in the Lewis case was justified because of "the *brutal* nature of the crimes themselves as well as Lewis' *callous, manipulating, adulterous, greedy, egregious* behavior (emphasis added)." In a court filing, he cited Lewis taking cash from her husband's wallet as he lay dying of his wounds and waiting 45 minutes to call the police.

He also pointed out that she was also having an affair with one of the triggermen.

Lynn Litchfield Divers called Cuccinelli's gratuitous accusation a variation of what is frequently called the "black widow myth." "Men and women can be charged for the same crime, and when there is sex involved, they will always give the woman a harsher sentence because they feel like she's pulling the strings," she explained. "And so, here you've got two men who did the killings, right? And one of whom had an I.Q. of [113], and Teresa had an I.Q. of 70. We don't execute anybody who has an I.Q. of 69 or below. She's one to two points too high, so the judge sentenced her to death, in his words, because she was the mastermind of this crime – the black widow."

Dr. Phillip Costanzo, a Professor of Psychology at Duke University, testified in a 2004 affidavit that Lewis, this purported criminal "mastermind," did not "possess the intellectual capacity to calculate and plan these murders." Dr. Costanzo also explained that, based on her I.Q. scores and a three-hour interview, Teresa operated at a "mental age" of a 12- or 13-year-old.

"Psychological test score data, life history data, interview data, and observational data converge and lead me to conclude that Teresa's participation in the murders was that of a follower, not a leader," he wrote in his conclusion. "She did not possess the intellectual capacity to calculate and plan these murders. She functions at a retarded level on the very intellectual skills most involved in the mediation of planning behavior. Indeed on some of those dimensions, she attains scale scores as low as 4, which translates to I.Q. equivalents of around 40 on those intellectual functions."

Professor of Psychiatry and Chair of Addiction Psychiatry at VCU, Dr. Elinore McCance-Katz, concluded her 2004 study of Lewis by writing, "In summary, this is a tragic story of a woman with limited intellect, dependent personality style, and severe drug addiction who exhibited very poor judgment, impulsivity, virtually no problem-solving skills, and had an ongoing desperate need to be cared for by others. Her deficiencies are simply not consistent with the idea that she planned and directed others in the murders of her husband and his son or that she was fully culpable for them in the same manner that persons without these disabilities might be. "

"Chap Lynn"

Lynn Litchfield Divers was already serving as the chaplain of the Fluvanna Correctional Center for Women when she got called to a special emergency meeting of the institutional leadership to inform her that since there were no facilities for women on death row at Sussex 1, a female death row prisoner was arriving there. "It was the only time I've ever been given a pre-sentence investigation report to read to learn a little bit about who someone was," she said. "Typically, my experience was never to read up on someone, but to let them teach me who they are in that moment and moving forward."

Divers was waiting at Fluvanna intake with the warden and several other senior facility leaders when Lewis entered, wrist, waist, and ankle shackled. When they removed her handcuffs to take her fingerprints, Divers asked the warden if she could approach her and speak to her. The warden consented.

Divers recalled that she walked up to Lewis and said, "I don't know what your life has been like to lead to this point. But may I offer you a hug?"

Lewis whispered, "Yes, please."

That was the first of only two hugs Lewis would receive in her seven years on death row.

Lewis was placed in Building 8, wing B, cell 103, an isolation cell at the far end of a long hallway, far away from any other inmates, behind a solid door with only a lockable meal slot.

This is where Chaplain Lynn, or "Chap Lynn" as she became known, visited Lewis. "I would visit her on Sunday nights after worship service," she recollected. "If I was lucky, they would open the meal tray slot. And so, I would get down on my knees and kneel on the concrete floor, or now and then, I'd finagle a chair from the officer's station."

Once there, Divers explained she reached her hands through the meal slot, and Lewis received them. "And she would rub my hands, rub them to her face, rub them just to hold them because they were the only hands that ever touched her in any act of kindness. She was only ever touched to be handcuffed to shower or taken outside for her recreation. So, physically, my hands were the only hands that touched her for six of seven years that she lived in isolation."

Divers explained her kindness gained a reputation among the women placed in the same hallway cells for infractions of some kind. "You know, in 'seg,' you got a lot of very unhappy women there, lonely, struggling, sometimes acting out. So, it can be loud and obnoxious," she recollected.

"And when I would walk down the hall, they would yell, 'Chap Lynn's here to see Ms. Teresa. Chap's here …' And they weren't doing that out of respect for me. They were doing that out of respect for Teresa, that this was an opportunity that Teresa had to have some time with her religious adviser. And most often, they were exceedingly supportive."

Divers also told of one visit she called a "full moon night," when the inmates were particularly rowdy. "Everything was louder and a little more rambunctious than usual," she described. "And Teresa loved to sing, and she had a lovely voice. And she would begin to sing one of her gospel country songs. And, you know, the holy spirit would echo through that place, and it would settle everybody right on down. It was really powerful to be a part of that and witness to it."

A model prisoner with a remarkable calming effect on the other inmates, Lewis became an effective counselor, although most of her counseling had to be done from her isolation cell, speaking through the ventilation system, just as the death row inmates at Mecklenburg and the old State Penitentiary had to do. As a death row inmate, she was not allowed to congregate with other inmates and spent her recreation time alone.

The Cockroaches Come Out

In that 2003 letter to an unnamed female, Matthew Shallenberger, on page 2, further described his aspirations to become a drug hitman and why he had sexual relations with Lewis:

> I figured why go to New York for 20,000$ a hit when I could do just one and make 350,000$ [unreadable]. This was the only reason I had sex with the mother. Like I said I am just not attracted to white women, especially fat, scary, ugly white women. It was just all part of the job. It was just part of what had to be done to get the money.

On Nov. 15, 2004, investigator Alfred C. Brown and attorney Maurie Levin interviewed Shallenberger at Wallens Ridge. In an affidavit, Shallenberger admitted that he "manipulated the whole thing" and would "take" Teresa from the moment he sized her up and noticed she was so easily controlled.

He then admitted that killing Julian and C.J. Lewis was his idea, not Teresa's. He admitted he killed for the money, but Teresa never spoke much of the insurance proceeds. "I take full responsibility," he repeatedly said.

After reading and signing each page of the affidavit, Shallenberger changed his mind. In a bizarre move, he tore his signatures off the pages and ate them.

In a Nov. 30, 2004 affidavit, Rodney Fuller swore that "Shallenberger was definitely the one in charge of things, not Mrs. Lewis." He also stated that Shallenberger "did talk about wanting to be a hit man. I didn't really think he was serious. After the killings he talked about going to New York and being an assassin for the gangs."

Most revealing, Fuller undercut the prosecution's entire murder-for-hire charge by stating that "No one hired me to commit a murder. No one paid me in advance or after the killings for taking part in the killings. No one promised me any payment in advance ... for taking part in the killings."

An acquaintance of Shallenberger and Fuller, Amin Goggins, swore in a Nov. 23, 2004 affidavit that "Ms. Lewis did whatever Matthew Shallenberger said. Personally, I don't think she had the sense to boil water without instruction."

None of these admissions made any difference, as Virginia's 21-day rule and Lewis's pleas nullified them. Her death sentence stood.

"I think when she was first convicted, nobody thought that Virginia was actually going to execute a borderline mentally challenged woman who didn't kill anyone herself," Divers claimed. "And then as appeal after appeal after appeal was denied in our tough-on-crime era of the early- and mid-2000s, it became more and more apparent to everyone that this really might happen, which is a hard thing to reckon with."

In 2006 Matthew Shallenberger committed suicide in prison.

Divers explained that as an employee of GraceInside, she was not allowed to advocate for the inmates or divulge the inner workings of the prison. That changed when it became apparent Virginia was going to kill Teresa, so she quit the organization to advocate for Teresa and be a whistleblower for crimes committed by prison staff against the female inmates.

"We had several 'majors' go to prison for sexual assault of women at Fluvanna," she recalled. "And I was trusted by the women at the prison enough to know who was doing what. And I ratted on them. That made my life difficult, and I ended up leaving. A senator got involved, and they ended up changing the warden, and the majors had to go to prison. Anyway, it was a mess and a half."

A Mockery

Reaction to the Lewis case among abolitionists was at first disbelief that, as Divers described, Virginia would carry through with such a grotesque miscarriage of justice. But by July 2010, when it became more and more evident that the execution would proceed on Sept. 23, voices rose against the execution. Requests for a commutation poured in from thousands of individuals, mental health groups, and especially the European Union. The website Saveteresalewis.org was created. Novelist and anti-death penalty advocate John Grisham wrote in the Sept. 12, 2010, *Washington Post* that the inconsistencies in the Lewis case "mock the idea that ours is a system grounded in equality before the law."

"In this case, as in so many capital cases, the imposition of a death sentence had little do with fairness. Like other death sentences, it depended more upon the assignment of judge and prosecutor, the location of the crime, the quality of the defense counsel, the speed with which a co-defendant struck a deal, the quality of each side's experts, and other such factors."

On Sept. 20, the U.S. Supreme Court rejected Lewis' final appeal, with only Justices Ruth Bader Ginsburg and Sonia Sotomayor voting to stop the execution.

I'm At Peace

The night of my crime I had Jesus telling me not to let this happen, and the Devil telling me to do it! Well, stupid me chose Satan's way.

-Teresa Lewis, in a written statement to her fellow Fluvanna inmates.

Lewis had been assigned another chaplain after Divers left GraceInside, so when she went back to visit Lewis at Greensville Correctional the day before her execution, it was the first time she had seen her friend for over a year.

"Teresa looked at me for a second, and then she was like, 'Oh, Chap Lynn,'" Divers remembered. "And there, they had bars in front of the death cells. So, I reached my arms through the bars, and I gave her our second hug. I stepped back and ... what do you say to somebody facing being executed the next day?"

"And she said, 'Look at me. How do I look?' And I didn't know what to say, so I said, 'Teresa?' And she said again, 'How do I look? Look at me. How do I look?' And I said, 'I don't understand.'"

"And Teresa said, 'Look at me, Chap Lynn. I'm at peace. I'm about to meet my Jesus.'"

"And she sang to me like we'd sung together before. And she sang five different songs. And she gave me the scripture passage that she wanted me to read at the service the next night where I would be holding vigil and meeting with other abolitionist folks at the death chamber outside on the lawn of the facility."

"And I remember she stood in front of me, and she had on her blue prison scrubs, and she sang with her arms stretched out, 'I sing because I'm happy. I sing because I'm free. His eye is on the sparrow. I know he's watching me.'"

Divers paused, her voice breaking. "As long as I live, I will never forget that moment."

Gov. Bob McDonnell refused to grant clemency, and Teresa Lewis died by lethal injection at 9:13 p.m. on Sept. 23, 2010.

No one denied that Lewis needed to be punished for the crime – she admitted she was wrong and should pay a price. However, no one believed that she was a future threat to society that deserved death.

"I don't know a single staff person, I don't know a single officer, I don't know a single administrator who was excited to see her execution or thought it was the right thing to do," Divers admitted.

"I was galvanized around her case because she did not pull the trigger," Fairfax Democratic party activist and public radio host Catherine Read asserted in a 2021 interview. "And the two men who did pull the trigger [were imprisoned]. And I'm like, what kind of justice is this? I couldn't believe it. I couldn't believe that the governor was not going to put a stop to it. What purpose did it serve when two men who committed murder turned state's evidence, and a woman is to put to death? That's the one that I said to myself, 'This has got to stop. This has got to stop.'"

Divers paused when asked what abolition of the death penalty meant to her personally. "No more Teresas," she finally answered. "No more women who have gotten the short end of every stick, being punished out of proportion for what's happened. No more

Teresas. No more Earl Washingtons ... And no more Lynn Litchfields, who are these chaplains desperately trying to save these people, who give their hearts and souls to the effort to end up getting beaten up, too. So, it goes for the attorneys and those who advocate, who understand the injustice. Maybe just a little more healing, a little less brutality for the officers, the staff, and the people who care about these folks. And a little more just in the justice system."

Witnessing Executions

Dr. E. C. Fisher
Dear sir,
Please be at the penitentiary at 7 a.m. Friday October 30, to witness the electrocution of Winston Green. Please regard this communication as confidential, especially as to the hour. Present this letter at the gate.
-Letter from penitentiary Superintendent J. B. Wood, Oct. 26, 1908.

Under Virginia law, executions could not be filmed or photographed, and no details were publicized as part of the secrecy laws. However, the superintendent invited approximately twenty persons to witness the act, including six to twelve "official" state witnesses, prison officials, guards, a chaplain, and the executioner. Women were not allowed to witness executions until 1962, with the electrocution of Carroll Garland.

"By statute, there are civilian witnesses," Jon Sheldon explained. "People can just apply to be a witness. There are law enforcement witnesses, and there are attorneys for the accused. The family for the accused cannot attend in Virginia, but victims [family] may attend, and they will [be] in a room, and there's a two-way mirror there, so nobody sees the victim's family."

Starting in 1908, in the State Penitentiary "A" basement, witnesses, including the press, filed in and stood in two rows less than six feet from the electric chair. Guards brought the prisoner in, and those witnesses saw the entire procedure of shackling and binding the prisoner into the chair, then the electrocution.

So many volunteered to witness the 1935 executions of gangsters Robert Mais and Walter Leganza that Penitentiary Superintendent Rice Youell decided to use separate groups for each execution.

Since the 1980s, up to four media witnesses acted as "pool witnesses" for reporters stationed outside the death house. In later years, media interest in executions diminished, and seats went empty, with not even a reporter waiting outside for a briefing. A notable exception was John Allen Muhammad, who was executed on Nov. 10, 2009. Dozens of reporters and satellite trucks from all over the world jammed Greensville Correctional Center's parking lot that night.

Sheldon described the witness section of the modern death chamber as a tiny movie theater the size of a living room. "They put a little grandstand on plywood so that apparently, if I'm in the fourth row, I can get a good view. For the witnesses, they put a piece of Plexiglas [between them and the injection gurney]."

"Right through a door there are three cells, and they're old-fashioned, [like in] 'The Andy Griffith Show.'"

What They Saw

Virginia Gazette **reporter, witnessing the April 13, 1753 hanging of Lowe Jackson for counterfeiting:** "Standing beneath the gallows, he addressed the spectators with a very moving and pathetic speech on the fatal consequences attending an early habit of vice, which had been the means of bringing him to that shameful and untimely end. He demonstrated an unusual composure of mind, and he died in a very penitent manner."

An anonymous Lima, Ohio reporter witnessing the Aug. 15, 1912 execution of Virginia Christian, the first woman executed in Virginia's electric chair: "Her face was absolutely calm, she gave a quick glance at the instrument of death, more in curiosity than in fear, lowered her eyes and stepped on the platform. A guard motioned her to be seated in the chair, and the negress sank into her place. Three guards hurried forward, one adjusted the knee, another strapped the woman's form into the chair, and the others clasped on the headpiece. A moment later, the body stiffened and twisted, a wisp of sickening smoke floated through the leather headpiece."

Penitentiary chaplain Russ Ford, on the July 19, 1990 execution of Richard Boggs and the Dec. 3, 1996 execution of Gregory Beaver: "Ricky Boggs has this unusual, mystical experience. He sort of floats in and sits down. But the execution got delayed. I asked Tony Barrett, 'Should we start raising hell or celebrating. Which is it?' And he said, 'The governor is having trouble deciding,' and I said, 'Well, can I go over and be with Ricky?' And said, 'Go. Russ, you can go over there.' So, I went over, and I'm holding Ricky's hand; I got my hand wrapped up around his shoulder, and I'm talking in his ear. He's got the mask on and all the equipment and everything."

"And all at once, I hear Eugene Grizzard, who was a warden out of Southampton at the time. And he says, 'Russ, no!' I lift my hands off Rick, and honest to God, I was maybe a foot away from him, and the electricity went right through his body."

"Just missed me, man. Just missed me."

Ford estimated he witnessed between 28 and 30 executions between 1984 and 2001. Another one that stands out is the 1996 electrocution of Gregory Beaver. Ford recalled that Beaver had just sat down in the chair when he removed his wedding band and handed it to him. "Greg just wanted to take it off and give it to his wife. I married them. [Warden Ron] Angelone sees this from afar, so he comes rushing over, saying, 'That can't happen!' It's like we're mugging somebody on the street corner or something. It was just childish. With all this going on, an execution, and this guy slips off his wedding band and hands it to the chaplain. You're like, 'What the fuck is going on?' Excuse my language. It was such a trivial thing to come over and be a real big rooster. And I never respected that when they got like that."

Beaver died wearing his wedding band. Later, it was removed from his finger at the State Medical Examiner's Office.

Father James Griffin, on the Dec. 10, 1992, execution of Timothy Dale Bunch and the Jan. 4, 1996 execution of Walter Correll Jr.: "Bishop Sullivan and I went to Tim Bunch's electric chair execution. And Bishop Sullivan said, 'Let's go in and watch it.' I said, 'I can't go in.' And I remember him saying, 'Oh, come on, that's why we're here.' I said, 'I wouldn't go see an abortion. Why would I see execution?' He said, 'Well, I'm going in.' So, he went in, and I stayed down the hallway. It was Greensville, and he came back out, and he said something I will always remember. He said, 'Oh, that wasn't too bad.' For Bishop Sullivan, it wasn't too bad."

> Cast into this sheer political abyss
> By the vengeful voices of our night
> With endless echoes of our darkness
> Yet still reflecting on the light!
> -Poem by Timothy Dale Bunch, Autumn, 1992, death row, Mecklenburg
> Correctional Center.

Griffin continued, describing Walter Correll Jr., who was executed in 1996 for the 1985 abduction, robbery, and stabbing murder of Charles Bousman Jr. in Franklin County. Correll was determined to have an I.Q. of 68. The two co-defendants, John Dalton and Richard Reynolds, testified that Correll killed Bousman by twice throwing a knife into his chest. But Correll's lawyers contend that Dalton and Reynolds blamed Correll for the killing to escape a death sentence.

"I talked to Correll ..." Griffin explained, "he wasn't Catholic, but he said, 'Can you pray the Hail Mary when I'm laying there?' And I said, 'Well, sure.' And it didn't register why he wanted it. So, they strapped him in and said, 'Father Griffin, you can talk to the inmate now.' So, I bent over and said, 'Do you want me to pray the Hail Mary?' And I started praying it, 'Hail Mary, full of grace [the Lord is with thee. Blessed art thou amongst women, and blessed is the fruit of thy womb, Jesus. Holy Mary, Mother of God, pray for us sinners, now and] at the hour of our death. Amen.'"

"That's why he wanted me to say that because it was at the hour of his death."

Griffin recalled that this moment still has a lasting effect on him. "That got to me. And five minutes later, he was dead."

Richmond News Leader **journalist Rex Springston, on the Jan. 19, 1993 electrocution of Charles Stamper, who had been paralyzed from the waist down in a fight with another inmate at Mecklenburg Correctional:** "He got stuck with a shiv or something when he was in prison ... but what was most memorable to me, most striking, was not the death, which was pretty clinical, but they brought him in, a guard on each side and his legs were just kind of scraping along the ground, so they had to just, sort of, drag this guy over to the chair. They put him in. I didn't see any steam or anything. You always hear about this. And it seemed like it was in seconds, poof, it's done."

Laura LaFay, on the June 17, 1993 electrocution of Andrew Chabrol and the Jan. 4, 1996 lethal injection of Ronald Bennett: "It was incredibly shocking in a number of ways. Chabrol was this small guy. [But] he's Mr. Toxic Masculinity, a tough guy. He's waddling to the execution chair because it's the most macho way to die. They put him in the chair, and his feet didn't reach the ground. And they strapped him in. Then just imagine a bunch of guys in suits standing around, talking on the phone, and waiting to push the button. This one guy told me, 'Oh, it ain't nothing, it's just like killing a deer, don't worry.'"

"There you are trapped in this little glass room, and there was a guy named David Bass who was kind of your host of the execution. He fancied himself a historian of the Virginia death penalty, and he would give a little talk about the chair and everything."

"They turn it on, and his arms, his ankles, everything just welled up immediately and turned red like a lobster, and then fire started coming out the top of his head, and nobody batted an eyelash. Then they turned it off, and that was that."

"I went outside to the parking lot where the AP reporter was briefing all the reporters at Greensville. And this reporter stood at the microphone and said, 'Andrew Chabrol died peacefully.'"

LaFay also witnessed the 1996 lethal injection of Ronald Bennett at Greensville Correctional.

"That was the last execution I ever went to see because I felt like too much of a participant. I thought it was barbaric. And lethal injection didn't seem much less barbaric because, in his case, they had all these curtains around this glass room that they would close and then open, and there he was, tied to the gurney. And then they closed them so they could stick in the needle, but there were a bunch of needle blowouts, which often happens. It was really messy, and they kept closing the curtains. We had no idea what the hell was going on. In the end, I think they must have just destroyed his entire arm, and there were several towels piled on top of it. From that point forward, I told the *Pilot*, 'I'm not doing it anymore. You want somebody to witness, find somebody else.' And they did."

Defense Attorney Steven Rosenfield, on the Sept. 28, 1995 lethal injection of Dennis Stockton: "He gets to the gurney, and I'm still walking with him because I was going to take his glasses ... and he sits on the gurney, and I take two steps announcing that, 'Dennis, let me get your glasses,' and these correctional officers treated it like an escape attempt."

Rosenfield went on to describe a most unbelievable incident. "The warden said, 'Okay, step back, counsel,' and they took the glasses and handed them to me. He's on the gurney, and then they close the drapes. They open them again [after] they've inserted the needles, and there's a phone on the wall not far from where the audience is seated."

"And the phone rings. Tony, my co-counsel and I looked at each other because we didn't know what we should do as lawyers, depending on what would be on the other end of the phone. And we could see the lips of the warden saying, 'wrong number.'"

"We had asked the governor to spare Dennis's life because we had a confession from somebody who said they had committed the murder. So, even though the governor turned us down, we thought he had second thoughts. But it was a wrong number."

"So, he hangs up and asks Dennis if he has any last words. Dennis mumbles some incoherent things. And before the warden could give the nod, the phone rang a second time. The warden had his back to us, but it took the same amount of time as it did minutes earlier – wrong number. And he hung up the phone and just nodded to the executioner."

Rumors trickled from the penitentiary in the days following Stockton's execution that the calls were not a wrong number at all but someone's idea of a cruel joke. The pervasive prison system corruption Stockton's death row diary exposed made many enemies.

"You know," Rosenfield explained, "that was part of the ghoulishness of a man, minutes away from being executed, and it's delayed because somebody called the wrong extension."

Sister Helen Prejean, on the July 23, 1997 execution of Joseph O'Dell:

I close my eyes and fold my hands in my lap and pray for God to take Joe quickly. Because of the tight strap, he cannot even draw one deep final breath of life. I pray for Lori [Urs]. I pray for Joe's sister, Sheila. I pray for the people of Virginia. I pray for the governor and the courts and all who are participants in this man's death."
- from her 2005 book "The Death of Innocents: An Eyewitness Account of
Wrongful Execution."

Chris Dovi, former journalist with the *Ashland Herald-Progress*, on the April 28, 1999 execution of Eric Christopher Payne:
"As I watched Virginia kill Christopher Payne by lethal injection on a metal gurney in a sterile, tiled room at Greensville Correctional Center, the murderer made no plea to be spared. By his own account, he wanted to die to end his suffering. That suffering became a matter of public record when he was just six years old, and Payne's father killed his mother before hanging himself.

It's undoubtedly true that, as a matter of assets, Payne's death was no loss for society. But neither did society gain by taking his life in this zero-sum exchange for the lives of his two victims, Sally Fazio and Ruth Parham.

If anything was lost, it was my faith in the death penalty as a deterrent to crimes like the ones Payne committed. In the dimly lit observation room, I'd come to watch Payne die. As the press representative, I sat in a hard-backed plastic chair just feet from a glass partition separating the handful of other witnesses – family members of one of the two victims, the lead investigator from Hanover County, and the prosecutor, Eddie Vaughn – from the execution room. As Payne's chest heaved his last breaths, someone gave a small sob. I watched as a plump tear rolled down Vaughn's cheek.

I recall feeling cold in that room. But I also recall wondering how this painless and relatively private death could possibly answer for the horrible suffering that Payne inflicted on his victims.

A state's reason to administer punishment for crimes has just four justifications: retribution, incapacitation, rehabilitation, or deterrence. Clearly, the death penalty does not rehabilitate. While it certainly incapacitates, so does life in prison – and stats show that even a long life behind bars is cheaper than execution. And execution hardly serves as retribution, as it essentially lets the guilty party off early. Not exactly clemency, but hardly a lesson learned by the guilty party to be employed later.

So how does state-sanctioned murder deter future crimes? Nobody was intended to be deterred from future crimes by Payne's death. Payne's presiding judge, Richard Taylor, said as much during sentencing: "He is entitled to be relieved of his misery," he said from the bench. "I think probably it is the best thing for everybody."

Taylor described no argument for the death penalty as retribution or a deterrent. Rather, it was an argument for state-assisted suicide. Taylor essentially described compassionate relief for a man who'd been dealt fatal wounds decades before.

And so it seems not unusual that on that chilly April night, 20 years after the violent deaths of Payne's parents, not even Payne's prosecutor left Jarratt reformed or the slightest deterred from crime by his execution.

As I made my way along I-295, cruising at just over the speed limit, I was overtaken by Eddie Vaughn, who passed me with enough speed that my car rocked in the wake of his Ford Crown Vic, as its red taillights disappeared over the horizon."

Larry Traylor, Director of Communications, Virginia DOC, on the Nov. 10, 2009 lethal injection of John Allen Muhammad (on Larry King Live, CNN television broadcast, Nov. 10, 2009, 9:00 p.m.) "Once he was strapped down, he was watching and looking around a little bit. Then the curtains were closed so that the team could come in and administer the I.V.s. During that time, he was just simply watching, curiously seeing what was going on. Once the I.V.s were administered and the curtain opened back up, he had his -- he was just lying down. His head was down. He had his head tilted slightly to the right and his eyes closed. I don't know specifically when he started doing that. But at that point, we were prepared to start. We asked him for a last statement. He did not even look at us or acknowledge us."

Richmond Times-Dispatch Journalist Frank Green, on the Jan. 16, 2013 electrocution of Robert C. Gleason Jr.:

> Execution team members led Gleason into the death chamber at 8:55 p.m., holding his heavily tattooed arms—the ink standing out on his prison-pale skin. Gleason was strapped into the wooden electric chair at his chest, arms, and ankles. He smiled, winked, and nodded at times toward his spiritual adviser sitting in the witness area ... The smile was more a leer, and the bravado came across as bizarre.
>
> ... His body tensed and his skin turned pink when the first cycle of electricity began. After a brief pause, a second ninety-second cycle was conducted. After five minutes, a physician put a stethoscope to Gleason's chest – just below a tattooed skull – and failed to detect a heartbeat.
>
> Gleason's smirk is my most indelible memory from the death house.
>
> -From Green's essay "Witnessing Executions," *University of Richmond Law*

Review, March 13, 2015.

Green wrote that between 1980 and 2017, he witnessed anywhere from 12 to 24 executions.

A Big Fat Hairy Goal

Abolition Now, Abolition Forever

> I felt like I was sort of the conductor of a symphony. The key is understanding how the symphony works together and then bringing in the key pieces, the prosecutors, the victim's family members, the conservatives, the media, grassroots activists, and our allies at the appropriate time. Just orchestrating that was certainly very satisfying.
> -former VADP Executive Director Michael Stone, on coordinating abolition in 2021.

Stone had 25 years of experience working for the Catholic Diocese of Richmond, four years' experience with the National Coalition to Abolish the Death Penalty (NCADP), and 18 months of experience as a house dad when he was hired on June 10, 2015, as the new executive director of VADP. "Ironically, in the 25 years I served at the Catholic Diocese, I was never the staff person in our office directly working on the death penalty," he said in a 2021 interview. "It was always one of my colleagues, either Rob Gabriel, BJ Brown Devlin, Kathleen Kenney, or Pat Slater. But in staff meetings, I learned a lot about the death penalty and became aware of the issues and the arguments against it."

That awareness suited him well when he left the Diocese and went to work as a field director for NCADP in 2011. "NCADP at the time was focused intently on Texas and Virginia. But my colleague in Texas and I also had additional states where we were in regular touch with the local leadership and provided technical assistance and training for them."

In addition to assisting VADP in Virginia, Stone worked with advocates in Pennsylvania, South Dakota, North Carolina, Florida, and Missouri, doing public education work mainly with the faith community and organizing public education events. He also worked to build VADP membership by assisting Steve Northup, the volunteer executive director.

In 2015, Stone was interviewed by Northup and the VADP search committee for the executive director position just as the NCADP grant money ran out. He recalled that decisive interview: "I was pretty clear understanding strengths and weaknesses of the organization. And in the interview, I hammered away on two themes. Number one, the legislature was firmly in Republican control at the time. [I said] 'Look, [VADP] is made up of a bunch of liberals. And if we are going to win in Virginia, we have to become more diverse politically as an organization.' And I had some ideas about how to go about doing that."

His second point was his assertion that he was an outstanding administrator and public educator but a lousy lobbyist. "If they hired me, I wanted money in the budget to hire a lobbyist to work during sessions," he insisted. "I was old enough to know what I was good at and what I sucked at."

Stone's visions of VADP fit well with Northup's in that he believed before Stone was even interviewed that abolishing the death penalty could come in as few as five or six years, and only if it was a bipartisan effort. "At the time, we could see a route to getting there, but it mainly involved persuading enough Republicans to come over because of common-sense reasons," Northup recalled. "Reasons that would appeal to conservatives, such as you don't trust big government, why would you trust the government to get [death] right?"

Northup also admitted that a significant advantage in hiring Stone was that he had worked for years with the Catholic Diocese of Richmond. "So many Catholics are conservative and Republicans. Michael knew how to talk Republican, particularly if they're Catholic."

Stone also knew when he took over that the organization needed to stop the fatal cycle of getting, spending, then running out of money to where staff had to be laid off. He set a goal to get VADP to where they could raise all the money they needed from supporters for base operations, then use any grant money for strategic initiatives.

The strategy started working. In just a few years, VADP continued to receive funding from the Death Penalty Mobilization Fund while Stone built up internal fundraising. "Raising additional money from churches was a big part of that," he admitted. "I think over a couple of years, we went from about $4,000 a year from churches to about $15,000 or $16,000."

About That 5-Year Plan

Stone knew at his hire that it had been four years since Virginia sentenced anyone to death. Accordingly, if capital defenders could keep any new people from being sentenced to death, by 2020, Virginia's death row could be empty. "I said that's a good time to launch an abolition campaign," he remembered, adding that it gave VADP five years to build up conservative support and get all the pieces needed to begin talking seriously about abolition. "I think in my first letter to the membership, I laid out that five-year vision, that we need your increased support for us to launch an abolition campaign in 2020, and laid out the reasons why."

He continued to use that messaging to excite donors, give them a sense of direction, and let them know that their donations were going to a specific goal. "In thank you letters, I always wrote, 'This will help us get us to where we want to be in 2020."

A handful of donors were annoyed at the thought of embracing conservatives and pro-lifers into the abolition effort and stopped donating. One relatively large donor stopped giving after VADP awarded Republican Sen. Bill Stanley "Legislator of the Year" in 2020.

Stanley had delivered an impassioned speech on the 2020 General Assembly session floor calling for an end to the death penalty because it violated conservative pro-life philosophy. In the 2021 session, however, his pro-life passion for abolition cooled when the Senate failed to pass mandatory life without parole (LWOP) for aggravated murder, a compromise he said he was not willing to make.

Stone noted that he was not doing anything revolutionary but continuing the establishment-oriented, policy-focused direction established by the organization a few years earlier. And, echoing Jon Sheldon, he also credited Ken Cuccinelli with opening conservative eyes to inequities in the criminal justice system.

"Even though he was a real right-wing zealot, he also believed in justice," Stone said of Cuccinelli. "When he found out about the wrongful conviction of Thomas Haynesworth (a Black man wrongfully convicted and sentenced to 75 years for five rapes he never committed), he went to bat to ensure that he was ultimately released. I think that highlighted for Republicans how the system does get things wrong, and we do get the wrong guys serving time in prison and on death row."

Stone credited shifting public opinion, the work of the media highlighting wrongful convictions, such as Haynesworth's, and the work of Witness to Innocence in helping shift conservative views on the death penalty over the last 12 to 15 years.

No Pushing

> If we execute the "worst of the worst," then what do we need Red Onion
> [prison] for? Why do we need Wallens Ridge?
> > -anonymous Libertarian, Arlington, Va. March 9, 2020.

With all of these pieces falling into place, VADP believed it still was not the time to push for total abolition or even call to slow it down. "We actively discouraged legislators from introducing abolition bills," he claimed. "We didn't want abolition to be seen as a joke at the General Assembly."

He pointed to the annual abolition efforts of Hanover Del. Frank Hargrove as an example. "God bless him, he would put in an abolition bill and get laughed out of committee on the first day of Courts of Justice. And you don't want that to be the image of abolition in the minds of legislators when you're really ready." Instead, VADP and its coalition partners encouraged legislators to look at incremental reforms to reduce the death row population.

The SMI Bill

> Thank you for your letter to abolish capital punishment for the mentally
> handicapped. I will consider such bills, but believe that the current defenses
> for mental incapacity are a sufficient protection.
> > -Letter from Gov. George Allen to VADP executive director Henry Hel-
> > ler, Jan. 30, 1989.

One of those incremental reforms was the Severe Mental Illness Exemption or SMI bill. In 2013 the ABA issued a massive report that contained about 30 specific recommendations for changing Virginia's death penalty system, and one was to exempt people with severe mental illness from execution. "There were other states working on that issue," Stone recalled. "And there was a lot of good research and national support that we could get if we pursued an SMI exemption legislatively in Virginia."

Mental illness and the use of the death penalty were inexplicably intertwined, and not just in Virginia. A study cited in a separate 2016 ABA report found that at least 20 percent of death row inmates nationwide at the time had a severe mental illness. In 2017, six of the 23 inmates executed in the U.S. were mentally ill. In 2018, it was ten of 25. In 2019, it was eight of twenty-two. Finally, in 2020, it was eight of 17.

Unlike "not guilty by reason of insanity" (NGRI), which sought to absolve a defendant of guilt, the SMI exemption addressed only the defendant's punishment, not guilt or innocence. The bill directed those defendants found guilty still must be punished and even receive life in a psychiatric institution or prison without parole. SMI took the death penalty off the table.

VADP and its partners, including the National Alliance of Mental Illness (NAMI-Virginia), the ACLU, the Catholic Conference, and others believed that the SMI bill presented a productive way to educate legislators about the flaws in the death penalty without directly addressing it. "It was sort of a sidelong attack," Stone explained. "It got us the opportunity to talk with supporters of the death penalty in a way that could cast doubt about the system without doing it directly. And I think that also helped soften the views of some Republicans about capital punishment."

The bill defined severe mental illness as "the exhibition of active psychotic symptoms that substantially impair a person's capacity to: 1) appreciate the nature, consequences, or wrongfulness of the person's conduct; 2) exercise rational judgment in relation to the person's conduct; or 3) conform the person's conduct to the requirements of the law."

As proven over and over, Virginia did not prohibit executions of persons who, at the time of their crime, had significant limitations in intellectual function caused not just by mental illness but by a disability such as traumatic brain injury or even dementia.

A coalition-produced sign-on letter outlined why conservatives should be against executing those diagnosed with severe mental illnesses. One point noted that there was no credible evidence to suggest that executions deterred those who do not understand their actions' consequences. Capital punishment was thus rendered utterly useless as a general deterrent to those stricken with those illnesses.

"Many pro-life conservatives believe that society's most vulnerable ought to be protected, not discarded," another point stated. "People with mental illnesses suffer from diagnosable psychological disorders. Their illnesses are not the result of their choices or their lack of personal responsibility."

Admittedly, the SMI exemption applied to a narrow segment of defendants. NAMI-Virginia and the American Bar Association's (ABA) Due Process Review Project in 2016 sponsored a forum, "Mental Illness and the Death Penalty." In it, former Commissioner of Virginia's public mental health system under Govs. Warner and Kaine, Dr. James Reinhard, explained that according to best estimates, only four percent of violence towards others is solely attributable to certain classes of mental illness, particularly to psychoses such as schizophrenia. Substance abuse and socio-demographic factors, such as poverty and family trauma, significantly contributed more to violent behavior than mental disorders.

The last person executed in Virginia, William Morva, was a textbook example of the commonwealth's willingness to kill a profoundly mentally ill person. Morva was sentenced to death for killing two people in 2006 during a prison escape while waiting to be tried on an armed robbery charge. On a trip to the hospital for an intestinal complaint, he overpowered the guard who had accompanied him and took his gun. He fatally shot a hospital security guard, Derrick McFarland, in the scuffle. On a subsequent search in Montgomery County, Morva also fatally shot a deputy sheriff, Cpl. Eric Sutphin.

At trial, jurors were told only that Morva was an "odd guy" and were not informed that he was actively psychotic in numerous ways. As a teenager, Morva became consumed by delusions, leading him to seek out living in the woods while believing he suffered from an intestinal disease that required him to eat large quantities of raw meat and pine cones. He claimed his real name was Nemo and that he was on a mission to save the world with his special powers. He believed those powers also made him the leader of a lost indigenous South American people. Morva was intently paranoid and thought that the George Bush administration was working with local police to kill him. "Someone wants me to die, and I don't know who it is," Morva told his mother in a phone call shortly before his escape.

He was right – it was the Commonwealth of Virginia.

After the conviction, with more and more awareness of Morva's disturbing mental state emerging, pressure grew on Gov. McAuliffe to commute his sentence to life without parole. Letters and petitions from 30,000 supporters deluged McAuliffe, including pleas from Rachel Sutphin, the daughter of one of his victims, to spare his life. Eighteen state legislators petitioned him for clemency. The United Nations called to stop the execution.

None of it worked. McAuliffe refused to grant clemency, stating in a boilerplate press release that "I personally oppose the death penalty; however, I took an oath to uphold the laws of this Commonwealth regardless of my personal views of those laws, as long as they are being fairly and justly applied."

15 Seconds

Shawn Weneta was an inmate at Greensville Correctional center when Morva was brought there from Sussex I to await his execution. He described a disturbing incident he witnessed from his cell window, which overlooked the yard: "On a Saturday morning, typically, it's normal operations. But we weren't allowed out of our cells on this Saturday morning, which was an indicator that they were bringing William Morva in a van to put him in the death house. And, when you are transported by the Department of Corrections, you have leg irons on, and there's a chain that goes around your waist, and then handcuffs get chained into that, to your waist chain, and then a chain that goes from your handcuffs down to your leg irons."

"There were five or six correctional officers that opened the door. And as Morva was stepping out of the van shackled and handcuffed, he shoulder-checked one of the officers."

Weneta could not believe what happened after that. "[The guards] yanked him out of the van, threw him on the asphalt, and beat him for about 15 seconds. Now doesn't sound like much, but he was shackled and handcuffed, so there was no reason to use that kind of force. But 15 seconds is an eternity when you're getting pounded on by four to six officers."

"I can't imagine what he was experiencing at that time. They seemed to be focusing on areas of his body that wouldn't be seen – the legs and body, not the face."

After Morva's gang-beating at the hands of corrections officers, Weneta reported they pulled the stunned and disoriented death row prisoner to his feet and manhandled him to the death house. "That's what I saw. And it was traumatic; it was disappointing and upsetting,"

Will Morva was executed on July 6, 2017. "Mr. Morva's execution brought no solace to me, but, instead, it strengthened my resolve that the death penalty needs to be abolished," Rachel Sutphin told *RVA* Magazine.

Corinna Barrett Lain addressed the Morva execution in a *Washington & Lee Law Review* article titled "Three Observations about the Worst of the Worst, Virginia-Style." She concluded that the execution was "a fitting final tribute to the death penalty in Virginia, an embarrassing execution that would mark the last gasp of an embarrassingly broken criminal justice practice."

A New Grant and a New Hire

> If you're not willing to knock on doors, get out your skinny clothes because you're going to starve to death.
>
> -old-school door-to-door sales trope.

A few months before the Morva execution, VADP received a generous grant from the Sisters of Bon Secours. They elected to double the paid staff (to two) by hiring a field director to take the SMI exemption bill to the public to raise awareness. This author, Dale Brumfield, was subsequently hired in late March 2017 and, after a month-long orientation, took the SMI bill on the road. His first trip was to the deep red North Carolina border communities of Danville, Pittsylvania County, and Martinsville.

Brumfield brought an eclectic skill set to the job. In addition to having several strong Republican contacts, he was the author of 11 books and had worked as a theme park engineering documentalist, magazine publisher, journalist, and an adjunct English professor with an MFA in fiction writing. He had also, for ten years, been a door-to-door supplemental insurance salesman, and in this field director position, those sales techniques found surprising new life.

Before arriving in Martinsville, he researched churches, civic groups, and community service organizations that may be good prospects. Knowing that most people believed in the death penalty theory but knew nothing about the actual processes, his goal was to get his foot in the door, start friendly conversations, then shut up, listen, and answer questions.

In addition to the civic groups, community service organizations, and faith groups, he searched for civic organizations such as Ruritans, Rotary, and Kiwanis. If they could pull three people together, he would talk to them.

After "beating the streets" of Martinsville for four days and making over 30 contacts, Brumfield saw many doors close, but he did manage to crack a few open, however tentatively. One of those cracked doors was a large county Ruritan Club, whom he kept in touch with until months later when they invited him to speak.

He penetrated six targeted Republican jurisdictions for two years, talking not about abolition but the SMI bill. Another critical contact during this time was the Virginia Federation of Republican Women (VFRW). He recalled being a vendor at their annual state conference in Richmond: "I arrived on Friday afternoon at the vendor's hall, and after getting set up, I realized that all the other vendors, with very few exceptions, were either hairstylists or makeup professionals," he explained. "So between the Mary Kay cosmetic representative and the Fantastic Sam's franchise owner was me, the death penalty guy – and the only man in the entire building."

As awkward as this arrangement seemed, it was a productive weekend. "I approached the placement and my subject matter with friendliness, appropriate seriousness, even humor, when necessary," Brumfield said. "I was never confrontational or adversarial, no matter how insistent some of the women were of how wrong I was. I always listened, thanked them for stopping by my table, we're all friends here, and please take a piece of candy." Many women told him on Sunday that they appreciated him being there.

As a result of this and their next state conference in Norfolk, Brumfield was able to secure speaking engagements at five VFRW chapters to talk and answer questions about SMI and, later, abolition. Many women, including the leadership, signed on to VADP's mailing list.

Brumfield also helped table at the 2017 and 2018 Conservative Political Action Committee (CPAC) with a national abolition group, Conservatives Concerned about the Death Penalty. Surprisingly, many of the younger Republicans at CPAC were entirely on board with abolition.

SMI Progress

The work not just of VADP but the entire coalition eventually netted notable results in the General Assembly after a couple of slow starts – only not enough to save William Morva. First introduced in 2016, the bill failed to pass committees until 2019, when it actually passed the Senate Courts of Justice, then passed on the Senate floor on a vote of 23-17. This vote was particularly notable as it was the first bill limiting the death penalty ever passed in the Virginia legislature. Unfortunately, it was passed by indefinitely in the House Courts of Justice Subcommittee 14-1.

In 2020, SMI passed the Judiciary Committee 9-4, then passed the full Senate with a startling vote of 32-7. Stone recalled that the victory in the Senate that year was attributable to Sen. Bill Stanley and his floor speech that flipped five Republicans who had opposed the SMI bill the previous year.

When the Democrats took control of the House and Senate, the new criminal law subcommittee chair, Del. Mike Mullin, being a prosecutor, was opposed to putting diminished capacity into the Criminal code. "And so while he supported the concept of SMI, he didn't want to write it into the code," Stone explained. "And he said, 'Look; instead, I really think we ought to just get rid of the death penalty entirely.' And he offered to patron the abolition bill in 2021. And so we took him up on that."

Virginia's Vanishing Death Penalty

A 2015 study by then-University of Virginia University law professor Brandon Garrett (now at Duke University) showed a striking decline in Virginia's death penalty between 2005 and 2014. Evidence pointed to better lawyering key in reducing the number and outcomes of capital cases, particularly in the sentencing stage, which had been cursory at best in decades past. With the advent of the capital defense offices, sentencing trials doubled in length (from an average of two days to averaging four days). Defense attorneys calling more expert witnesses introduced specific evidence that included issues of mental health, substance abuse, and childhood trauma.

The report also noted that only seven counties in Virginia imposed death sentences during that decade, and nine of the 11 death sentences were imposed in the most populous jurisdictions. "Smaller jurisdictions clearly lost their taste for capital trials first, but now almost the entire commonwealth has followed their lead," Garrett told the Oct. 19, 2015 *UVA Today* news service.

The report also showed disturbing trends in the kinds of evidence still used in capital cases, with many relying on procedures found to be unreliable or susceptible to abuse, including unreliable or coerced informant testimony, undocumented police confessions, and mistaken eyewitness identifications.

The last death sentence handed down by a Virginia jury was in 2011. That year Mark Lawlor was convicted of the brutal murder of Genevieve Orange in Falls Church. The court sentenced Lawlor to die, but a 2018 federal appeals court ruled that the original trial judge had wrongly prohibited Lawlor's lawyers from presenting evidence pertaining to the defendant's future dangerousness. A new sentencing trial was ordered, but simultaneously, Fairfax County elected a progressive new prosecutor, Steve Descano, who ran on a criminal justice reform platform and promised to never to seek the death penalty. With Descano's approval, Lawlor was resentenced to life without parole on two counts, capital murder in the commission of rape and capital murder in the commission of abduction. He also waived any rights to seek early release.

Descano's decision – and others – triggered howls of protest from far-right-wing media outlets, such as American Liberty News, Powerline blog, and Newspunch, who alleged he was a "trojan horse" prosecutor planted by billionaire George Soros. They claimed that in 2016 Soros began a quiet overhaul of America's criminal justice system by bankrolling "soft on crime" commonwealth attorneys and prosecutors to go easy on vicious murderers and child molesters.

Statistics from 2015 to 2020 show how dramatically the death penalty had fallen from favor. In those five years, 34 offenders were convicted in Virginia of capital murder. Of these, 32 received a sentence of life in prison. The court suspended the life sentences for the remaining two, ordering prison terms of 36 and 38 years each.

While Michael Stone had anticipated an empty death row by 2021, there were instead only two death row inmates left – Thomas Porter and Anthony Juniper. A far cry from the 55 inmates sitting there in 1999.

Porter was convicted in 2005 of shooting a police officer three times. Juniper was convicted in 2004 of a quadruple murder, including a two-year-old and a four-year-old. Both cases had been hung up in appeals for over 13 years due to serious questions about guilt, prosecution misconduct, and witness tampering.

More Pieces Fall: Commonwealth's Attorneys on Board

The election of the progressive Descano was a philosophical switch for Fairfax, considering that since 1976 the county ranked fourth out of 133 jurisdictions statewide for death sentences, with six executions. This election was one of many in several critical jurisdictions across Virginia that showed profound commitments to reforming Virginia's criminal justice system.

Another elected progressive was Amy Ashworth, who replaced Prince William County prosecutor Paul Ebert after retiring in 2018 after 52 years in office. During Ebert's five decades, he was known for his wry wit and aggressiveness in pursuing death at all costs, winning 13 death sentences with nine executions. Because of this one man, Prince William was not only number one in Virginia but one of the top death penalty jurisdictions in the entire nation.

Ebert failed to secure a death sentence in his last capital case just before retirement in a fitting end to his lethal career. "The demographics of Prince William were relatively conservative all those years and much more pro-death," Ebert lamented. "And I always knew someone on the jury. Now, I seldom know someone on the jury."

In January 2020, Descano and Ashworth joined ten other progressive prosecutors (Anton Bell, Hampton; Buta Biberaj, Loudoun County; Parisa Dehghani-Tafti, Arlington County and Falls Church; Howard Gwynn, Newport News; James Hingeley, Albemarle County; Stephanie Morales, Portsmouth; Joseph Platania, Charlottesville; Bryan Porter, Alexandria; Shannon Taylor, Henrico County; and Gregory Underwood, Norfolk) in signing a letter to General Assembly leaders endorsing sweeping criminal justice reforms in the then-upcoming 2020 session. These included automatic expungement of criminal records for "formerly system-involved community members;" an end to mandatory minimum sentences; an end to cash bail; an end to the "three strikes" felony enhancement for petty larceny offenses; and, most importantly, abolition of the death penalty.

Stone credited Kelson Bohnet and Rob Poggenklass with organizing reform prosecutors to support abolition.

While 12 commonwealth's attorneys out of 133 across Virginia does not sound like enough to influence all those crucial reforms, it is essential to realize that this small group of prosecutors represented 43 percent of Virginia's population. Three former attorneys general and five former commonwealth's attorneys also joined these 12.

As a result of these signatories, the Virginia Association of Commonwealth's Attorneys (VACA), who had for years consistently and loudly opposed any death penalty-limiting legislation, remained neutral on abolition. This neutrality was a crucial part of the "perfect storm" of events leading to abolition in 2021.

More Pieces Fall: Advocating During a Pandemic

> Virginia Republicans meet in churches. Democrats meet in schools and government buildings. Libertarians meet in bars.
>
> -VADP field director Dale Brumfield.

2020 started gangbusters for Brumfield, securing no fewer than 12 speaking engagements just in the first eight weeks. Then on March 9, after addressing a group of Northern Virginia Libertarians in where else but an Arlington bar, it all came crashing to a halt.

The Coronavirus pandemic shutdown forced VADP and their partners to pivot and find new ways to advocate and educate with their abolition target session looming just months away. Like most everyone else, they embraced virtual meetings through Zoom to accomplish that.

In May, after the conclusion of the 2020 session, Brumfield began contacting legislators and their aides to set up Zoom meetings with himself, Stone, and VADP lobbyist Virginia Podboy to gauge support for abolition and answer questions. Many legislators responded that they supported the current death penalty laws and saw no reason to meet. Others said they fully endorsed abolition and saw no reason to meet. But in the end, VADP met virtually with 52 Senators and House Representatives, both Democrats and Republicans.

Many legislators had never voted on or even considered death penalty legislation before, and some had little idea how the death penalty even worked. These 15–25-minute meetings critically honed VADP's ability to describe the process and the inherent problems succinctly and then answer any legislators' questions. The talks were honest, and there were no attempts to sway a legislator out of their opinion, whatever it was. Some admitted they personally saw a need for the death penalty but were willing to listen to their constituents or caucus leadership on the matter. Some were avid supporters of abolition, some were on the fence, but far fewer than anticipated expressed hardcore opposition.

If a legislator seemed wobbly, Brumfield usually knew political action committee members in their district from his fieldwork who could mobilize constituent contact to confirm their support for abolition to them.

Stone maintained a tally sheet of these meetings, and closing in on the final days before the 2021 session, it appeared that the votes were there to pass abolition in House and Senate Committees. The vote count on both floors, however, was far too close for comfort.

There was more work to do.

More Pieces Fall: Black Lives Matter Meets a Penitent Governor

"Are you sitting down?"

"Yes."

"The governor is going to endorse death penalty abolition in his State of the Commonwealth address."

-Phone conversation between VADP lobbyist Virginia Podboy and Executive Director Michael Stone on the eve of Gov. Ralph Northam's State of the Commonwealth address.

On May 25, 2020, 46-year-old George Floyd, a Black man, was killed by a white Minneapolis police officer, Derek Chauvin. Chauvin kneeled on Floyd's neck for almost nine minutes after he allegedly tried using a counterfeit $20 bill in a convenience store.

This video-recorded murder of a Black man under the knee of a white policeman, along with several other high-profile police shootings of unarmed Blacks, sparked a global protest movement against historical racism and police brutality under the banner "Black Lives Matter," or BLM. These protests roared into Richmond, with demonstrations centered around the city's own symbols of historic racism, the Confederate monuments. BLM ground zero was the massive Robert E. Lee monument at Monument and Allen Avenue, renamed Marcus Davis Peters Circle after a Black Richmond man who a police officer gunned down during a mental health crisis.

The grass circle surrounding the 40-ft tall monument soon became a living, breathing protest of historical racial inequity. Displays of Blacks nationwide murdered by police, a garden, a basketball hoop, and almost continuous projections on the granite graffiti-adorned pedestal expressed 150 years of pent-up anger, disgust, and frustration with the way things had been and were going.

The traditionally solemn reverence of that circle became instead a symbol representing all Richmond and all Virginia, not just the supremacist whites.

"When the nation became riveted on the police murder of George Floyd, people saw first-hand an example of the fatal use of government power against a black man," Stone said at the 2021 VADP victory luncheon. "When protests against police abuses erupted in Virginia and around the nation, reluctant legislators suddenly embraced reform of our deeply flawed legal justice system."

VADP had been speaking loudly and as clearly as possible that any race-based criminal reform efforts had to include the abolition of the death penalty, with its ugly roots in white supremacy, racism, and lynching. A month after Floyd's murder, in June 2020, VADP issued a statement written by Stone and board chair Kristina Leslie, titled "The Nation's Racism, Virginia's Death Penalty." In part:

Sadly, once again, with the horrific murder of George Floyd, we are reminded of these outrages. And we are again committed to their eradication. ... According to the Death Penalty Information Center, among those executed for interracial murders in the United States, 295 black people were executed for killing white victims. Only 21 white perpetrators were executed for killing Black victims.

Of the 1,390 documented executions carried out in Virginia since 1608, only four involved a white person killing a black man or woman, all of them since 1997.

Thus, it took 390 years for the Virginia criminal justice system to determine that the life of a Black person, in limited circumstances, was equivalent in value to that of a white person.

The death penalty is a poster child for everything wrong with our criminal justice system – blatant racial disparities, police and prosecutor misconduct, and the propensity for convicting innocent men and women.

We urge all of those who believe capital punishment is a gross abuse of power to join us as we salute those on the front lines of change.

Catherine Read observed that after the George Floyd murder and the racial unrest, "people suddenly woke up and said it's not like we weren't aware that racism was everywhere, that it was in our workplace, in our various communities; it's not like we didn't know it, there was just nothing that motivated them to demand change. Well, then that happened, and there was enormous momentum. And then people suddenly felt like they weren't alone."

Virginia embraced institutional racism for decades and has sometimes struggled unsuccessfully to divest itself of it. In 1940, the 1878 James Bland song "Carry me Back to Ole Virginny" was bizarrely adopted as the state song by House Joint Resolution No. 10. This happened despite the presence of not just outdated and offensive slang such as "darkey" and "massa," but the point of view the song projected of a formerly enslaved man who longed for his pre-emancipation days. He pined for being back on the plantation ("There's where I labored so hard for old massa") and of his desires to be free from modern worries and join "massa and misses" at "the bright and golden shore."

The first bill former Gov. Douglas Wilder introduced as a freshman Senator in 1970 was to abolish that song – but he was unprepared for the blowback, and the bill died. Incredibly, the song defied legislative efforts to replace it every year from 1988 until 1997, when the General Assembly considered making lyric changes to make the song sound less like a Black man longing for slavery days and more like general nostalgia for the old Virginia of the past.

The legislature failed to pass any of those changes but compromised to retire the song as "State Song Emeritus," where it remains today.

Called on the Carpet

Gov. Ralph Northam became embroiled in a major controversy when a 1984 photo surfaced on a right-wing website purportedly showing him at an Eastern Virginia Medical School event dressed in Blackface, standing beside another person in Ku Klux Klan robes.

The photo set off a firestorm of bipartisan controversy, with political leaders from all sides urging, even demanding, that Northam step down. While first admitting guilt and apologizing, he later backtracked and claimed that the Blackface student was not him but that he was "99%" sure who it was.

Northam rejected calls to resign, pledging instead to focus his administration on racial justice issues. Brutal listening sessions with Black Virginians around the state, including legislators, community leaders, and citizens slowly resurrected his political career. He announced the formation of a commission to review how public schools taught African American history, and he created the position of a cabinet-level Diversity Officer. Another commission was created to find and weed out racist language in Jim Crow-era statues still on the books.

In these initiatives, the governor admitted that he was a product of a white-based state educational system that had insidiously, over decades, institutionalized racism to the point where it was no longer recognized.

"Northam's rebirth," a Jan. 9, 2022 *Washington Post* story stated, "was driven partly by an extraordinary effort to connect with Black constituents across Virginia, a process that Northam says broke him down and built him back a better person — more aware of the ugly reality of race in America."

These ugly realities in the history of Virginia slavery and race relations Northam and many others encountered had foundations in Virginia's decision in 1948 to let the General Assembly take direct control of public-school textbook production. The Assembly that year established a commission, under the oversight of the segregationist Harry F. Byrd, to hire authors and edit manuscripts for three statewide textbooks on Virginia history, geography, and government.

According to the 2018 *Richmond Times-Dispatch* story "Happy slaves? The peculiar story of three Virginia school textbooks," journalist Rex Springston wrote, "One common thread of the books was the adulation of Confederate Gen. Robert E. Lee. 'General Lee was a handsome man' who 'sat straight and firm in his saddle,' said the fourth-grade text, 'Virginia's History.' It added that Lee's horse, Traveller, 'stepped proudly, as if he knew that he carried a great general.'"

The only women mentioned in these texts were Pocahontas (portrayed extremely incorrectly) and Martha Washington.

Newly-emerging civil rights legislation received almost no mention in this government-produced propaganda as a way of ignoring or diminishing the impending policies of President Harry S. Truman. With the onset of the post-war communist scare and the activities of Sen. Joseph McCarthy and the House Unamerican Activities Committee, these politicians saw their work as keeping teachers from spreading progressive (i.e., communist) ideas.

At least two generations of Virginia schoolchildren learned incomplete and whitewashed history from these ridiculously biased texts before they were finally phased out in the early 1970s.

Virginia also fought fiercely throughout the 1950s to keep schools segregated, with "Massive Resistance" going so far as to close some of them rather than integrate, depriving hundreds of Black children of formal education. Virginia could not repeal a miscegenation law prohibiting interracial marriage until pushed into a corner by the U.S. Supreme Court in 1967. The commonwealth continued practicing eugenics, or involuntary sterilizations of those considered "unfit to breed" (which, like the death penalty, overwhelmingly targeted Blacks, the poor, and the mentally ill), until 1979.

Fittingly, the Black Lives Matter movement sought to irrevocably demolish these racist "Virginia way" relics of the past. The Virginia Senate finally, in *2020* (emphasis added), stopped honoring enslaver Robert E. Lee "as a great Virginian and a great American." Schools, streets, and highways named for Confederate leaders and segregationists are being renamed. The Confederate monuments are now gone from public rights-of-way, and the capstone of racial inequities, the death penalty, is history.

Northam's bold decision to endorse abolition gave cover to many of those legislators shaky on the issue. Many expressed personal opposition to the death penalty but were concerned of what their constituents would think.

"His endorsement put a huge jolt of energy into our efforts," Stone said. "Black legislators, in particular, intuitively understood the importance of death penalty abolition for larger reform of the legal justice system. They needed reassurance that a vote to end the death penalty would not hurt them back in their home districts."

More Pieces Fall: Coalition Partners, Local and National

The Virginia General Assembly punted abolition in its 2020 session due to the growing pains of new Democratic leadership, Covid-19, and a packed schedule of big-ticket items that included gun rights, ERA, abortion, and LGBTQ protections. VADP and its partners knew that they had to start early and be diligent to ensure that abolition would (at least) be seriously debated in 2021.

VADP worked closely with three main local allies: the Virginia Interfaith Center for Public Policy, the Virginia ACLU, and the Virginia Catholic Conference. While the Catholic Conference was busy playing defense on several causes the Democrats were looking to dismantle, they did not play a significant role in abolition. However, for many years before 2021, they had been true stalwarts, both for SMI and abolition.

The Virginia ACLU stepped up in 2021 after a few years of relative inactivity on abolition issues. Since public opinion was high on some legislators' list of deciding factors on abolition, they managed to get a grant from the national ACLU to run a last-minute poll in those target districts.

"We didn't have enough [money] to do a comprehensive statewide survey," Stone said, "but we were able to focus on the districts where those legislators who had asked us for information."

A Christopher Newport poll on numerous legislative issues also found 53 percent favoring abolition – results reflected in the ACLU poll. "[This] really surprised me, given how the question was worded," Stone explained. "So I think that helped us."

The Virginia Interfaith Center for Public Policy joined the coalition in the spring of 2020. VADP helped secure funding for them to hire a full-time justice reform organizer, Reverend Dr. LaKeisha Cook, whose job, among many, was to mobilize Black clergy. "She was an absolute rock star in the short time where she was working," Stone said. "She mobilized over 300 pastors to support death penalty abolition, many of them Black."

Dr. Cook also organized five separate prayer vigils at execution and lynching sites around the state, all of them led by Black clergy. These vigils, including one at the former Virginia State Penitentiary site in Richmond, brought much-needed media attention to abolition. Contributing too was the work of Ben Hoyne (also of the Interfaith Center) with the Legislative Black Caucus. "[The Black Caucus] had always supported death penalty reform and abolition," Stone observed. "We also had Sen. Louise Lucas and Sen. Mamie Locke say they would support having abolition a priority for the Black Caucus."

Stone noted that the advocacy of the Black Caucus and Black clergy helped convince Gov. Northam to embrace abolition publicly.

Abolition got another push from a group called Justice Forward VA. Founded by Arlington defense attorney Brad Haywood, Justice Forward VA is a criminal justice reform advocacy organization created to be a counterweight to the powerful Virginia Association of Commonwealth Attorneys (VACA).

"The first things we focused on were all this in-the-weeds procedural stuff, like jury sentencing and probation rules," Haywood said of the organization's 2017 beginnings. "We never really thought that the big-ticket stuff was possible, given Virginia legislature's attitude towards criminal justice. It wasn't just the Republicans who were bad on criminal justice. It was a lot of Democrats, too. We saw [abolishing] the death penalty as a pipe dream, and when they started talking about it, it sounded like a political football. But, I'm glad it wasn't."

Haywood and his organization saw abolition in Virginia as "profoundly symbolic." "Being the capital of capital punishment and being the first Southern state to abolish it... it's a demarcation between the past and the future. [Abolition] could be a domino-type thing, also. A few other states aren't going to be too far behind."

VADP and coalition partners were supported nationally by Laura Porter and the 8th Amendment Project, a national abolition organization. Founded in 2014, it is committed to bringing together "dozens of national, state, and local partners around a shared strategy to achieve repeal and discourage use of the death penalty by working to change the public discourse about capital punishment in the United States." Porter worked closely with Virginia partners on almost daily Zoom meetings and conference calls before and during the 2021 Assembly, offering support and advice based on her experience with other successful state abolition campaigns.

Another strategy embraced by the coalition included submitting guest op-eds to various Virginia news outlets advocating for abolition. Del Mike Mullin wrote one for the Feb. 2, 2021 *Washington Post* titled "Virginia must prevent wrongful executions." In it, he said, "But as long as we have a system that relies on human beings, with all of their frailties and biases, we can never eliminate the risk of wrongful conviction completely. The death penalty is a permanent response within an imperfect system."

More Pieces Fall: Murder Victim Family Members

From the earliest days of Deans' Murder Victims Families for Reconciliation to the 1996 Journey of Hope to 2021 abolition, the roles of murder victim family members in the abolition discussion have been critical and greatly appreciated.

Murder victim families know the pain and anguish of losing a family member to a senseless and violent crime. Many have seen their own lives and those around them crumble due to that crime. And while they have every right to encourage prosecutors to seek the punishment they deem necessary, a growing number of them speak out, and instead of demanding a death sentence, they advocate for the killers' lives.

Rachel Sutphin said that William Morva's execution forced her to grieve two deaths – her father's and his. "My moral and religious convictions led me to plead with then-Gov. Terry McAuliffe to change Morva's sentence to life without parole," she wrote in a Nov. 22, 2019 *Washington Post* op-ed. "I believed that clemency and a change in sentence were a fair and just punishment for the man who murdered my father."

Sutphin, who has spoken twice before the General Assembly on the impact of the death penalty on families, also wrote that Morva's death sentence left her and her family abandoned. "Instead of supporting my family and me when we needed it the most, the commonwealth devoted its resources to the trial and appeals that lasted more than ten years. Year after year, I was retraumatized by the uncertainty and repeatedly forced to relive the worst day of my life." Sutphin also noted that her pleadings to Gov. McAuliffe to commute Morva's sentence remained unanswered.

Death penalty proponents often speak of "offering closure" to murder victim families by seeking death. Conversations with many of those families reveal that no amount of killing brings back their murdered loved one, robbing them of that empty promise. Instead, many speak of seeking peace, not closure, and a desire not to let this atrocious crime and their anger toward it rule their lives.

Harrisonburg resident Linell Patterson and her sister Megan Smith's father and stepmother, Terry and Lucy Smith, were tortured and murdered in Pennsylvania in 2001. Both answered with a resounding "No" when Lancaster County District Attorney Craig Stedman asked whether they wanted their father's three murderers put to death. Stedman ignored them and pursued death sentences anyway. Two of them received life sentences, and the remaining one, Landon May, received death.

Throughout the trial, Stedman stressed that "justice was being done" for the sisters and their families and that he sought the death penalty in their name, which was a slap to their faces. They felt their voices no longer mattered, leaving them "silenced and disempowered by a criminal justice system that cast us aside."

"It makes me so angry to hear that the death penalty is for me," Patterson said. "Often, victims' family members are grouped into one category — one that desires another death to obtain justice. Speaking with other victims' families, I know we have different feelings about capital punishment, but another death will not assist in my healing. I will not feel justice when capital punishment has been implemented. It will not make me feel safer, or less angry, or facilitate healing. It will not bring me peace. It will not bring my loved ones back."

In a Feb. 21, 2015 interview with the *Morning Call*, Smith said, "I've figured out what justice actually is: It's everyone getting what they need to heal. In a story like mine, it's a victim's surviving family members being supported in the aftermath of a terrible crime. It's guidance on how to navigate the funeral, the trial, the money, the grief. It's the community getting what it needs in the form of safety and crime prevention programs, and the offenders being taken out of the community. It's also the offenders getting what they need – accountability, counseling, safety as well. All of these needs can be met without the death penalty."

White supremacist James Fields Jr. drove his car into a crowd of protestors in Charlottesville during the 2017 Unite the Right rally, killing Heather Heyer. Phone records and social media posts showed that Fields did not act spontaneously but in a concerted effort to inflict harm to a group of counter-protesters.

Despite this hateful and deadly act, Heyer's father, Mark Heyer, did not want the death penalty for his daughter's killer. "I don't relish the thought of him getting the death penalty. That's my belief," Heyer told BuzzFeed News before the verdict was reached. "I'd rather him get his heart straight and get life [in prison]."

Fields was sentenced to life plus 419 years plus $480,000 in fines.

Eight murder victim family members served as representatives in the 2021 General Assembly session. All eight of them voted for abolition. Sen. Janet Howell directly challenged supporters' arguments that the death penalty helped victim family members by describing her own painful personal experience. In the House, Delegates Chris Hurst and Mark Levine gave emotional speeches about the homicide of their loved ones and concluded their stories by urging an end to capital punishment.

It's Go Time: the 2021 Assembly session

> Abolishes the death penalty, including for those persons currently under a death sentence. The bill provides that no person may be sentenced to death or put to death on or after its effective date for any violation of law. The bill incorporates HB 1779 and is identical to SB 1165.
> -Summary as passed of HB 2263, introduced by Del. Michael P. Mullin,
> 2021 General Assembly session.

A legislator with a (D) after their name was never a guarantee they would automatically be in favor of abolishing the death penalty. However, the 2019 Democrat sweep made the 2021 General Assembly much more conducive to abolition, with a window of opportunity open further than it had ever been. When the Assembly convened on Jan. 13, Democrats held a 21-18 majority in the Senate and a 55-45 majority in the House.

Democrats also controlled the executive branch, with a governor who had agreed to sign abolition legislation. In addition, Virginia was only one of 28 state legislatures where neither party held a veto-proof "supermajority" in both chambers.

In the Senate, Sen. Scott Surovell introduced SB 1165, "Death penalty; abolition of current penalty." In the House, Del. Mike Mullin introduced an identical bill, HB 2263. In addition, Del. Lee Carter introduced his own abolition bill, HB 1779, which later merged into Del. Mullins' bill.

Both bills sought to abolish the death penalty and commute the sentences of the two remaining inmates on death row to life in prison. These proposed commutations were a worrisome sticking point to the coalition, and they feared a last-minute compromise could have left their death sentences intact. To their relief, this compromise was not necessary.

Life Means Life (Without Parole)

Just as a (D) after a legislator's name does not automatically make them against the death penalty, an (R) after the name also does not automatically make them support it. As mentioned previously, Southwest Virginia Republican Sen. Bill Stanley announced on the Senate floor in 2020 that he would support death penalty abolition in the 2021 GA session and encouraged his pro-life colleagues to join him. This announcement was crucial in securing more Republicans, profoundly increasing the chances of abolition passing, and most importantly, making it truly a bipartisan effort.

On January 31, 2021, Stanley wrote an impassioned op-ed for Roanoke.com titled "A Conservative Viewpoint on Ending the Death Penalty" that reiterated his stance. "Opposition ... is consistent with my conservative principles," he wrote. "This reasoning is based upon three basic principles: my strong faith in God and the gift of life; my appreciation that our criminal justice system is not infallible; and my firm belief that capital punishment empowers the government with an awesome authority to which it is not entitled."

He fervently described that the death penalty was counter to his unabashed pro-life stance. "I am for life. And life means 'Life' to me."

The editorial, however, closed with a curious tacked-on caveat that effectively invalidated his argument. "I am supporting the current legislation pending in the General Assembly to end to [sic] the death penalty, so long as those convicted of aggravated murder are never allowed to be set free, and so long as they are sentenced to life without the possibility of parole. If that is the bill, then I will support it; if it is not, then I will not."

Stanley would vote for abolition only if life without parole (LWOP) was amended to definitively mean no parole. During the debate, Democrats had rejected attempts from Republicans to amend the bill, including Stanley's proposed changes that would have guaranteed a mandatory minimum life sentence for aggravated murder without the possibility of parole. Without that guarantee, Stanley, who had initially co-patroned the abolition bill, not only pulled his support but angrily spoke out against it. "This could have been ... a bipartisan effort to end the death penalty. Instead, it's a party-line effort," he complained.

Stanley and other Republicans' hard-line stances may have been bolstered by the testimony of Michelle Dermyer, whose husband Chad Phillip Dermyer, a Virginia State trooper, had been murdered. She told the Senate Judiciary Committee that the man who killed her husband was sentenced not to life but 36 years in prison. She cautioned that "A sentence of life in prison does not always mean a sentence of life in prison."

Despite losing Republican support, the bill passed the Senate Judiciary Committee on Jan. 18 by a 10-4 vote. It then was referred to and passed the Finance and Appropriations Committee on Jan. 26 by a 12-4 vote. After an emotional and lengthy floor debate, the bill passed the Senate on Feb. 3 by 21-17.

Sen. Bill Stanley did not vote.

In the House, the Subcommittee on Criminal Courts recommended the bill on Jan. 29, 2021on a 6-2 vote. The bill then passed the Courts of Justice Committee on Feb. 3 with a 15-6 vote. Then, on Feb. 5, it passed the House by an overwhelming vote of 57-41.

"Our champions, Sen. Scott Surovell and Del. Mike Mullin were masterful in coordinating floor speeches," Michael Stone said at the VADP victory luncheon.

During those floor speeches, Del. Mark Levine tearfully shared emotional testimony of how his brother-in-law murdered his sister Janet. He closed by saying that the bill was not about him or the victims but that Virginia may kill innocent people. "Killing someone else doesn't bring Janet back to me," he said.

Mullins, a prosecutor, also said that the risk of executing an innocent person kept him awake at night.

One aspect of the chamber's floor debates that surprised many legislators and observers was the lackluster opposition to abolition. Republican Del. Jason Miyares, who many suspected was angling to be Virginia's next attorney general by showing how tough on crime he was, led the charge by resorting to emotional arguments and bloody crime scene photos depicting brutal, high-profile homicides. Miyares and other Abolition opponents ignored the questions of racial bias, deterrence, cost, and innocence while singularly insisting that only death could bring justice to the family members of murder victims.

A passionate death penalty supporter, Republican Albemarle Del. Rob Bell, said in a hearing that the two remaining death row inmates, Porter and Juniper, were watching the debate with "rapt attention." He claimed that the inmates' cheering "could metaphorically be heard at the gravesites of those five crime victims ... We have five dead Virginians ... that this bill will make sure that their killers do not receive justice."

After "crossover," the Senate passed the House bill on a 22-16 vote, and the next day, on Feb. 22, the House passed the Senate bill on a bipartisan 57-43 vote.

Gov. Northam promised to sign the bill.

Virginia Becomes First Southern State to Abolish the Death Penalty

On March 24, 2021, inside a tent in the shadow of the state's execution chamber at Greensville Correctional Center, Gov. Ralph Northam signed death penalty abolition into law.

"Ending the death penalty comes down to one fundamental question: Is it fair?" he said after touring the execution chamber and seeing the electric chair and the lethal injection gurney. "For the state to apply this ultimate, final punishment, the answer needs to be yes. Fair means that it is applied equally to anyone, no matter who they are. And fair means that we get it right, that the person punished for the crime did the crime."

"But," he noted, "we all know that the death penalty cannot meet those criteria. That is why it is time in the Commonwealth of Virginia to end the death penalty."

VADP vice president Jayne Barnard spoke at the signing and credited the work of VADP and many others, especially faith leaders, religious groups, and murder victim family members such as Rachel Sutphin, for their untiring work to make abolition possible.

Gov. Northam's chief legal counsel, Rita Davis, quoted Martin Luther King Jr. when she said, "The arc of the moral universe is long. But today, in the Commonwealth of Virginia, it bends sharply towards justice."

Sen. Jennifer McClellan, the vice-chair of the Virginia Legislative Black Caucus, released a statement that said in part: "This is a historic moment for criminal justice reform in Virginia as we finally end a barbaric system that disproportionately punished Black and Brown people."

Claire Guthrie Gastañaga, executive director of the ACLU of Virginia, told the *Richmond Times-Dispatch* that "While the wheels of justice often turn slowly, we are grateful to be closing the chapter on this racist and inhumane practice."

"The Virginia story is a microcosm of what we are seeing nationally," Brandon Garrett said in the same article. "American death sentencing continues to disappear. I suspect that Virginia's historic repeal will be a sign of things to come from other formerly steadfast death penalty states."

"It was like a breath of fresh air and optimism," said Tzvia Schweitzer, an activist for the Loudoun County Democrats who supported abolition for many years. "And oh my gosh, this wonderful thing. And it made me feel the longer I live in Virginia, the more I like it here. And it also made me feel again that during a time that I felt there were problems with the country's leadership, there is leadership, and Virginia is doing the right thing."

Robert Dunham, director of the Death Penalty Information Center, told CNN in a story headlined "Why Virginia's abolition of the death penalty is a big deal for the state and the US" that Virginia's repeal had "extremely important implications for race relations in Virginia." He described the symbolism of Virginia as the "gateway" to abolition in the remainder of the former Confederacy.

In an April 17, 2021 op-ed in *USA Today*, Martin Luther King III wrote, "I commend

Northam and Virginia lawmakers. When they were confronted with their own state's immoral history, they did not look away. They did not hide or deny. Instead, they confronted Virginia's racist past and vowed to do better. Ending capital punishment in Virginia is a decisive step toward the racial reckoning that our country desperately needs. The rest of the South should follow suit."

Long-time abolitionist and VADP board member Dr. Todd Peppers told the *New York Times* that Virginia's death penalty was "a long, bloody history, and it's astonishing that a state like Virginia, a former Confederate state, a state that so enthusiastically embraced the death penalty, is abolishing it."

"I never thought I'd see this."

Sen. Scott Surovell, the Senate patron of the bill, also spoke at the signing ceremony. He told the assembled crowd that "Someone should write a book about Virginia's death penalty."

Afterword: Making it Stick

In 35 years of crossing the country trying to stop the death machine, I've come to see capital punishment as "the lid on the garbage can." I believe that once we take that lid off that can, people will see into the rotten, stinking, maggot-infested mess that is our criminal justice system and be forced to do something about it.

-Actor and death penalty abolitionist Mike Farrell, in his keynote address,
VADP Awards Luncheon, March 24, 2019.

In 2022, one year after abolition, Virginia survived the first attempt to reinstate the death penalty. In January, Republican Sen. Bill DeSteph introduced Senate Bill 379, "Capital murder; death penalty for willful, deliberate, etc., killing of a law enforcement officer."

Simultaneously, in the House, Republican Del. William Wampler introduced HB 661 with the identical title. Both bills intended to authorize punishment by death for the "willful, deliberate, and premeditated killing of a law enforcement officer."

The timing could not have been worse – less than two days before these bills dropped in their respective galleries, a young mentally ill Ashland man shot and killed police officer John Painter and Campus Safety Officer J.J. Jefferson on the Bridgewater College campus.

However, despite the timing and the emotions swirling around these murders, the Senate Judiciary Committee defeated SB 379 on a 9-6 party-line vote. The House Courts of Justice Committee never held a hearing on HB 661.

One possible explanation for the defeat of these bills was there simply were not enough votes to get them out of committee. Another possibility was that the Republican House leadership did not want to waste time on bills they knew would never pass the Democrat-held Senate.

One has to wonder if the sponsors of these bills were aware of the costs and logistical challenges of reinstating the death penalty. Outgoing Gov. Ralph Northam donated the electric chair, lethal injection gurney, and associated paraphernalia to Richmond's Virginia Museum of History and Culture on Arthur Ashe Blvd. The DOC has already converted death row and the execution chamber to protective custody housing. The lethal injection drugs have been destroyed.

Reinstatement would come with a considerable price tag, not just to re-outfit the death chamber and procure all the drugs and equipment back into service but to create and re-staff at least one capital defense office with attorneys, mitigation experts, and investigators.

Legislators may well be hesitant to appropriate the several million dollars needed to bring back a barbaric practice of previous centuries. But the move is not without precedent: in May 2015, the Nebraska State Legislature abolished their death penalty.

Republican Gov. Pete Ricketts vetoed the legislation, but the legislature overrode the veto 30–19.

Later that year, a group called "Nebraskans for the Death Penalty" circulated a petition to repeal the bill, and Ricketts and his father bankrolled the initiative. The petition's organizers submitted enough signatures to suspend the new law, and then in the Nov. 16, 2016, general election, the public rejected the abolition bill by over a 30-point margin.

A prominent Republican told the state's abolition director, Stacey Edwards, to not take it personally but that Nebraska's Republican party believed that bringing back the death penalty was an excellent way to raise money.

Nebraska had no clue what it was doing and had to resort to smuggling to obtain the badly-needed execution drugs. They managed to execute Carey Dean Moore in 2018 but used drugs illegally obtained from a compounding pharmacy called Community Pharmacy Services, which distributed medications to long-term care facilities. Currently, the state is mired in court proceedings and is medicinally stymied, unable to find anyone to sell them the four-drug cocktail.

In the face of what happened in Nebraska, VADP remains vigilant at least until 2024 to guard against reinstatement.

Do You Think it can Come Back?

Faith leader Debbie Simpson: "Abolition is a recognition of the worthwhileness and the freedom of each individual. This is huge for Virginia, but there are still many people in Virginia who would say, 'Oh, I'll go back to the death penalty tomorrow.' You know, that's why I say it's an individual, interior thing. You as an individual have to come to the point where you know that each of us is worthwhile. As Sister Helen says, each of us is worth more than our worse act."

Attorney Rob Lee: "It seems that that's certainly possible it can come back. And the extremes seem to be taking control, particularly on the right. If someone finds it expedient or has some political gain to playing this issue, I think they would bring it back without much hesitation. But Virginia had already lived without the death penalty for ten years."

Journalist Laura LaFay: "It would be a dark day for me to see the death penalty come back to Virginia."

Capital defense attorney Kristina Leslie: "It's such a momentous time. My children will grow up in Virginia, where we don't have the death penalty. That is a huge human rights victory, which normally takes sometimes decades, centuries to accomplish, and we've managed to do that in a state that killed the first documented person. Ultimately, it's not going to come back as long as everyone just stays on their toes."

Former VADP executive director Michael Stone: "All it takes is one truly horrific crime. Another John Allen Muhammad, a series of sniper shootings, or someone to shoot up a movie theater, or someone to barge into a local government center and start popping off multiple homicides. That's all it takes for people to get emotionally wound up and an opportunity for cynical politicians to exploit that for votes by saying, 'Well, you know, this just shows why we have to reinstate the death penalty. And you know, by gum, I'm the guy to do it. So vote for me, give me money.' All it takes is a mass killing, and that could change. We have to remain vigilant."

Faith Leader Robert More: "It was so significant that we had finally done the right thing in relatively short order. People worked on it for years and years, of course, but all the pieces that [were] put in place, and others, getting the death penalty defense bar to change [so] that prosecutors didn't feel the need to pursue the death penalty. The fact that the death penalty became almost a moot issue as far as actual criminal practice was concerned. And then people say, well, if it's not being used, but it's costing us all this money, what's the point? And then [the] efforts of reaching out to people across the spectrum, particularly conservatives, and winning them over is just very significant."

Activist Catherine Read: "We need to create a place where everybody can survive, thrive, and succeed. And when you have the death penalty hanging out there, and it's so arbitrary ... I've known from the beginning that it was never about justice; it was about penalizing. It was about revenge. It was about thinking you're going to feel better to take the life of someone you believe deserves to die. But who deserves to die?

"And, why do any of us think that we're in a position to decide who needs to die?"

Final Word

After the civil war, into Reconstruction and the Jim Crow era, when hangings were held openly in the jurisdiction where the crime occurred, local sheriffs frequently let the condemned prisoner speak to the gathered crowd. Facing imminent death on the gallows, the person held a commanding moment in a previously anonymous and suppressed life for the first time. In the Black communities, he was seen as a martyr, and his speech, sometimes permitted for as much as one hour, had authority never realized before.

The last man hanged in Virginia was Joel Payne, a Black man who had been sentenced to death in 1909 for the murder of his father-in-law. Payne took full advantage of the sheriff's generosity. After a deputy led him from the Bedford County jail at 6:00 a.m., he stopped at the foot of the gallows, turned, and admonished the hundreds of people who surrounded him to lead lives of "virtue and uprightness." He encouraged those who were married or were contemplating marriage to make a home for themselves "and never live with your father-in-law."

He ascended the scaffold. He spoke again in full view of the noose and his coffin, claiming that while he acted in self-defense, he was regretful and confident of divine forgiveness.

He then led the crowd in the hymn "Nearer my God to thee."

This "last words" practice ended when Virginia privatized executions in the State Penitentiary. Still, sometime over the years, it became customary for the warden to allow the condemned man or woman a final statement. While most of these "famous last words" are lost to history, a few are documented.

Nat Turner, executed in 1831. "Was not Christ crucified?"

W. D. Totty, executed in 1860. "Leave whiskey alone."

Timothy Webster, executed in 1862 after the rope broke on the first attempt. "I suffer a double death."

William Jackson, executed in 1873. "This is nothing strange! I saw this rope in my dreams Sunday night. Father in heaven, catch my soul!"

Lucinda Fowlkes, executed in 1881. "No more but to bid all farewell."

Charles Beaver, age 16, executed in 1883. "Farewell, friends and fellow creatures."

Joe Hampton, one of the Martinsville Seven, executed in 1951. "Everything's all right. We'll see you on the other side."

Linwood Briley, executed in 1984. "I am innocent."

Michael Marnell Smith, executed in 1986. "Forgive me, Lord. I come to thee."

Wilbert Lee Evans, executed in 1990. "I am taking Justice Marshall's dissenting opinion with me to the electric chair and to my grave. To the Truesdale family, I am dead and they don't have to hate me anymore. I am sorry to have caused all the hardship."

Willie Lloyd Turner, executed in 1995. "When is it going to start? Will I feel it?"

Richard Townes, Jr., executed in 1996. "I am innocent. That's all I have to say. I am innocent."

Lem Tuggle Jr., executed in 1996. "Merry Christmas!"

Joseph O'Dell, executed in 1997. "Governor Allen, you're killing an innocent man. I want to say this to Eddie Schartner, the victim's son, 'Eddie, I did not kill your mother.' ... I'm sorry your mother's dead. But I didn't kill her."

Ronald Watkins, executed in 1998. "I just want to say I'm sorry, to the McCauleys and my family, for the pain that I have caused them."

Douglas Buchanan Jr., executed in 1998. "Basically, let's get the ride started. I'm ready to go."

Bobby Ramdass, executed in 2000. "[The] Redskins are going to the Super Bowl."

Derek Barnebei, executed in 2000. "I am truly innocent of this crime. Eventually, the truth will come out."

Christopher Goins, executed in 2000. "There's no God but Allah."

Thomas Akers, executed in 2001. "I thank the Lord Jesus Christ [for coming into my life]."

Bobby Swisher, executed in 2003. "I hope you can all find the same peace of Jesus Christ as I have."

James E. Reid, executed in 2004. "I forgive you for what you are doing, but I don't forgive you for what you think, or for what you feel, or what you say, or what you do. I forgive you because God has forgiven me."

John Schmitt, executed in 2006. "Come on with it."

Roger Keith Coleman, executed in 2006. "An innocent man is going to be murdered tonight. When my innocence is proven, I hope Americans will recognize the injustice of the death penalty, as all other civilized countries have."

Christopher Emmett, executed in 2008. "Tell my family and friends I love them. Tell the governor he just lost my vote. You all hurry this along; I'm dying to get out of here."

Kent Jermaine Jackson, executed in 2008. "You all can't kill me. I am the king. Remember me like you remember Jesus. I'll be back."

Robert S. Yarbrough, executed in 2008. "Tell my kids I love them. Let's get it over with. Make people happy."

Darick D. Walker, executed 2010. "I don't think y'all done this right, took y'all too long to hook it up. You can print that. That's it."

Teresa Lewis, executed 2010. "I just want Kathy to know I love you and I'm very sorry."

Robert C. Gleason Jr., executed in 2013. "Kiss my ass ... Put me on the highway going to Jackson and call my Irish buddies ... God bless."

Alfredo Prieto, executed in 2015. "Get this over with."

William Morva, the last person executed in Virginia, when asked if he had any last words, 2017. "No."

Sources

Many thanks to the following people for generously giving their time for an interview for this book: George White; Joe Giarratano; Denise Giarratano; Calvin Arey; Laura LaFay; Rob Lee; Shawn Weneta; Steve Northup; Gerald Zerkin; Kristina Leslie; Matthew Engle; Debbie Simpson; Michael Stone; Steven Rosenfield; Henry Heller; Bob More; Catherine Read; Elise Cleva; Tzvia Schweitzer and Harry; Virginia Rovnyack; Bruce Smith; Peter Wallenstein; Beth Panilaitis; Jon Sheldon; Julie McConnell; Fr. James Griffin; Brad Haywood; Kent Willis; BJ Brown Devlin; Kathleen Kenney; Carissa Phillips; Russ Ford; Phil Hirschkop; Rex Springston; Lynn Litchfield Divers; and Jack Payden-Travers.

Also special thanks to Jodi Boyle, Supervisory Archivist, M.E. Grenander Department of Special Collections & Archives, University at Albany, SUNY and James Acker, Emeritus Distinguished Teaching Professor, School of Criminal Justice, University at Albany. Thanks also to VADP, executive director Michael Stone, and the VADP Board for the time and resources needed to create this work. Thanks also to Bruce Cruser, Virginia Rovnyack, Debbie Simpson, and Steven Rosenfield for the archival records provided.

Special thanks also to Doug Dobey at Dobey Design in Richmond for the front and back covers and Hunter Brumfield for his assistance.

Interview transcriptions by Speechpad.com.

Bibliography

Due to space limitations, many sources cited in the text are not duplicated here.

"Del. Frank Hargrove, R-Hanover, recently entered HB 1827, which would abolish the death penalty. We asked him about it." *Style Weekly*, 31 Jan. 2001.

"Diary of John Blair." William & Mary College Quarterly Historical Magazine, Vol. VII, Jan., 1899.

"ExecutedToday.com." *ExecutedToday.com 1786: Hannah Ocuish, Age 12*, 2008, www.executedtoday.com/2008/12/20/1786-hannah-ocuish-age-12/.

"Life on Death Row." *Christianity & Crisis* magazine, Vol 40 no. 11, 23 June 1980.

"Noose Slipping in Lynchburg's 'Legal Lynch' Case." *Muhammed Speaks*, 28 Jan. 1966.

"Some English Conditions Surrounding the Settlement of Virginia." American Historical Review. 1907

"The Code of 1919." The Virginia Law Register 1919, pp. 97

"The Execution of Reed and Clements." *Richmond Dispatch*, 24 Apr. 1852. p. 2.

Adalberto Aguirre, Jr. Slave executions in the United States: A descriptive analysis of social and historical factors, *The Social Science Journal*, 36:1, 1-31. 1999

Agrahackar, Vishal. "The Use of Solitary Confinement in Virginia Is Inhumane and Unlawful." *ACLU Speak Freely*, 6 May 2019, www.aclu.org/blog/prisoners-rights/solitary-confinement/use-solitary-confinement-virginia-inhumane-and-unlawful.

Alice McGill, "Murray v. Giarratano: Right to Counsel in Postconviction Proceedings in Death Penalty Cases," 18 *Hastings Const. Law Quarterly*: pg. 211 1990. https://repository.uchastings.edu/hastings_constitutional_law_qua-terly/vol18/iss1/5

Ankur, Desai and Brandon L. Garrett, "The State of the Death Penalty," 94 *Notre Dame Law Review* 1255-1312 2019.

Bair, Toni V., Professional Correctional Management Operating a Death Row Popula-tion: Putting Theory into Practice, 73 *Wash. & Lee Law Review*. 1189, 2016, https://scholarlycommons.law.wlu.edu/wlulr/vol73/iss3/6.

Banner, Stuart. *The Death Penalty: An American History*. Cambridge, Mass., Harvard University Press, 2003.

Barrett Lain, Corinna and Doug Ramseur. "Disrupting Death: How Dedicated Capital Defenders Broke Virginia's Machinery of Death." Draft document. 2021.

Beagle, Ben. "Court asked Execution Law to be Specific." *Roanoke Times & World News*, 11 Aug. 1982.

Beck, Julie. "The Grisly, All-American Appeal of Serial Killers." *The Atlantic*, 21 Oct. 2014, www.theatlantic.com/national/archive/2014/10/the-grisly-all-american-appeal-of-serial-killers/381690/.

Bedau, Hugo A. "The Case Against the Death Penalty." Capital Punishment Project, American Civil Liberties Union pamphlet, 1984.

Bell, Karen Cook. "Gender, Civil Rights, and the Case of Odell Waller." 26 Feb. 2018. https://www.aaihs.org/gender-civil-rights-and-the-case-of-odell-waller/

Bessler, John D. *Kiss of Death: America's Love Affair with the Death Penalty*. Boston Northeastern University Press, 2003.

Blanton, Wyndham B. "Epidemics, Real and Imaginary, and Other Factors Influencing Seventeenth Century Virginia's Population." *Bulletin of the History of Medicine*, Vol. 31, No. 5, Symposium On Colonial Medicine: In Commemoration of the 350th Anniversary of the Settlement of Virginia (Sept.-Oct., 1957), pp. 454-462. Johns Hopkins University Press. https://www.jstor.org/stable/44449175.

Boggs Jeremy. "We the White People: Race, Culture, and the Virginia Constitution of 1902." Master of Arts Thesis, Virginia Polytechnic Institute and State University, 2003.

Bonnie, Richard J. "Foreword: Psychiatry and the Death Penalty: Emerging Problems in Virginia." *Virginia Law Review*, vol. 66, no. 2, Mar. 1980.

Borgmeyer, John. "Working Himself to Death." *C-Ville Weekly*, 18-24 June, 2002.

Bovee, Marvin H. Christ and the Gallows, Or, Reasons for the Abolition of Capital Pun-ishment. Gale Ecco, Making Of Mode, 2010.

Bowers, William J, et al. *Legal Homicide: Death as Punishment in America, 1864-1982*. Boston, Northeastern University Press, 1984.

Braden, Anne. "Free Thomas Wansley: A letter to white southern women from Anne Braden." SCEF publication, Dec. 1972.

Braden, Carl. "Legal Lynching." *The New South Student*, Dec. 1967.

Breen, Patrick. Nat Turner's Revolt: Rebellion and Response in Southampton County, Virginia. 2005.

Brumfield, Dale M. "An Executioner's Song." *Richmond Magazine*, April, 2016.

Brumfield, Dale M. "Stopping Sanism." Guest editorial, *Richmond Times-Dispatch*, 4 Sept., 2016.

Brumfield, Dale M. Railroaded: The True Stories of the First 100 People Executed in Virginia's Electric Chair. Richmond, Va, HJH Media, 2020.

Brumfield, Dale M. *Virginia State Penitentiary: A Notorious History*. Charleston, SC, History Press, 2017.

Bryant, Samantha M, "Black Monster Stalks the City:' The Thomas Wansley Case And Racialized Politics of the Press, 1960-1980." 2018. *ETD collection for University of Nebraska - Lincoln.*
https://digitalcommons.unl.edu/dissertations/AAI10793365

Bucklew v. Precythe, No. 17-8151, Brief of Amici Curiae Pharmacy, Medicine, and Health Policy Experts in Support of Petitioner, 23 July, 2018.

Campbell, C.J. Rogers v. Commonwealth, 183 Va. 190. 9 Oct. 1944.

Carrington, Charles MD. "The History of Electrocution in the State of Virginia." Lecture transcript, 41st annual session of the Medical Society of Virginia, Norfolk, Oct. 25-28, 1910.

Cassuto, L. "The inhuman race: The racial grotesque in American literature and culture." New York: Columbia University Press. 1997.

Chammah, Maurice. Let the Lord Sort Them: The Rise and Fall of the Death Penalty. New York, Crown, 2021.

Channing, Rev. Henry. Sermon Preached at New-London Dec. 20, 1786 Occasioned by the Execution of Hannah Ocuish, T. Green, 1786. www.hathitrust.org.

Chapin, Bradley. *Criminal Justice in Colonial America, 1606-1660*. Greece, University of Georgia Press, 2010.

Childs, Dennis. Slaves of the State: Black Incarceration from the Chain Gang to the Penitentiary. Minneapolis: University of Minnesota Press, 2015.

Christian, W. Asbury. *Richmond, Her Past and Present*. Richmond: L. H. Jenkins, 1912.

Clarke, Alan W. "Virginia's Capital Murder Sentencing Proceeding: A Defense Perspective." *University of Richmond Law Review*, vol. 18, no. 2, 1984, scholarship.richmond.edu/lawreview.

Cleary, Ben C. "Death in the Spring." *Style Weekly*, 19 Feb. 1985. https://www.bencarloscleary.com/death-in-the-spring.

Cleary, Ben C. "Down the Hall from Death." *Style Weekly*, 1985.

Cohen, Dov and Richard Nisbett. "Self-Protection and the Culture of Honor: Explaining Southern Violence." Personality and Social Psychology Bulletin 20(5): 551-567. 1994.

Coppola v. Commonwealth. 30 Aug. 1979.

Coulson, Hilary L. "Will She Hang? Women Sentenced to Death in Pennsylvania and Virginia, 1800–1900." Pennsylvania History: A Journal of Mid-Atlantic Studies, vol. 86, no. 3, 2019.

Deets, Lee Emerson. "Changes in Capital Punishment Policy since 1939." *Journal of Criminal Law and Criminology (1931-1951)*, vol. 38, no. 6, Mar. 1948.

Denno, Deborah. 2007. "The Lethal Injection Quandary: How Medicine Has Dismantled the Death Penalty." *Fordham Law Review* 49: Pg.76.

Derrida, Jacques, et al. *The Death Penalty: Volume I*. Chicago; London, University of Chicago Press, 2014.

Earley, Mark. L. "A Pink Cadillac, an IQ of 63, and a Fourteen- Year-Old from South Carolina: Why I Can No Longer Support the Death Penalty." *University of Richmond Law Review* 49, 2015: pp. 811-823.

Edds, Margaret. "Remembrance: Marie Deans." *Style Weekly*, 11 Apr. 2011.

Edds, Margaret. An Expendable Man: The Near-Execution of Earl Washington, Jr. New York, New York University Press, 2003.

Elvin, Jon. "Doubts Raised in Virginia Death Row Prisoner Case." *The National Prison Project Journal*, 1990.

Erickson, Mark. "Death Shrouded in Mystery." Daily Press, Sept. 15, 1996.

Erickson, Phil. "A Tale of Two Deaths." *Raleigh Review*, 1982.

Espy, M. Watt, John Ortiz Smykla. *Executions in the United States, 1608-2002: The Espy File*. Fourth Edition. Ann Arbor, MI: Inter-university Consortium for Political and Social Research, 2004.

Farrell, Mike. Keynote Presentation for VADP Awards Luncheon. VADP 2019 Awards Luncheon.

Filler, Louis. Movements to Abolish the Death Penalty in the United States. Sage, 1952.

Galliher, John F., Gregory Ray, Brent Cook, "Abolition and Reinstatement of Capital Punishment During the Progressive Era and Early 20th Century," p. 83 *Journal of Criminal Law & Criminology*. 1992-1993.

Garrett, Brandon L. "The Decline of the Virginia (and American) Death Penalty." *SSRN Electronic Journal*, 2015, 10.2139/ssrn.2674604.

Garrett, Brandon L. "Virginia's Vanishing Death Penalty." Slate.com, 30 Oct. 2015.

Giarratano, Joseph M. "Landmark Case Decided, 6-4," *Southern Coalition Report on Jails & Prison*, Vol. 15, No. 3, Summer 1998.

Goodman, Michael L. "An Argument against Allowing the Families of Murder Victims to View Executions." *Journal of Family Law*, vol. 36, no. 4, 1997.

Green, Frank. "Witnessing Executions." *University of Richmond Law Review* 2015.

Green, Laura. "Stereotypes: Negative Racial Stereotypes and Their Effect on Attitudes Toward African-Americans." Richmond, VCU. Negative Racial Stereotypes and Their Effect on Attitudes Toward African-Americans - Scholarly Essays - Jim Crow Museum (ferris.edu)

Gregg v. Georgia. Oyez, www.oyez.org/cases/1975/74-6257.

Grinnan, Dr. A. G. "The Burning of Eve in Virginia." *Virginia Historical Magazine*, June, 1896. (www.archive.org).

Gross, Samuel R., et al. "Race and Wrongful Convictions in the United States." The National Registry of Exonerations, Newkirk Center for Science and Society, 2017.

Guild, Jane Purcell. "Black Laws of Virginia." The Committee for the Advancement of

Negro Education, Richmond, Va. 1936.

Harris, LaShawn. "The 'Commonwealth of Virginia vs. Virginia Christian:' Southern Black Women, Crime & Punishment in Progressive Era Virginia." *Journal of Social History* 47, no. 4. 2014: 922-942.

Hefferman, Jim. "Killing the death penalty: Alumni lead the charge to end four centuries of capital punishment in Virginia." *Madison* magazine, online only, 16 March, 2021. https://www.jmu.edu/news/2021/03/16-alums-help-end-death-penalty-in-va.shtml

Hirschkop, Philip J., and Michael A. Millemann. "The Unconstitutionality of Prison Life." *Virginia Law Review* 55.5 June, 1969: pp. 795-839.

Hopkins, Evans. "Notes From a Prison Cell on the Coppola Execution." *Washington Post*, 22 Aug. 1982.

Jameson, Franklin J., Ed. *Original Narratives of Early American History 1606-1625*. Barnes & Noble, Inc. New York. 1907.

Joint Legislative Audit and Review Commission of The Virginia General Assembly. *Review of Virginia's System of Capital Punishment*. Commonwealth of Virginia, 2000.

Joyner, Nancy. "The Death Penalty in Virginia: Its History And Prospects." *University of Virginia Newsletter*, vol. 50, no. 10, 1974.

Karp, David J. "Coker v. Georgia: Disproportionate Punishment and the Death Penalty for Rape." *Columbia Law Review*, vol. 78, no. 8, Dec. 1978, p. 1714.

Keve, Paul W. *The History of Corrections in Virginia*. Charlottesville: University Press of Virginia, 1986.

Keve, Paul. "Slave Clem, 12-Year-Old Executed in Surry County." Received by M. Watt Espy, Virginia Commonwealth University, 12 Sept. 1984, Richmond, VA.

Kidwell, Roland. "Court Assents to Death Plea." *Roanoke Times & World News*, 11 Aug. 1982.

Kilpatrick, James J. "Joe Giarratano/ An Execution That Serves No Purpose." *Roanoke Times*, 3 Feb. 1991.

LaFay, Laura, et al. *Unequal, Unfair and Irreversible: The Death Penalty in Virginia*. the American Civil Liberties Union of Virginia, Dec. 2000.

Lain, Corinna Barrett. Three Observations about the Worst of the Worst, Virginia-Style, 77 *Wash. & Lee Law Rev. Online* 469, 2021. https://scholarlycommons.law.wlu.edu/wlulr-online/vol77/iss2/8

Lifton, Robert Jay. "Death in Life: Survivors of Hiroshima." University of North Carolina Press, Chapel Hill, NC. 1991.

Lindholm, Jeff. "Briley Execution Brings Out the Worst." *ThroTTle* Magazine. November, 1984.

Lloyd, James T. Jr., Questions Surrounding Virginia's Death Penalty, 17 *U. of Richmond Law Review*. 603 1983. http://scholarship.richmond.edu/lawreview/vol17/iss3/8.

Mailer, Norman. "The Executioner's Song." Boston, Little Brown and Co., 1979.

McAtlin, Barbara Jean. "Written in Blood, Stamped in Unfairness... Virginia's Infamous 21-Day Rule." *Justice: Denied*, N.D., www.justicedenied.org.

McCarthy, Colman. "A Defender on Death Row," The *Washington Post,* 15 Apr., 1989.

McCartney, Martha. "The Starving Time." Encyclopedia Virginia. Virginia Humanities, 28 Jun. 2018. Web. 2 May. 2020.

Messner, Steven F., et al. "Distrust of Government, the Vigilante Tradition, and Support for Capital Punishment." *Law Society Review*, vol. 40, no. 3, Sept. 2006.

Mogul, Joey L. The Dykier, the Butcher, the Better: The State's Use of Homophobia and Sexism to Execute Women in the United States. *N.Y. City Law Review*. 473. 2005.

Monroe County Va. Court of Oyer & Terminer. *Rebecca v Coalter,* 2 May 1825. National Death Penalty Database.

Morton, Oren F. "The Monroe County History." Ruebush-Elkins Co., Dayton, Va. 1916.

Morton, Oren F. "A History of Monroe County, West Virginia." United States, McClure Company, Inc. 1916.

Ogletree, Charles J. Jr. "Black Man's Burden: Race and the Death Penalty in America." *Oregon Law Review*, vol. 81, no. 1, Spring 2002, p. 15-38. HeinOnline.

Papers of Gov. James Pleasants, 1822-1825. Box 288.

Partington, Donald. "The Incidence of the Death Penalty for Rape in Virginia." *Washington & Lee Law Review*, vol. 22, no. 1, 1965. https://scholarlycommons.law.wlu.edu/wlulr.

Payden-Travers, Jack. "Reflections on the End of the Death Penalty." *LA Progressive*, 27 Mar. 2021, www.laprogressive.com/end-of-the-death-penalty/.

Peppers, Todd and Margaret Anderson. "A Courageous Fool." Vanderbilt University Press, Nashville, 2017.

Peppers, Todd C. The Commonwealth of Virginia v. Joseph Michael Giarratano: A Cautionary Tale, 73 *Washington & Lee Law Review* 1119 2016. https://scholarlycommons.law.wlu.edu/wlulr/vol73/iss3/3

Phillips, Ulrich B. "Slave Crime in Virginia." *The American Historical Review*, vol. 20, no. 2, 1915, pp. 336–340, www.jstor.org/stable/1835473.

Phillips, Ulrich B. Slave Crime in Virginia. The American Historical Review, Jan., 1915, Vol. 20, No. 2 Jan., 1915, pp. 336- 340 Oxford University Press on behalf of the American Historical Association

Pieterse, J. N. "White on black: images of Africa and blacks in western popular culture." New Haven, Conn.: Yale University Press. 1992

Pilkington, Ed. "States Are Stockpiling Lethal Injection Drugs That Could Be Used to Save Lives." *The Guardian*, 20 Apr. 2017, www.theguardian.com/world/2017/apr/20/states-stockpiling-lethal-injection-drugs-arkansas-execution.

Pokorak, Jeffrey. Probing The Capital Prosecutor's Perspective: Race and Gender of the Discretionary Actors, Cornell Law Review, 1998. pg. 83.

Porta, Madeline. "Not Guilty by Reason of Gender Transgression...,"319 CUNY Law Review, vol 16 no. 2 Summer 2013. CUNYLR_16.2_Complete.pdf (cunylawreview.org).

Radelet, Michael (editor). "Facing the Death Penalty: Essays on Cruel and Unusual Punishment. Philadelphia: Temple University Press. 1989.

Radelet, Michael. "Twenty-five Years After Gregg." Amnesty International USA Study Guide, 2001.

Rankin, Hugh F. "Criminal Trial Proceedings in the General Court of Colonial Virginia." *The Virginia Magazine of History and Biography*, vol. 72, no. 1, 1964, pp. 50–74.

Rexroat, Barbara. Unpublished genealogy of the Seat Family, sections 3-6, 2014.

Richer, Alanna Durkin. "Execution costs spike in Virginia; state pays pharmacy $66K." AP News, 12 Dec. 2016. https://apnews.com/article/7879b7bd0e7a400ea23136b32d7ba64d.

Rise, Eric. The Martinsville Seven and Southern Justice: Race, Crime, And Capital Punishment in Virginia, 1949-1951. 1992.

Rogers v. Commonwealth, 183 Va. 190. 1944. Supreme Court of Appeals of Virginia· Record No. 2855.

Rogers, James C. "Human Sacrifice U.S.A." Lyceum Publications, 1984.

Ross, William E. "End the Death Penalty." *The Virginia Law Register*, 5 Dec. 1905.

Rutyna, Richard. *"The Capital Laws of Virginia: An Historical Sketch."* Virginia State Crime Commission Advisory Committee on Capital Punishment, 17 Sept. 1973.

Sarat, Austin. "A Mostly Untold Story: Botched Executions and the Legitimacy of Capital Punishment." *Life of the Law*, https://www.lifeofthelaw.org/2013/10/a-mostly-untold-story-botched-executions-and-the-legitimacy-of-capital-punishment. 30 Oct. 2013.

Sawyer, Jeffrey K., "'Benefit of Clergy' in Maryland and Virginia. *American Journal of Legal History*, Vol. 34, No. 1, Jan. 1990, pp. 49-68. https://ssrn.com/abstract=2443963

Schafer, Judith Kelleher, and Philip J. Schwarz. "Slave Laws in Virginia." *The American Historical Review*, vol. 102, no. 5, Dec. 1997.

Scott, Ned Jr. "An Eye for an Eye: The Strange death of Frank Coppola." ThroTTle Magazine, 1 Sept. 1982.

Scott, Arthur Pearson. *Criminal Law in Colonial Virginia*. United States: University of Chicago Press, 1930.

Segura, Liliana. "The Long Shadow of Virginia's Death Penalty." *The Intercept*, 11 Apr. 2021, theintercept.com/2021/04/11/virginia-death-penalty-abolition/.

Shallenberger, Matthew. "Untitled Letter." Received by unknown, Aug. 2003.

Shallenberger, Matthew. *Affidavit of Alfred C. Brown*. 30 Nov. 2004.

Shannon, Margaret, "Matters of Life and Death." *Atlanta Journal Constitution*, 23 Apr. 1972

Shepherd, Joanna M. "Deterrence versus Brutalization: Capital Punishment's Differing Impacts among States." Michigan Law review, Vol. 104, no. 2, 2005.

Sherman, Richard. "The Case of Odell Waller and Virginia Justice, 1940-1942." *William & Mary Magazine*, vol. 60, no. 1, 1 Nov. 1992.

Shires, Carl. "Electric Chair, after 232 Executions, Loses 'Elegance'." *Richmond News Leader*, March 8, 1961.

Sinclair, Melissa S. "Blood Sisters." *Style Weekly*, 15 Sept. 2010.

Smith, Capt. John. The Generall Historie of Virginia; the Fourth Book. London. 1624

Snyder, Jonathan. "The Death Penalty: An Historical and Theological Survey, And: Against the Death Penalty: Christian and Secular Arguments against Capital Punishment." *Human Rights Quarterly*, vol. 21, no. 2, 1999.

Staff "Group Claims Southern Myths Back Death Penalty." *Suffolk News-Herald*, 16 Dec. 1976. P. 1-2.

Staff report. "Jury Gives Wansley Life." *The Southern Patriot*, April, 1967.

Staff. "Christian Virginia vs. Virginia Christian," *The Crisis* Magazine, Sept. 1912, 237–239.

Staff. "35 Years Later: "Mecklenburg Six" Prison Break and Its lingering Impact on Virginia." *WRIC Online*, 13 May 2019.

Staff. "A Woman Hanged." *The Los Angeles Times*, 17 July 1896.

Staff. "An Inhuman Mother." *Chattanooga Press*, 24 July 1896.

Staff. "An Old Question Is Up Again: Is Death Penalty Justified?" *Richmond Times-Dispatch*, 8 July 1951.

Staff. "Campaign for Beattie." *Alexandria Gazette*, 11 Nov. 1911.

Staff. "Capital Punishment." *Clinch Valley News*, 17 Nov. 1911.

Staff. "Capital Punishment." *Richmond Times-Dispatch*, 5 Aug. 1936.

Staff. "Chair Claims First Woman Victim Today." *Richmond News Leader*, Aug. 16, 1912.

Staff. "Christian Girl Must Die To-Day." *Richmond Times-Dispatch*, Aug. 16, 1912

Staff. "Diabolical Murders." *The Carolina Sentinel* (New Bern, NC). 2 Feb. 1822.

Staff. "Electric Chair may get Eight Negroes." *Daily Press* (Newport News), March 13, 1909.

Staff. "Electrocution in Penitentiary Friday." *Newport News Daily Press*, Oct. 31, 1908.

Staff. "Finney's Sentence has been Commuted." *The Evening News* (Roanoke), Oct. 10, 1908.

Staff. "Group Opposes Death Penalty." *Staunton News Leader*, 16 Jan. 1977.

Staff. "House Committee hears Death Penalty Arguments." *Staunton News Leader*, 31 Jan. 1977.

Staff. "How it Feels to Die in the Electric Chair." *Richmond Times-Dispatch*, March 5, 1916.

Staff. "Last of Doomed 7 Says 'Meet me in Heaven.'" *Richmond Afro-American*, Feb. 10, 1951.

Staff. "Lawyers for executed Virginia man say he may have died painfully." *Reuters*, 19 Jan. 2017.

Staff. "Martinsville Trial." *Danville Register*, June 6, 1950.

Staff. "Robert Faulkner Commits Suicide." *Richmond News Leader*. 30 March 1908. P.1

Staff. "Secrecy Behind Executions." *New York Times*, 29 Jan. 2014.

Staff. "Triple Slave Execution in Brentville, Va." *The Baltimore Sun*, 17 Feb 1857.

Staff. "Two Murderers Hanged." *National Police Gazette*, 15 July, 1885.

Staff. "Va. House Panel Votes Expansion of Death Penalty." *Daily Press*, 1 Mar 1977.

Staff. "Va. Prisoner Beats Electric Chair, Hangs Self." *Jet*, 1954.

Stern, Jeffrey E. "The Cruel and Unusual Execution of Clayton Lockett." *The Atlantic*, June, 2015.

Stevens, Linda. "Groups Stimulate Move for Abolition of Death Penalty." *Fredericksburg Free Lance-Star*, 31 May, 1970.

Strachey, William. "A true reportory of the wracke, and redemption of Sir Thomas Gates Knight, in Hakluytus posthumus, or, Purchas his Pilgrimes, compiled by Samuel Purchas, London, 1625," posted by *Encyclopedia Virginia*,

Streib, Victor L. "Death Penalty for Female Offenders." *University of Cincinnati Law Review*, vol. 58, no. 3, 1990. HeinOnline

Streib, Victor L. "Juveniles' Attitudes Toward Their Impending Executions." Excerpted from "Facing the Death Penalty." Philadelphia: Temple University Press, 1987.

Streib, Victor L. The Juvenile Death Penalty Today: Death Sentences and Executions for Juvenile Crimes, January 1, 1973 - April 30, 2004. Ohio Northern University College of Law, Ada, Ohio. 2004.

Sussex County Virginia. Commonwealth vs Hartwell Seat's Clem. 14 Apr. 1787. Archives.albany.edu.

Tarter, Brent and the Dictionary of Virginia Biography. "Sir Thomas Dale (d. 1619)." Encyclopedia Virginia. Virginia Humanities, 23 Sep. 2013. Web. 1 May. 2020.

Trigilio, Joseph and Tracy Casadio. *Executing Those Who Do Not Kill: A Categorical Approach to Proportional Sentencing.* American Criminal Law Review, Vol. 48: 1371. 2011.

Trotti, Michael A. "The Scaffold's Revival: Race and Public Execution in the South." *Journal of Social History* 45 no. 1. 2011.

Troy, Anthony, et al. Petition for Conditional Pardon for Joseph M. Giarratano Jr. 4 Sept. 2009.

Va. Dept. of Corrections. *Operating Procedure, Execution Manual.* 17 Feb. 2017.

Vollen, Lola., Turow, Scott. "Surviving Justice: America's Wrongfully Convicted and Exonerated." United States: McSweeney's, 2015.

Wallenstein, Peter. "Slavery Under the Thirteenth Amendment: Race and the Law of Crime and Punishment in the Post-Civil War South." *Louisiana Law Review* 77, no. 1. Sept. 2016.

Wansley v. Miller, 353 F. Supp. 42. 1 Jan. 1973.

Warden, Rob and Daniel Lennard. "Death in America under Color of Law: Our Long, Inglorious Experience with Capital Punishment." Nw. J. L. & Soc. Pol'y: Pg. 194. 2018. https://scholarlycommons.law.northwestern.edu/njlsp/vol13/iss4/

Webb, George. *The Office and Authority of a Justice of Peace ...:.* United States: W. W. Gaunt, 1736.

Williamson, Eric. "As He Rose in His Career, Bonnie Made Case Against Capital Punishment." University of Virginia School of Law. 2 April 2021. https://www.law.virginia.edu/news/202104/he-rose-his-career-bonnie-made-case-against-capital-punishment.

Willis, Anne Romberg, "The Master's Mercy: Slave Prosecutions and Punishments in York County, Virginia,1700 to 1780." 1995. Dissertations, Theses, and Masters

Projects. Paper 1539625945.

Willis, Anne Romberg, "The Master's Mercy: Slave Prosecutions and Punishments in York County, Virginia, 1700 to 1780." 1995. Dissertations, Theses, and Masters Projects. Paper 1539625945. https://dx.doi.org/doi:10.21220/s2-8eh2-0488

Wood v. Zahradnick.

Wood, Amy Louise. "The Spectacle of Lynching: Rituals of White Supremacy in the Jim Crow South." *The American Journal of Economics and Sociology*. Vol. 77, No. 3-4. May-Sept. 2018

Woodford County, Virginia. Oyer & Terminer. 25 June, 1791. National Death Penalty Archive.

Web and Digital Collections

Ancestry.com

Case.law

Death penalty information center (http://deathpenaltyusa.org/usa1/state/virginia)

ExecutedToday.com

Find a Grave Cemetery records (http://findagrave.com)

Google scholar (www.scholar.google.com)

Hathitrust digital library (http://hathitrust.org)

Internet Archive digital library (http://www.archive.org)

Internet Archive Scholar (http://scholar.archive.org)

James Madison University lynchings website (https://sites.lib.jmu.edu/valynchings/)

JSTOR.org

Library of Congress (http://loc.gov/)

Library of congress digitized newspapers (http://chroniclingamerica.loc.gov/)

Library of Virginia online digitized newspapers (http://virginiachronicle.com)

Murderpedia encyclopedia of murderers (http://www.murderpedia.org)

Newspapers.com digitized newspapers (http://www.newspapers.com)

The National Death Penalty Archive, M.E. Grenander Special Collections and Archives, University at Albany, State University of New York (https://archives.albany.edu/description/repositories/ndpa)

Virginia Center for digital history (http://www.vcdh.virginia.edu)

Virginia Heritage Guides to Manuscript and Archival Collections in Virginia (http://vaheritage.org/)

Index

Dale M. Brumfield was formerly executive director for Virginians for Alternatives to the Death Penalty after serving over three years as field director. This is his twelfth book.

CPSIA information can be obtained
at www.ICGtesting.com
Printed in the USA
BVHW012013130522
636832BV00009B/2